KORN FERRY
Institute

THE
INCLUSION
PARADOX

3RD EDITION

The ^post Obama Era
and the Transformation of
Global Diversity

Andrés T. Tapia

Praise for *The Inclusion Paradox*

"Andrés Tapia has emerged as a rising star in business strategy. In *The Inclusion Paradox*, Tapia challenges us to call out our differences as a critical step to achieve inclusion. This book is a call to action. The megatrends are identified. The sustainable strategies are defined. The probing questions are outlined. Tapia equips the reader to lead change rather than be the victim of it. I recommend it to executives who are serious about being competitive by embracing and leveraging diversity."

– Gloria Castillo, President and CEO, Chicago United

"*The Inclusion Paradox* is a significant contribution to the field. Andrés' uncanny ability to weave together the unique tapestries of various cultural perspectives has helped to enlighten, inspire, educate, and even transform our understanding of a topic that can often be complex and controversial."

– Mary-Frances Winters, CEO, The Winters Group

"Andrés is an insightful and provocative thought leader in diversity and inclusion. Based on his personal and professional experiences, he challenges the conventional approach. In clear and direct language, *The Inclusion Paradox* describes a new way to drive real results in your diversity and inclusion efforts."

– Jorge Figueredo, Executive Vice President, HR, McKesson Corporation

"In *The Inclusion Paradox*, Andrés masterfully examines American corporations' challenges with diversity. He astutely analyzes the difference between diversity and inclusion, and the importance of recognizing differences rather than minimizing them."

– Mellody Hobson, President, Ariel Investments

"*The Inclusion Paradox* is a must-read for all who want to keep ahead of the forces of change. Andrés has focused his keen mind on the most critical issues that are creating global societal change today."

– Carol Evans, former CEO, Working Mother Media and Diversity Best Practices

"Andrés Tapia is indeed one of today's most dynamic and exciting thought leaders in the area of diversity and inclusion. He has transmuted talents as a communicator, journalist, and human resources expert and consultant into an imprimatur and brand that is much in demand. His presentations are exciting and arresting. They encompass a rare combination of South American flair and romantic passion with a keen North American corporate insight to come up with a unique viewpoint of how inclusion can be embedded into all facets of business to make them more productive and profitable."

> *– Robert L. Ingram, Multimedia Sr. Sales Director Corporate Responsibility, Black Enterprise*

"Andrés Tapia is one of the preeminent thought leaders working in the diversity space today. His unique approach to promoting diversity and inclusion in organizations makes what is often an uncomfortable and contentious topic into a productive, liberating conversation. *The Inclusion Paradox* is a must-read for anyone looking to promote diversity and inclusion in their company or organization. His writing is clear and engaging, and best of all, completely informative."

> *– Jim Hirsch, Executive Director, Chicago Sinfonietta*

"This book hits the nail on the head! In the ever-growing conversation of diversity and inclusion, this book captures the true essence of the dilemma. You can't have diversity if people are not comfortable enough to bring their full selves to the table...hence the need for inclusion."

> *– Katherine W. Phillips, Columbia Business School, Paul Calello Professor of Leadership and Ethics*

"Andrés is the consummate diversity and inclusion professional with a unique way of challenging traditions that are not driving new thinking. His thought leadership in the areas of cultural competence and inclusion is moving diversity and inclusion practice to the next level. Visionaries are not MADE, they are BORN to LEAD...that is Andrés Tapia."

> *– Eric Watson, Vice President of the Office of Diversity & Inclusion, Delhaize America*

"This book takes a topic that can be perceived as feel-good liberalism and contextualizes it as crucial for even the most conservative business mind. Tapia explains how demographic, social, economic, and political forces have come together in a perfect storm that can drown and shred the best businesses, as we've already seen. He provides clear rationale, strategy, and practical steps for navigating the storm to penetrate new markets, grow existing ones, and attract and retain the best talent."

> *– Dianne Hofner Saphiere, creator of the Cultural Detective® series, and Principal, Nipporica Associates LLC*

"*The Inclusion Paradox* provides a provocative and shrewd perspective on global diversity. It provides a lucid picture of the globalized world and is a definitive handbook for business and diversity executives who want to succeed in shaping an inclusive work environment. The analysis provided in this book is illuminating, far reaching, and most importantly, absolutely correct. Tapia's book is notable for its emphasis on a global diversity perspective as a driving catalyst for economic growth in corporate America."

　　– Dr. Robert Rodriguez, author of Latino Talent: Effective Strategies to Recruit, Retain and Develop Hispanic Professionals *and* Diversity Executive *magazine columnist*

"*The Inclusion Paradox* provides a compelling, 21st century perspective towards an age-old question: How can the United States and our global community create a truly inclusive environment across the vast span of cultural differences? The solution, according to the author, is to engage the minds and hearts of all people through the constructive management of our differences. In order to do this effectively, intercultural competence is essential. Tapia provides needed information on why we need to rethink how inclusion operates in our workplaces and gives us personal stories that show how different cultural perspectives dramatically impact relationships in our families and organizations. The book also provides practical solutions. This book is, quite simply, required reading for leaders today."

　　– Dr. Mitch Hammer, co-creator of the Intercultural Development Inventory (IDI), and CEO of Hammer Consulting

"Today's educators shape tomorrow's quality citizens and corporate employees and executives. Andrés Tapia's expertise challenged us to rethink our priorities and practices as we strive to prepare our students for the 21st century. Andrés, an outstanding facilitator, is also a wonderful storyteller who immediately connects with others. While developing a warm, safe, and comfortable environment, he is capable of pushing participants to reflect on the challenging implications of an increasingly dynamic global reality. *The Inclusion Paradox* speaks directly to educators charged with preparing all students to succeed in a world where diversity must be, as he says— understood, embraced, and 'called out' so that crosscultural competence emerges as a result. It is a must-read for individuals seeking to foster equity and striving to achieve personal and systemic excellence."

　　– George V. Fornero, former Superintendent of Schools, Township High School District 113, Highland Park, Illinois

"Learning from and working with Andrés Tapia has been very impactful for me. While I have been involved with diversity and inclusion for many years as part of my HR role, and as part of my own personal passion around the power of respecting and valuing teamwork, I had a lot to learn about the way to optimize these principles in a global company. Andrés provided me with a worldview and an appreciation for awareness of self and others that helped me in my quest to leverage diversity and inclusion on work teams. He has amazing insights and is able to probe deeply into the subconscious biases of individuals and organizations."

– Laurie S. Simpson, Vice President and Chief Compliance Officer,
Deere & Company

"Thanks to Andrés, we now have a vehicle to open more paths into an authentic dialogue between artists and corporate audiences. Since the arts embrace diversity by allowing exploration and revelation of culture and self, it is an essential and necessary conversation for creating greater inclusion in organizations. And a word on Andrés' Latino background: like we have done in dance, in exploring and sharing our culture, we create new insights that help all see each other in new ways."

– Eduardo Vilaro, founder of Luna Negra Dance Theater and Artistic Director of
Ballet Hispanico

"In *The Inclusion Paradox*, Andrés Tapia leaves no stone unturned in addressing the thorny issues of diversity and inclusion, including how they've evolved and why corporations must and *can* do better in making them a more organic part of business in the 21st century. Tapia's advice is not only sound, but delivered with great intimacy and insight. That's because, given his Peruvian roots and successful rise in corporate America, diversity and inclusion are deeply personal matters—and have been for the almost decade I've known him as both a friend and a colleague. He has been a real pioneer in this area, talking about how to find the synergy between our gender, faith, sexual, age, and cultural differences long before it was fashionable, asking hard questions, offering contemplative answers, and advocating for an approach that goes beyond just forming committees and day-long diversity training."

– Jill Sherer Murray, Communications Practice Leader, The Trion Group, and
author/blogger of "Diary of a Writer in Mid-Life Crisis" on WildRiverReview.com

"Andrés has skillfully translated his innovative views on inclusion and diversity into a set of practical approaches that form a valuable road map for change. This is definitely required reading for anyone who wants to take a leadership role in creating and driving an inclusive culture."

   – *Jeanne Mason, Ph.D., Corporate Vice President, Human Resources, Baxter International Inc.*

"*The Inclusion Paradox* is brilliant! The distinguished author, Andrés T. Tapia, has elevated the subject matter to bring meaning in a very unique way to it, as well as many, many associated terms. I find the book a wonderful read, both from an educational and entertainment point of view. I congratulate Andrés for writing what could become a definitive treatise on the subject matter."

   – *The late Maestro Paul Freeman, founder, Chicago Sinfonietta, Czech National Symphony Orchestra*

KORN FERRY
Institute

THE
INCLUSION
PARADOX

3RD EDITION

post

The Obama Era
and the Transformation of
Global Diversity

Andrés T. Tapia

The Inclusion Paradox

The Obama Era and the transformation of global diversity
3rd Edition

Twitter: @AndresTTapia
LinkedIn: LinkedIn.com/in/andrestapia1
Web: kornferry.com/diversity
Blog: inclusionparadox.com

www.kornferry.com
www.kornferry.com/institute

Library of Congress Control Number: 2016908125
ISBN-10: 1946229857
ISBN-13: 978-1946229854

Printed in the United States of America

Item number L84849

To Lori –

mi vida, who keeps it real

A Marisela –

m'hija quien vive y celebra la paradoja de las diferencias

One life

But we are not the same

We get to

Carry each other

One, U2

Table of contents

Author's note
Introduction to the 3rd edition

The post-Obama Era:
Diversity and inclusion are here to stay

Regardless of one's own personal political preferences, the first time Barack Obama was elected president was historic. The second time marked true cultural change. And now, we enter the *post*-Obama Era that will continue to be a time of unprecedented diversity, but its impact will go beyond the shock-and-awe of a radically changed demographic landscape to the institutionalization of the implications of this diversity.

This, of course, doesn't mean that all welcome the changes. Change can be disruptive, chaotic, mistaken. But it is also inevitable, and so we must understand why it has occurred and its implications. This is what inspired in me, a student and practitioner of culture change, to publish the first edition of this book, *The Inclusion Paradox: The Obama Era and the transformation of global diversity*, a few years ago as the US's first Black president began his maiden term.

The election of Barack Obama was a defining moment that captured—both metaphorically and literally—the zeitgeist of the times. This unprecedented moment came to be known as the Obama Era, a period in history that was as much about the demographic changes in society that made possible the election of the United States' first Black president as about the man and leader himself—a man whose own multidimensional biography would come to define diversity in the early twenty-first century.

That first election was certainly historic. It was a massive break through the barriers of color. But it was too soon to tell if it was going to lead to being understood as being anything beyond a flash-in-the-pan stroke of luck. After all, Barack Obama's election took place in the context of an imploding, out-of-control economy hemorrhaging 700,000 jobs a month.[1] In desperation, millions were willing to take a what-the-hell bet of voting for the non-White person who could maybe magically save the nation.

While the insurgency of the 2008 Obama election brought us to the tipping point of a new way of understanding a contemporary and diverse society, as the governing road got tougher and steeper, evidence began to mount that Obama's historic election could end up being an outlier episode rather than a transformative era.

As typically occurs when societies are at the tipping point of a tectonic shift, powerful countervailing forces emerged to prevent this impact from happening. We saw this societal dynamic emerge through the zealous Tea Party phenomenon, which led to major setbacks to the President's agenda in the midterm elections. Conventional wisdom dictated that the Obama adventure wouldn't last more than one term.

But for all the headwinds the country's first Black president faced, the pundits and the opposition fell well short of their predictions. While theories abound of political strategy missteps, it's clear that the biggest oversight by one side—and the greatest asset of the other—was in how they responded to the shifting of diversity demographics.

As many wondered if the 2008 election and the four years that followed were going to end up being an episodic blip, or instead be the first surge of a rising and lasting tidal wave of change, the results of the 2012 election provided the answer. The demographic shifts were here to stay. Barack Hussein Obama swept back into office with the following diverse votes: 90 percent of Blacks, 70 percent of Asians, 70 percent of Latinos, 65 percent of voters under 40, 55 percent of women.

Obama's second election, with its gay marriage victory, the election of the first lesbian US senator, and the election of the greatest number of women to Congress, ended up being the thunderclap announcing that true cultural change had arrived.

And now, even as massive political forces fiercely debate who will lead the post-Obama Era, regardless of who wins the 2016 US presidential election, the changes we saw during the Obama Era are not merely novelties, but patterns woven into the fabric of society for generations to come.

This cultural shift is a lesson that should not be lost on business leaders as they examine their talent and marketplace goals.

Diversity is leading to permanent policy changes

Demographics are destiny. They affect the economy, the schoolhouse, the workplace, and the voting booth. The diverse demographic tsunami with its waves crashing against our electoral shores was a dramatic announcement that the long-predicted diversity of the US had finally arrived. The 2012 election only solidified this reality.

If diversity before the Obama Era had been about a feel-goodism, the embrace of multicultural celebrations, and the paralysis of political correctness, then today's shifting demographics have implications that go far beyond kumbaya moments and exotic cuisine. They head straight into public policy decisions about education, the healthcare system, the financial system, and the nation's tax structure that affect everyone's lives. Regardless of where one stands philosophically or politically, there can be no denying that these massively shifting demographics have upended the policy agenda, creating both deeply seated support as well as opposition. In fact, the vociferousness of the opposition is actually an indication of how real and deep these cultural changes have been.

Consider the following:

- Education reform—with its signature Race to the Top program—has been disproportionately benefitting kids of color as the focus is on failing schools, which have been graduating less than 50 percent of African-American and Latino students.

- Financial reform in 2010 had within its provisions the creation (for the first time ever) within the Federal Reserve System the Office for Minority and Women Inclusion in each of the Federal Reserve Banks. Not only did it call for greater diverse representation in its workforce and leadership, but also for the Fed to press their banks to commit to advancing diversity.

- President Obama signed an Executive Order in 2011 that established a coordinated government-wide initiative to promote diversity and inclusion in the federal workforce that, in his words, is intended "to develop and implement a more comprehensive, integrated, and strategic focus on diversity and inclusion as a key component of their human resources strategies."

- In 2012, nearly one million young undocumented Latinos living in the United States were offered a reprieve from deportation under a presidential executive order.

- In January 2013, Secretary of Defense Leon Panetta lifted the ban on women serving in combat roles, thus removing one of the greatest obstacles to career advancement for women in the military. Then, in 2015, the first-ever female Army Rangers completed what is considered the most grueling physical endurance test in the military.

- The healthcare reform law of 2014 has so far insured over 10 million previously uninsured Americans—a disproportionate number of which are people of color.

- In 2015, the US Supreme Court made same-sex marriages legal in the entire country.

While many will disagree with the merits or values behind the culture changes, for better or for worse, the point has fully tipped. Whatever one's political preferences, we were all players in this culture-change drama. Its myriad implications for the economy, education, energy, immigration, and individual and collective responsibilities—while still happening in fits and starts—are irreversible.

To prove that this embrace of diversity will continue in the post-Obama Era, his second Inaugural ceremony featured the first Latina Supreme Court Justice to administer the Vice President's oath of office, the first Black female to give the invocation, and the first Latino, who is also openly gay, to recite an Inaugural poem.

In addition, the first Black president was also the first president to refer to Gay Rights in an Inaugural speech, the first to advocate for the equal rights for women, and the first to address citizenship rights for the millions of undocumented Latino immigrants. He tied it all together in a stunning statement, referring to the Civil Rights legacy that ran "through Seneca Falls, and Selma, and Stonewall."

This is an upside-down time. If before in the diversity field we singularly focused on how minorities or those traditionally on the margins of society were affected by or were at the mercy of the choices of the majority, we now see this emerging New Mainstream bending the arc of history as they challenge the rules of engagement for those who have traditionally held power.

This, of course, does not mean that the actual solutions are obvious or that they won't require vigorous debate of how best to address. But when African Americans, Latinos, Asians, LGBT, youth, and single women decide the election for president for a second time, and when in the 2016 election there are two Latinos, one African American, and one woman as contenders on the Republican side, and on the Democrat side a woman has a high probability of becoming the first female president, then we can say the agenda has been set by a changing generation of voters for what needs to be addressed for the United States.

People on both sides of the political and philosophical divide agree that they want the United States to remain economically competitive in a world where change—demographically, economically, politically, technologically—is happening at warp speed. What they don't agree on is how best to do this. But one thing is clear: Those who have traditionally been marginalized and whose voices were either not heard or dismissed, given their sheer numbers, cannot be ignored any longer.

And here's where I pivot to the implications for business. The hyper-diversity of the workforce and the marketplace are completely upending long-held beliefs and practices in human resources, marketing, and product development.

Since the publication of the first edition of this book, I moved from the position of Chief Diversity Officer at Hewitt Associates to the post of President of Diversity Best Practices and now I am a Senior Client Partner and Global Practice Leader for Korn Ferry's Workforce Performance, Inclusion and Diversity Practice. Then as now, I've had the opportunity to serve as an executive diversity and inclusion consultant to the C-suite of dozens of Fortune 500 companies. I have stood in front of thousands of leaders and employees around the world from companies such as John Deere, Marriott, McKesson, Barilla, Baxter, United Airlines, IBM, Discover, and dozens more including multinationals from India, China, South Korea, and various European countries.

These experiences allow me to say even more confidently that the ideas and solutions presented here are not just theoretical or hopeful. *They work.* And not just for corporations, but also for not-for-profits, government institutions, schools, law enforcement agencies, and healthcare organizations.

Many of today's problems are legacy outcomes—the results of policies and philosophies that have little to do with today's realities. So the way out is through divergent thinking, through the ability to see our issues in new ways never seen before. The best way to do this? Tap an unprecedented diversity to bust through calcified, narrow-vision traditional thinking. 'Cause same old will continue to mold.

The mold buster is indeed the diversity that too many still fear. If unleashed, leveraged, and managed well, diversity and inclusion can lead the way to breakthrough creativity and innovation. Here's how one of the poster children of the new economy, Indian-born, Ivy-League-educated, US-based CNN political scientist and commentator, Fareed Zakaria, sees the US as narrated on his show *GPS* right after Obama's reelection: "edgy, experimental, open-minded—and brilliantly diverse."

And here's how the namesake of the Obama Era sees it as stated in his reelection acceptance speech in Chicago on election night in 2012: *"I believe we can keep the promise of our founders, the idea that if you're willing to work hard, it doesn't matter who you are or where you come from or what you look like or where you love. It doesn't matter whether you're Black or White or Hispanic or Asian or Native American or young or old or rich or poor, able, disabled, gay or straight, you can make it here in America if you're willing to try."*

The work of diversity and inclusion has never been more important or relevant. Many already see it and are reaping and spreading its benefits, but too many still don't. This is why we still have work to do.

As you open up this third edition with its updated facts, figures, up-to-date current event references, as well as enhanced with new Korn Ferry research and thought leadership, I believe more than ever that diversity and inclusion hold the keys to strengthening our organizations, our markets, our economies, our families, our relationships, and our nations.

What is required to move forward are influential, well-informed, committed, and passionate leaders like you.

¡Adelante! (Forward!)

Foreword

By Michael C. Hyter

Washington DC office Managing Director and Senior Client Partner, Workforce Performance, Inclusion and Diversity, Korn Ferry

I've spent my entire professional career (both in the corporate world and as a strategic consultant/thought leader) engaged in advancing Diversity and Inclusion globally. While next-generation diversity, which is the focus of this book, is about addressing the inclusion of individuals from all traditionally underrepresented groups, I got my start primarily in the successful development of people of color and women. This has been my passion, influenced a great deal by my own experiences of facing exclusion and then being on the receiving end of support from mentors and sponsors throughout my career who were committed to helping me find, and achieve, the fullness of my potential.

Over the years, in spite of the efforts expended by so many of us within the D&I field, the dismal lack of progress in the representation of women and professionals of color within the executive leadership ranks continues to be a significant concern.

So often the perception has been that a well-developed and facilitated D&I training program was the answer. However, training alone is not, nor has ever been, the only answer, since behavior change can't be advanced merely by an event. Instead, true behavior change is a result of a process that includes clearly defined standards, objectives, and clear accountabilities being managed day in and day out.

Even though finding and hiring talent is the easiest thing to measure, it isn´t enough. What is essential, yet gets much less attention given its difficulty, is the retention of talent by creating an environment where diverse talent can thrive.

Throughout my personal journey of consulting with senior executives over the years, I continue to hear from CEOs and their teams that they believe their organizations are "true" meritocracies. Yet when talking to many professionals within their respective companies and looking at the results, the reality of meritocracy is the farthest from the truth.

Derailing the achievement of meritocracy are issues such as the lack of clarity about expectations as well as the failure to position people for success through challenging assignments that are visible, complex, and important. This simply doesn't happen in a consistent way within organizations.

I have observed that the decision makers are blind to the reality that those within an organization who reflect the majority are given special allowances for high-risk opportunities and support through failure at a significantly different rate than those who do not reflect the majority. But because their intentions are honorable, they are clueless of the impact that this imbalance has on those who aren't advancing.

And a cycle is perpetuated based on the assumption that those who aren't advancing is because of their innate inability as opposed to their lack of positioning...and the downward reinforcing cycles continue. To stop this cycle, the real opportunity for truly improving D&I is a sound, effective talent management process that incorporates the understanding and acceptance of differences within the recruitment, onboarding, development, and succession planning systems. That's the key ingredient in creating processes that result in a sustainable outcome where all talent is in alignment with the business strategy needs of an organization.

As I built the D&I practice as the CEO of Global Novations, my team and I were successful in aiding major organizations in addressing D&I as an integral part of talent management (vs. it being a bolt-on set of solutions). When we successfully sold our business to Korn Ferry in 2012, we had the privilege of providing these services to companies around the globe, in 78 offices and 37 countries.

Along the way, I came across Andrés Tapia when he was the Chief Diversity Officer for Hewitt Associates. He turned out to be one of the most innovative, process- and strategic-oriented leaders that I had ever witnessed. His speaking tours and his thought-provoking writings about diversity with a global lens created a huge platform for him and truly impacted many who benefited from his teaching.

So when Andrés joined our D&I practice at Korn Ferry, it was an absolute honor for me to have him as part of the team where he and I are colleagues. Combining the best of what we have to offer to our clients has been a dream come true.

Andrés' commitment to the development and advancement of everyone is a gift, yet his understanding of how that can be done within the complexities of business structures is his unique gift. Andrés codified his approach in this book, *The Inclusion Paradox: The Obama Era and the transformation of global diversity.* In this third edition, Andrés includes updated information based on our collective work together, incorporating Korn Ferry's extensive research, new client stories, and contributions from many of our thought leaders in the Firm.

Andrés' passion, leadership, and clear voice is timeless as an answer to how each of us can play a key role in the success of leveraging diversity within our clients' organizations in a world undergoing vast transformative change.

Enjoy this wonderful body of work, written by one of the leading voices in D&I and multiculturalism in our modern times. I am honored to claim Andrés as a colleague, but more importantly as a friend.

Mike Hyter
Washington, DC

Introduction

It turns out that the warm, let's-all-just-get-along connotations of inclusion are misleading. Achieving true inclusion is hard—very hard. It's harder, in fact, than achieving awareness, tolerance, and sensitivity. It's harder than diversity itself. Ironically, at the same time, it's actually become easier and more hip to talk about diversity and inclusion. Around the world, corporations, not-for-profits, educational institutions, police departments, governments, and the military are catching on that the workforce is changing in dramatic, unstoppable ways. After years of ignoring the swelling demographic tsunami, finally they grasp that these changes raise myriad implications for how organizations hire, manage, develop, promote, and reward their workers in ways that will motivate them to stay and do their best.

Over the past decade, think tanks, boutique consultancies, magazines, and books have showcased stories of winning strategies and programs. Conferences are abuzz with high-voltage diversity energy, while across organizations, an array of initiatives—from mentoring and diversity training to diversity councils and affinity groups—sprout up like mushrooms in the forest after a rainstorm. Stories abound of CEOs making brave statements about their organizations' commitment to diversity, of innovative strategies and programs that crack the glass ceiling, and of members of traditionally marginalized groups landing on career platforms and performing to their full potential. All this has indeed resulted in organizations becoming more diverse overall.

Such accomplishments give us plenty to celebrate, if only for a moment. After a generation of diversity work, organizations increasingly worry that—despite their success at bringing diversity in the door—even the most diligently executed initiatives will not be enough to shatter the glass, concrete, bamboo, tortilla, and rainbow ceilings. Despite years of incremental progress, truly meaningful breakthroughs remain elusive, with managerial and leadership ranks falling *far short* of reflecting what should be the most diverse workforce in the history of civilization. Increasingly, top-of-the-house leaders realize if they don't get this right—if they fail to tap into the ranks of diverse talent around them—their organizations face weakened financials at best, and extinction at worst.

As a leader in the diversity and inclusion space and consultant to many multinational organizations, I've witnessed firsthand how employers across the United States, Canada, India, South Korea, China, and various countries across Latin America and Europe—even those who have heartily embraced diversity—were caught off guard by the implications of an increasingly diverse workforce. As they seek to portray themselves as being open to a workforce that *looks* different, they have done little to adjust to a workforce that *thinks* different. Such thinking leads to different behaviors, which, in turn, further churn up the usual organizational undercurrents.

Consider the complexities of the following scenarios: White females managing African-American males, who in turn manage White males, Latina women, and immigrant- and US-born Asians—all of whom are charged with delivering profitability for an enterprise statistically still run by White males. Then there are Indians managing teams in the United States, Argentineans shaping the global financial system of a US-based multinational, and Muslims making global real estate decisions from their offices in Dubai.

These workforce shifts take place amidst massive global demographic, political, and economic changes, where trends in each of these arenas accelerate those in another. For example, the Obama Era—a time when the US had its first-ever Black president—carried with it profound cultural implications, both in the United States and globally, that affected not only personal, group, and institutional relationships, but also how we do our work strategically and day-to-day. Among the populations most significantly impacted has been the emerging workforce. An increasingly multicultural workforce requires a deeper cultural understanding from many different angles—not only what cultures are in the mix, but also what individuals believe, how they act, and *why* they act that way.

The Inclusion Paradox: The Obama Era and the transformation of global diversity 3rd edition explores the impact of the Obama phenomenon from a cultural—rather than political—perspective. Sure, there are myriad political observations to be made on blue state/red state shifts and in the many legitimate yet contentious policy debates swirling in Washington. But whether our views align more with the Tea Party, the Occupy Wall Street crowd, or the uncategorized, regardless of how such matters end up getting hashed out politically, there's an undeniable, transformative story that has been unfolding that includes all of us globally. Whatever one's political preferences or passions, we're all unwitting players in this culture-change drama.

In the context of extensive consulting and speaking, I have
cultural implications that I believe have been hallmarks of the
believed these to be true at the start of the Obama Era, and as
to the post-Obama Era, I believe that these will continue to be tr

1. Inclusion is a transformative force.

2. Our actions have global impact.

3. Diversity and inclusion require intentionality.

4. We'll experience a renaissance of values-driven decision making.

5. We must have a heightened focus on results.

6. The bottom-up is as important as the top-down.

7. "Both/and" trumps "either/or."

8. True diversity and inclusion require calling out our differences, not
    minimizing them.

Because he is a full reflection of today's contemporary, pervasive diversity—
Kansas-born White mother, Kenya-born Black father, single-mom raised,
Hawaii-shaped, Indonesia-influenced—let's explore these hallmarks in
more detail, using Obama's own biography-influenced words to frame the
discussion.

Admittedly, the selections are from the aspirational moments—some of which
have been bound to crash head-on into harsher realties. But these aspirations
reveal forces of diversity unleashed in this era that are unprecedented, so
much so that they also generate counterforces of resistance that further
confirm that we are in the midst of a transformational era.

Inclusion is a transformative force*

"If there's anyone out there who still doubts that America is a place where all things are possible; who still wonders if the dream of our founders is alive in our time; who still questions the power of our democracy, tonight is your answer. It's the answer told by lines that stretched around schools and churches in numbers this nation has never seen, by people who waited three hours and four hours, many for the very first time in their lives, that their voice could be that difference. It's the answer spoken by young and old, rich and poor, Democrat and Republican, Black, White, Latino, Asian, Native American, gay, straight, disabled, and not disabled."
– President-elect Barack Obama's Acceptance Speech in Grant Park, Chicago, November 4, 2008

Changing demographics have radically transformed the workplace. Massive immigration and aging populations have significantly changed the face of the American workforce. More generations are in the workforce than ever before, forcing organizations to deal with and benefit from the differing perspectives of Traditionalists, Baby Boomers, Gen Xers, and Millennials. At the same time, women and racial/ethnic minorities account for a rapidly growing portion of the workforce, with some reaching the upper echelon of their organizations. Xerox, Yahoo, HP, Kraft, and PepsiCo all have strong female CEOs, while Merck, United Airlines, and MasterCard have African-American, Latino, and Indian chief executives.

It's no coincidence that we're seeing these demographic trends. A generation ago, women and minorities were achieving breakthroughs in the arenas of sports and entertainment. Today, gender and color glass ceilings are cracking in the corporate and political arenas of power. With this new talent comes

....

* Since that historic night, President Obama has continued to speak about the transformative force of diversity: *"An America that doesn't simply tolerate people of different backgrounds and beliefs, but an America where we are enriched by our diversity. An America where we treat one another with respect and with dignity, remembering that here in the United States there is no 'them' or 'us'; it's just us. An America where our fundamental freedoms and inalienable rights are not simply preserved, but continually renewed and refreshed.... Put simply, we must be the America that goes forward as one family, like generations before us, pulling together in times of trial, staying true to our core values and emerging even stronger. This is who we are and this is who we must always be."*
– President Obama's remarks during Iftar dinner, August 10, 2011

And

"For we know that our patchwork heritage is a strength, not a weakness. We are a nation of Christians and Muslims, Jews and Hindus—and non-believers. We are shaped by every language and culture, drawn from every end of this Earth; and because we have tasted the bitter swill of civil war and segregation, and emerged from that dark chapter stronger and more united, we cannot help but believe that the old hatreds shall someday pass; that the lines of tribe shall soon dissolve; that as the world grows smaller, our common humanity shall reveal itself; and that America must play its role in ushering in a new era of peace." – President Obama's Inaugural Address, January 20, 2009

new styles of leadership, new business strategies, new corporate policies, and new approaches to creating more inclusive environments.

When there are more people who "look like me" up the succession path, more employees can hope that they, too, have a chance to succeed. Just over 15 years ago, Linda DeLavallade, an African-American diversity practitioner whose career trajectory has included meaningful stints at Hewitt and Allstate, was working for a major bank. She was told she could not aspire to a certain role because "we only have one Black man and one Black woman in the executive recruiting organization at a time." This meant she had to wait until the Black woman who currently occupied the position resigned.

In the wake of Obama's 2008 and 2012 elections, Linda reflected on how different corporate America feels now, compared to that time at the bank. "I've received quite a bit of support in recent years from the diverse teams I've been on," she said. "Not only have I seen greater opportunity, the leaders of those teams supported me by letting me be me and not force-fitting me into a certain mold."

Our actions have global impact

"Throughout human history, societies have grappled with fundamental questions of how to organize themselves, the proper relationship between the individual and the state, the best means to resolve inevitable conflicts between states. And it was here in Europe, through centuries of struggle— through war and Enlightenment, repression and revolution—that a particular set of ideals began to emerge: The belief that through conscience and free will, each of us has the right to live as we choose. The belief that power is derived from the consent of the governed, and that laws and institutions should be established to protect that understanding. And those ideas eventually inspired a band of colonialists across an ocean, and they wrote them into the founding documents that still guide America today, including the simple truth that all men—and women—are created equal.

"But those ideals have also been tested—here in Europe and around the world. Those ideals have often been threatened by an older, more traditional view of power. This alternative vision argues that ordinary men and women are too small-minded to govern their own affairs, that order and progress can only come when individuals surrender their rights to an all-powerful sovereign. Often, this alternative vision roots itself in the notion that by virtue of race or faith or ethnicity, some are inherently superior to others, and that individual

identity must be defined by 'us' versus 'them,' or that national greatness must flow not by what a people stand for, but by what they are against.

...

"The ideals that came to define our [North Atlantic] alliance also inspired movements across the globe among those very people, ironically, who had too often been denied their full rights by Western powers. After the Second World War, people from Africa to India threw off the yoke of colonialism to secure their independence. In the United States, citizens took freedom rides and endured beatings to put an end to segregation and to secure their civil rights. As the Iron Curtain fell here in Europe, the iron fist of apartheid was unclenched, and Nelson Mandela emerged upright, proud, from prison to lead a multiracial democracy."

– President Obama's remarks to European youth at the Palais des Beaux Arts Brussels, Belgium, March 26, 2014

The US election was followed with deep, vested interest by people in capitals, towns, and hamlets outside the United States with the understanding that the choice made in both Novembers in 2008 and 2012 would have an impact not only for Americans, but for people around the world. From the beginning, Barack Obama got this, as evidenced in his 2008 acceptance speech: *"To all those watching tonight from beyond our shores, from parliaments and palaces to those who are huddled around radios in the forgotten corners of our world—our stories are singular, but our destiny is shared."* Similarly, choices made at multinational corporate headquarters in London, Stuttgart, Paris, New York, Mumbai, Shanghai, Chicago, and Los Angeles have great impact on the far-flung global corners of their companies.

In a world where events in Washington, Delhi, São Paulo, Athens, and Dubai have instant impact everywhere, the challenges that President Obama has faced have been, in some ways, similar for all business leaders. Our words, decisions, and actions have immediate impact on employees' commitment and enthusiasm, and, by extension, on the quality of their work. "This challenges us as diversity leaders to step it up and come up with transformative ways of doing things," says Deb Taylor, former Director of Global Diversity at Deere & Company.

Pauline Kiejman, a global human resources consultant and a French citizen working in the UK, viewed the dawn of the Obama Era in light of its effects on global diversity: "Obama's election simply gave me hope. In a gloomy economic climate, watching the world celebrate this election together was truly uplifting. It made me feel there's hope for the values of diversity, for real change in how we interact with each other. As I looked around me in our

London office, I thought about how diverse we are as a team—from Australians to Indians, Swedes, French, English, Scots, Irish, and Americans—and I hoped this could go even further in the future."

Diversity and inclusion require intentionality

"To realize more fully the goal of using the talents of all segments of society, the Federal Government must continue to challenge itself to enhance its ability to recruit, hire, promote, and retain a more diverse workforce. Further, the Federal Government must create a culture that encourages collaboration, flexibility, and fairness to enable individuals to participate to their full potential.... By this order, I am directing executive departments and agencies to develop and implement a more comprehensive, integrated, and strategic focus on diversity and inclusion as a key component of their human resources strategies. This approach should include a continuing effort to identify and adopt best practices, implemented in an integrated manner, to promote diversity and remove barriers to equal employment opportunity, consistent with merit system principles and applicable law."

– President Obama, Executive Order 13583 – Establishing a Coordinated Government-wide Initiative to Promote Diversity and Inclusion in the Federal Workforce, August 18, 2011

True inclusion begins with a deliberate proclamation, but it can't end there. It must then be followed by relentless intentionality at every level of the organization.

When I first met Russ Fradin at the start of his tenure as Hewitt's CEO a few years ago, he told me about his commitment to diversity, stressing that he was not so much for talking about it than doing it. "As I create my leadership team, I plan to have a diverse executive council," he said matter-of-factly.

Sure enough, his intentionality surfaced when four of his nine direct reports were women and two were people of color. "Hewitt has a proud legacy of inclusion that is part of what makes us a special company," he said then. "Our strong and long-standing commitment to creating a diverse workforce is not only the right thing to do, but it's good for business." He added pragmatically that Hewitt's clients spanned the majority of the Fortune 500—"a diverse set of companies with a diverse set of employees. We find that reflecting this same diversity in our own workforce allows us to approach our work from multiple perspectives."

Many other CEOs have led with this point of view, including Korn Ferry's CEO Gary Burnison. "The world is more diverse than ever before, a multicultural mosaic of endless variety," he says. "Celebrating the richness of that diversity is the heritage of trailblazing societal changes that have empowered people to stand up for themselves and their identities. But diversity, alone, is not enough. Inclusion is diversity's companion. While diversity honors our differences, inclusion bridges them. When a particular work environment or society is inclusive, there is a seat for everyone at the table. Conversations become enriched and exchanges of ideas gain texture as people contribute viewpoints and perspectives from how they see, experience, and participate in the world."

Korn Ferry's clients agree, plus add their own rationale. Says Bob Lane, Deere & Company's former Chairman and CEO, "If we're to succeed in today's very competitive environment, which requires us to have the best talent from as many different diverse pools as possible, we need to treat diversity with the same focus and dedication as we have put into our company hallmarks, such as quality."

Sodexo's Chief Diversity Officer Rohini Anand reflects further on what this means in terms of changing the way organizations have operated in the Obama Era and beyond. "It might mean reframing how work is getting done. It's a new day in many ways, and I think that we're seeing a new generation, a generation of folks who have not necessarily seen the hardships of the Civil Rights movement. I think we know that there's a lot more work to be done, but we need to reframe how that's done. And think about new strategies to get there."

We'll experience a renaissance of values-driven decision making**

"We the people declare today that the most evident of truth that all of us are created equal—is the star that guides us still; just as it guided our forebears through Seneca Falls and Selma and Stonewall; just as it guided all those men and women, sung and unsung, who left footprints along this great mall, to hear a preacher say that we cannot walk alone; to hear a King proclaim that our individual freedom is inextricably bound to the freedom of every soul on

....

** Here the President continues the oft-repeated theme regarding the common bonds Americans share, and which represents his deeply felt value that we are each other's keepers. *"There are mothers and fathers who will lie awake after their children fall asleep and wonder how they'll make the mortgage, or pay their doctor's bills, or save enough for college. There is new energy to harness and new jobs to be created; new schools to build and threats to meet and alliances to repair. The road ahead will be long. Our climb will be steep…but America—I have never been more hopeful than I am tonight that we'll get there. I promise you—we as a people will get there. So let us summon a new spirit of patriotism; of service and responsibility where each of us resolves to pitch in and work harder and look after not only ourselves, but each other."*
– President-elect Barack Obama's 2008 Acceptance Speech

Earth. It is now our generation's task to carry on what those pioneers began, for our journey is not complete until our wives, our mothers, and daughters can earn a living equal to their efforts. Our journey is not complete until our gay brothers and sisters are treated like anyone else under the law, for if we are truly created equal, then surely the love we commit to one another must be equal, as well. Our journey is not complete until we find a better way to welcome the striving, hopeful immigrants who still see America as a land of opportunity, until bright young students and engineers are enlisted in our workforce rather than expelled from our country."
- President Obama's, 2nd Inaugural Speech, January 21, 2013

Recently, a CEO prefaced a presentation regarding some tough decisions about cost management by saying, "Speaking from my heart..." He went on to explain how his leadership team had considered the tight economy and how difficult it would be for laid-off workers to find jobs. As a result, the company chose to offer voluntary reduced hours and unpaid sabbaticals, so employees would be able to keep their jobs and full-time healthcare benefits.

During the global financial crisis that began in 2008, Pricewaterhouse Coopers (PwC) pledged to lay off people only as a last resort, and instead asked every employee to take responsibility for making hard cost-reduction decisions within their spheres of influence. Other companies made similar choices. As Pauline Kiejman observes, "As we work with leaders, part of the message now, more than ever, is the need for them to speak from the heart and, rather than draw on people's worst fears, draw from their best hopes."

Today's Millennials in particular are demanding nothing less than for corporations to act as moral players who care for their people, the communities around them, and the planet. A company's track record of making values-based decisions is as carefully scrutinized as their job offers, and what they find could either clinch or break the deal of whether they say yes or not. These rivers of doing social good run deep. Neither symbolic gestures nor inconsistent policies around common-good impact are tolerated as good enough. And as Millennials hopscotch into being half of the world's workforce and, therefore, move more fully into leadership and management, they won't be asking for values-based leadership—rather simply just doing it themselves.

We must have a heightened focus on results***

"I feel confident in being able to say that every one of the agencies in this government has been focused on how do they improve, get smarter, get better, get faster, become more focused on delivering good value to the end user."

– President Obama's remarks before the President's Council on Jobs and Competitiveness, January 17, 2012

The Obama Administration has faced huge challenges in terms of the economy, the environment, terrorism, healthcare, and retirement. Every organization faces some of these same issues, albeit on a smaller scale. How do we come out stronger following a worldwide recession? How do we harness our know-how—our core knowledge and skills—to help our customers, clients, and constituents better address these huge challenges and still remain viable and financially strong?

Diversity and inclusion must not merely inspire, it must also contribute tangibly to business and organizational objectives. "Clearly in these tough economic times, heightened focus on results applies to diversity and inclusion as well. It's not immune from the need to deliver results," says Sodexo's Anand. "We have to focus on the bottom line. And yes, in addition to contributing to profits, the work must lead to tangible and visible improvement to a company's representation and culture of inclusion. Results must positively impact on our clients' and customers' quality of life."

In 2008, Robert Parkinson, then Chairman and CEO at Baxter International Inc., launched the 75-year-old company's sustainability philosophy and strategy. His approach is typical of an emerging mindset that puts its stake in the powerful combination of both a results- and values-driven orientation. Here's how Parkinson framed it on Baxter's website:

No global corporation can afford not to act responsibly in today's marketplace. Baxter's approach to sustainability reflects the quality of our management, our people, and our company culture. It also reflects the responsibility and accountability we must demonstrate to remain a global leader in our industry. We also see sustainability as a way to

....

*** The President, like business leaders everywhere, is assessed on his results. Diversity is no exception to this political and business reality. *"America, we have come so far. We have seen so much. But there's so much more to do. So tonight, let us ask ourselves—if our children should live to see the next century; if my daughters should be so lucky to live as long as Ann Nixon Cooper* [the 106-year-old voter he referred to earlier in the speech], *what change will they see? What progress will we have made?"*
– President-elect Barack Obama's 2008 Acceptance Speech

attract and retain talent and make Baxter a rewarding place to work and develop. Ultimately, we believe our efforts in sustainability enhance shareholder value by making Baxter a more competitive company in an increasingly challenging business environment. Our efforts to bring lifesaving therapies to countries where many people still go untreated for conditions such as hemophilia, kidney disease, and others are not altruistic. It's our business. But the goal is similar to other elements of sustainability—to save and sustain lives. It's this higher purpose that binds everyone at Baxter together as a company and as global citizens.[1] 🙲🙲

In his presentations to employees, Parkinson also emphasized diversity and inclusion's role in creating a sustainable and profitable culture.

The bottom-up is as important as the top-down

"And above all, I will ask you to join in the work of remaking this nation the only way it's been done in America for 221 years—block by block, brick by brick, calloused hand by calloused hand. What began 21 months ago in the depths of winter must not end on this autumn night. This victory alone is not the change we seek—it's only the chance for us to make that change. And that cannot happen if we go back to the way things were. It cannot happen without you."
– President-elect Barack Obama's 2008 Acceptance Speech

For the diverse crowd of 250,000 in Chicago's Grant Park on election night, the emotion of the night went beyond history-in-the-making or even beyond a partisan victory. What seemed to come from deep in the hearts of homemakers, professionals, janitors, executives, massage therapists, hip hop teenagers, actors, homeless people, college students, retirees, able-bodied and disabled people, and gay and straight people was the visceral sense that this moment wouldn't have been possible without each group and each individual having actively chosen to participate. The consensus analysis of the 2012 election result was that this was even more critical the second time around.

Obama grounded his inclusion philosophy in the American national motto of "Out of the many, one" *(E pluribus unum)*. Empowerment is much more than a state of mind. In the case of Obama's election, it yielded a tangible historic result. When traditionally marginalized individuals are given an opportunity to have their voices heard and their talents showcased, the potential that is revealed will make what seemed impossible, possible—not just for them, but for the world around them. The culture's sense is that we're all part of making this happen.

There's a lesson here for organizations seeking diversity breakthroughs. Baxter's former Vice President of Global Inclusion and Diversity Don Wilson explains, "As much as we look to our leaders to set the course, no matter how right the path may be, it means nothing unless all of us, regardless of our role or pay band, find our place to contribute and step into it."

"Both/and" trumps "either/or"

"For it's precisely the pursuit of ideological purity, the rigid orthodoxy, and the sheer predictability of our current political debate that keeps us from finding new ways to meet the challenges we face as a country. It's what keeps us locked in 'either-or' thinking: the notion that we can have only big government or no government; the assumptions that we must either tolerate 46 million without health insurance or embrace socialized medicine. What's needed is a broad majority of Americans—Democrats, Republicans, and Independents of goodwill who are reengaged in the project of national renewal and who see their own self-interest inextricably linked to the interests of others.... I imagine they are waiting for a politics with the maturity to balance idealism and realism, to distinguish between what can and cannot be compromised, to admit the possibility that the other side might sometimes have a point. They don't always understand the arguments between right and left, conservative and liberal, but they recognize the difference between dogma and common sense, responsibility and irresponsibility, between those things that last and those that are fleeting."

– From *The Audacity of Hope: Thoughts on Reclaiming the American Dream*
   by Barack Obama, 2006

Through this mindset, Obama attempted to chart a course to move the discourse from either/or to both/and possibilities. Admittedly, this has proven significantly more difficult that anyone had imagined. However, as elusive as this has been, the only way out of polarized either/or debates and thinking is both/and.

While his realm is in politics—attempting new ways of addressing foreign policy, abortion, gay civil rights, healthcare—this also creates new possibilities in organizations. "There's speed, quality, and low cost," the workplace adage says, "but you can only have two out of the three." Today's upside-down, fast-paced world is rejecting this either/or choice. The times demand solutions that can deliver all three.

Both/and allows us to celebrate individual accomplishments, while still reveling in being our brothers' and sisters' keepers—to celebrate a working woman for her accomplishments as a mother *and* her success as a senior executive of a leading corporation; to create a more inclusive definition of diversity that goes beyond race and gender, but that still addresses the unfinished business of underrepresentation in management and leadership. That moving forward the work of diversity does not entail doing it at the expense of the White male, but rather including him in it in ways that he also benefits.

True diversity and inclusion require calling out our differences, not minimizing them

Here's Obama on race:

"For the African-American community, *that path means embracing the burdens of our past without becoming victims of our past. It means continuing to insist on a full measure of justice in every aspect of American life. But it also means binding our particular grievances—for better healthcare, and better schools, and better jobs—to the larger aspirations of all Americans—the White woman struggling to break the glass ceiling, the White man who's been laid off, the immigrant trying to feed his family. And it means taking full responsibility for our own lives—by demanding more from our fathers, and spending more time with our children, and reading to them, and teaching them that while they may face challenges and discrimination in their own lives, they must never succumb to despair or cynicism; they must always believe that they can write their own destiny.... In the* White community, *the path to a more perfect union means acknowledging that what ails the African-American community does not just exist in the minds of Black people; that the legacy of discrimination—and current incidents of discrimination, while less overt than in the past—are real and must be addressed. Not just with words, but with deeds—by investing in our schools and our communities; by enforcing our Civil Rights laws and ensuring fairness in our criminal justice system; by providing this generation with ladders of opportunity that were unavailable for previous generations. It requires all Americans to realize that your dreams do not have to come at the expense of my dreams; that investing in the health, welfare, and education of Black and Brown and White children will ultimately help all of America prosper."*
- Senator Barack Obama's "A More Perfect Union" Speech, March 18, 2008

Here's Obama on sexual orientation:

"No longer will our country be denied the service of thousands of patriotic Americans who were forced to leave the military—regardless of their skills, no matter their bravery or their zeal, no matter their years of exemplary performance—because they happen to be gay. No longer will tens of thousands of Americans in uniform be asked to live a lie, or look over their shoulder, in order to serve the country that they love. As Admiral Mike Mullen has said, 'Our people sacrifice a lot for their country, including their lives. None of them should have to sacrifice their integrity as well.' ... Finally, I want to speak directly to the gay men and women currently serving in our military. For a long time your service has demanded a particular kind of sacrifice. You've been asked to carry the added burden of secrecy and isolation. And all the while, you've put your lives on the line for the freedoms and privileges of citizenship that are not fully granted to you. You're not the first to have carried this burden, for while today marks the end of a particular struggle that has lasted almost two decades, this is a moment more than two centuries in the making."

– President Obama's remarks at the signing of the repeal of the Don't Ask, Don't Tell Act, December 22, 2010

In the Obama Era, effectively calling out differences matters more than ever—not just in our interpersonal relationships, but also in product design, development, and marketing. Pharmaceuticals, for example, are realizing they need to address differences in their clinical trials, because the bodies and chemical levels of homogenous male participants respond differently than women's bodies, and the physiological response of African Americans to certain medicines may be different than those of Africans or Latinos.

Likewise, BASF, the German chemical company, had a breakthrough on behalf of its client Adidas when it tuned into the reality that Asian feet are different from Western feet. That explained why Adidas running shoes were not selling well in Asia. As soon as the company redesigned the shoes to the realities of Asian feet, sales skyrocketed.

The same concept applies to people. For people to feel included in their work organizations, we must get better at constructively calling out the differences among the talent in our midst. This, in turn, will help us shape programs and opportunities that entice the best talent to come work for us, and then to do their best work and thrive. More than ever, organizations must build platforms that give voice to their diverse populations, which are still highly concentrated in the lower levels of our organizations.

"The Obama election taught us that we need to recognize and tap into the various different constituencies and their unique needs and points of view," says Edie Fraser, CEO of STEMconnector® and its Million Women Mentors (MWM) initiative. "So, it's very clear that the active participation of women, Hispanics, LGBT, and so many others in the electoral process—there's recognition that in order to win, you've got to include diversity and inclusion in terms of volunteers, money, and votes. And so you've got to have the policies that call out and address the unique needs of various different groups."

This quote of then Senator Barack Obama from his seminal speech on race, "A More Perfect Union" delivered at Constitution Center in Philadelphia, Pennsylvania on March 18, 2008, captures the diversity and inclusion ethos of the Obama Era which is that calling out differences constructively rather than either destructively or, conversely, minimizing them as inconsequential, is much more effective: *"I believe deeply that we cannot solve the challenges of our time unless we solve them together—unless we perfect our union by understanding that we may have different stories, but we hold common hopes; that we may not look the same and we may not have come from the same place, but we all want to move in the same direction—towards a better future for our children and our grandchildren."*

What is the Inclusion Paradox?

This brings us to the concept of the Inclusion Paradox, which will be used throughout the book to explore the various cultural dimensions of the Obama Era and beyond.

Before we can define the paradox, however, we must first distinguish between diversity and inclusion. These terms are often bandied about as synonyms. While they relate to the same ultimate goal, they are in no way synonymous. In *The Inclusion Paradox,* I offer a differentiated view of these two terms—one that has resonated with clients in diverse industries and different countries:

Diversity is the mix. Inclusion is making the mix work™.

Many diversity best practices have focused on bringing those who are different in the door. Many of these efforts have been quite successful, and companies have achieved diversity—the mix. But in many places, the mix is not working well. We end up with *diversity without inclusion.* Here, diversity's promise—that greater diversity leads to greater innovation and profitability—dies.

Our inclusion deficiencies show up in higher turnover rates for people of color across the board, and for women in certain companies and industries. The non-budging nature of the different ceilings (glass, concrete, bamboo, tortilla, and rainbow) attests to the fact that inclusion has fallen short of its promise.

Without inclusion, advancement becomes difficult. Good management and leadership skills often are not recognized when they are manifested differently than the organization's mainstream. And, rather than leading to new ways of doing things, "different" ends up being defined as poor performance.

How do we achieve both diversity and inclusion? For starters, we must challenge the long-standing "best practice" belief that to achieve inclusion, *we need to minimize differences.* Differences based on gender, race, ethnicity, nationality, faith, income, education, sexual orientation, physical abilities, military experience, and other dimensions are too ingrained, too hard-wired into what makes us and shapes our thinking. Trying to submerge these for the sake of a definition of inclusion rooted in sameness is unrealistic.

In other words, in order to have inclusion, rather than minimizing differences, we need to call them out constructively. *This is what I refer to as the Inclusion Paradox.*

Calling out differences has significant implications for workforce policies and programs. "The diversification of the workforce means that the term 'average employee' is fading away," says Andy Hiles, former National Benefits Leader at McKinsey & Company and now VP Strategy, Actuarial and Underwriting, National Accounts at Aetna. "Workforce policies and programs designed to support the 'average employee' increasingly miss the mark in meeting employees' needs and desires."

Calling out differences unleashes the true creative contributions of diverse perspectives that play off each other and lead to better work relationships, greater innovation, and profitability that benefit individuals, teams, and organizations.

And throughout this book's discussion, the Obama Era and its legacy will be the canvas against which we'll explore how to apply the Inclusion Paradox.

A three-step approach to mastering the Inclusion Paradox

The foundation for creating true inclusion lies in organizations and individuals who can manage these called-out differences. They must possess a bundle of skills—referred to as *crosscultural agility*—which entails three fundamental steps for navigating the Inclusion Paradox. Because the levels of awareness are interdependent and sequential, we must master these three steps in the following order:

1. **It's all about me.** Know who you are and what you believe. What is the foundation for these beliefs? How do you put these beliefs into action? How do others perceive you and your actions?

2. **It's all about them.** Know how others are different. What do you see in others? Why do they act as they do? How are their beliefs reflected in their actions?

3. **It's all about us.** Know how to navigate the gap. Since you can't know everything about everyone, consider how you can bridge the gap between what you know and don't know. When is an issue personal, cultural, or something else? How do you make sure that what you said is actually what is heard? How do you resolve cultural differences to arrive at mutually satisfying solutions?

These three steps, coupled with the eight Obama Era implications, will help equip you for the lifelong journey of mutually transforming yourself, the people around you, and the organizations of which you are a part. Becoming culturally competent is an essential skill in our global, multicultural, multigenerational diverse world. Those who master it will be best positioned to thrive in this transformative time.

Site map for book

I wrote this book from the perspective of a get-it-done, strategy-focused, corporate officer and later C-suite consultant. It's geared toward stimulating paradigm-shift thinking to achieve diversity and inclusion breakthrough in the workplace. At the same time, it is not a book about best practices and not intended as a detailed road map for change.

Every workplace is unique. What works for some may not work for others. Rather, *The Inclusion Paradox* looks beyond best practices and gets readers to open themselves to new ways of thinking about common and vexing challenges. In *The Inclusion Paradox,* I share stories as well as strategic steps that individuals, teams, and organizations can take to create true inclusion.

The Inclusion Paradox is divided into five major sections:
 Part 1: The urgency of inclusion
 Part 2: Calling out differences in relationships
 Part 3: Calling out differences in groups
 Part 4: Calling out differences in organizations
 Conclusion: Be the change you wish to see in the world

There's a logical build from the first to the last section, but the chapters within Parts 3 and 4 are written topically, which means they stand on their own and can be read in any sequence based on what interests you the most.

Part 1: The urgency of inclusion

The emerging workforce is more diverse, virtual, autonomous, and empowered than ever, yet it is also smaller and less skilled. In this section, I lay out the business case for addressing the major global forces—demographics, technology, longer life spans, and financial risk management by corporations and government—that require a fundamentally different approach to the workplace. While drastic changes will be needed to engage and harness the energy of this emerging workforce, this book focuses on the need to create more powerfully inclusive environments.

Part 2: Calling out differences in relationships

Workplace clashes are *inevitable*. The seemingly minor mismatches and judgments of those who are different contribute to underlying tensions between people. When these differences are minimized rather than called out, "going along to get along" often leads to greater conflict and frustration rather than resolution. This section focuses on ways to create profitable interpersonal relationships in the workplace. It touches on the various ways in which we're different—gender, race/ethnicity, nationality, sexual orientation, and ability—and how this plays out in relationships among people who work together.

Part 3: Calling out differences in groups

In this section, I explore the challenges and opportunities related to today's multicultural, diverse teams. I examine the sociological characteristics of diverse groups, as defined by gender, race/ethnicity, nationality, sexual orientation, age, and ability—and how these play themselves out in intergroup interactions. By calling out differences and managing them effectively, organizations can achieve true inclusion and successful group relationships, which in turn leads to more profitable products and services.

Part 4: Calling out differences in organizations

Organizations have a compelling story to tell. In this section, I highlight those that have effectively, legally, and profitably utilized differences to execute human resources programs such as recruiting, performance management, benefits, leadership development, succession planning, and employee engagement. By recognizing differences, organizations can more effectively evaluate the success of their corporate brand, communications, and performance management processes, and as a result, can attract, engage, and retain the best talent from all backgrounds.

Conclusion: Be the change you wish to see in the world

I conclude this book on a note of hope. While the threats of the new world order are evident, so are the possibilities for an exponential explosion of creativity, innovation, and life-improving products and services birthed through the union of diversity and inclusion. Embracing the mix and knowing how to make it work will give us the power to create an alternative, uplifting, and creative vision.

On a more immediate note, I'd like to leave you with the message that corporations, not-for-profits, government, law enforcement, and the military will have to attract and retain the best talent from multiple labor pools if they are to survive the Talent War—and the key to attraction lies in creating truly inclusive environments. However, don't be fooled by how soft and effortless that sounds—inclusion is one of the hardest things to achieve.

"This is our moment. This is our time," Obama proclaimed as he closed his 2008 acceptance speech. In a world where rules are changing at a dizzying rate and we find ourselves facing unparalleled and simultaneous threats and opportunities, the question of the moment is this: In the urgency of now, in your life and in your work, what new possibilities do you see? *The Inclusion Paradox* is meant to help you answer this question. ⬭

PART 1:
THE URGENCY
OF INCLUSION

Part 1: The urgency of inclusion

Context is everything. Words, actions, gestures. Policies, pronouncements, punditry. Their impact—or lack of it—is given life by the ground on which the seed falls. In Part 1, I delve deeper into the overture of themes sounded in the book's introduction. What are the specific trends that shaped the Obama Era? How are these trends shaping the current and future emerging workforce? What implications do they have on diversity and inclusion? And what does it all mean for each of us, both personally and in the work that we do?

In the pages that follow, I present a holistic view of how today's environment—steeped in economic crisis, unstoppable globalization, and wildly escalating diversity—has upped the ante and created both greater peril and unprecedented opportunity for organizations and individuals.

No country is an island. The interconnections among us and among our countries and institutions are inextricable. Much like Chaos Theory posits that the flutter of a butterfly's wings can trigger a chain reaction, potentially leading to hurricanes and other natural disasters, the flutter of decisions made in the boardroom can lead to massive job losses or gains anywhere in the world. Financial decisions made on Wall Street sweep through Main Streets from London to Lhasa. A misinterpreted gesture can result in the loss of a multimillion-dollar deal. A misplaced word can ruin a relationship for a lifetime.

Before we get into specific strategies for addressing implications of the mix and making it work, we must first understand the context in which we live and work. It doesn't matter if you're a small, independently owned and operated mom-and-pop store or a major multinational chain. Nor does it matter if you're a CEO, a manager, or an entry-level employee. Context affects everyone regardless of size, geographic location, or position. To make smart decisions, we must be grounded in context.

At the same time, the global reality needs to be contextualized to each individual country, or specific diversity and inclusion issue. Granted, there is demographic change worldwide, but how it manifests itself shows up differently depending on the area in which it occurs.

Organizations must recognize these differences when formulating their inclusion strategies or they run the risk of seeing their efforts backfire, resulting in employee turnover and alienation. They must factor in the challenges that other countries face that are unique to their own demographics and that may not always parallel those of the United States.

The Inclusion Paradox requires that we not only acknowledge the differences among us, but also that we learn to navigate those differences to make the mix work. To meet the challenge of difference—to navigate the paradox of inclusion—we need the foundational skill of crosscultural agility. It's not a skill that comes naturally, but it can be learned.

Join me as we take a closer look at today's context and examine crosscultural competence, a critical capability that is essential for successfully navigating the post-Obama Era. ♀

AN UPSIDE-DOWN WORLD

Chapter 1
An upside-down world

The world is not flat – it's upside-down.

An African American has now been President of the United States, twice. To be a minority is to be the majority; to be young is to be more experienced; to be a woman is to be rising in opportunities; to be disabled is to be differently-abled; to be a Veteran is to be honored; to be out is to be in. Economic instability rocks the most advanced economies. Dubai is now a capital of innovation. Financial behemoths on Wall Street in New York and in The City in London disappeared overnight à la Lehman Brothers, were swallowed up by others, or were hammered with charges of wrongdoing.

Meanwhile, countries that had been considered third world—beset by violence, dictatorships, and dysfunctional economies—are now bursting with economic booms. China surpassed the United States as the largest economy in the world in 2014.[1] Brazil and India are economic powerhouses. Even the small are becoming mighty. Colombia, a country with a reputation as a failing state ridden with drugs and crime, is as of 2015 making tremendous economic progress. Colombia's economy is thriving and, along with Peru's, has become the fastest-growing economy in Latin America.[2]

All of these economic double-takes, plus China holding about 7 percent of US Treasury securities[3] (making it the nation's largest creditor), the Middle East upheavals redrawing boundaries and alliances, the election of a black US president who rose with a power base in the grassroots and not in Washington, and a raucous anti-establishment US 2016 presidential election clearly indicate that the old economic and political order is being dismantled and new ones are rising. But there is deep uncertainty about what the new order in these various contexts will mean for the next generation.

Daily, even hourly, we feel the relentless aftershocks of changes at work—in our retirement portfolios, in municipal budgets, in therapy sessions. Myriad questions remain about our futures, but we can't help feeling in our bones that changes of historic proportions are transforming the economic, political, and social landscapes. Even the weather's topsy-turvy behavior in the convulsions of climate change has both real and metaphorical messages to it.

That leaves us with the following question: How relevant is the work of diversity and inclusion in this upside-down world where most assumptions of what works and why have been rendered inoperative?

We have many reasons to worry. Many diversity and inclusion best-practice "givens" once seemed as solid as Lehman Brothers, AIG, and a soaring retirement nest egg. Now, they too are poised to disappear at worst or lose altitude at best. But I believe that rather than a total wipeout, the breakdown of the old financial, political, and cultural order and the rise of the new mean a greater—not lesser—urgency for diversity and inclusion.

In this time of reckoning for so many industries and institutions, we must take stock of diversity and inclusion work. One thing is for sure: Conventional diversity and inclusion wisdom will no longer be sufficient, as the new global order demands new thinking and a wrenching self-examination of diversity and inclusion work.

In the midst of the 2008 financial market meltdown, a European senior leader for a large investment firm was called to an urgent meeting in London, sponsored by one of the organization's Chinese leaders. The European leader recalls, "There we were in the meeting and *he* was telling *us*—a dozen White male Europeans in the financial capital of Europe—what economic sectors to invest in, which ones to get out of. I realized right then and there that my world had changed overnight." Sharing the story with a group of diversity and inclusion leaders, Ernst & Young's Chief Diversity Officer at the time, Pierre Hurstel, summed up the significance of the encounter as follows: "Money is moving faster than our business, and diversity and inclusion processes, structures, ideas, and beliefs, can keep up with. Diversity and inclusion needs to be rethought in the context of the restructuring of the financial system."

Changes in business and the economy are not just about the squeeze being placed on diversity and inclusion budgets. They are also about the urgent need to offer relevant and compelling answers to the huge economic challenges organizations face. Before we wrestle with how best to provide value through diversity and inclusion, we need to ground ourselves in the current, yet rapidly changing, context of this work.

Tectonic shifts caused by global demographic, economic, sociopolitical, and technological megatrends are shaping an emerging workforce unprecedented in its processes and behaviors. Changes in birth rates, retirement trends, and job requirements are reducing the size of the workforce and creating significant skill shortages, while eased trade barriers, telecommunications advances, and the knowledge economy are producing a highly global and virtual workforce. At the same time, loosened cultural norms about work "suitable" for men and women, higher minority birth rates, and unprecedented migration waves around the world are creating a thoroughly diverse workforce. This cultural shift, coupled with the knowledge economy, social media technologies, and new kinds of employment contracts are giving rise to the most autonomous, empowered group of workers ever seen.

Indeed, the emerging workforce is vastly diverse. But there is much more to it than that. Other characteristics must be considered if we're to shape high-impact strategies and programs for making the most of this talent.

Before delving into the specifics of this new workforce, let's first explore five megatrends that are turning the global workplace and workforce upside down:*

- Economic and political volatility
- Multifaceted, unprecedented diversity
- Fewer government and corporate guarantees
- Rapidly evolving, game-changing technology
- Globalization

....

* *Note.* This chapter draws substantially from the research and insights of Hewitt Associates' Robert Gandossy, Tina Kao, and Elissa Tucker. Much of this content originally was published in various Hewitt books and white papers, including "Next-Generation Talent Management: Insights on How Workforce Trends Are Changing the Face of Talent Management" by Elissa Tucker, Tina Kao, and Nidhi Verma, 2005, and *Workforce Wake-Up Call: Your Workforce Is Changing, Are You?* by Robert Gandossy, Elissa Tucker, and Nidhi Verma, 2006.

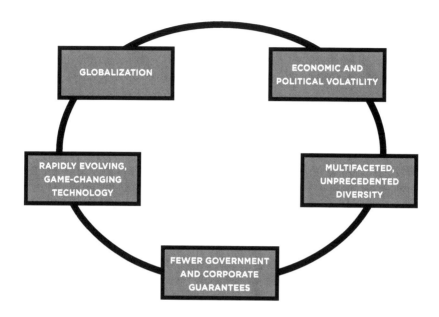

Megatrend #1 – Economic and political volatility

Life is less predictable

Having grown up in a Latin American country—where we survived a 12-year dictatorship along with press censorship, states of emergency, and dusk-to-dawn curfews and where the booms of car bombs jarred us from sleep in the middle of the night—my mother's home country of the United States seemed like a bastion of stability and security. In this upside-down world, however, that is no longer the case. Domestic and foreign terrorists have struck in multiple cities in the US; a presidential election result was contested all the way to the Supreme Court; for nearly a decade, the political system has been asphyxiating in the clutches of the double strands of policy polarization; natural disasters such as hurricanes Katrina and Sandy decimated New Orleans and parts of New Jersey and New York City. As if that wasn't enough, California—one of the world's ten largest economies with some of the most gorgeous natural wonders—is in the midst of one of the state's worst droughts in the past century with water shortages in a tinderbox of forest fires. The United States has not exactly been a bastion of security in the early twenty-first century.

Volatility is everywhere. In Latin America, elections lurch from right to left and back again. Political polarizations split countries or pit country against country. The Republics of the former Soviet Union have armed themselves against attempts to bring them back into the fold with the Ukraine barely holding on. The Middle East boils over with myriad political fissures as the

Arab Spring has moved to a stage of great ferocity and uncharted waters of the way forward with the rise of ISIS. In addition, several African countries still contend with genocide and famine; the European Union wrestles mightily with whether the "Union" part of its name is worth it as it ambivalently intervenes in preventing a Greek financial apocalypse and subsequent Continental financial contagion. All this as it struggles mightily to cobble together a unified and strategic response to the refugee crisis caused by the civil wars in Syria and other Middle Eastern countries. Meanwhile, global terrorism and global warming continue to inject greater instability in every corner of the world.

By their very nature, both the human and nature-made acts of devastation surprise us, with no part of the world safe as terrorists have targeted Bali, Madrid, Baghdad, London, Islamabad, and Mumbai increasingly so with the randomness of lone wolf attackers; cyclones, hurricanes, earthquakes, and tsunamis have hit Japan, Thailand, Taiwan, Jamaica, New York and New Jersey with unprecedented fury. Who knows where will be next?

With nonstop, instantaneous coverage of these events feeding our apprehension that anything can change at any time in any place, it's no wonder our safety, health, retirement, and jobs are thrown into question in an instant.

Megatrend #2 - Multifaceted, unprecedented diversity

We are more different

Suddenly, it seems the global demographic tsunami is upon us. While it is certainly reaching its peak, it has been coming for some time now.

In Latin America, regional migration is creating new labor force dynamics as Peruvians show up in Chile, Brazilians in Argentina, and Bolivians in Paraguay. In Chile, immigration from neighboring countries has doubled over the past decade, reaching 24 percent or 185,000 people, despite its small population.[4]

Across Europe, the aging and declining population is becoming more racially and ethnically diverse due to the swelling influx and higher birth rates of immigrants from Africa and the Middle East. In Britain, 70 percent of population growth is driven by migration, but the population overall is declining.[5] In Germany, nearly 20 percent of babies are born to immigrants from North African, Middle Eastern, and/or Muslim families.[6] A Pew Research study predicts that Muslims will nearly double their numbers in Europe—to more than 10 percent—by 2050.

Globally, the number of Muslims is expected to increase by 73 percent—from 1.6 billion in 2010 to 2.8 billion in 2050. In 2010, Muslims made up 23 percent of the global population. Four decades later, they are expected to make up 30 percent of the world's people and to outnumber Christians worldwide by 2070.[7]

In the United States, the Census Bureau confirms the Latino population is not only continuing to grow in the traditional bastions of California, Texas, and Illinois, but will also grow by 57 percent from 2015–2050,[8] making Latinos one-fourth of the US population. Some projections put that number at one-third. Symbolically, it's now not uncommon to see statues of the Virgin de Guadalupe, the patron saint of Mexico, in traditionally homogenous Connecticut, Washington State, and Kansas. In fact, in terms of its demographics, not even Kansas is in Kansas anymore.

Such demographic shifts create implications for employers and workers. Small and large companies are grappling with the implications of multicultural work teams. In 2012, nearly 70 percent of new entrants into the US workforce was comprised of women and minorities,[9] while Europe's only population growth currently comes from Middle Eastern and North African migrants.[10] Of course, this raises profound questions about European identity. It is clear that Europeans can no longer ignore the racial and ethnic tensions that surround them.

Obama's two elections unwittingly brought some of these tensions to the fore, not just in the United States but also around the world. Black people living in France, for example, live in a society that philosophically seeks not to call attention to racial/ethnic differences. Nonetheless, his election all the way across the Atlantic attracted attention to their economic and social plight.[11] These kinds of status-quo-changing demographics strain existing organizational and governmental programs that were built around the needs of a more homogenous workforce.

With rising demographic numbers comes greater economic and political power. In certain locales, Muslims in England can now resolve their disputes through a sharia court.[12] Women around the world are exerting greater influence.[13] In Europe, for example, women now represent half the workforce and are a driving force behind government efforts for gender pay equity and quotas for women on boards in various countries.

In the US in 2008, Latino voters tipped New Mexico, Nevada, and Colorado toward Obama, delivering those states' first Democratic victory in several elections.[14] By the 2012 election, Latinos in those battleground states and others, like North Carolina, Wisconsin, Virginia, and Ohio, also voted decisively for Obama.[15] The Latino influence was so decisive in the 2012 election that both Democrats and Republicans acknowledge that Latinos have permanently changed the political landscape and electoral equations.[16] The 2016 presidential election cycle should cement this very point with bigger numbers and the likelihood of record-breaking turnout, given the immigration issues at stake for Latino families.

And on the list goes: The Lilly Ledbetter Act guaranteeing equal pay for women. The repeal of Don't Ask, Don't Tell in the US Military which caused a cascade of pro-gay marriage legislation and referenda between 2010 and 2014 that ultimately culminated in the US Supreme Court gay marriage legalization in 2015. There has also been a massive focus on the growth and strengthening of community colleges to make higher education more affordable for those from lower incomes.

One doesn't have to agree with the particular policies to see that demographics are having a major impact on policies. A generation ago, gender and color barriers were broken most often in the fields of sports and entertainment. Today, it's happening in the power arenas of business and politics. It's been said that demographics are destiny. Indeed, Obama's elections signaled the cresting of a demographic tsunami that has had a tangible impact on many areas of society.

Megatrend #3 – Fewer government and corporate guarantees

We are more on our own

Everywhere we turn, someone is taking something away. Companies are freezing corporate pensions, not-for-profit pension payouts are continually being reduced,[17] and retiree medical insurance is being grandfathered out. While the United States traditionally has had more of a fend-for-yourself mentality, it still has provided an extensive safety net. That net is shrinking, however, in every state and with each congressional budget. Financial planners are telling us not to count on Social Security when planning for retirement because no one knows if Social Security will be solvent by the time many are ready to golf nine-to-five.[18]

Corporations face a massive rise in benefit costs just as they're struggling against the headwinds of aggressively managing operating costs. Municipalities, school districts, and airlines are cutting back on services and making customers pay for each "perk," such as in-flight meals or baggage checking. One airline even began charging for using the in-flight restroom![19]

To face their economic challenges, companies have begun moving from a paradigm of corporate benefactor to one of personal responsibility—first by asking employees to cover a greater slice of their healthcare coverage costs, and more recently by putting nearly the entire retirement savings burden on employees. While they're willing to match savings up to a point—typically 4 to 6 percent of what employees put into it—organizations will do so only if the employee participates. And even when they do, the average contributions will not be enough to cover their employees' retirement needs.

While financial advisors have recommended saving enough to cover roughly 80 percent of our current costs in retirement, an Aon Hewitt projection in 2009 suggested a more accurate figure being somewhere around 130 percent. This is because people are living longer, and future healthcare costs will eat up a larger-than-planned percentage of their retirement income.[20] This presents quite a different picture from when companies provided full pensions that covered all retirement costs for loyal, lifelong employees.

Of course, that's when the concept of cradle-to-grave employment was still alive and well. Lifelong employment is no longer in the realm of reality. Not only are we not guaranteed a lifelong job, but also the job itself is not guaranteed to stay in the country, as offshoring continues to be a fact of life. Employees nowadays are free agents and are treated as such, owning responsibility for their own benefits planning, development, and career management. And Millennials are already operating with this assumption. Their "job hopping" is said to be the new normal. Millennials expect to stay in one job for less than three years, meaning they could have between 15–20 jobs over the course of their time in the workforce.[21]

This fend-for-yourself trend has been challenged during the Obama Era, and the philosophical debate it engendered has been at the heart of what turned into a hyperpolarized decade in the political realm. Candidate Obama spoke against the culture of "fend for yourself," frequently declaring his belief that we are each other's keepers. This philosophy is, in part, what feeds an expectation by many that the US government needs to address the uninsured status of millions; needs to grant tax breaks to companies who keep jobs here rather than sending them overseas; and needs to continue the wave of interventions to keep the auto companies from going bankrupt or preventing families from losing their homes. These expectations that these communal interventions are desirable and expected are diametrically in contrast to the opposite faction with its values of individualism and self-reliance that shows this kind of support is neither desired nor effective.

The level of government involvement in the well-being of its citizens is one of the major debates of this time. But regardless of how things end up regarding the particulars of different political debates, there will be no going back to the days when a state or company adopted a paternalistic role providing for our needs more fully. Pensions are not coming back and more and more of the costs for healthcare security will be pushed to individuals and away from organizations. The Obama Era belief that we should not be left to fend for ourselves is still tempered with the other side of the debate that citizens must take personal responsibility for their own needs and those of their family.

Put simply, the time of generous benefits is gone.

Megatrend #4 – Rapidly evolving, game-changing technology

Anytime, anyplace, anything

Providing a global platform on which work could be shared, the Internet was the first modern technological inflection point. Now, we've moved on to broadband wireless, which allows workers to untether themselves from the workplace. This newfound flexibility comes not just from being able to connect with any other worker or source of information, but to ever-larger items. The size of document attachments no longer matters. Time lags are absent. It's now possible to have seamless communication between any two locations nearly anywhere in the world—with no delay.

Still, two things have stood in the way of fully untethering the workforce: cost and policy. The cost issue is being resolved as prices for networked broadband wireless computing have come down as network upgrades are implemented. In the policy arena, corporations are struggling to keep control as young workers bring their own devices to work and simply want to be able to connect them to the enterprise's network to do their work. While at first the motivation by corporations was more a knee-jerk reaction to have tight control for branding and employee behavior monitoring, now the dilemmas are even more vexing, given we live in an era of cyber-attacks and massive data leaks that demand even tighter controls in a time when employees are demanding less of it.

With broadband wireless, you can be at the airport, home, cabin, taxi, beach, or yes, even the office, and still do your work. It also makes it possible for far-flung teams to work together as if in the same location—though no one has yet solved the twelve-hour time zone differences that guarantee meetings at midnight and dawn for half of the participants. Work can be digitally disseminated across the globe—Europeans can pass data to Argentineans to crunch, those numbers are then picked up by Indians for analysis and distributed globally for interpretation. As the number of employees working offshore grows, so will employee power in those locations. Already, Indian and Polish back offices demand front-office accountability and decision making. With power shifts and cultural differences across borders, global diversity tension buzzes through billions of bits and bytes, pulsating through transatlantic fiber-optic cables and Wi-Fi networks.

While Web 1.0 was primarily about content aggregation, Web 2.0 or the interactive web, which is social media, is about two-way communication that generates new content. It allows for the "wisdom of crowds" to be scalable out to millions. In the Obama Era, this inflection point sped up action to support the belief that bottom-up is just as important as top-down as we have witnessed with #ArabSpring, #OccupyWallStreet, and #BlackLivesMatter. No longer will policy influencing be confined just to Washington and the corridors of Congress. Twitter is in the house.

To leverage social networking, the Obama Administration sought out web-savvy citizens who could be mobilized to influence legislation, speak up on policy, and empower themselves to participate in the innovation of the times. President Obama's campaigns used the cutting edge of social media and technology and applied this thinking to his administration. He was the first president to use Twitter with the American public via his @POTUS handle (acronym for President of the United States) as a way for him to engage directly with the American people. He also created the US Digital Service and tasked them with remaking the digital experience that Americans and businesses have with the American government by hiring some of the most accomplished talent in Silicon Valley.[22]

President John F. Kennedy's challenge of "a man on the moon within ten years" was met by technology elites in the hallowed halls of NASA. The Obama Era equivalent, to "be energy independent within ten years," is being achieved both by top-down efforts but also by the masses. Equipped with broadband wireless and social networking tools, technology whizzes in basements, dorms, cafes, corporate cubicles, and garages are driving the energy revolution from the bottom-up. At the same time, it's being driven top-down through the most massive drive toward clean energy in history via direct investments, incentives, and regulation.[23,24] The United States is now on track to be energy independent by 2030,[25] possibly even sooner.

Technology serves to amplify diverse voices so they can be better heard above the din, not just in the political and societal sphere, but increasingly within companies as well.

Megatrend #5 – Globalization

We are the world

It was once said that when the United States sneezed, the rest of the world would catch pneumonia. In an upside-down world, no country can make a move without affecting other nations. In today's diverse world, any country or region can sneeze and spread pneumonia everywhere else—including to the United States.

Our financial markets are linked. Our labor supply chain is linked. Our technologies are linked. Our ability to access products and services is linked. One look at the world's roller-coaster stock market indices proves we're completely and intrinsically linked. Asian markets wake to respond to the previous day's financial happenings in Europe, and Americans respond to what happened overnight in Asia.

Jobs, too, are rapidly moving around the globe. Since 2005, some 2.6 million manufacturing jobs have moved overseas. Analysts predict that in the next 15 years, American employers will transfer 3.3 million white-collar jobs and $136 billion in wages to places like India, China, and Russia. Developing countries could be on the receiving end of about 25 percent or 30 to 40 million American offshored jobs, according to Dr. Alan Blinder, who served on President Clinton's Council of Economic Advisors.[26] What's more, the International Labor Organization (ILO) World Employment Report (2014) predicts that by 2025, there will be 1.2 billion new entrants to the world labor market. But only 3 percent of the 460 million new job seekers in the next ten years will hail from Europe and North America, while 75 percent will come from Asia.[27]

It should be noted, however, that this trend has begun to slow somewhat with some jobs actually being brought back as offshoring has lost some of its cachet—politically, socially, and economically. This is due to instability in parts of India and elsewhere, rising wages in emerging markets, declining wages or even wage depression in the United States, the high cost of transportation, and Obama Administration policies aimed at rewarding companies that keep or bring back jobs to the United States.

2014 was the first year in the last 20 that the United States had a net increase of at least 10,000 manufacturing jobs. Walmart is a key driver of this trend and Boston Consulting Group estimated that Walmart's move to buy an additional $250 billion in US-made products over the next ten years could create up to 1 million direct and indirect American jobs.[28]

But even this reverse trend is disruptive, since it once again forces a wholesale rewiring of labor strategies and policies. Plus, it won't be enough to reverse the redistribution of global jobs taking place.

Characteristics of the twenty-first century workforce

These megatrends have implications not only for economics, politics, and society, but also for a new workforce whose characteristics are very different from those of the late twentieth century. Not only does it differ in what it looks like, but also in the challenges it faces and how it gets its work done. Today's workforce is:

- Smaller and less skilled
- Highly global and virtual
- Vastly diverse
- Autonomous and empowered
- Burdened with multilayered responsibilities

While the "diverse" characteristic comes as no surprise, it cannot be the only focus of a successful diversity and inclusion strategy. Such efforts will be incomplete if they don't account for all the major dimensions of the emerging workforce. Let's explore each one in detail.

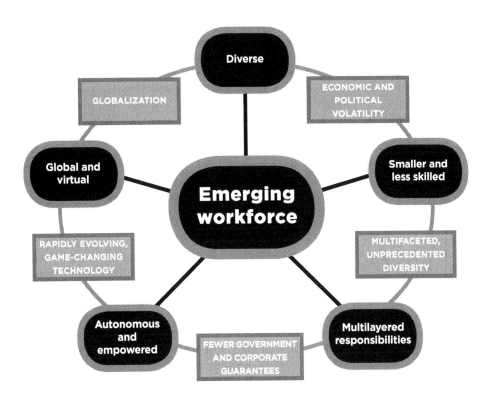

Workforce trend #1 – Smaller and less skilled

Smaller

We can't predict the short-term impact of the current economic challenges, yet long-term demographic trends still show that, given current population growth, a certain number of workers will be needed to deliver the products and services the population needs. Despite the deep recession of 2008–2009, most experts anticipate a continuing talent shortage, primarily due to the vast number of Baby Boomers who are retiring, leaving behind far too many jobs for the much smaller Generation X to fill while Millennials face some experience gaps. When the decline of Boomer workers hits bottom, member nations of the Organization for Economic Cooperation and Development (OECD) will have experienced a combined reduction of 65 million people from the workforce.[29] At the same time, those countries with increasingly restrictive immigration policies may be unwittingly undermining their ability to meet talent needs. To remain viable, organizations will need to nurture and surface talent in all labor pools. Doing so is one of the key business cases for diversity.

Less skilled

As Millennials fully enter the workforce and more fully step into managerial and leadership positions, coupled with the Gen Xers already in place, the gross numbers are there for there to be enough of them to make up for the dearth of Baby Boomer workers who are now retiring at a rate of 10,000 a day.[30] But while they have the numbers, not enough Millennials will possess the skills and experience demanded by the Digital Economy. By 2018, the United States will have 46.8 million job openings. Thirty million of these jobs will require some kind of postsecondary education, and there will be a shortfall of 3 million.[31] And 60 percent of employers report that candidates applying for jobs lack the necessary skills to fill available positions.[32]

Consider the engineering talent crisis. Technology and utility companies are seeing waves of experienced, knowledge-rich Baby Boomers activate their pensions and retire. Yet looking at the pipeline of current college students pursuing engineering degrees, it's clear these industries will not find enough replacement workers in the coming decade. Even more worrisome, according to Ron Glover, former Vice President of Global Workforce Diversity for IBM, "The process to produce an engineer with the capabilities we need really starts at kindergarten and goes right through high school. Because if you don't get the kids in sufficient quantity getting the fundamental math and science curricula that they need at that point, you have no chance of producing enough people with the skill sets at the end of the university pipeline. And everything that we saw starting in 2008 around what was in the pipeline in the United States, caused us to be pretty alarmed."

Jobs for scientists and engineers are expected to increase at a faster rate than employment in all other occupations between 2010–2020, according to the National Science Foundation.[33] That means companies fueled by these specialized skills must tap non-traditional engineering labor pools, such as women, minorities, immigrants, and expatriates, to try to meet their needs. So far, they are falling short.

It's not just engineers and scientists either. Industrialized nations are experiencing acute shortages of nurses and other highly skilled professionals. And developing countries are short on accountants, lawyers, and business administrators. In Peru, for example, unprecedented decentralization by the federal government has put more tax revenues under the control of the *departamentos* (provinces). Yet ambitious plans for long-needed sustainable irrigation, potable water, electricity, and manufacturing projects remain unaddressed. Despite finally overcoming more than 200 years of limited access to tax revenues, these provinces simply don't have enough people with the requisite skills to make plans for spending the money as intended. Due to this talent gap, in 2012 they left over 30 percent of their infrastructure budgets unspent.[34]

It's not just book-learning or new technical skills that are needed in the new economic order. Technological breakthroughs are creating new products at warp speed. Rapidly changing local and global politics and economics affect everything, from the price of oil to the Dow Jones Index to immunization plans. Companies will continue to restructure, re-engineer, de-layer, off- and on-shore work. The competencies of problem solving, adaptability, flexibility, learning agility, and innovation are more critical than ever. Unfortunately, these competencies are in short supply. From the C-suite to the shop floor, the most valuable workers will be those who solve never-before-seen problems and flex, bob, and weave with the constantly evolving marketplace. Further, the generational transition will be painful, given the vast worldview differences between the Baby Boomers—who embedded their now outdated views of how the world works into the systems they are leaving behind—and that of Xers and Yers.

Workforce trend #2 – An increasingly global and virtual workforce

Global

As technology and economic reform enables a full global reach, traditional geographic workplace boundaries crumble fast. Without those boundaries, a truly global job market is rising. No longer are workers limited to marketing their skills solely within one country or region—they can market themselves to organizations anywhere in the world.

Mobility and migration are on the rise, with workers far less likely to remain in one physical location throughout their careers. Over the past 40 years, global migration of less skilled and highly skilled workers has doubled.[35] Among developed nations, the United States is by far the biggest recipient of labor inflows, but other nations are also increasing their share of migrant labor as talent shortages heighten.[36]

And what about the jobs these workers follow?

Increasingly, the jobs themselves are being relocated to places that best match company needs in terms of labor, skills, costs, and capacity. Low-cost communication technologies and rising education levels in developing nations make it not only possible but also financially attractive to move jobs across the globe. We have all felt the repercussions of these relocations by either losing jobs or seeing many coworkers and friends lose theirs. Many jobs in IT, Customer Service, HR, Finance, and Accounting have primarily gone to countries in the Asia-Pacific region, which boast large populations of college-educated workers along with low labor and operational costs. And as talent in those markets gets tapped out and their wages rise, the global economy is finding more talent in Latin America, Eastern Europe, and Southeast Asia,[37] and more recently in Africa.[38]

In the Obama Era, President Obama worked at balancing the paradox of wanting to protect American jobs with acknowledging and even capitalizing on an exceptionally mobile global workforce and his belief in free trade as evidenced by the signing of the 10-nation signatory Trans-Pacific Partnership which accounts for 40 percent of the world's GDP. In addition to the trends mentioned above, something new has been taking place where it's become attractive for emerging markets to offshore certain work *to* the United States. While wages are higher (even if they've stagnated in the United States, they're still significantly higher compared to other countries), the services and innovation American workers offer those markets, given their edge in university education and innovation, have been pivotal to this reverse trend.

Before policies were enacted to discourage offshoring, this trend showed no signs of slowing. The number and types of jobs offshored and the nations to which they're offshored had been broadening. Jobs outsourced globally have become increasingly sophisticated.[39] Some estimate that up to 25 percent of American jobs are susceptible to offshoring.[40] Consider IBM's example. The technology giant eliminated 4,000 jobs and let laid-off workers take jobs in another country if they were willing to work on local terms and conditions.[41] Already, half of IBM's workforce is located outside the United States.[42]

While global offshoring is mostly an American trend—three-fourths of offshored jobs originate in the United States—other nations are expected to adopt the practice.[43] As offshoring increased, so, too, have concerns about its negative impact on the workforce. Not surprisingly, global outsourcing reportedly has boosted worker stress and competition and diminished worker engagement in the countries doing the offshoring.

Global musical chairs: Labor migration

A *New York Times* article a few years ago[44] explored Romania's severe talent shortage, which surfaced when the European Union eased labor migration laws. At that time, talent-hungry Spain capitalized on the situation by enticing Romanian workers into its borders. To plug this talent hole, Romania began flying in Chinese workers. China, in turn, started importing workers from Africa to make up for *its* loss.

Peruvians are in Chile. Brazilians are in Argentina. Americans are going to India—not on expat assignments or to visit the Taj Mahal, but to get hired for the very jobs that were offshored there.[45] So, while labor migration benefits many recipient countries, it creates a vicious cycle in that those countries that export their labor force discover that this process diminishes their own resources.

Canada's Alberta province is one of those talent hungry regions luring talent from elsewhere. Alberta's labor shortage is so severe that McDonald's must pay $15 an hour to keep its workers. Stores close at 4 p.m. because there are not enough workers to mind the shop. And it doesn't end here—this labor shortage extends from the St. Lawrence Seaway to the Pacific Ocean. Sadly, this trend in declining labor is nothing new: in the last 25 years of the twentieth century, the Canadian labor force grew by 226,000 per year. During the first decade of the twenty-first century (2000–2009), it only grew by an average of 123,000 a year. By 2010, it grew a measly 42,000. By 2016, growth will be nearly zero.[46]

The result is a zero-sum game. One country's—or province's, state's, city's, or company's—gain is another's loss.

Highly virtual workforce

The definitions of "coworker" and of being "at work" are changing as workers connect via the latest communication technologies. Across the world and across industries, workers are "freed" from their desks and relieved of their traditional nine-to-five schedules. Growing use of wireless phones, high-speed broadband connections, and smart phones is redefining the concepts of "workplace" and "workday."

No longer is a fixed physical location a requirement for work. Instead, workers are laboring from their cars, at client sites, in hotel rooms, at home, and even while on vacation. There has been a significant upsurge in remote working. Telecommuting rose 103 percent between 2005 and 2014 and makes up nearly 4 million workers and growing, according to statistics from the American Community Survey.[47] According to a report by the Conference Board, the number of remote workers in the United States has nearly doubled and more than tripled for some professions, such as insurance underwriters and records clerks.[48]

Workers now can work at any time. A growing number of workers are on call all the time. Multitasking like never before, they switch seamlessly back and forth between their work lives and their personal lives. They check their Outlook email and then watch the next movie in their Netflix queue. They respond to emails while waiting at the dentist's office and log back in to work after the kids are in bed.

For some workers, this capability brings a new level of work-life synchronization and satisfaction. For others, it's fostering unhealthy workaholic tendencies. A 2012 survey by the Center for Creative Leadership found that 60 percent of professionals with smart phones kept in touch with work for a full 13.5 hours per day, and then spent another 5 hours juggling work email each weekend.[49]

Good Technology, a mobile-software firm, found that 68 percent checked work email before 8 a.m., 50 percent checked it while in bed, and 38 percent routinely did so at the dinner table. In another study conducted by the American Psychological Association, 44 percent of working adults surveyed reported that they check work email daily while on vacation—about 1 in 10 checked it hourly.[50]

Together, virtual co-working and the virtual workspace are creating an "always on" workforce that sees no limits to jobs.[51] Many workers are simply afraid to slow down—afraid to disconnect for fear of losing job security in an increasingly competitive, global labor market. Unfortunately, the consequences of an "always on" workforce can be dire—leading to "lousy employees: tired, depressed, mistake-prone, resentful, and eventually burned out."[52] On the upside, workers have more flexibility to take care of their work, home, and other personal demands. In fact, some studies[53] indicate many workers view this flexibility as the ultimate perk.

With the ubiquitous availability of broadband wireless Internet and social networking, the tools are there, and capital investments are being made to keep up. The emerging workforce is pressing for a shift in mindset and a change in policy. (For more, see Chapter 15, "Work-life flexibility: The mother of all battles.")

To grasp how much technology has driven our ability to connect and make things happen, one need only look to the Obama campaign's unprecedented use of social networking to mobilize a seamless, virtual volunteer force—one better organized and more powerful than anything preceding it.

On the "Get Involved" page of the "Obama for President," website, supporters in *any* part of the country were able to choose a project, such as Women

Calling Women in Ohio or Latinos Calling Latinos in Nevada. With the click of a mouse, a phone list of registered voters in the selected state, with the defined demographic profile, popped up on the screen. Alongside the list was a script for the volunteer to follow. Depending on the campaign, the goal varied, with volunteers filling out appropriate details about each call recipient on a form they submitted electronically.

The forms—filled out by tens of thousands of volunteers working from whatever location and using their own phones—were converted into actionable lists for the Obama team's field offices. These scrubbed lists then guided a door-to-door campaign effort. As a result, volunteers didn't waste their time knocking on doors where the voter no longer lived or where the voter was already set on voting for John McCain in 2008 and Mitt Romney in 2012. And, surprisingly, these electronically scrubbed lists helped the volunteers to avoid the homes of those who had already indicated enthusiastically they were voting for Obama. (After all, you don't want to waste time preaching to the choir.) Instead, volunteers zeroed in on leaning voters and the undecided—the swing voters who ultimately decided the election. This new method of voter volunteerism was unprecedented micro targeting.

How can we harness these same technologies to achieve similar results for our organizations? What can companies accomplish if they truly untether their workforces and outsource certain types of work to the multitudes?

Cisco, the digital networking company, is using its untethered workforce to test its virtual network of web, high-definition video, and social media. By using it real-time, employees provide ongoing, continuous input regarding the way they use the tools. This data instantly becomes part of Cisco's real stories sales pitch and feeds their technology-hungry backbone and design teams, who eagerly seek ways to differentiate Cisco from competitors. "As life and work get mashed together, we want to create 'anywhere computing,' where what employees experience at home or work is the same," said Lance Perry, Cisco's former Vice President of IT Customer Strategy and Success.

Procter & Gamble has been creating a virtual workforce of 120,000 self-selected innovators from more than 175 countries who are not even on the company payroll. In addition to its legendary R&D group, the company now taps into the entire world by posting technology challenges—such as how to print a message on a Pringle potato chip—to its website. Winners receive cash rewards if their ideas are implemented. "Since 2006, the company was deriving at least 35 percent of its ideas from outsiders," write the authors of *We Are Smarter Than Me: How to Unleash the Power of Crowds in Your Business.*[54]

Workforce trend #3 – A vastly diverse workforce

We now are experiencing the most diverse workforce ever in terms of age, gender, ethnicity, and life pursuits. Workers are entering the workforce earlier and staying longer—as many as four generations are in the workforce at once. In the United States, growing consumerism, coupled with the rising cost of education, is motivating more teenagers to enter the workforce. Labor force participation of American youth (16 and 24 years old) is roughly 60 percent,[55] and a similar trend has been noted in Europe.[56]

As workers enter the workforce at increasingly younger ages, older workers are bucking the tradition of retiring at 65. Motivated by longer life expectancies (in Japan, 60 percent of the population is age 65 or older[57] and by 2055 that number will be 40 percent,[58] and in China, more than 126 million people are age 65 or older),[59] changing cultural expectations, shrunken retirement savings accounts, and the availability of knowledge and service work, they're working longer.

In the United States, workers are staying on the job for an average of 15 years beyond age 55,[60] and more people age 50 to 79 are going back to work either to fulfill financial needs due to the ravages of the Great Recession of 2008–2012 or simply to stay active.[61] Going forward, 80 percent of US Baby Boomers expect to keep working past 65.[62] Outside the United States, older workers aren't employed to such an extent, but that, too, is expected to change.

With so many generations in the workforce at one time, older workers are finding themselves the brunt of stereotypes and discrimination. In the United Kingdom, age discrimination now tops the region's list of work-related discrimination claims. And in the United States, age discrimination claims over the past five years have consistently accounted for over 20 percent of all discrimination charges.[63]

Age represents only one diversity element. Motivated by the trend toward equitable cultural norms and out of economic necessity, large numbers of women have entered the workforce in recent decades. Women now represent 55 percent of the global workforce, according to the World Bank. Today, 70 percent of women in the developed world and 60 percent in the developing world are engaged in paid employment.[64] It should be noted, however, that the variance across the developing nations is vast. In North Africa and the Middle East, women are no more likely to have a paying job than they were 20 years ago. In Japan, only women hold 10 percent of managerial positions, compared to 43 percent in the United States.[65] But women in Latin America are now 20 percent more likely to be part of the workforce, and in Colombia, which was once one of the countries that was least open to female workers, women are 50 percent more likely to be employed than they were in 1995.[66]

As more females enter the workforce, men and women are increasingly choosing occupations previously dominated by the opposite gender. Today, women participate in all industries, professions, and job levels. They are asking for combat roles in the military, lifesaving roles in firefighting squads, and pole-climbing roles for utility companies. They comprise half of the enrollment in law, medical, and MBA programs. At the same time, given the decimation of manufacturing jobs that have been traditionally held by men, the guys are increasingly taking on what were traditionally female roles—becoming librarians, secretaries, nannies, preschool teachers, nurses, paralegals, and typists. Unfortunately, many men in historically female roles report high levels of stress and discrimination,[67] while 56 percent of women believe their job opportunities are not equal to those of men.[68]

Race and ethnicity increase the mix. Migration levels and high birth rates are boosting the proportion of ethnic minorities in the developed world. Since 1975, global migration has doubled.[69] Since 1970, US migration has tripled.[70] As of 2013, 232 million people—3.2 percent of the world's population—lived outside their country of origin.[71]

Yet another trend is more diverse in terms of lifestyles or life patterns. Fewer workers are following life's traditional path—education, then work and family, followed by leisure. Instead, they're mixing and matching stages in personalized sequences.[72]

Current organizational structures and processes are calcified into forms that support a far more homogenous workforce. Stress fractures have appeared as the new workforce has been pushing against these rigid processes.

Workforce trend #4 – An autonomous and empowered workforce

The more governments and corporations push the burden for retirement planning, healthcare coverage, and career development to employees, the more these individuals are going to equip themselves to play the game, and they are using a variety of work-oriented social media sites to do so. For example, salary.com allows them to see if their salary measures up to others in the same position. Using LinkedIn, they can share their résumés and personal profiles with other like-minded individuals.

Increasingly, workers are taking responsibility for the direction and substance of their professional lives. Recognizing that they have job- or profession-specific expertise their managers do not have, knowledge workers are becoming the logical decision makers in their organizations. Using the Internet and intranets, these workers access competitive intelligence and business trend information, thereby increasing their decision-making abilities.

As the Internet and information literacy reduce job search costs, the revised employer-employee contract minimizes personal and professional job-switching costs. Ushered in by the downsizing of the 1980s, the new employment contract lets employees change jobs with relative ease and minimal sacrifice. No longer are employees limited to one corporation or career path as their sole route to promotion and increased rewards.

No longer an indicator of a problem employee, searching the external job market has become a sign of business acumen. In fact, the new norm is for workers to search the job market continually for better opportunities. Rather than being loyal to one brand, many workers use the employment intelligence they earn on the job to seek better offers. According to the Glassdoor Employment Confidence Survey 2014, more than 1 in 3 employees looked for a new job in 2015 when they did not receive a pay raise. This shift came as employees felt more confident than they had in the job market since the Great Recession, as half of employees reported optimism in their ability to find a new job matched to their experience and compensation levels.[73]

During an economic downturn, management might take the shortsighted view that dissatisfied workers are "lucky to have a job." However, this stance has been backfiring as the economy recovers, making it a lose-lose approach. Through effective diversity and inclusion strategies, organizations can turn this "changed and charged" dynamic into a win-win.

Workforce trend #5 – A workforce with multilayered responsibilities

Without government and corporate guarantees, workers exert extra energy providing for their own stability, squeezing in errands during work hours, and struggling to balance work and home. Many workers face added responsibilities as members of the "Sandwich Generation"—adults who find themselves caring for aging parents and young children at the same time. Employers contribute to the stress: no longer are workers recipients of healthcare and retirement benefits so much as *consumers* of benefits, who must become educated buyers to ensure they are taking care of their family's needs. At the same time, employees find work increasingly intruding on their home lives via text messages in the evening and middle-of-the-night overseas conference calls.

As work interrupts personal life and personal life interrupts work, the work-life divide vanishes. Workers can best shuffle these multilayered demands if their jobs offer sufficient flexibility. "Employers need to enable their employees to tend to life from work, and work from life," says Perry.

The Obama Era brought recognition that work-life boundaries had been erased. As the "First Couple," Barack and Michelle Obama juggled high-visibility roles, young children, and one still-living elder parent who moved in with them to the White House, while still tending to their relationship. The First Couple went to great lengths to negotiate the demands of home and office, from the President making time to eat with family to the couple exercising together. As they visibly demonstrated ways to deal with these kinds of multilayered responsibilities, the Obamas actually influenced organizational culture. As they took time for date nights or joined their kids on the neighborhood Halloween walk, they helped dismantle outdated expectations of how leaders and workers spend their time and juggle work-life responsibilities.

The Obama Era has been characterized by the ability to juggle various issues at once. Just as President Obama has had to tend to healthcare, the economy, education, wars, terrorism, the environment, immigration, infrastructure, and global relationships, *and* his family, workers must learn to manage their own multilayered responsibilities.

Taken together, the five workforce trends outlined above—smaller and less sufficiently skilled; global and highly virtual; vastly diverse; autonomous and empowered; and laboring under multilayered responsibilities—define a workforce radically different from that of even recent times.

Employers will need to rethink their approach to managing this talent. To do so requires diversity and inclusion approaches that are broader in scope, bolder in reach, and interdisciplinary in their solutions. It requires a different mindset and skill set, to which we turn our attention in the next chapter. ♀

SUMMARY POINTS

- The world isn't flat; it's upside-down. Change is happening so rapidly in so many areas that no one—no organization, no geographic region, and no society—can afford to avoid or ignore it.

- Five megatrends are roiling through workplaces around the world:
  - Economic and political volatility
  - Multifaceted, unprecedented diversity
  - Fewer government and corporate guarantees
  - Rapidly evolving, game-changing technology
  - Globalization

- Correspondingly, five megatrends are shaping an emerging workforce:
  - Smaller and less skilled
  - Highly global and virtual
  - Vastly diverse
  - Autonomous and empowered
  - Multilayered job responsibilities

SHAPING YOUR STRATEGY

- How are these megatrends showing up in your organization? Are leaders and managers making decisions that take them into account? If not, what can you do to influence one key leader?

- What's the makeup of your organization's emerging workforce? In addition to their racial/gender/generational/sexual orientation makeup, how are their preferred work styles enhancing and/or challenging the workplace?

- What can you do to surface a key need that's currently being overlooked?

SUSTAINABLE DIVERSITY
RELEVANT, PROFITABLE,
AND GAME CHANGING
SUSTAINABLE DIVERSITY
RELEVANT, PROFITABLE,
AND GAME CHANGING
SUSTAINABLE DIVERSITY
RELEVANT, PROFITABLE,
AND GAME CHANGING
SUSTAINABLE DIVERSITY
RELEVANT, PROFITABLE,
AND GAME CHANGING
SUSTAINABLE DIVERSITY
RELEVANT, PROFITABLE,
AND GAME CHANGING
SUSTAINABLE DIVERSITY
RELEVANT, PROFITABLE,
AND GAME CHANGING
SUSTAINABLE DIVERSITY
RELEVANT, PROFITABLE,
AND GAME CHANGING
SUSTAINABLE DIVERSITY
RELEVANT, PROFITABLE,
AND GAME CHANGING
SUSTAINABLE DIVERSITY
RELEVANT, PROFITABLE,
AND GAME CHANGING
SUSTAINABLE DIVERSITY
RELEVANT, PROFITABLE,
AND GAME CHANGING
SUSTAINABLE DIVERSITY
RELEVANT, PROFITABLE,
AND GAME CHANGING

2

Sustainable diversity: Relevant, profitable, and game-changing

It was a hospital built for White people.

Not that they had intended it that way. But that's what they got. In their rapid expansion into the fastest-growing cities in the United States, the large hospital chain had failed to hard-wire inclusion into their growth plans. They had correctly identified expanding metros, but had not made note that the growth was due to the demographic tsunami of growing racial/ethnic representation. How could this affect their ambitious business plans?

During one strategic diversity and inclusion session, one astute real estate guy pulled out the template blueprint for their hospitals. Can you figure out why? Just what could a blueprint have to do with diversity and inclusion?

Considering the concepts behind the Inclusion Paradox, ask yourself this: What differences were not being considered in this hospital's services? For example, what happens in the waiting room when patients of different cultures get wheeled into surgery?

It turns out that, according to various studies, if the patient is White, there will typically be one or two people in the waiting room. If it's an African-American patient, there could be six or seven people waiting. When it's a Latino, it could be more than a dozen! In looking at their designs, the business strategists realized they were about to build hospitals in rapidly growing racially diverse neighborhoods—the very thing that was fueling their market growth opportunities—that inadvertently catered to White cultural preferences.

This realization was the turning point in their inclusion work. Once they pulled on the thread of cultural assumptions about the proper size of waiting rooms, they began to see that many other day-to-day hospital interactions—from the intake process to the layout of the emergency room to parking rules—were replete with cultural assumptions. Differences in beliefs and behaviors regarding modesty, faith, authority, illness, family support, and more had multiple implications for what would create a welcoming and comforting hospital environment. By discovering the mission-critical reason for diversity, this hospital chain has embarked on a diversity effort that, in large part, will be about offering crossculturally competent healthcare. Their focus on the diversity implications of their mission led right back to the need for a diverse staff at every level of the hospital and the need for all employees to be culturally competent in order to do their jobs effectively. This is what sustainable diversity and inclusion can look like.

Grounding diversity strategy in a products and services perspective, rather than in a human resources perspective, poses quite a challenge—but the payoff can be of astoundingly high value. In the case of hospitals, it can literally save lives.

As discussed in Chapter 1, "An upside-down world," a new financial and political order demands a new diversity and inclusion order. Creating pathways to sustainable diversity must be a characteristic of this new order. In the Obama Era and beyond, solutions have to yield unequivocal, tangible benefits both to employees and to the bottom line.

Many diversity and inclusion professionals aren't aware just how vulnerable the work is if it remains on its present course. It is a time of contradictory trends in the diversity field. On the one hand, plenty of signposts point to a diversity and inclusion renaissance. In response to some of the megatrends shaping the emerging workforce, an explosion has taken place in the number of Chief Diversity Officer (CDO) appointments,[1] CEO statements championing diversity, and diversity and inclusion coverage in both the business and mainstream media. The rising tide of US and global diversity is transforming the social and workforce landscape in ways that even the biggest skeptics can no longer ignore.

On the other hand, the financial shakeout of 2008–2012 has resulted in a diversity initiative crash similar to that of the dot-coms in the 1990s. While many things were riding on the World Wide Web wave, not all were equally financially sound or even good ideas to begin with. When the day of reckoning came, the non-sustainable ideas quickly imploded.

How do we ensure that the new diversity and inclusion order is relevant to the core of the business agenda and not continued to be built on shaky foundations? The answer to this question is critical.

During the dot-com implosion, winning ideas from Google, Amazon, Apple, and other Silicon Valley start-ups redefined the marketplace and positioned these companies for sustainable growth and evolution. The same will be true for diversity and inclusion. To survive the current transformation that diversity and inclusion is undergoing, we must make the shift from *programmatic* diversity to *sustainable* diversity by focusing on the approaches, ideas, processes, strategies, and tools that will lead to sustainability. The time for deep reexamination and restructuring is now. In the same way that there have been winning technology companies, there are also winning companies in diversity and inclusion that have been pioneering the steps that follow.

Making the shift

Programmatic diversity means affinity groups, diversity councils, diversity learning, and heritage month celebrations. It means successful programs such as minority and women mentoring programs, diversity recruiting fairs, and Safe Space[2] for lesbian, gay, bisexual, and transgender (LGBT) employees.

These programs are—and will continue to be—important. But they're just the scaffolding for the structure that needs to be built. Eventually, as the building takes shape, the scaffolding will be dismantled. While it was once a necessity, where the structure is built to last with diversity and inclusion built right into its foundation and supporting beams, the scaffolding of programs will be less vital as it will be replaced by the shiny new Otis elevator.

Consider the dot-com scaffolding—putting "e-" in front of everything, subscription-based access to "e-mail," and dial-up connections. All this was just scaffolding for the real structure: 24/7 online, customizable, self-service shopping, movies, music, and travel; the ability to find like-minded souls anywhere in the world through Facebook; open and free portals to anything; networking with tens of thousands through LinkedIn; ubiquitous broadband wireless connectivity.

In terms of our work, the equivalent sustainable edifice is a structure where diversity and inclusion is:

- Hard-wired into the organization's mission, growth, and profitability strategies and into the creation, design, marketing, and selling of the company's products and services.

- Embedded into every process and practice that touches employees, from their initial contact with the organization to the time they're brought in, oriented, trained, promoted, and made to feel part of the overall enterprise.

In the same way that the "e-" became assumed in every online interaction, sustainable diversity will be characterized by how much it has become part of how we do business and manage people. No longer will we have to put "diversity" in front of everything. "Diversity recruiting" will be replaced by "recruiting" with diversity sourcing and hiring fully integrated into how things get done. And "diversity management" will become just good management, where differences are taken into account proactively, with wisdom and savvy.

We can't get rid of the scaffolding just yet, however, as we are still laying the foundation for sustainable diversity.

Laying the foundation for sustainable diversity

Decisions regarding funding, staffing, and executive support must be grounded in the "business case." This is shorthand for "How will the investment required to do what you're proposing for diversity and inclusion bring greater value to the organization via higher revenue, cost savings, margin improvement, and/or enhanced corporate brand?"

In diversity and inclusion circles, there has been plenty of talk about the business case for diversity for quite some time now. It sounds something like this: "Society is getting more diverse; therefore, the workforce is getting more diverse. In the midst of a growing skilled talent shortage, we must hire the best talent from as many labor pools as possible. Demographic growth is in the emerging workforce populations, but traditionally, we have not known how to tap into its top talent." The more advanced version adds, "An organization's workforce should mirror the increasingly diverse marketplace the company is trying to sell to."

Compelling arguments, for sure. But they're incomplete.

As we've seen, the skilled talent shortage will be massive. Companies that cannot hire the talent they need will falter, fall behind, or even disappear. The case for inclusion is incomplete, however, because it's focused only on the talent dimension of the business case—what I call the "*talent* business case"—rather than a more holistic approach.

When it comes to the question, "What is the business case?" diversity work must have as compelling an answer as contained in the competing requests for greater investment in new technology, a new advertising campaign, or a new product. When partnering with our clients to shape a global diversity and inclusion strategy, the first task is to ensure a rock-solid grounding in the business case. The question we must answer before doing anything else is:

> *Why is diversity important to you, specifically in the business that you are in, for the kind of company you are?*

Before they can reply, I offer the following caveat, "There are three answers you cannot give: 'Right thing to do'; 'War for talent'; 'Compliance.'" Such answers, while part of the answer, are insufficient. They're generic, rote reasons that any company in any industry in any part of the world could give. It's crucial that each company finds the differentiated reason for how diversity and inclusion will help them achieve their own specific business and mission goals, within the context of their particular products and services, for how they run the business. I call these the "*marketplace* business case" (and for not-for-profits and government, the "*mission* case") and the "*operations* business case." Along with the *talent* business case, they give us the comprehensive framework to lay the foundation for sustainable diversity.

The business case for diversity and inclusion

WHAT WE SELL

Culture – What we believe and why

Marketplace business case
Impact on products and services

Talent business case
Impact on talent (engagement, retention, advancement, etc.)

Operations business case
Impact on internal systems and processes

Culture – What we believe and why

WHO DOES THE WORK

HOW WE RUN THE BUSINESS

The foundation for sustainable diversity and inclusion

Let's look at the structural elements of sustainable diversity in more detail.

The *marketplace* business case: Hard-wiring diversity to products and services

Diversity as solely a human resources thing will wither on the vine.

Not only do people strategies need to support the business and mission, but also organizations that fail to take the megatrends and their impact on the marketplace into account risk losing relevance. Like the hospital at the beginning of this chapter, they may discover that consumers with different cultural worldviews are looking for different features and values.

Many Fortune 500 leaders understand the importance of diversity and are clear about its impact on their businesses. CEO Brian Moynihan of Bank of America saw an important link to customer satisfaction: "When internal diversity and inclusion scores are strong, and employees feel valued, they will serve our customers better, and we'll be better off as an organization."[3] And it shows. With a diverse workforce, BOA can serve their customers better;

through their products and services, Bank of America meets their Latino clients' needs with in-house language support. They provide online tools—such as the Spanish version of the Home Loan Guide, among others—and they train their customer service employees to help them deliver a clear and consistent customer experience through the use of proper Spanish terminology and grammar. This has led to a very large market penetration with Latinos.[4] Today, Bank of America serves 8.3 million Hispanic/Latino customers, and has more primary banking relationships among Hispanic/Latino customers than its industry peers.[5]

Former IBM Chief Diversity Officer Ted Childs now runs his own consultancy, Ted Childs® LLC. He is widely recognized as the pioneer of hard-wiring diversity to the business. He has trademarked the following statement: "Workforce Diversity: The bridge between the Workplace and the Marketplace®." Childs' leadership and vision has served as a catalyst for many market penetration initiatives. Among them, while at IBM, an LGBTQ+ sales initiative targeting LGBTQ+ small business owners, which resulted in the sale of millions of dollars' worth of computer equipment and services. IBM was wise to take this step. In 2015, LGBTQ+ purchasing power was estimated to be $830 billion in the US and $3 trillion worldwide.[6]

People with disabilities provide another opportunity for marketplace inclusion. Marca Bristo, Executive Director of the disability advocacy group Access Living in Chicago, points out that people with disabilities are "a customer base with a bigger niche market than the coveted 'tween market." She is quite right, as the market of the 54 million people with disabilities is estimated to be $1 trillion, two times that of teens and seventeen times that of tweens.[7] Yet as Bristo explains, "Virtually no market research is ever done on people with disabilities, and they are missing out on a huge consumer base that is only going to grow as Baby Boomers age. They are already experiencing disability because of their parents and grandparents, and now they will be experiencing their own disability."

This type of sustainable inclusion can only happen if differences are constructively called out using the principles of the Inclusion Paradox. It's not only at the moment of sale that signage needs to be produced in Chinese, Spanish, or Polish, but also during the creation of the product or the go-to-market approach. Here's a look at how a few companies are figuring this out:

- Japanese gaming company **Koei Co.** sought to expand its market share in Canada and the United States by developing product beyond its popular samurai games. However, executives knew up front the company wasn't good at making the kind of "gritty, realistic fare" preferred by Westerners. They worried the new games would miss the cultural mark. To overcome this challenge, they expanded their team in Toronto—which consisted primarily of a "handful of animators working on Japanese games"— hiring two dozen Canadians to design Western-market games. Granted, these Canadian designers are still entrenched in a Japanese working environment—complete with various daily rituals, including morning team exercises—but they are allowed a wide range of artistic control. They are trusted by executives to handle details, both large and small, which make games appealing to a Western market.[8]

- **Northwestern Mutual** is placing a big bet on its ability to attract, retain, and advance Latino talent. Not only for the sake of getting the best talent, but also to seize the $1.3 trillion Hispanic market opportunity in the US—the 15th largest economy in the world growing at a rate of $200 billion a year. Northwestern Mutual's bet entails an extensive outreach program to attract Latino talent and consumers. In the coming years, all their sales managers will go through crosscultural agility training in order to gain a better understanding of Latino talent and customers. They also seek to do the same for African Americans, Asian Americans, and the LGBTQ+ community. These crosscultural agility trainings are intended to be an enabler for sales managers who will be accountable for attracting, retaining, and advancing diverse talent as well as growing Northwestern Mutual's marketplace share of non-White consumers.

- At **Sodexo,** Senior Vice President and Chief Diversity Officer Dr. Rohini Anand works closely with the business to add a competitive differentiator to the food services and facilities management it provides to universities, schools, hospitals, and corporations. "We assist our clients with their own diversity and inclusion strategy development," says Anand. "Our diversity and inclusion efforts, which include offering cultural competency training for our clients' employees who are working both with our and their own diverse employee base, have strengthened our relationships with them. This increases our chances of renewing contracts when they are due."

- In July 2010, President Obama issued Executive Order 13548, establishing the goal of hiring 100,000 people with disabilities in the federal workforce by 2015. Later, in 2013 the Department of Labor introduced a hiring goal for federal contractors and subcontractors: that 7 percent of each job group in their workforce be qualified individuals with disabilities. Government contracts to supply drugs are an important part of **Walgreens'** business. Hence, Walgreens developed a plan to recruit a diverse workforce made up of at least 20 percent workers with disabilities in two of its distribution centers. For example, in Windsor, Connecticut, Walgreens ended up employing over 400 employees, over 50 percent of whom have a disability, including individuals with seizure disorders, autism, hearing impairments, visual impairments, cerebral palsy, intellectual disabilities and mental health disabilities.

• Since **Korn Ferry** is in the talent and leadership business, Korn Ferry has asked itself, "What implications does diversity and inclusion have on the very work of executive search, high potential identification, succession management, and leadership and management development that we do?" Clearly, the points of intersection are myriad. In fact, as the designer of the best practices in human capital processes and tools, we recognize that we operate within the very context necessary to embed diversity and inclusion right into the structure of the human capital edifice. Korn Ferry helps our clients understand that different things may motivate members of different demographic groups. Their lack of representation in management and leadership begs the questions, "Why does the gap exist?" and "How do we close these gaps?" The answers lie in organizational and leadership capabilities to ensure leaders are truly inclusive through awareness of their unconscious biases and through developing the competencies necessary within crosscultural agility.

There cannot be true, sustainable inclusion until leaders, managers, and employees understand and believe that diversity is the key to their business and mission success. A mission-grounded rationale for diversity de-escalates many of the contentious issues surrounding the subject. Regardless of whether they're part of the majority or minority, employees see the relevance of diversity in their own day-to-day responsibilities. Such a rationale also shifts diversity from being about various constituencies to being about the whole enterprise.

The *operations* business case: Hard-wiring diversity to processes and structures (it's sexier than it sounds)

The hospital built for White people featured at the beginning of this chapter is a clear example of just how vital it is to consider diversity and inclusion when determining how to provide services *and* run a business. Not only do doctors and nurses need to provide crossculturally competent care, but those designing the buildings and parking lots and providing wireless connectivity need to consider that people from diverse backgrounds and experiences will respond differently to their environments.

One powerful influence in the movement to incorporate diversity into business management is the late Dr. R. Roosevelt Thomas Jr., author of the groundbreaking book *Beyond Race and Gender: Unleashing the Power of Your Total Workforce by Managing Diversity* (AMACOM, 1992). Since his book's publication more than 20 years ago, Dr. Thomas has worked with innumerable corporations, spearheading conversations and serving as a catalyst for addressing diversity and inclusion issues inherent in operational strategies, such as vendor and supplier relationships, branding, and mergers and acquisitions. Despite his best efforts, Thomas said, "Companies are still significantly overlooking how much addressing diversity issues in their operational areas can yield significant results."

Here are some examples of where and how to do this.

Mergers and acquisitions

One area that could definitely benefit from a closer examination of diversity issues is mergers and acquisitions. Fifty percent of all mergers do not achieve their promised financial value creation. Their failure is rarely due to a lack of financial or technological synergy, but due to cultural incompatibility.[9] It turns out that the due diligence required in determining financial and marketplace compatibility rarely includes looking at the various cultures of the merging companies—a diversity and inclusion issue if ever there was one.

There are too many tales to tell of painful, wrenching mergers, where bad blood lingered long after the ink had dried. Rather than referring to the new name of the merged company, people were still identified by whether they were "Legacy Company A" or "Legacy Company B."

"In a survey we conducted of corporate development and human resource professionals involved in a merger, they ranked cultural integration as the second top contributor to transaction failure, just behind failure to pay appropriate attention to workforce issues," says Elizabeth Fealy, Principal, Human Capital and Americas New Services Leader at Ernst & Young. "Diversity and inclusion embedded into the M&A work can help mitigate these types of hiccups or convulsions. While culture can be viewed as amorphous, in our methodology we quantify cultural differences, identify the desired go-forward culture, and orchestrate an implementation process that fosters diversity and inclusion. It significantly increases the chances that the merger will succeed in achieving its financial objectives."

In a 2014 Korn Ferry survey, 72 percent of executives agreed that culture is extremely important to organizational performance, yet only 32 percent believed their own organization's culture is aligned to its business strategies.[10]

"The concept of organizational culture has never been more critical or more complex," says Senior Partner Dave Eaton, Korn Ferry's Practice Leader of Cultural Transformation. "And in that, the need to manage the deep implications of diversity and inclusion within organizational culture. Omnipresent globalization, mergers and acquisitions, joint ventures and outsourcing make it imperative to bottom-line results that companies focus on identifying, aligning, and communicating a common culture. They must then cascade and integrate this culture skillfully through crosscultural agility across their enterprise; and then tie that culture back to business strategy."

He adds that the various diverse subcultures can play a key role if harnessed proactively: "Driving culture transformation depends on engaging the workforce to embrace the change by helping them understand what's in it for them. Informal leaders within the organization need to be identified who can be engaged in the change effort and serve as culture champions. These can come from the informal subcultures within an organization, such as affinity groups."

Additionally, Eaton continues, national cultures can create massive headwinds that can effect the required culture change. "Just look at the M&A change efforts of Lucent of the USA and Alcatel of France, Daimler of Germany and Chrysler of the USA, Nissan of Japan and Renault of France. They all experienced major cultural challenges due in large part to an inability of the two merging organizations to adeptly, in a mutually reciprocal way, navigate through their cultural differences and successfully build a third culture."

Top five reasons why M&A transaction goals were not achieved

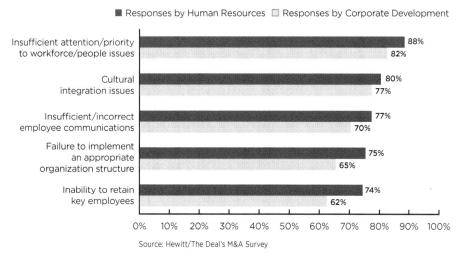

Source: Hewitt/The Deal's M&A Survey

Procurement

The name of the game in procurement is to get the greatest amount of services for the least amount of money. At the same time, corporations now are making a conscientious effort to use diverse suppliers directly or ask their middlemen to do so, and the US government is leading by example. Over the two Obama Administrations, we have witnessed an increased commitment to diversity within the federal government, and within that, increased focus on supplier diversity for procurement.

Diversity in the area of procurement is not just about using diverse suppliers, however. It's also about helping them to learn the ropes of large-scale business, which creates win-win situations for the suppliers, buyers, and other groups. One person who is doing this with high-impact results is Douglas Freeman, CEO of Virtcom Consulting, a strategy management consultancy. He helps companies make and save millions of dollars on marketplace strategies and operational efficiencies by reexamining how they structure and run their processes.

His differentiator? Diversity. (See the sidebar for an example of how Freeman helped one client achieve $400M in new revenue through his application of the diversity *operational* business case.)

A $400 million case study of the *operations* business case

"Our core philosophy can be summed up as 'diversity-focused,' where we seek to help our client generate profit through diversity," says Douglas Freeman, Founder and CEO of Virtcom Consulting. Freeman uses the experiences he gained as a senior consultant at Deloitte Consulting, as an investment banker at JPMorgan Chase, and as the head of Business Development and Operations for Mondus, where he helped raise more than $170 million in private equity financing.

Freeman recognized that minority-owned businesses were inadvertently being shortsighted in their strategies for keeping their expenses down. As a result, they were losing out on a government mandate that 23 percent of federal agencies' procurement dollars must be spent with diversity vendors (spread across nine different categories).

The rub was that vendors qualifying as "minority-owned" businesses don't normally accept credit cards for two major reasons: 1) They want to avoid paying transaction fees that can amount to thousands of dollars, and 2) Most of them simply are uncomfortable accepting credit cards, due to a lack of experience with them. Instead, they typically take payment through direct deposit or checks, not procurement cards.

Here's where they were missing out. Because checks and direct deposits involve cumbersome processes to set up and use, government agencies were reluctant to do business with anyone who used the less streamlined check-writing process. They had the motivation to meet the mandate, but not the patience to work with outdated approaches.

Using hard data, Virtcom helped change the perception of diversity vendors in terms of the real costs of waiting 90 days for payment, the often-overlooked result of the check-paying process. By waiting three months, vendors were, in effect, paying interest charges on the unpaid invoice. When comparing the cost of the transaction fee on credit card charges (2 percent) to the cost of waiting for payment (2 to 5 percent), they were able to clearly show that accepting credit card payments resulted in cheaper transaction costs.

Virtcom then partnered with a major credit card company to develop a procurement card—a specialized credit card used by government agencies or large companies to purchase big-ticket goods and services costing more than $5,000—specifically for the African-American market. Virtcom initiated a supplier enrollment program that targeted and trained more than 2,000 diversity vendors. They also partnered with federal agencies to market the idea of procurement cards and trained bank sales force teams and processors.

Early in the process, Virtcom had to debunk the myth that diverse business-to-government suppliers (B2G) were a higher credit risk. Virtcom showed the banks, the processors, and the credit card company that the B2G market had a 0.0007 default rate. In other words, it was virtually risk-free. Based on the biased belief that diverse suppliers posed a higher credit risk, credit card companies had been charging a much higher transaction rate.

In the end, the card proved beneficial to suppliers and buyers, as well as the credit card company that issued it. Participating vendors now get their money in about two days, improving their cash flow and financial strategic management, while reducing the costs of not being able to pursue new business or make investments while waiting for payments to be made.

Boasting less expensive transaction costs (about $60 less expensive than a non-credit card transaction/payment), the procurement card saves the government billions of dollars, while significantly reducing the complexity of the process. Meanwhile, credit card companies have discovered a new revenue stream, since diversity vendors are now able to accept credit card payments for large purchases. The first year the diversity card was utilized, the credit card company gained $79 million in new revenues. Over a period of four years since it was implemented, revenue has amounted to more than $400 million—all from what was just recently a totally untapped market and revenue stream.

According to Freeman, "We specialize in an area that we call 'blind spots'—missed business opportunity linked to diversity. In working with any large enterprise, we usually find six to ten of these. We propose quantitative value around those blind spots."

And in this case study of the *operations* business case for diversity, more than $400 million worth of blind spots.

Regionalization

Think about the regionalization that's taking place in multinationals as they move away from country-specific structures to regional structures. Rather than have every function staffed in every country, they're spreading out. The IT function for all of Latin America may be in Buenos Aires, while the HR function is in Mexico City, and the Finance organization is in Santiago. Although they may speak Spanish and do the sign of the cross before praying, you will find variations in how Argentineans, Mexicans, and Chileans perform their jobs. It's clear that any cost savings garnered by regionalizing will be undercut by cultural and diversity breakdowns.

Consider the management consultancy that's merging the Real Estate, HR, and Technology areas of their Italian, Spanish, and Portuguese practices. The offices in each of these countries have to figure out how they're going to serve all their constituencies across deep language, cultural, and regulatory differences. In order for it to be accomplished successfully, this operational strategy desperately needs diversity and inclusion embedded into it.

We can bring them in, but we can't keep them: Hard-wiring diversity into all people strategies

Once grounded in the *marketplace* and *operations* business cases, diversity and inclusion can be more effectively realized as part and parcel of a company's talent strategies. Even top leadership has become adept at recognizing the connection. Many now say that they have proof diversity improves their business performance. Few will disagree with statements like this: "The talent and skills necessary to successfully drive our business are found in diverse people with different backgrounds." Or this statement, from a vice president at Bell South, "For us, inclusion is not only fundamental to our employee workforce, but also to our leadership structure, our supplier base, our charitable and corporate social outreach, and among the customers who make up our marketplace."[11]

So far, much of the diversity and inclusion work has been focused on getting those who are different in the door—hence, the focus on recruiting fairs, CEO proclamations on "the power of diversity," and tapping into affinity groups to help with the act of recruiting itself. Many of these efforts have proven quite successful at attracting greater diversity—the mix.

But inclusion—making the mix work—continues to elude most employers because, unfortunately, it's possible to have diversity without inclusion. If the members of a company's community do not feel they're full partners in the well-being of the corporation, if they feel their differences create both invisible and visible barriers to their ability to contribute fully their abilities and ambitions—then there is no inclusion. Conversely, we can have inclusion with no diversity when homogenous groups surround themselves with the comforts of their shared experiences.

"Some leadership teams don't realize how insular they are," says Korn Ferry Senior Partner and Talent Strategy Practice Leader Ilene Gochman. "Their understanding of the range of diversity is quite narrow—personality, industry experience, schools they went to—compared to the myriad of possibilities and what would enhance the team's success. It's vital that in our work we extend their field of vision about what diversity encompasses and what implications it has for their business."

The key to fostering inclusion is for the entire system to enable and nurture the mix. Even when attitudes are changed and majority members "get" the diversity business imperative, outdated systems and processes are still in place about how people join and grow within organizations. They are the legacy of the culturally bound wisdom and preferences of groups of people who were not very diverse at the time. In large part, HR processes themselves may be perpetuating old results, not because of their current intentions, but because of what they've inherited. Thus, although diverse talent comes in, it leaves at a higher rate.

Korn Ferry Senior Client Partner and Regional Managing Director for the Mid-Atlantic Region Michael Hyter (who has written two books on inclusion—*The Power of Choice* and *The Power of Inclusion*) says, "Inclusion and diversity have to become embedded into the normal processes and procedures within the talent management system. It's the only way to ensure measureable outcomes in a sustainable way."

Chapter 3, "Deeply embed D&I into your talent management systems," takes a detailed look at a few HR processes where we must hard-wire diversity and inclusion.

But before we go there, a few final thoughts on how organizations can pull together the marketplace, talent, and operational business cases into a cohesive whole.

Pulling it all together

"Increasingly, CEOs and CHROs are seeking to align their human capital strategies to their overall organizational strategies," says Ilene Gochman. "For too long, talent programs have been disjointed—even working at odds with one another—in the absence of having been developed as cohesive enablers to where the organization has declared it wants to go. Diversity and inclusion programs must also follow this same strategically aligned glide path. When they do, they will be well positioned to have the true sustainable impact diversity and business leaders seek."

In July and August of 2015, Korn Ferry conducted a comprehensive, global survey of views on leadership development.[12] The responses—over 7,500 from 107 countries—identified the following top organizational challenges that keep leaders up at night:

Rank the most pressing, strategic business priorities in your organization

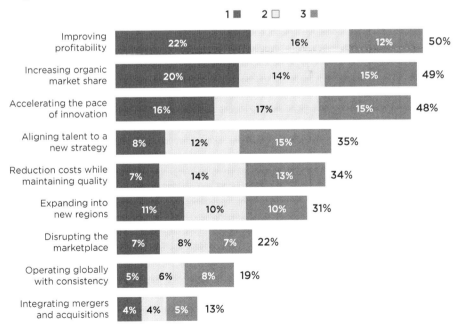

1 ■   2 □   3 ■

	1	2	3	Total
Improving profitability	22%	16%	12%	50%
Increasing organic market share	20%	14%	15%	49%
Accelerating the pace of innovation	16%	17%	15%	48%
Aligning talent to a new strategy	8%	12%	15%	35%
Reduction costs while maintaining quality	7%	14%	13%	34%
Expanding into new regions	11%	10%	10%	31%
Disrupting the marketplace	7%	8%	7%	22%
Operating globally with consistency	5%	6%	8%	19%
Integrating mergers and acquisitions	4%	4%	5%	13%

Take a careful look at the top priorities. Most not only intersect with talent issues, but also with diversity and inclusion. In fact, diversity and inclusion can be a vital enabler to addressing several of these top challenges:

- *Increasing organic market share*: As I have mentioned before, the new, underpenetrated markets are those representing the new diverse demographics. If companies neglect to understand the unique needs, wants, and aspirations of these consumers, they can say goodbye to aspirations to grow market share organically.

- *Accelerating the pace of innovation*: As you have heard, this is one of the most commonly cited reasons by Business, HR, and D&I leaders as key to the business case for diversity and inclusion.

- *Aligning talent to a new strategy*: With human talent being increasingly diverse and shaped by experiences, traits, and drivers that differ from those of more traditional talent, organizations will falter at alignment if they assume similarity and underestimate the need for diversity knowledge and crosscultural agility to mobilize the talent to get behind the new business strategies.

- *Expanding into new regions*: By definition, these new regions are about going into places abounding with differences at every level: population, talent, cultural, political, economic, geographical, and environmental. Being highly skilled at diversity, inclusion, and crosscultural agility is not just a nice to have—it is vital!

- *Disrupting the marketplace*: This will require alternative thinking, perspectives, experiences, networks, and people. Disruption cannot happen with status-quo thinking or leadership teams.

- *Operating globally with consistency*: Ironically, the ability to manage diversity is key to managing consistently. It requires a significant amount of sophisticated thinking and decision making to determine where to draw the line of what will be consistent for operational effectiveness and what will be allowed to remain at the discretion of the local offices and teams. In other words, "consistency" also requires smart variance management.

- *Integrating mergers and acquisitions*: Bringing two different organizational cultures together is rife with inclusion challenges. So serious, in fact, that not managing these cultural gaps effectively often derails achieving the financial goals sought from the M&A in the first place.

Make no mistake—the hypercompetitive global marketplace has not just been a market thing. It's a "people thing" as well. We have the inevitable difficult decisions regarding job eliminations, treating laid-off workers with dignity, and maintaining a focused and engaged workforce for those who remain. It's a time when diversity and inclusion must be tended to—not in spite of the financial crisis, but because of it.

We have a desperate need for perspectives, skills, and worldviews that currently don't exist in organizations in order to interpret and prosper within this new upside-down world order.

Without diversity and inclusion, this desperate need will not be realized. ♀

Stay with us! Marriott targets LGBT travelers

Nancy Trejos, USA TODAY, *June 2, 2014*

Marriott International is going after the Lesbian, Gay, Bisexual, and Transgender community with a new social media and marketing campaign that launches today, joining a number of major hotel chains aggressively trying to lure the lucrative clientele. #LoveTravels will feature images wrapped around five hotels in Washington, D.C., print ads in LGBT media, an online portrait gallery and other ads in various US cities. The ads will feature openly gay NBA player Jason Collins, among other spokespeople. Images and videos plus personal stories will be available at LoveTravels.Marriott.com and at Marriott.com/gaytravel.

Marriott's campaign is the latest example of the hotel industry stepping up its efforts to lure LGBT travelers. While the company says it is targeting the community to make LGBT travelers feel more welcome, there's also a business incentive. According to Out Now Global, an LGBT marketing specialist group, the potential value of the LGBT travel market was set to reach $181 billion last year.

The Supreme Court's striking down of the Defense of Marriage Act and the expansion of marriage equality has sparked more businesses to publicly reach out to the community. "It's almost expected at this point in the LGBT community," says David Paisley, senior research director at Community Marketing and Insights, an LGBT marketing research firm.

Since its start in San Francisco in the 1980s, Kimpton Hotels & Restaurants has been at the forefront with its support of community organizations advocating for the LGBT community.

But many other hotels have followed suit.

Preferred Hotel Group launched the Preferred Pride program in 2011 with more than 120 gay-welcoming independent hotels and resorts in 20 countries. OUT NYC has called itself the first gay hotel in New York City. Hilton Worldwide has a gay travel package and a website dedicated to helping LGBT guests plan their vacations. Marriott's campaign will run through November. Braden Summers, a celebrity photographer, shot the photos of Collins, fashion model Geena Rocero, and Marriott employee Talisha Padgett-Matthews.

"Our goal is really to educate and engage and shift perception of our portfolio brand," says Kristine Friend, senior director of segment marketing for Marriott International. "We've decided to kick off a holistic campaign that really helps celebrate inclusiveness and beautifully illustrates our desire to make people feel at home at our hotels." Rick Stiffler, Preferred Hotel Group's Vice President of Leisure Sales, says hotels have no other choice but to pay attention to the LGBT traveler given how much they spend on travel.

"It's in the billions and that really has a lot of people paying attention to the LGBT market," he says. "I think if you're not paying attention, you're definitely missing the boat. For us, it's not only the right thing to do, it's the smart thing to do." Collins, who spent part of last season with the Brooklyn Nets, calls Marriott's outreach program "important not only to the LGBT community but to society in general." He adds, "When I travel with a boyfriend, we really want to feel that sense of inclusiveness regardless of our sexual orientation or religion. We want that feeling of being welcome."

SUMMARY POINTS

- Sustainable diversity is different from programmatic diversity, although the two are linked.

- For diversity to be sustainable, it must be hard-wired into an organization's mission, growth, profitability, and operational strategies. It must have compelling answers to how greater diversity and inclusion can be an enabler for achieving business goals.

- Diversity and inclusion is extremely relevant to business leaders and managers in order to help them meet their most important objectives.

SHAPING YOUR STRATEGY

- How much of your strategy relies on programmatic approaches, rather than the sustainable approach of hard-wiring diversity to your talent, business, and operational imperatives?

- As you think about marketplace growth and operational priorities, where do you think diversity and inclusion can add something of value?

- What would it take to help leaders and managers understand how much diversity and inclusion can help them with their business needs?

- In emphasizing the benefits for traditional majorities if they address diversity and inclusion, how can you avoid too far of a pendulum swing in ways that soften the urgency of diversity and inclusion and, in the process, minimize the real challenges of achieving equity within the organization?

Chapter 3

Deeply embed D&I into your talent management systems

In the previous chapter, we explored how the business case for diversity and inclusion is not just based on talent, but can also be an enabler to reach both marketplace and operational goals. In addition, we briefly touched on how HR and diversity and inclusion need to be enablers to making this happen. Despite their potential, HR systems are infected with unconscious bias legacy gremlins that can sabotage the most well-intentioned diversity and inclusion goals.

In this chapter, we zero in on the talent systems themselves—sourcing and recruiting, high potential identification, succession management, and employee benefits. Further, we focus on how to ensure diversity and inclusion is systematically hardwired into them.

First, let's look at a foundational gap within the human resources function that often prevents its high-performing practitioners from seeing that their valued best practices may actually be hindering the advancement of diversity and inclusion. The gap is about limited crosscultural agility, including lack of awareness of how unconscious bias may be playing a part.

A key gap: Diversity management skills for constructively calling out differences

The White, middle-class recruiter was convinced the candidate lacked confidence and, in fact, seemed like he was hiding something. When asked why, rather than give examples tied to the candidate's narration of his career history, the recruiter demurred to a gut feeling: "I don't know, I just didn't feel he was being straight with us. And he sure seemed nervous." When pressed further to identify what was informing her gut, she finally clicked into the specific behavior. "He totally avoided eye contact with all of us!" It turned out that the candidate came from an Asian culture in which direct eye contact with someone in an authority position—such as an interviewer—would be considered rude and disrespectful. The recruiter's gut—her intuition—that had served her so well in her career had failed her here.

In *Blink: The Power of Thinking Without Thinking,* Malcolm Gladwell lays out a treatise on how our intuition can serve us powerfully yet lead us tragically astray. When we're observing and acting based upon our frames of reference— our *worldviews*—we often misinterpret what we're seeing. A certain trait or behavior—such as avoiding eye contact—that indicates respect in one culture can mean something quite different in another. And the consequences can be serious.

The Inclusion Paradox demands that we know how to call out our differences in order to create sustainable diversity. Doing so requires *crosscultural competence*, which I define "The ability to discern and take into account one's own and others' worldviews, to be able to solve problems, make decisions, and resolve conflicts in ways that optimize cultural differences for better, longer-lasting, and more creative solutions."

An overall organizational lack of crosscultural competence contributes to keeping the glass ceiling from shattering. To create inclusive environments, we must first address the traditional issue of *power*. That's because the work required to eradicate the *-isms* of prejudice rests within the realm of those in power. In fact, many best-known diversity strategies and programs—such as the call for CEO commitment plus the creation of affinity groups, inclusion councils, and mentoring programs—are aimed at reducing the barriers to greater access and connection to those in power.

Even when leadership has embraced the need to promote diversity and become personally involved, the most well-intentioned efforts will quickly hit the limits of their ability to bring about change. Good intentions are simply not enough, because diverse representation is still lacking in management and leadership.

The *-isms* within the realm of power play a part in the hindrances to diversity and inclusion, but they don't explain the whole story. White, male cultural preferences define the attributes of strong leadership. This is not an indictment, but rather an observation that every culturally bound group— Latinas from Miami, Ivy-league educated African Americans, Japanese businessmen in Tokyo, White males in Omaha—has a preferred leadership style that they believe has contributed to their success. But where White males have to accept the greater burden of responsibility of addressing this is that they have been the prevailing group leading corporate organizations in the United States and Europe and therefore shaping the cultures that dictate how talent and leadership are assessed, shaped, rewarded, and promoted. So when those who are not White and male are stuck below the glass ceiling, this systemic bias must be recognized and owned by those currently in power to dismantle their exclusionary impact.

In a multicultural, global world, however, the diverse employees coming through an organization's doors and moving up in organizational ranks are going to exhibit great managerial and leadership qualities that often are not recognized as such because they look different from the cultural norm of the majority group currently in the leadership position.

Creating crossculturally agile individuals and organizations is essential for ushering in sustainable diversity. Only through crosscultural agility can employees and leaders gain the language, concepts, and tools for skillfully addressing cultural differences. This agility provides the tools they can use to navigate the difference.

Keeping in mind this culturally biased perspective of what constitutes true leadership, let's now look at a few of the talent systems through a new lens.

Performance management: The phenomenon of overlooking talent

To uncover the inadvertent assumptions that prevent the mix from working, we must explore the wiring of the performance assessment process.

As companies focus on their key or high potential talent, they run the risk of perpetuating underrepresentation if this select group is not adequately diverse. The view that 20 percent of talent yields 80 percent of results has plenty of merit—it informs a strategy that an organization can get an even bigger payoff by focusing on this top talent. But if not managed in a way that diversifies who ends up in this talent pool, true inclusion will be elusive.

Korn Ferry's Senior Client Partner Michael Hyter explains, "There is a tendency for senior leaders to believe that their organizations are meritocracies, but that thinking reinforces the false notion that the best talent—regardless of their background—will naturally rise to the top. These 'talented few' then are believed to merit an intense focus. The problem is that this small group has not been the result of meritocracy. If it had, it truly would have been representational of the diverse talent available. But it's not. And in this, high-performing talent that comes from traditionally underrepresented groups get overlooked through conscious and unconscious biases that then result in intense development for the few 'gifted' ones who perpetuate the homogeneity of who will get the attention to move ahead."

Inclusion Paradox principles clearly apply here. By design, the focus on key and high-potential individuals shrinks the pool of talent that receives special attention and developmental resources. How can we ensure these pools are diverse? Here, we still need some scaffolding to ensure sustainability. Along with the high potential assessment, a multicultural talent review (MCTR) must be undertaken. The MCTR provides a macro view of the distribution of one's multicultural talent, and considers the following questions:

- How many potential top multicultural talent leaders do you have?
- In comparing different groups to one another, what is the bell curve of their performance levels?
- What are the turnover rates?
- What are their engagement scores?

Very high top performers who happen to be people of color or people with disabilities already will have been identified during the high potential assessment. Studies on the success of talent from traditionally underrepresented groups have shown that these individuals tend to be superstars who stand out dramatically. The potential blind spot is overlooking the strong—but not superstar—talent among these very same underrepresented groups. Due to their different ways of thinking or acting, their strong performance is often not recognized as such.

As Russell Bennett, Vice President of Latino Health Solutions at UnitedHealthcare®, says, "In corporate society, it's easy to find leaders and managers who say they strongly support the concept of diversity. They want people who look different, but corporations still reward for conformity and are often uncomfortable with non-conformity."

We need to ferret out this overlooked talent. But the question remains: Are managers able to tell the difference between a performance issue and a crosscultural misunderstanding? Think about the following performance assessment sound bites:

"Trust"

"High performing"

"Pay for results"

"Proactive"

"Executive presence"

"Nice"

"Assertive"

"Fire in the belly"

On the surface, these are all seemingly strong, positive traits. However, as we'll see later in the book, these sound bites are often tagged to individuals and can label them for the rest of their careers. Each is loaded with culturally biased assumptions that may inadvertently filter out positive assessments of diverse employees because the manner in which they express themselves may not fit an organizational view of what these traits look like when wielded effectively.

On the flip side, negative sound bites may sound like this:

"Aggressive"

"Not a team player"

"Clients don't feel comfortable with her"

"Shy"

"Passive"

These, too, are terms that can mean different things depending on the culture from where the individual originates. For example, was the individual's behavior truly aggressive? Or was it actually a respectful and effective way of achieving business results within the context of their culture? Was the individual demonstrating passive participation in a meeting, or was he or she displaying effective, face-saving, influential leadership? By focusing specifically on diverse talent, an MCTR can create an opportunity to call out differences. This enables a company to be better positioned to look more accurately at talent that could, ironically, be overlooked by the very nature of an individual's differences.

For a business to be truly successful—through the Obama Era and beyond—it needs to draw on a diverse talent pool. Not only that, but it also needs to make sure this diversity of talent feels included in the culture of the organization. If this is the case, Baxter's former CDO, Don Wilson, said, "These diverse individuals will become talent magnets for you," creating a win-win scenario for everyone.

Succession management

"Your next CEO could be a woman currently in Mumbai," says Senior Partner Jim Peters, Korn Ferry Hay Group's Global Lead for Succession Management. "But given how poorly companies are managing diversity and inclusion in their organizations, the chances are high they will overlook her—and the many other high potentials from traditionally underrepresented groups that are in their midst in every nook and cranny of their organizations."

In fact, the Achilles' heel for any organization that genuinely seeks diversity in leadership is not putting a laser focus on how to ensure that their high potential and succession pools are diverse. Look at the diversity of these pools and one can predict whether leadership teams will remain as homogenous as the current status quo. "Sure, hiring diversity is a way to try to accelerate diversity of leadership," says Peters. "But in addition to the unintended consequences of hiring diverse talent into an organization that has not nurtured an inclusive culture to ensure they are successful, it is the diversity within the succession pools where the more sustainable long game toward full diversity in leadership lies."

When Peters, who has worked on succession management with CEOs and other executives from hundreds of the largest organizations, engages them in this very conversation of the diversity of the pools, typical objections pop up. One of them is the spoken or unspoken assumption by those managing the high potential and succession pools that only a handful had true "potential." This statement, often made in the context of diversity pools, is not only rife with conscious and unconscious biases, but it is simply wrong. Peters argues:

> I often get asked, 'is potential immutable?' Immutable is not a word I use on a regular basis, so I had to fire up the synapses in my brain to dig out a definition. My wiki head told me 'unchanging, fixed, or rigid.' In other words, the question gets at the historical nature versus nurture controversy. People are born with potential and others are not is one point or view. Or, conversely, potential can be developed, enhanced, and nurtured. It's the latter that I believe—we are all born with potential and then thrust into a world in which our potential is enhanced, neutralized, or thwarted. While our research tells us that potential is comprised of seven signs,[1] we know all seven can be developed. Some of them are harder to develop but they can be. As a result, I reject the notion that potential is 'immutable.'

The other dynamic that tends to derail the consideration of traditionally underrepresented talent in the high potential and succession pools is the requirement regarding mobility. Peters points out that for many companies, once they create their first draft of high potentials and then those on it are asked if they are mobile to take on new assignments, if they say "No thanks" or "That is not an option for me right now for x reason," they take the person off of the high potential list. In effect, they punish them. "Therefore, I believe that using mobility as a criterion for potential has an adverse impact on gender diversity in particular," he says.

And the negative impact goes both ways. Either the person said he or she was not mobile at the time, or ironically, the organization makes assumptions that he or she won't be able to, without ever asking him or her. I witnessed the executives of a Fortune 50 manufacturing company do precisely this when a woman's name came up for consideration to run a factory in a city in which she did not currently live. As much as they had praised her performance up to that point and considered her next logical career step runoff managing a factory, they simply moved her off the list once one of the decision makers pointed out she had just gotten married, and "Certainly she won't want to move." Once it was pointed out to them how this unilateral decision was made on her behalf, they cringed at how obvious their unconscious bias had gotten the best of them. They put her back on the list and asked her. Turns out, she was very willing to relocate in order to seize the opportunity.

But still, there are those who indeed won't be able to relocate. How do we resolve the dilemmas for those that are not mobile at the key point in their career development without negatively affecting their advancement opportunities? Here's Peters once again:

> " Arguably, your ability to develop a track record of formative experiences would be enhanced through mobility, but it is not necessary. Maybe one cannot move from Indianapolis to Hong Kong—due to child requirements, spousal careers, aging parental needs, family medical considerations, or other such normal things people have to deal with in life.... And yes, immersion is a great way for one to understand the Asian market. But, let's get creative here. How about the person works on a cross-functional/regional project team chartered with drafting a strategy for the Asian market and is willing to spend two weeks every quarter in the region? What companies need to do is to become developmentally creative to enhance the potential of people, not arbitrarily thwart their development. "

Benefit programs can also be culturally biased

Crosscultural competence also means that organizations can clearly see the implications of diversity on programs that have not traditionally been thought of as culturally influenced. Inclusion is lacking, for example, when it comes to employees' optimal use of benefits. In the United States, although 401(k) and 403(b) retirement savings benefits and preventive care are available and communicated equally to all, African Americans, Latinos, and women tend to under-save and exhibit behaviors that often sub-optimize their return on investment, according to research by Aon Hewitt and Ariel Investments.[2] These studies have also shown that different demographic groups under- or overutilize preventive care. Whether it's about health or wealth, these types of utilization disparities are evidence that we do not have inclusion, even in benefits that are available and accessible to all employees.

While there are socioeconomic reasons for these gaps, cultural differences are also at play. How benefits are designed, communicated, marketed, and accessed inadvertently conforms to—and is optimized by—the worldview of the traditional majority culture. Sustainable diversity demands that we be aware of why and how this is happening. As a result of this awareness, we can create solutions that make these essential well-being programs work equally well for all. We'll explore these phenomena and solutions in depth in Chapter 14, "Why not acknowledging differences can make us sicker and poorer."

There are other ways in which benefit programs can be tailored to meet diverse needs. In addition to its standard benefits package, Xerox has given employees $10,000 for allocation to different programs.[3] This gives non-traditional families the flexibility to tailor benefits to their personal needs. Meanwhile, Merrill Lynch and Bank of America have instituted "extended family benefits." These flexible plans let employees add other household members to the plan, be it a domestic partner, an elder parent, or a grown child.[4]

The cultural bias within benefits is not a trivial matter. As healthcare costs rise and a greater burden is placed on the new workforce to take responsibility for their retirement planning, the long-term well-being of employees needs to be a hallmark of sustainable diversity—even once they're no longer employed by the company providing these benefits.

Flexibility and virtuality

Almost all diversity and inclusion issues point to the need for greater flexibility—not only in terms of benefits programs and the length of time they are extended, but also in advancement opportunities, set retirement age, and fixed job descriptions. Calling out differences among a growing number of groups can quickly become complicated, particularly as we expand beyond the categories of race and gender. Two generations ago, the call for flexibility came from working moms. Now, it's coming from working dads, Millennials, Gen Xers, near retirees, and singles—in essence, everyone! This implies that it's less about tweaking systems and processes for greater flexibility and more about creating systems that are flexible by design. Meanwhile, nano and Web 2.0 technological breakthroughs challenge the paradigm that flexibility automatically means greater cost.

The 2008 financial meltdown accelerated the need to provide greater flexibility as organizations asked employees to do more with less. Work hours are increasing both out of need and fear, and flexibility can now be offered as a reward in a time when pay increases and benefits are reduced. (Check out Chapter 15, "Work-life flexibility: The mother of all battles," where I explore this further.)

Sourcing and recruiting

I left this particular talent process for the end of the sustainable diversity discussion since it is where those seeking fast solutions for diversity and inclusion go first—and often stay here as if it were the panacea.

However, we now do need to come back to sourcing and recruiting as an essential aspect of recruiting diversity. My intent here is not to travel well-trodden territory on diverse sourcing and recruiting best practices (there are a lot of highly valuable, proven best practices that have been well documented); rather, I wish to explore some next practices emerging today.

"As the workforce evolves and employees identify themselves with a broader lens that goes beyond gender, ethnicity, and traditional affinity groups, recruiting and sourcing strategies must be innovative and next-generation," says Germayne Cade, Vice President, Client Solutions at Futurestep, a middle management search firm and recruiting process outsourcing provider that is part of Korn Ferry. In fact, executive search firms such as Korn Ferry are feeling the appropriate heat and rising to the challenge to ensure its candidate reach be as broad and deep as possible, through using both traditional and unconventional approaches to finding talent outside the usual resources.

"The secret to alternative diversity sourcing is to create targeted 'talent communities,'" says Neil Griffiths, Global Practice Leader for Korn Ferry's Futurestep Talent Communications and Employer Brand Practice. Griffiths explains:

> It's not enough to say you want a diverse slate. Organizations need to be very specific about which talent segment they are looking to engage and attract. Whether it's women in Engineering, Latinas in Finance, African Americans in Marketing, or Veterans in Supply Chain, a targeted value proposition is key. This requires the need to understand your audience and their channel behavior as well as clearly defining the reason they should join an organization. This is not to say organizations should not strive to have all forms of diversity for their many roles, but here I am talking about the power of micro targeting. Learning from Google and Facebook's best social media science, organizations need to identify the specific demographic they are after. This yields significantly superior results compared to blanket attempts to bring in 'more' diversity.

"A talent community approach can be beneficial for several reasons. First, it attracts the passive candidate through ongoing education of an organization's brand. It also allows talent to understand what it takes to succeed in an organization before arriving.

"For example, when Kraft approached us to help attract Veterans to their organization, we set about developing a key value proposition to tell the story of the opportunities Kraft could offer. By inviting returning Veterans to register in the online talent community, we could share with them the skills required to succeed, and allow ex-military talent working at Kraft to tell their story of transitioning into a role in civilian life.

"The results were a ready-made talent pool, educated on the company's brand, values, and culture. They were also well briefed on the job openings available straight away. The talent community became a sourcing channel and shortlists of candidates included more diversity of skills than before.

Bryan Proctor, Senior Client Partner and Global Leader of the Financial Officer Center of Expertise, diversifies the talent pools his team pulls together for Korn Ferry's clients by tracking the very best sitting and future CFOs. "It is incumbent upon us to know who is on the rise, particularly those individuals who bring diverse backgrounds, experiences and points of view. We systematically identify the best of the best, and diversity is always a meaningful part of the equation. This puts an appropriate burden on Korn Ferry. Search firms like us must be proactive in bringing the best diverse candidates to the attention of corporate America."

But the path forward is tough. "The financial crisis of 2008–2009 created a setback for the advancement of diversity at the board level," says Victor Arias, Senior Client Partner in Korn Ferry's Board Placement Practice and Leader of the Diversity and Inclusion Center of Expertise. "Companies recruited board members with crisis-management capability. Turnover was low during the few years following the crisis. Underrepresented groups such as Hispanics did not make progress at top board level participation during these years. But things are changing. Savvy companies are beginning to look at board recruitment differently in order to grow ethnic minority leadership representation, no longer only focusing on a narrow scope of former CEOs or CFOs."

But there is one other dimension that must be brought up carefully. Without allowing this next point to be an excuse for not sourcing enough diversity, in addition to sourcing diverse slates every which way, organizations can also use a diversity and inclusion lens even when the choice has come down to the top two candidates—for legitimate "best candidates" reasons—being members of the majority. And this evaluation filter would be: Which of the two is the more inclusive leader? In other words, companies can legitimately evaluate which one has the track record as a savvy and skilled champion of diversity and inclusion and, therefore, who would be the most likely to do the same in the new organization.

Implications for HR and diversity and inclusion practitioners

What does this type of sustainable approach to diversity and inclusion mean for the practitioners in the field?

As I've argued throughout this chapter, we must tackle the work of diversity and inclusion in a different way in order for it to be sustainable. Those in diversity work need to build new capabilities and take on new experiences. "The chief diversity officer should have responsibilities that extend beyond traditional people issues," says 25-year veteran diversity consultant

Mary-Frances Winters, CEO of the Winters Group. "The role should include international government relations, trade relations, manufacturing, design issues, selection of location, security, ethics, and global marketing."

This applies not only to CDOs, but also to all HR leaders. Diversity is not something to be tended to on the side, but an integral part of managing all the dimensions of human capital which HR professionals and people managers are responsible for. It must also be coupled with *operations*, with how the business is run, and with what an organization produces and sells.

HR leaders are beginning to grasp the importance of diversity and inclusion. In the fall of 2008, the Society for Human Resource Management (SHRM)—the leading global association of HR professionals with more than 100,000 members—convened a group of the top 100 diversity leaders and practitioners to give advice on how best to integrate diversity into their highly regarded HR certifications. This is a public acknowledgment that there had been an increasing number of HR professionals taking over the diversity agenda and seeing it as an inherent part of their responsibilities. This has led to the development of three new HR diversity and inclusion organizational standards, which in 2013 were finalized by SHRM in cooperation with the American National Standards Institute.[5]

Korn Ferry Senior Client Partner George Atkinson from the Executive Search Practice who specializes in placing HR executives has seen the evolution happen during his 19 years of experience. He says, "Just as we've seen a tremendous increase in interest from CEOs to elevate the role of the HR leader because talent is now viewed as the company's greatest driver of success (or failure), diversity within the leadership ranks has been prompted by the need to relate to a vastly more diverse customer base. There's much greater buy-in for D&I for concrete business reasons, not just because of political correctness."

He goes on to cite many examples, including a 15,000-employee strong hospital system that increasingly sees patients and their families coming in from the Middle East. "There's so much cultural sensitivity required there that can actually make the difference between life and death."

This signals a fundamental shift in how HR professionals are viewing the need to get intimately and personally involved with diversity and inclusion.

Increasingly, I am asked to facilitate strategic sessions for HR professionals on how to move diversity and inclusion forward. What is telling about these invitations is that many of them are initiated by the SVPs of HR, not the CDOs. Clearly, HR leaders are feeling ownership for diversity and inclusion as never before. Why? In part, it's because they're not getting the results they expected from their long-distance sponsorship and support for diversity and inclusion work. It's also because they're seeing diversity and inclusion issues spill over into every area of HR. They're seeing that to lead in HR means to lead on diversity.

"There is no question that HR and business leaders are stepping up their diversity and inclusion game," says Hyter. "I am both excited for the diversity and inclusion field, but at the same time worried for the diversity practitioners I have known for a long time. Having this owned by others other than the D&I office—it's exactly what we have been striving for. But as it begins to happen, the diversity and inclusion practitioners need to reposition themselves in becoming directly aligned to the strategic direction of the business versus just a support role."

Diversity and inclusion practitioners, in fact, have to take their work toward a place of more sophisticated vigilance. Sure, it's a breakthrough practice when CEOs use their position of power to advocate for diversity and inclusion. But they should take care to ensure their efforts are not getting caught up in superficiality. This may happen when companies showcase diverse people in their marketing materials, offer minority scholarships, attend minority career fairs, subsidize minority internship programs, and fund minority community outreach programs. All of these are key and commendable efforts, but from a sustainability perspective, they don't engage the organizational machinery that defines the way things get done.

Programs come and go. In the process, they raise issues, maintain interest, and mobilize people into action. Such programs must lead to systemic changes to existing processes or the creation of new ones to ensure inclusion of the mix. Programmatic diversity is like riding a wave on a surfboard. It can be a spectacular, memorable thrill. But sustainable diversity requires harnessing the demographic wave to change the coastline itself. ⌇

SUMMARY POINTS

- Addressing diversity is much more than getting diverse talent in the door through sourcing and recruiting.

- Every HR discipline has the potential to perpetuate the lack of diversity or to accelerate it.

- Unconscious biases inadvertently get systemically embedded and reinforced in talent management systems.

- There are new ways to address the sourcing and recruiting of traditionally underrepresented talent.

- While diversity missteps may be unintended, they're still very real. This can be evidenced in the gap between majority and non-majority employees' use of company benefits.

SHAPING YOUR STRATEGY

- How **crossculturally agile** are your HR practitioners? If they're not, how much are they aware of the issue? What can you do to build a case for them to be crossculturally competent and then help them achieve that goal?

- Has your HR function done an **unconscious bias audit** of its various talent processes? Doing so would uncover quite a bit that needs to be addressed. And when it is addressed, the impact will be positive for generating greater diversity and inclusion.

- As you look at the **benefits** that are available and how they're used, are they truly inclusive in addressing the needs, wants, and aspirations of the various different demographic groups in your organization?

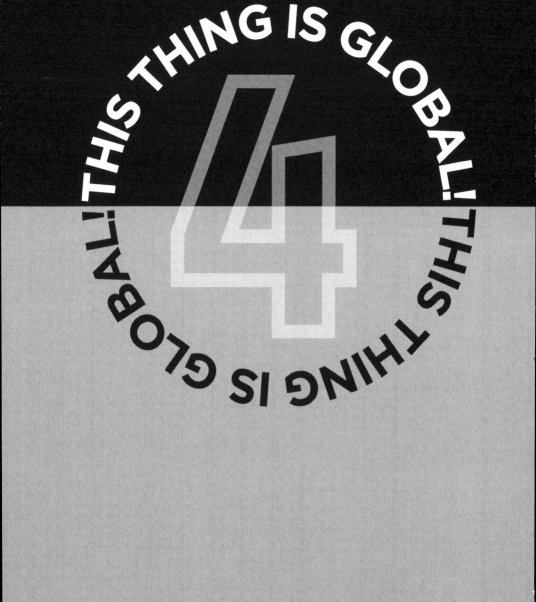

THIS THING IS GLOBAL! THIS THING IS GLOBAL! THIS THING IS GLOBAL! THIS THING IS GLOBAL!

4

Chapter 4
This thing is global!

The Obama Era has marked the globalization of most dimensions of our lives. Customer support for our cell phone can just as likely come from Gurgaon, Manila, or Albuquerque. The diagnosis of our chest X-rays can come from a radiologist in Bangalore or in Tacoma. Even our local city council news can come in the form of virtual reports from Filipinos watching council proceedings in Buena Vista, California. Americans are simultaneously managing virtual teams of workers in Buenos Aires, Brussels, Beijing, and Mumbai. Indian leaders, without having to repatriate, are directing American teams.

Diversity and inclusion must consider these labor realities. While it's important to address diversity issues within a country, we must also address them across countries. Global teams may make sense in terms of overall compensation costs, round-the-clock coverage, and local language support, but we mustn't forget they are complex organisms where inclusion/exclusion issues materialize in ways that affect both the quality of relationships and the work performed by these teams.

As US-based multinationals begin planting the diversity flag in their operations outside the United States, they run the risk of inadvertently—and somewhat ironically—dismissing alternative national interpretations of diversity. While there's good reason to celebrate the global diversity push by American multinationals, many of whom have strong diversity track records in the United States, there are pitfalls that could undermine the successful globalization of diversity and inclusion, if left unchecked.

During the past few years, I've given a number of presentations on diversity issues and trends to nearly hundreds of multinational client contacts in my native Latin America, Europe, and Asia. Speaking in Buenos Aires, Santiago, São Paulo, Mexico City, San Juan, London, Vienna, Zurich, Shanghai, Seoul, Beijing, and Delhi, I've heard these issues play out in a variety of ways. "This diversity thing is an American thing," is a common complaint outside the

United States. "We don't see how the race issues in the United States are relevant to us—and yet we are being held accountable for targets for racial diversity that are not relevant for our workforce demographics."

A breakdown has occurred somewhere between the inspiring workforce and people strategies and the execution of diversity as a business imperative. As a result, we're beginning to see an increasingly resentful backlash against the American version of diversity abroad. In addition, there's an ironic blind spot that has emerged. While American companies are aggressively pushing diversity messages, many are failing to make the connection between the message of inclusion and long-standing complaints that HR policies, communication campaigns, and common business processes are culturally insensitive to Latin American or other non-US organizational and cultural contexts.

Four approaches to global diversity

In examining both the successful and unsuccessful approaches to global diversity, it's helpful to break them into four distinct archetypes: Isolationists, Idealists, Imperialists, and Globalists.

While members of all four archetypes are highly committed to the ideals of diversity, the differences lie in how they approach it.

Isolationists and Idealists

Isolationists tend to have a limited view of the world and don't think very much about diversity outside the 50 states. To them, diversity is exclusively defined in the common US terms of race/ethnicity, gender, sexual orientation, and physical ability, with a nod to secondary diversity issues such as thinking styles. These organizations may also take a more compliance-driven approach to diversity.

Idealists acknowledge that diversity issues must be addressed abroad, yet they have a naïve understanding of how that could and should play out. Idealists tend to believe that programs that have proven successful in the United States will be equally effective when implemented abroad. Neither the Isolationists nor the Idealists have much power in the global diversity arena, though some may have power within the context of the United States. Whether they have true power or not, their limited exposure to life outside the United States undermines their ability to have a significant impact on diversity on a global level.

Imperialists and Globalists

Imperialists and Globalists are the most interesting and powerful of the diversity strategy groups. Members of both groups are highly experienced and committed to global diversity, yet they differ in their diversity missions.

The Imperialists have earned their stripes through deeply committed work in forging cutting-edge diversity strategies built around thoughtful metrics, tough accountability, minority and women leadership, and succession planning. They have been so successful in the United States that they're now setting their sights abroad, where they seek to implement all they've accomplished stateside.

Many members of this group are "inadvertent" Imperialists in that they would never describe themselves as such. While they may espouse values of inclusion, their actions belie a more Imperialist nature. For example, using Latin America as a case study, some demand that their company's offices in the region develop metrics of representation and plans for how they're going to bridge the diversity gaps in their offices. In doing so, they often describe the diversity requirements in terms of African American, Latino, and Asian representation.

With the exception of Brazil, Latin America does not have the same degree of racial diversity as the United States, making these demands impossible to meet. And even where race is involved locally, in Latin regions, diversity issues tend to be based more on class than race. During Colonial times, people of color could purchase certificates of whiteness, which then gave them a host of economic privileges such as the right to own property. While this practice certainly acknowledged race as a factor, it placed greater emphasis on an individual's economic status in terms of privilege.[1]

The pitfall in Imperialistic diversity lies not only in reactions to specific diversity messages, but also in corporate behaviors—including HR business and HR policies—procedures, and guidelines that Latin Americans may view as culturally insensitive. Ironically, many companies with an Imperialistic bent fail to see the contradiction between their emphasis on diversity and their cultural insensitivity in the deployment of other corporate initiatives.

Though both Imperialists and Idealists believe the US approach to diversity is better, Idealists take a more social justice approach, rather than a pragmatic business approach, which results in less of an impact on the organization. In some ways, Globalists and Imperialists are cut from the same cloth—although both grasp the strategic importance of diversity to their businesses, they differ in their level of focus on measurement and accountability and in their cultural sensitivities. Globalists do not assume that what has worked in the United States will work elsewhere. Their first inclination is to deconstruct diversity—to unearth its true meaning in each country or region—rather than rely exclusively on the American definition.

With this approach, Globalists have been able to surface not only the crosscultural issues between their non-US offices and their American counterparts, but also the issues existing among the countries *within* the various global regions themselves. For example, as US multinationals regionalize corporate work in Latin America, cultural differences are surfacing between professionals in Argentina and Mexico. Latin American business and HR leaders have been caught off guard, having assumed the barrier would be low due to a common language, similar histories of being colonized by the Spanish, and cathedrals at the hearts of their cities.

"We were wrong," one Mexican business leader told me. "We are discovering in a painful way that there are very big differences between how business is conducted in Mexico and South America." For example, there are often relational misunderstandings between the more typically expressive South Americans and the more typically taciturn Mexicans.

Despite trying to be sensitive to the spirit of diversity, companies often make unintentional missteps. A corporate video produced in the United States and intended for a Puerto Rican audience featured a moving interview with an employee who had sacrificed a lot to cross the Rio Grande and seek a new life in America. He talked emotionally about his dream of one day becoming a US citizen. For Puerto Ricans, who are already US citizens and do not see themselves as having to resort to illegal immigration, this was a serious insult. Several people walked out of the screening. A Globalist approach would have avoided the assumption that what works for Latinos in the United States, where they are the minority, will also work for Latinos in Puerto Rico, where they are the majority.

The way forward

Diversity and inclusion offer a new platform for conversation and understanding among all involved. Diversity practitioners are strategically positioned to help broker new ways of talking about crosscultural issues that have long vexed multinationals conducting work outside the United States. However, those diversity professionals who have not had much exposure to life and work outside the US are going to be at a significant disadvantage in stepping into this breach. Thus, chief diversity officers aspiring to lead diversity globally must make this developmental task a priority.

Setting a Globalist tone, rather than an inadvertently Imperialist one, can happen quickly in initial conversations on diversity. A variety of declarations have proven effective at disarming predisposed defensiveness against the perceived US diversity Imperialist message. They include: "The key is for you to define what diversity means to you, your region, your country, your group," or "Our starting point will not be what diversity means in the United States," or "Diversity can open up new avenues for conversation on crosscultural conflicts between those in our region and US Americans."

However, including a disclaimer on diversity does not negate the fact that every organization, regardless of its location, experiences some degree of resistance to change. There is a very real element of individuals and organizations digging in their heels and using the accusation of Imperialism as an excuse to avoid having the difficult conversations and making the hard choices. Yet, no matter how uncomfortable, it's something we must do if organizations and workers are to thrive in the emerging environment, and if we are to continue building on the gains made so far.

Globalist views

While US-based diversity practitioners wrestle with what it means to make their strategies global—versus exporting an "American thing"—non-American, non-European multinationals are confronting diversity challenges of their own. Much like the Americans and Europeans who preceded them during the first modern multinational expansion in the '60s, these new multinationals from emerging markets did not consider diversity issues as they mapped out ambitious global product launches and marketing strategies from their home countries. Yet here they are, running right smack into them.

It's not just cross-country, global diversity issues that are popping up, either. As the demographic tsunami ripples throughout various countries around the world, hidden issues are beginning to surface. National inclusion realities are percolating at a local level in parts of the world where diversity talk had been dismissed.

In just four years' time—the time it takes to go to college and get a professional degree—a woman in India or China could find herself in a completely different place in terms of personal and economic power. As multinationals hire women in large numbers, a profound social change regarding gender roles is taking place. Income earned in this woman's name and deposited in her bank account means greater individual power. This, in turn, lets her be more independent about the choices she makes, where she lives, and even whom she chooses to marry or when she chooses to marry, if at all.

The impact is not just societal. Glass-ceiling issues are increasingly sprouting up in these emerging economies as women succeed and expect to move up. In Latin America, for example, half of the workforce is comprised of women. Now that they've been in the workforce for one-and-a-half generations, Latina women are starting to hit the glass ceiling. Women hold just 6 percent of listed board directorships[2] and only 22 percent of senior-level corporate positions in Latin America. Latina women can't help but wonder why.[3]

As the world continues to shrink, a male bias in these traditionally male-dominated societies poses a real challenge for organizations. Without a change in their mindset, companies that fail to embrace women in the workforce—particularly in upper-management positions—are going to fall behind those that do. "I see gender mismanagement as a global geographic liability. Women offer an extraordinary opportunity for access to talent," says Ted Childs, the former Chief Diversity Officer at IBM. "And these male-dominated cultures or male-dominated companies, in both cases, are going to find that this attitude is a liability."

In Canada—a country rightfully proud of its tolerant and welcoming culture—the diversity conversation is catching Canadians off guard as they begin to glimpse a fundamental gap between their inclusion ideals and their inclusion results. Here, the metaphor of the multicultural mosaic—where people retain their sense of group identity, yet together construct a beautiful social array—was intended to contrast with the American ideal of the proverbial melting pot in which immigrants were expected to shed their accents, dress, and customs and conform to Main Street ways. But Canadians are facing the stark reality that the mosaic is not displayed as expected in the managerial and senior ranks. Roughly only 16 percent of corporate officers are women, even though women represent nearly half of the Canadian workforce,[4] and in 2015, Prime Minister Justin Trudeau appointed a cabinet that was 50 percent women.[5] Meanwhile, only 3 percent of Canada's visible minorities hold senior management positions, despite representing more than 15 percent of the Canadian labor force.[6]

Sourcing talent from long-excluded groups in Canada

Canada's one-million-strong Aboriginal population comprises 4.3 percent of the population and 3.3 percent of the labor force. Yet, Aboriginals are underpaid compared to their White counterparts and face significantly higher levels of unemployment compared to the national average.[7] According to the Canadian Human Rights Commission, roughly 15 percent of Canadians with disabilities who are employed report being discriminated against because of their disability. At the same time, the number of Canadians with disabilities is expected to grow from around 4 million in 2009 to roughly 6 million by 2026.[8]

Headquartered in Regina, Conexus is an integrated financial services provider with more than 50 locations throughout Saskatchewan. After years of watching its workers lured away to work in the Alberta oil sands, Conexus decided to tap into a ready source of talent right in its own backyard: the Aboriginal population at a nearby community.[9] Gayle Johnson, Executive Vice President of Human Resources, Marketing, and Community Development, admits the program required some trial and error before it ran smoothly. However, she attributes its ultimate success to these key initiatives:[10]

1. Before the recruitment process began, HR representatives from Conexus met with senior tribe members to explain the initiative. Only after garnering their endorsement did Conexus representatives begin meeting with community members.

2. Conexus introduced education and awareness training for its staff two years in advance of the effort, to help them understand and respect Aboriginal culture. More intensive training was provided to managers immediately before the arrival of the first group of Aboriginal employees.

3. To ensure companionship and support during the onboarding period, Aboriginal employees were hired in groups of ten.

4. Conexus brought in tribe elders to assist with communication during the ten-week training program it provides its Aboriginal employees. The program covered more than banking; it also provided social skills and personal financial training, like budgeting and how to use a checking account.

5. A First Nations liaison was hired to act as a "cultural intermediary" and advise on how to resolve issues. Since Aboriginal employees have a more relaxed attitude toward time, this made Conexus' standard 8 a.m. start time a challenge, for example. To avoid what was sure to be tardy showings for the group during their onboarding process, Conexus moved their starting time to 9 a.m.[11]

Thanks to the initiative, Aboriginals not only make up a significant portion of the Conexus workforce, they now hold financial services and administrative positions as well. Moreover, Conexus has a workforce that more closely mirrors the community—and a new customer base, to boot!

Even Europeans, who have been outspoken in questioning the relevance of diversity for them, feel the buffeting winds of an aging workforce, declining population, gender pay gap, and rising diversity through massive waves of immigrants from North Africa and the Middle East. The ideals of German meritocracy, British common sense, and French *liberté*, *égalité*, and *fraternité* face uncomfortable challenges to their credibility.

The mix and making it work – Localizing diversity and inclusion

Talking about *global diversity* first requires shifting from an ethnocentric, US-based perspective "United States-to-the-world" to a "world-to-the-world" global perspective. In today's upside-down world, diversity is flowing every which way.

"Diversity" and "inclusion" mean different things to different people. Some reject the word itself as reflecting American corporate imperialism that has nothing to do with non-US realities.

In her extensive travels across the globe, Monica Francois Marcel, a deeply experienced interculturalist and co-founder of the consultancy Language and Culture Worldwide, sees signs that organizations are grappling with the varied aspects of inclusion. "Everyone is going to struggle with diversity within his or her own workforce," she explains. She goes on to say that while other countries, regions, and companies will have to face diversity and inclusion as they define those terms, "It would be ideal if they could glean from the United States' lessons learned without feeling as though the United States is pushing lessons on them—in other words, if they can take what they will from the experiences of the United States, they can improve upon them in their own regions and contexts."

Regardless of whether I'm speaking in Latin America, Europe, Canada, India, or the United States, I frequently ask audiences if they are willing to set aside their working definitions and see if they can agree to the definition of the two terms I introduced at the beginning of this book: Diversity is the mix, inclusion is making the mix work™.

With this approach, each location can define the mix and how it's working. Three concentric circles typically appear: mainstream things that pretty much everyone brings up, like gender; outlier topics that those on the margins in the group eventually bring up, like race in Brazil and sexual orientation in Spain; and taboo issues that no one brings up, like race in Peru and sexual orientation in India.

Here's a bit more of what I have encountered in a few of the countries where I have engaged in this conversation:

India – While race/ethnicity predominates when evaluating an individual's background in the United States, race rarely appears on that list in India. Rather, the top considerations are likely to be religion, caste, and geographic region. Each of India's 28 states has its unique predominant language and dialects (more than 300 in the whole country), as well as variations in cuisine, attire, and cultural focus. Understanding and dealing with such a broad spectrum of diversity presents a tremendous challenge in and of itself. The more expressive Punjabis, for example, are likely to dominate in the workplace, compared to the more taciturn folks from Uttar Pradesh. Managers from Northern Indian states have been known to say they will not hire anyone from a Southern state. Variances in corporate experience also cause discord. Those who grew up in outsourced, offshored roles tend to clash with those who did not. The one-up dynamics of this issue are real and can be blatant.

"While inclusion presents an opportunity—as well as a tangible business case—to move past traditional barriers, it must be framed within the context and realities of the unique cultures of the country or location," says Sodexo's Senior Vice President and Chief Diversity Officer, Dr. Rohini Anand. "For example, in India, where one of the defining issues is caste, some customers may be reluctant to eat food cooked by someone of a different caste, and this directly impacts us as a food service provider."

Brazil – Geographic region is also a top consideration in Brazil. The traditional rivalry between *Paulistas* from São Paulo and *Cariocas* from Rio—and the way both look down on *Mineiros* who come from the agricultural and mining interior of Minas Gerais—plays out in unproductive ways in the workplace. In a roundtable discussion with a group of employees in Uberlândia in Minas Gerais, *Mineiros* talked with feeling about how morale is affected by what employees believe are superior attitudes on the part of coworkers and customers from the big cities. The put-downs are both subtle and explicit, creating a mix that is not working well. And productivity suffers as a result.

Japan – In the Land of the Rising Sun—where only 10 percent of managers are women[12] and 70 percent leave the workforce when they have children[13]—rigid workplace gender roles and the aging population are placing extraordinary pressures on Japanese society. With a negligible immigrant influx that has resulted in one of the most racially homogenous countries in the world, Japan's greatest source of diverse talent for managerial and senior roles are women. But Japanese corporate culture is still a long way from creating pathways for women to rise to the leadership ranks. Fortunately, companies are beginning to recognize the problem. A few years ago, for example, Japanese electronics giant Sony appointed a head of diversity in Tokyo to address gender issues in its Japanese workforce. In addition, Prime Minister Shinzō Abe has made the advancement of women in business leadership one of his top priorities.

Falling into the same traps? Multinationals from emerging nations

As multinationals from emerging markets continue to spread their global reach, they will continue to face the kinds of diversity and crosscultural challenges American and European multinationals have been facing— and often not addressing—for decades. Remember Chevy's failed push to introduce the Nova in Latin America? (After all, who would want a car that, in Spanish, means "Doesn't run?")? Or Braniff's "Fly in Leather" campaign that invited Latin Americans to *"Volar en Cuero"* ("Fly Naked"!)?

Now the shoe is on the other foot. When Telefónica of Spain took over the state-run Brazilian telephone monopoly in 1998, it made the mistake of misspelling its own name on the logo plastered throughout the city, as well as on stationery and printed materials. They used the Spanish *Telefónica* instead of the Portuguese *Telefônica*. A public outcry forced them to get it right. Even Latin American multinationals, *multilatinas*, are falling into the same traps as their American and European counterparts as they regionalize their corporate work in their own regions. They, too, are running into differences that are not apparent visibly, yet are very real in what people assume and believe that go deeper than the Argentinean term *che* and the Peruvian equivalent *compadre*. Software development companies from India risk losing big accounts because their programmers are failing at crosscultural communications. Frequent misunderstandings occur regarding whether deadlines can truly be met, because junior Indian team members in a rigid hierarchy are conditioned that it's not appropriate to say "No" to an American boss.

So how can emerging-market companies strengthen their globalization by being competent in diversity? These companies already are positioned to help broker new ways of discussing crosscultural issues that have long vexed multinationals. After all, they experienced firsthand what happened in their countries when the first multinationals arrived. And as Dr. Mitch Hammer, the co-creator of the Intercultural Development Inventory, which is widely used to measure intercultural competence, says, "The ability to bridge across differences at the national, the ethnic, and other levels of difference is what is really going to determine our effectiveness in meeting global needs."

Emerging-market multinationals bring their cultural strengths and offer perspectives that could be mutually beneficial. For example, Brazilians exporting the country's spirit of *jogo de cintura* (a term from soccer-fevered Brazil describing soccer hip and waist feints used to get past an opponent) could offer just the right mindset and skill set we all need to adapt to an unpredictable, global business world mutating at a dizzying rate.

Emerging-market multinationals must take crosscultural agility seriously. It is the bedrock that will improve interpersonal communications between workers, open new ways of thinking about product design, and sharpen sales pitches. Companies are beginning to awaken to this realization. The Indian company I referred to earlier, for example, now puts its teams and those of its US clients through intensive crosscultural working sessions.

New rules for the changing game

Everyone is spinning off-center in this new game. Emerging countries are facing global diversity, while Americans watch their long-cherished diversity assumptions and programs evolve and become owned by others. All players need to put their own house in order. Companies working to grow and prosper in this increasingly globally diverse world must deconstruct diversity and culture to unearth the true meaning in their own country or region, rather than relying exclusively on each country's past definitions.

What rules can we glean from this new space?

Listen to employees in your home country and global offices with regard to how they perceive each other. Is there a shared sense of collaboration, or are colleagues convinced their peers in other countries simply can't get it right? Are workers blaming each other as the cause of low-quality work or slow response times, citing their "peculiar" way of getting things done? If so, your company may need to build crosscultural agility and instill some global diversity savvy.

Pay attention to local offices' diversity issues. Companies that have addressed diversity issues in a progressive way within their own countries tend to be better positioned for anticipating and addressing those issues on a global scale. If we define *diversity* as the mix and *inclusion* as making the mix work, what is the desired mix of your workforce and customer base given, say, Brazilian demographics? Do you have a workforce that reflects, as Brazil's national motto says, the land of *Ordem e Progresso (Order and Progress)*? Are women in managerial and leadership positions? Do they feel they're able to bring their full spectrum of talents to your company's business issues? With 50 percent of the population being Afro-Brazilian, are Black people well represented in your pipeline? If you have the mix right, how well is it working?

In Brazil, private companies with more than 100 employees are obliged to hire people with disabilities. Quotas vary between 2 percent and 5 percent of the labor pool, depending on each employer's total number of employees.[14] Yet companies struggle to find enough skilled people from this group to employ for the jobs they have. Out of their own initiative, progressive companies are creating programs to equip this workforce before hiring them.

Be a student of the major demographic shifts in the markets you want to serve. In Latin America, the major demographic shifts are age-related, as a large influx of young people has entered the workforce just as an older generation prepares to leave, creating generational clashes. The Chilean postal service, a 100-year-old state institution, realized that its patronage-style, family-based tradition of offering lifelong employment was not going to provide the workforce needed to modernize operations for the digital age. It needed college graduates with specific technical skills to help re-engineer its way of doing business. The postal service was unprepared for the generational and culture clash that resulted between those who claimed the company as a family entitlement because "my grandfather worked here" versus those newcomers who came in with a different, more competitive mindset.

In the United States, progressive, diverse companies have recognized the emerging marketplace flourishing in their midst. Financial institutions, for example, are seeing their greatest growth coming from the rising Latino population (projected to comprise nearly one-third of the United States by July 1, 2050).[15] Many Latinos have embraced the role of entrepreneur. According to a 2014 report by the Partnership for a New American Economy, there are more than 3 million Latino-owned businesses in the US, and that figure is expected to double in five years.[16]

What new market needs is emerging in your country due to the demographic shifts?

Hard-wire it to HR. A growing number of Latin-American employees are declaring that diversity, along with work-life balance, is a critical factor in what attracts them to an employer. According to Hewitt's Best Employers in Latin America study, one of the top five characteristics of a Best Employer was its commitment to diversity and work-life balance. Some 87 percent of employees at Best Employers said their "organization is committed to creating a work environment that embraces diversity and differences" versus 67 percent of those who were not deemed Best Employers.[17]

The path to inclusion lies in talent sourcing, recruiting, onboarding, compensation, and development processes that are fair, accessible, culturally appealing, and relevant to the various groups within your organization. Make it a priority to involve HR and business leaders in your diversity efforts.

Bringing it home

Diversity has become exponentially more complex as it has gone global. As Dr. Hammer explains, "The global leader today is somebody who is able to shift cultural perspective and adapt behavior appropriately to cultural context in order to accomplish goals that are important to the organization. Now that's a simple definition. But it's a very complex kind of capability." Along the way, some American diversity practitioners, while savvy and supportive about global diversity issues, have expressed a private fear that United States diversity issues will be ignored because US-based race and ethnicity issues present unique challenges. If one's diversity view is US-to-the-world, that fear is legitimate: the United States will not be able to sustain its specific diversity issues on the top of the global agenda. But, in a world-to-the-world diversity view, where the United States is just one among many global regions that must address their own diversity issues, then the specific diversity issues found only in the United States remain a high priority regionally.

"Think global. Act local," says a popular slogan. But in an upside-down world, we must also follow all the permutations of this wisdom:

- Think global. Act global.
- Think local. Act global.
- Think local. Act local.

These variations may not make for a nifty, pithy bumper sticker, but they make for far more effective global diversity strategies that truly will make the world more inclusive. ⊙

SUMMARY POINTS

- In addition to addressing diversity issues within a country, we must deal with diversity and inclusion issues across national boundaries.

- Enterprises that are committed to diversity may assume one of four distinct archetypes: Isolationists, Idealists, Imperialists, and Globalists.

- Diversity and inclusion may take on different meanings to different people around the world. One definition that rings true across industries and societies is: *Diversity is the mix. Inclusion is making the mix work™.* This definition enables every entity to define the mix and make the mix work for them.

- Multinational organizations from emerging markets may face diversity and crosscultural challenges similar to those that enterprises from developed markets have been addressing.

SHAPING YOUR STRATEGY

- Think about how your company and your competitors have been approaching global diversity. Which of the four archetypes do they embody?

- If your company is an Isolationist, Idealist, or Imperialist, what actions or steps must you take to shift your diversity and inclusion approach to a Globalist perspective?

- What is the mix in the various places where your company has a major presence? How does it compare and contrast to the mix in the United States? How well is it working? In areas where it is not working well, what steps can you take to surface those issues and begin addressing them?

PART 2:
CALLING OUT DIFFERENCES IN RELATIONSHIPS

Part 2: Calling out differences in relationships

What makes us uniquely human is our ability to put into language what we're thinking, feeling, and imagining. Strings of words are woven into stories that capture our fears, our desires, our destructions, and our creations. Since the beginning of civilization, we have used stories to pass history and values from generation to generation.

Our lives are resonant with stories—bedtime stories ease children into slumber; news stories inform us; reality TV stories seduce us.

Business is also about stories. We are fueled by the narratives of how our competitors and we are doing in the marketplace—we celebrate the thrill of client wins; we feel the impact of narrow losses. Around the world, employees play both leading and secondary roles in their companies' stories of growth and decline, mergers and acquisitions, and stagnation and transformation.

Diversity and inclusion both compels and repels because, at its essence, it's about the intimate topic of identity—of individuals, groups, nations, and organizations. In other words, diversity and inclusion is about how we seek to define what makes us who we are. Ultimately, diversity is about biography— one's unique life path that shapes how each of us understands how the world works and how we choose to be actors in it.

In the Obama Era, biography more than ideology becomes essential in our ability to connect in a global world. However, ideology has taken some big hits in recent history—from the fall of the Berlin Wall to the fall of Wall Street. In an upside-down world where the old rules are null and void, where we face challenges and issues never faced before, those ideologies that were shaped when the world was right-side-up have little relevance. It is in one's personal story where we now seek answers.

To read Obama's autobiography, *Dreams from My Father: A Story of Race and Inheritance*, is to experience an intensely personal discovery of identity. The man who would be president wrestled profoundly with what it meant to be the biracial child of a White Christian woman from Kansas and a Black Muslim man from Kenya. How did his growing up in Hawaii and Indonesia shape how he viewed the world? What inheritance did he receive from the different influences in his formative years?

Obama is not only the first Black US president; he's also the most global one. Obama's search for his roots did not take him to the Deep South. It took him to Kogelo, Kenya. In this narrative, we begin to see the contours of a life experience that shaped a leader who can move successfully across racial lines in the United States, walk just as comfortably through Ivy League halls as along inner city streets, and who can be seen as "one of us" by the 200,000 Berliners who came out to watch him deliver a speech at the city's Victory Column during the 2008 campaign.

It is in Obama's story that he came to understand his place in the world—and thus, how we can come to understand him. In the same way, the Inclusion Paradox demands we know our own biographies in ways that provide insight for ourselves and for others about our own places in the world. We need to be able to tell our own stories.

Inclusion is about both individual and collective stories. It is about our identities as men, women, parents, members of families, religious adherents, community members, citizens of nations and the world. In addition, it is about our identities in the workplace—as colleagues, coworkers, frontline managers, and leaders—from the shop floor to the executive suite. It is about exploring who we are in the midst of so many changes, celebrating that discovery, and valuing the journey.

The most powerful story is an individual's narrative of identity—of discovering and celebrating who he or she is. Regardless how different it may be from our own, each person's story contains something inherently valuable. Each story contains our individual quests to discover life's meaning and our relation to the universe. Through this discovery, we learn how to fit into the larger structures of society, which in turn helps us recognize those things in others' stories that we can relate to.

In diversity work, stories help us personalize controversial political or philosophical issues so we don't dehumanize them. These "controversial issues" make up the lived experiences of our neighbors, siblings, friends, and coworkers—people just like us who are trying to survive and thrive during their finite time on earth.

Growing up in a bilingual/bicultural home with family in Peru and in the United States, I attended the American High School of Lima, FDR Roosevelt, with the sons and daughters of multinational executives, diplomats, spies, and missionaries. Having Peruvian grandparents in Lima and American grandparents in Washington State, I constantly crisscrossed physical and invisible boundaries between countries, organizations, and people. These relational and cultural junctions forged my understanding of worldview differences and how to navigate them successfully and profitably—thus leading to my creation of the Inclusion Paradox.

As I laid out in the Introduction, there's a three-step process to mastering the Inclusion Paradox. We must learn that:

1. It's all about me.
2. It's all about them.
3. It's all about us.

In Part 2, we focus specifically on the first step—learning that "it's all about me." We cannot begin to make interpersonal and group collaborations work with people different from us if we don't know *ourselves* as cultural beings. Many spiritual traditions and leadership books reveal that the secret to enlightenment, wisdom, power, and followership is self-awareness: Who am I? What has shaped me? What motivates me? How do I understand the world?

Only after we answer these questions can we begin to compare and contrast ourselves with others. In doing so, we learn to understand them better and help them better understand us. Armed with this understanding, we can address the implications of these differences among groups, which is the focus of Part 3, and among organizations, which we'll explore in Part 4.

The linchpin to inclusion exists in our ability to manage the differences between ourselves and those ahead of us. Speaking at the Diversity Best Practices' Diversity Leadership Awards Gala on November 17, 2005, Civil Rights icon Dr. Dorothy Height summed up our journey, explaining that legislation was just the beginning: "We need to turn the laws into relationships—and the relationships into opportunities." ⬭

5

and

I NEED **YOU**R DIFFERENCES
need
mine

Chapter 5

I need your differences ... and you need mine

How could I have missed it? I really thought I had agreement from the group. After all, one of the team members had even said, "Andrés, I agree with you 100 percent." Yet when I started acting on the agreement I was sure we had, the emails and voicemails started flying in: "What are you doing? We did not agree to this!" Confused, I replied, "What part of 100 percent didn't I understand?"

As a Latino in corporate America, I once again had broken some unspoken rule, missed some commonly understood signal, and a foul was called. I was yellow carded. But unlike on the soccer field where I know why, on the corporate field I had no idea. Making things even more difficult: My colleagues weren't even aware I did not know what had gone amiss.

What had gone amiss—I was to learn through much trial, error, and observation of the Midwestern, European-American corporate culture—was that I was a middle-class Latin-American guy with a direct style of communication inside an indirect-communication-style corporate environment. What I had missed were the body language and code words signaling disagreement that people with similar cultural backgrounds intuitively interpret, but which were lost on me. I had my own body language and code words that other Latin Americans would interpret correctly, but that my European-American colleagues had missed and misinterpreted on their end.

And so it went. They thought I was confrontational. I thought they were duplicitous. They thought I was disruptive. I thought they were inefficient.

Every minute, somewhere in the corporate world, someone who is different from the mainstream, someone whom the corporation wanted in their midst because diversity is a business imperative, is not feeling included. We're making missteps that lead to the raised eyebrows, the sidelong glances, the "tsk, tsk" of "doesn't she have a clue?"

Not only must we acknowledge that we're different from one another in vital ways, but we must navigate these differences to succeed together. This is a must-have skill in the Obama Era. Whether in government, academia, nonprofits, or the corporate world, never before have we seen such an intersection of powerful, competent, and ambitious talent working together on behalf of common organizational missions—but with wildly differing ways of going about it. The requisite bundle of skills and behaviors is what's referred to as *crosscultural agility*, and it's something that must be exhibited by both individuals and organizations.

What exactly do I mean by "crosscultural agility"? As I shared earlier, it's "the ability to discern and take into account one's own and others' worldviews, to be able to solve problems, make decisions, and resolve conflicts in ways that optimize cultural differences for better, longer-lasting, and more creative solutions."

How can companies bulk up talent and organizations in this competence? Not surprisingly, most initial answers will veer toward the need for training. In these transformational times, however, pinpoint solutions will not be enough. Building crosscultural agility is a developmental task similar to building great managers and leaders. One classroom or online learning experience won't do the trick. It requires a systemic approach that changes underlying assumptions about managing differences, how we assess and reward people, the kind of talent we hire, the structures and processes we put in place to get things done, and yes, the learning we provide employees. Even the learning must be staged out with the realism and respect this competence demands, however. In the same way that most of us would not be able to handle algebra without first learning basic arithmetic, so it is with learning how to navigate our differences in truly inclusive ways. The first thing we must tackle is our underlying belief about what we need to learn to do.

Since more than $8 billion has been spent on diversity learning yearly in the United States alone,[1] let's start by examining the ROI we've gotten for this investment.

The faulty paradigm of tolerance and sensitivity

Say "diversity training" and many people will immediately think about learning experiences based on a paradigm of tolerance and sensitivity. This approach made sense 25 years ago when more women and racial/ethnic minorities began to enter sectors of the US workforce once dominated by White males. As they did, they encountered intolerance and insensitivity. Hence the birth of "sensitivity training." Born out of the Civil Rights era and the transformative feminist movement, sensitivity training taught how to be tolerant toward differences. It was appropriate for the first generation of diversity work. The guys *did* have to be made aware that the pin-up calendars had to come down, that their sexist and racist banter about women and Blacks had to stop, and that a female worker getting pregnant didn't mean she was not committed to her career. It was a disruptive time for old-timers and newcomers alike, as the workplace erupted in dislocations, antagonisms, fear, and explicit prejudice.

A generation later, tolerance and sensitivity work has established mechanisms for addressing the isms.

Tolerance is a good antidote to resistance and defensiveness on the part of majorities toward those who are different. It's a place of *truce* rather than *truth*. It's manifested in statements such as: "I won't resist you anymore." "I'll tolerate that you're here." "I'm okay, you're okay." "We'll agree to disagree." "Live and let live." It's the answer to, "Why can't we all just get along?"

Sensitivity takes it further. It finds its voice in statements such as: "I will work at understanding that you have unique needs and preferences." "When you say something bothers you and it doesn't make sense to me, I accept that it is important to you." "I won't question your views, and I won't resist them." In between the lines it says, "I'll let you have that gimme."

As a result of this approach, much *explicit* prejudice in the workplace has subsided or gone underground. Unfortunately, however, this paradigm has spent itself. It has been taken as far as it can, and it will not be enough to enable the transformation of global diversity. Why has this paradigm run out of juice? A few reasons:

- **Paralysis.** Regardless of what opinions people may harbor, employees generally know what is and is not appropriate to say. Political correctness has paralyzed us from talking in constructive ways about the very real differences between us. Even those who have welcomed diversity often don't know how to move beyond the obligatory, "I'm glad you're here."

- **Impractical.** Tolerance and sensitivity aren't very helpful when facing a colleague whose mother taught him the exact opposite of what yours taught you to do. It's an attitude, not a skill, that's condescending at worst or superficial at best, as we sponsor international and ethnic food potlucks and teach each other our culture's dance steps.

- **US-centric.** Tolerance and sensitivity do not serve us well in developing a platform for global diversity. It's a construct that flows out of the Civil Rights movement that gets sniffed out as too American as soon as it crosses the border. Don't get me wrong. Americans are right to be proud of the movement. In global work, however, this approach is limited due to its historical context.

- **Finger-pointing.** Tolerance and sensitivity undermine Inclusion because of its implied audience. Who is it that needs to be more tolerant and sensitive? The White heterosexual male, of course! So he's in the audience, thinking, "Okay, I get this. This is all about me, but I don't feel part of it." Right there in inclusion training, an important part of the community is being excluded.

It's time for more powerful concepts that go beyond, "You've got yours and I've got mine." We need to create a voice that asks, "What is ours—*together?* Out of our differences, what new progress can we create—*together*? How can I make how you view the world a part of how I see it, too?"

What could replace this limited, spent paradigm? Today's global world requires a shift toward the paradigm of crosscultural agility.

The benefits are many:

- **Competency-based.** Crosscultural agility is not about an attitude or stance, but discrete, observable, and trainable skills and behaviors.

- **Pragmatic.** It's applicable to resolving daily diversity issues. When facing that same colleague who learned something different on his mama's knee, it provides a means of resolving differing worldviews.

- **Globally relevant.** No matter where in the world I've presented or consulted, audiences readily acknowledge there are real differences in their midst—and they could use some skills to navigate them. Take Europe, for example. Europeans may have been quick to criticize diversity as an American thing, but crosscultural agility certainly resonates on a continent where cultural differences have led to wars, caricatures, and exasperation for a long time.

- **Versatile.** Given the expanding definition of diversity and the all-embracing nature of inclusion, it can be used in navigating all kinds of differences, not just traditional diversity issues. It's the same skill required to navigate differences in thinking styles, functional roles, organizational cultures coming together in a merger and acquisition, and so on.

- **HR system-compatible.** Crosscultural competency can be embedded into an organization's performance, reward, recognition, and development system. Presented as just another set of expectations on which employees will be measured, the connection to work, expected outcomes, and pay rewards can be made clear.

- **Not accusatory.** No group, no matter how marginalized, has an inborn crosscultural gene. The implied audience in crosscultural agility is all of us. So the White male is in the audience, thinking, "Ah, okay, I need this but so does everyone else."

With crosscultural agility, individuals and organizations can begin to see that we all need each other's differences. It's not a matter of simply tolerating, accepting, or even appreciating those differences in some esoteric way, but rather understanding on a fundamental level that we need those differences for our very survival. This puts an entirely different spin on diversity and inclusion.

Crosscultural agility requires us to look at our cultural differences, call them out, ask deep questions about their underlying assumptions, and suspend our own cultural judgments. (We all have them.) We then need to tackle business or professional challenges based on what we've learned. It's an ongoing, ever-evolving practice with no finish line. It's the hard work required to succeed in the Obama Era and beyond.

Korn Ferry Managing Principal Peggy Hazard, who has done crosscultural work around the world with myriad executive teams, says, "The first step is recognizing that crosscultural agility goes way beyond the dos and taboos, like how to exchange business cards. It's about understanding that culture influences nearly everything they do at work. Once they recognize how it can make or break their global expansion efforts, efforts to build leadership pipelines in emerging markets, achieve true value-creation post mergers and acquisitions, tap new markets, etc., it is seen as vital rather than a nice to have."

The payoff can be both personally and professionally profitable in these upside-down times. The crosscultural and intercultural fields have much to offer us in terms of tools and models to more competently navigate the cultural differences surrounding us.

Diversity across national cultures: Ayayay! Why are the French so French, the Mexicans so Mexican, and the Americans so American?

Fons Trompenaars and Charles Hampden-Turner, European authors of *Riding the Waves of Culture: Understanding Diversity in Global Business*, were intrigued by how multinationals with strong corporate cultures, such as IBM, still struggled with national differences getting in the way of being able to work as effectively as they wanted. To better understand what was going on, they created an extensive survey with a series of "What would you do?" scenarios.

Here's one: You're riding in a car with a friend who you know is speeding. Suddenly, the flashing lights of a police car appear in the rear-view mirror. After pulling the car over, the officer asks you, "Was your friend speeding?" What would you answer? The answer depended on one's nationality. Ninety-seven percent of Swiss would say, "Yes, my friend was speeding," but only 32 percent of Venezuelans would give the same answer.[2] What's going on?

The authors came up with seven different cultural dimensions to explain the different ways people from different cultures would approach the same scenario. In the case of the speeding car, they developed a construct that identified what individual cultures determine is fair. Some cultures believe that rules apply to everyone equally. Trompenaars and Hampden-Turner referred to them as *Universalist*. Other cultures determine what is fair based on the context of the situations. These, they referred to as *Particularist* cultures.

In returning to the case of the speeding ticket, one can now imagine the judgments flying. The Universalist turns to the Particularist and says, "How dare you lie to a police officer!" while the Venezuelan turns to the Swiss and retorts, "How dare you betray a friend!"

Both want the same thing—fairness—but they have different ways of interpreting what fairness is. In their book, the authors explain how these kinds of worldview clashes happen daily in the workplace, as workers try to figure out whom to confer status to, how to get work done, and how to manage time, projects, and emotion.[3]

Here are the headlines from Trompenaars and Hampden-Turner's Seven Cultural Dimensions:

How do we define what's fair?
Universalism vs. Particularism
Focus on the rule vs. focus on the particular context.

How do we get things done?
Task vs. Relationship
Focus on the destination (outcomes) vs. focus on the journey/quality of the relationship.

How do we confer status?
Achievement vs. Ascription
Focus on the accomplishment vs. focus on the title.

Where do we get our sense of identity?
Individualism vs. Communitarianism
Identity comes from the self vs. identity comes from the group one is a part of.

How do we manage emotions?
Neutral vs. Affective
Focus on restraint in showing emotions vs. focus on showing them.

How do we define time?
Sequential Time vs. Synchronous Time
Time is linear; focus on one thing at a time vs. time is circular; focus on the big picture.

How do we manage our environment?
Internal Control vs. External Control
Focus on dominating the environment vs. focus on accepting whatever comes.

Before going any further, let me make a distinction between *archetypes* and *stereotypes*. An archetype is the tendency of a group of people to behave in a certain way. A stereotype is the belief that all members in a cultural group behave according to the archetype for that group. For example, people from Latin America are more likely to show emotions publicly than people from Japan. But this does not mean all people from Latin America show public emotion or all people from Japan do not.

As individuals and organizations use the Seven Cultural Dimensions framework to diagnose cultural clashes, they find language and concepts to interpret and analyze the situation, back off the judgment, and then are able to resolve their differences. When this occurs, amazing things can happen.

An example can be found at furniture maker Herman Miller, where designers had been trapped in the Universalist mindset that they designed one-size-fits-all chairs based on an assumption of five-foot-nine-inch medium-framed males. Michelle Hunt, the company's Senior Vice President for People during the 1980s, recalls, "This, of course, left out a lot of people and limited sales." Once they started seeing the market through more Particularist eyes, they began designing chairs that adjusted to a multiplicity of body shapes. Their sales exploded.[4]

The tenets of the Seven Cultural Dimensions have also helped me to be more successful in the corporate world. For several years, my friendships were hindered by different interpretations of how to demonstrate respect through the management of time. Soon after arriving in the United States to attend college, I found myself bewildered by a new European-American friend looking at his watch in the middle of a heart-to-heart conversation about our life aspirations. "Omigosh, Andrés, it's 12 o'clock. I've got to go. Here's my half for lunch," he exclaimed, plunking down his money and taking off. I was hurt and offended. How dare he leave in the middle of an intimate conversation just because the clock said it was 12 o'clock? "Cold, rude, impersonal Americans!" was my judgment.

As I soon discovered, I was causing hurt and offense on the other end as well. Later that same day, I showed up at another European-American's apartment to hang out. He opened the door and was clearly upset: "Andrés, what's the matter with you? It's 7:30. We were supposed to meet at 6 p.m. You're an hour and a half late!" In all likelihood, his judgment was something along the lines of, "Irresponsible, disorganized, inconsiderate Latino!"

This went on for *two* years. In comparing notes with other Latin-American students, I soon learned they were experiencing the same thing. We were having two different interpretations of time. European Americans tend to be "clock-oriented" people, where time is defined by seconds, minutes, and hours. Conversely, Latin Americans are more "event-oriented." Things, such as a conversation, last as long as they need to and the rest of the day adjusts to that. Using Trompenaars and Hampden-Turner's language, the first is a Sequential view of time, the latter a Synchronous view of time.

Armed with this insight, conversations with my European-American friends changed. Not only did we have a better understanding of how we viewed time—and, therefore, that we were not being intentionally disrespectful to one another—but we also now had language to navigate through the differences:

"Hey, let's get together this weekend!"

"Okay. Gringo time or Latino time?"

"Well, it depends. If it's dinner and a movie, let's make it gringo time because if we're late for dinner, we'll be late for the movie. And that's no fun for anybody."

"Okay. But if it's 'come to our place to hang out,' let's make it Latino time, so we're not running around getting all stressed out, you getting your place ready, and me battling traffic to hurry up to start right at 7 o'clock so we can...relax!"

These seemingly minor mismatches and mutual judging of those who are different contribute to the underlying tensions between people. Its effect is to make inclusion more elusive. It's also part of what contributes to the common phenomenon of higher turnover among those who are culturally different from the majority. Employees who are different from the norm often are assessed as poor performers at worst or just not top-notch talent at best. Depending on the dominant culture of the organization, they may be seen as too abrasive or too passive, too controlling or too submissive, too standoffish or too friendly. And on and on, the judgments go.

Not only is this detrimental to diverse individuals, it also hurts the organizations that hire them. This leads to higher turnover among people of color across all industries in the United States and among women in male-dominated industries around the world.[5] Not only do employers have to deal with the costs of their replacement, but they also lose out on alternative ways of doing work. Baxter's former CDO Don Wilson explains, "If you're trying to solve your inclusion or diversity problems by just focusing on talent acquisitions, you're not going to solve it. The acquisition piece only impacts less than 15 percent of your workforce. If you have a turnover of only 15 percent, that's what you're going to be replacing every year. If the turnover is 20 percent, that's what you will be replacing. What about that 80 percent or whatever percentage of your workforce that exists today—how are you going to deal with that?"

In other words, employers can't think they're solving their diversity issues by merely bringing diverse talent into the workforce, only to have them leave in a year's time because they don't feel their different approaches are being understood or appreciated. This only contributes to a vicious cycle of replacing staff, which adds to the cost of replacement and frustrates existing employees—that 80 percent—that continually have to adjust to a revolving door of new team members. Especially in a world where the rules are changing by the hour, we need innovative ways of looking at things. It requires seeing it through the very same perspectives many of us have been judging in negative ways.

Cultural dimensions can also explain different cultural groups' tendencies with regard to preventive health or with their long-term savings plans, a topic I turn to in a later chapter. Or trust, as you will see in the "Crosscultural agility: How trust-building differs across cultures" sidebar in this chapter.

. . . .

Crosscultural agility: How trust-building differs across cultures

By Tony Malinauskas, Manager of Interactive Solutions, Korn Ferry

A manufacturing manager from a company headquartered in the United States was visiting the subsidiary in Japan and was puzzled when he encountered a roomful of apparently never-used production equipment at the factory. When he asked a Japanese colleague about the equipment, he was told that it was for a few projects that headquarters had cancelled before manufacturing for the project had begun. The subsidiary felt they had to purchase the equipment despite the cancellation of the projects to preserve the trust their local equipment vendor had in them.

The importance of trust in business relations is well accepted, but this incident illustrates that trust-building can look very different when working across cultures. So, how can one become more proficient at intercultural trust-building when there can be differences that are totally unexpected? First, let's look at the elements that generally foster trust. Here are Korn Ferry's "Four Elements of Trust" *without* a crosscultural lens to interpret them:

- Competence: You are capable of producing desired results in an effective manner.
- Reliability: You are consistent in your delivery of competent performance.
- Openness: You readily share relevant information with others.
- Support: You understand and have an interest in the other party's interests and goals.

Now let's look at these four elements through the different Japanese and American cultural lenses and how they end up being interpreted in an opposite way:

- **Competence:** For the stability-seeking Japanese, cancelling the order quickly would make the subsidiary appear incompetent of planning properly. Conversely, for the risk-oriented US headquarters, initiating action quickly and making adjustments along the way is how any competent organization operates.

- **Reliability:** For the relationship-oriented Japanese subsidiary, the impact on the people involved in the implementation would be foremost in their minds. For them, being able to take into account how decisions may affect other people is seen as a hallmark of reliability. Conversely, to the task-oriented US headquarters, a change in direction can be excused and seen as reliable, effective decision making if some degree of advance notice is provided along with a logical rationale.

- **Openness:** For the Japanese, cancelling the order would make the subsidiary appear like it was not forthcoming with information. Members of high-context cultures (many things seen and unseen do matter) like the Japanese may share information with close contacts (such as prized vendors) on a "*nice*-to-know" basis so each knows the background of happenings with the other. However, members of low-context cultures (only the one item being considered matters) like the Americans tend to share on a "*need*-to-know" basis, such as when action is required.

- **Support:** For the Japanese, cancelling the order would make the subsidiary appear uncaring. In hierarchical cultures like in Japan, the vendor may have an expectation that the subsidiary, being "above" them on the hierarchy as a customer, would to some extent "protect" the vendor so the vendor could faithfully serve the subsidiary. Conversely, in egalitarian cultures such as in the US, such an expectation is much less prevalent.

Complicated? You bet. Manageable with the right amount of crosscultural agility? For sure.

While much intercultural research has focused on exploring cultural differences between citizens of countries, frameworks like Trompenaars and Hampden-Turner's can also be applied to differences of cultures within a country. Granted, very little has been done along these lines. However, Thomas Kochman, a White sociologist, has done some pioneering work in looking at the cultural differences between African Americans and European Americans.

In his book, *Black and White Styles in Conflict*, Kochman asserts that Black and White Americans use two different communication styles for establishing trust: truth over peace or peace over truth.[6] Though his book was written more than 20 years ago, Kochman's more recent research corroborates what he identified back then: that while both Blacks and Whites are looking to establish trust in communication, each group interprets and demonstrates the value of "trust" differently. Archetypically, African Americans seek open and direct interactions, even to the point where vigorous disagreement occurs: truth over peace. The rationale is that, "I can trust a person who is this open—this honest—with me." However, White Americans generally seek to establish trust with a more indirect style focused on achieving peace. When approaching a point of conflict, they might simply agree to disagree. Peace is sought and valued. Their rationale is that, "I can trust a person who defers his or her position for the harmony of the relationship."

Given these differences, a White American with an indirect communication style might come away from an interaction with a Black American demonstrating a more direct style, thinking, "Why is this person being so aggressive?" On the flip side, the African American might come away thinking, "What is this person trying to hide?"

This concept can be applied in exploring the interactions of any two cultures where direct and indirect styles of communication come into play: US East Coast vs. US Midwest. US American vs. Indian. German vs. Japanese. The list goes on.

For the past several years, some colleagues and I have presented at the National Black MBA conferences. In discussing the cultural differences between African Americans and European Americans, we introduce the Seven Cultural Dimensions. During the audience participation section, the group usually determines that in six out of the seven dimensions, African Americans and European Americans are on opposite sides. The same pattern emerges when doing this exercise with Latino and Indian audiences. No wonder there's so much misunderstanding!

Everything is relative to something else

Along the way, I've realized that these dimensions serve as a relative scale between two cultures. As a Latino from an affective culture (one manages emotions by showing them), I've always viewed European Americans as being from a neutral culture (one where emotions are not displayed). Compared to Latinos, they are. In working in Canadian and UK offices and meeting with local clients, however, I've learned that both Canadian Anglophones and the British see European Americans (their racial kin) as "emotional"—or to use the crosscultural terminology, "affective." Compared to Anglos in Canada and England, they are.

These interpretations cannot be static. They must be dynamic. Compared to Northern Indian culture, are the French or Germans task- or relationship-based? Compared to Aboriginal Canadian culture, are Francophone Canadians sequential or synchronous? And how do Francophone Canadians compare on this same cultural dimension to Anglophone Canadians? The answers matter if one is to effectively navigate across various cultures. Not that one has to master every possible cultural permutation, but when work or personal circumstances bring us face-to-face with a new culture, success requires we possess this skill.

Why are affinity groups—among the most widely used diversity strategies—resisted so vehemently in France?

For the French, affinity groups are a strange concept. By contrast, Americans historically have had a mindset that makes them more naturally predisposed to affinity groups. In 1835, sociologist Alexis de Tocqueville (who was ironically French) wrote in *Democracy in America* how he marveled at how Americans got things done through the power of "free association." Americans accomplished things via what were basically *affinity groups* brought together by a common purpose.

Americans are naturally wired to organize themselves as groups to enact change. When discussing history, Americans frequently talk about affinity groups—Pilgrims, slaves, "Indians," Italian immigrants, Irish potato famine refugees, undocumented Latinos. This is particularly true in politics, as evidenced by CNN's digital voting map on election night. It offered an intense analysis of voting patterns by affinity group, answering questions such as, "What do low-income, White women from Appalachia want?"

By contrast, French history lacks a pattern of connection by affinity. Rather, family bonds were emphasized, so villages were organized and wars fought along bloodlines: the Hapsburgs vs. the Bourbons, for example. And election results are based more on right and left ideological votes than on voter demographics.

So why does an individualistic culture, such as that of America, paradoxically gravitate so easily toward communal affinity groups? To answer this question, let's compare American individualism to French individualism by contrasting heroes. American individualistic heroes stand for society. Loner John Wayne fights for his community, not himself. Batman defends Gotham City. Captain America defends the nation. Even the Most Valuable Player of a sporting contest is positioned in the spirit of a team win.

"In contrast, French individualism is significantly more shaped by the French philosophers, and by a sense of personal exploration which is the purpose of one's life," says Helene Baudet, a French national working as Project Leader for Diversity and Inclusiveness, in Ernst & Young's Global Diversity team. She explains that the "I think, therefore I am" worldview, where the self is at the center, leads away from communal heroes and toward French individualistic anti-heroes.

One such anti-hero is the comic book character Asterix, a non-muscular, disheveled iconoclast who fights for the village clan, rather than an affinity-based community. Baudet continues, "Other French heroes, like Le Petit Prince, Jean-Jacques Rousseau in 'Les Confessions,' Cyrano de Bergerac, Antoine Doinel (recurrent hero of Truffaut's films), have this in common: They are lonely products of a difficult childhood and no known parents. They are single men whose ambition is not to save the world, but to be the authors of their own lives. They spend a lot of time exploring their own emotions and speculating about the emotions of others, continuously debating the choices that will build their own identity and shape the relations they have with other individuals. Their goal in life seems to be to do things a la *premiere personne (in first person)*—that is in the 'I' or 'me' sense. Truffaut himself says, 'I see life as a very tough thing. I think one should have a very simple, very basic ethic: Say yes, yes to all, and do only what one wants to do.'"

"Mon dieu!" the action-oriented John Wayne would say in his own way to these French iconic figures. While "The Duke" may never have *joined* an affinity group himself, his raison d'etre was to help affect a win for people from a similar background.

As they encounter each other in global organizations, could American and French perspectives influence each other and converge at some point in the future? If, after all, the spirit of diversity work is to bring about positive change, does it really matter whether it happens through affinity groups making their voices heard or through individuals fighting for an ideal that benefits others?

Bicultural is more powerful than bilingual (though, of course, it helps to be bilingual)

For generations, parents have encouraged their kids to learn other languages for the sake of opening up their horizons and creating opportunities to connect with people from other lands. While English has been the *lingua franca* of global business, there's an emerging power language that's commanding attention: Chinese. (You thought I was going to say Spanish, didn't you?) In an example of how emerging markets are bypassing the United States in their dealings with other markets, Chinese language academies are proliferating in Peru. *"El idioma del futuro es el chino,* the language of the future is Chinese," a student told the Peruvian news magazine, *Cuarto Poder* after mouthing his first-ever Chinese words.

Being bi- or multilingual does indeed open up new opportunities, but language should be seen as only the tip of the iceberg of the deeper knowledge of other people's worldviews within their cultures. While knowing more than one language is valuable in multiple ways, the benefit will be curtailed unless we also learn a country's worldview. "It's not enough to know the language, but also the culture," the student went on to tell *Cuarto Poder*, "to understand the Chinese way of thinking, which is so different to our Latin sensibilities."

Says Dr. Milton Bennett, "I call it 'feeling of appropriateness.' And the assumption is that this is typically lodged in embodied ethnocentrism. How do we get to have the feeling of appropriateness in another culture? If we are going to go do business in China, for example, it's one thing to have the minimal and not very useful wallet card that says, 'When in China, do this/don't do that,' etc. It's a little bit better to have been through the program that says, 'Here's about US culture, here's about Chinese culture, and here are the differences that you should be paying attention to.' But it's unclear that that really brings us to the point of being able to go to China and feel what the appropriate thing to do is there. And yet for us to operate competently and effectively in that context, that's what we need to be able to do. But how do we get there?"

Language actually contains the keys to these cultural insights. We may know how to say fluently, *"No gracias, estoy lleno"* ("No thank you, I'm full") when offered a third serving at a Latin-American home, but fluency may create an easier way to be disrespectful. In a culture where "no's" are frowned upon, a "yes, please" in English would yield better results.

American vs. Indian debate: Are project plans necessary?

Accepting that differences exist and learning to call them out constructively sheds light on myriad daily interactions in increasingly multicultural teams, particularly when they involve teams from India. Much guidance about the differences between Indian and American cultures centers on tip-of-the-iceberg matters that, while important, are superficial. Numerous websites and travel guides offer advice such as, "Don't pick up food with your left hand," "Remove your shoes before entering private homes, places of worship, and even some shops and stores," and "The Western side-to-side head shake doesn't always mean 'no.'"

But these bits of advice don't explain the tension between Americans and Indians when it comes to project plans. Profound, below-the-waterline differences in worldviews come to a head among talented people on both sides with regard to how the work is going to get done. At Hewitt, I had the opportunity to work in-person on crosscultural tensions surfacing with both sides of an implementation team in Gurgaon, India and Lincolnshire, Illinois. All were highly committed to performance excellence, but misunderstandings and judgments were hindering progress.

"What is the thing that is most frustrating you about working with the Americans?" I asked the Indian team members.

"It's the project plans!"

"What about them?"

"They keep asking for them."

"And?"

"We haven't produced them yet."

"Why not?"

"We've got so many other more important things to be doing—the coding, the batch processes, the quality testing. We don't really have the time to create these detailed project plans they are asking for."

"Anything else?"

"It just feels like they don't trust us."

"Why do you say that?"

"We can't help but feel that by their repeated asking for it, they don't really believe that we can do the work. Rather than worrying about this document, about what we are going to do, we would rather just be doing it! We are all so committed to the project and we don't want to let anyone down, especially our

American colleagues. We will work 'round the clock if we need to, including the weekend, to get it done. A project plan is just a piece of paper. We have told them we will get it done. Why don't they believe us?"

Back in the United States, I got in front of the other half of the team:

"What is the thing that is most frustrating you about working with the Indians?" I asked the American team members.

"It's the project plans!"

"What about them?"

"We keep asking for them."

"And?"

"They haven't produced them yet."

"Why not?"

"We just don't know! They keep telling us that we'll have them soon, but still nothing."

"And why do you think this is?"

It was in this moment that the assumption of similarity started to generate its uncomfortable side effects. If something so "simple" and "commonly understood" as project plans were not being produced, what explanations could there be for this except for… No one wanted to say. Someone changed the topic.

"The other thing that's frustrating is that when we go over there, there's a lot more socializing than we feel there's time for. We're only there for a few days, and we need to make the most of our time."

With both groups, I introduced various crosscultural concepts and models, including the Seven Cultural Dimensions. After talking them through these, I asked the Americans, "So, as a task-oriented group, how can you get comfortable spending a little more time socializing with your Indian colleagues so they feel respected?"

We went 'round and 'round until finally an astute American said, "I know! I'll make relationship building a task that goes into my project plan, maybe with a subtask of going out to dinner the first night we're there. And maybe with a note to self that says, 'Don't talk too much about business. Keep it personal.'" To which another American added, "Yeah, and when we get back to the hotel from dinner, we can pull out our project plan and check it off!" Amidst the laughter of self-recognition, there was relief.

In India, I asked the group there, "So, as a relationship-based group, how can you get comfortable creating that project plan for the Americans in order to reduce their anxiety?"

We went 'round and 'round until finally, an astute Indian said, "I know! For the sake of the relationship, we will create the project plan."

Not only does mutual adaptation improve team dynamics, it actually enhances each of the sub teams' performance. Project planning invites consideration of time off due to holidays, vacations, and illness. At the same time, it triggers contingency planning to account for the upcoming monsoon season's weather-related power outages. Relationship building on the front end invites greater benefit of the doubt when time zone, language, and cultural differences create tears in the project's fabric. Personal connection reverses the emotional energy that, rather than ripping the fabric further, channels it toward mending the tear.

As a guy who moves through time in an event-oriented way, learning about clock-oriented time has enhanced my ability to execute my visionary ideas more efficiently and effectively. Conversely, the clock-oriented people in my life have found their experiences enriched by more consistently discovering the gestalt of the event itself.

In the end, it's not enough to tolerate differences or learn more about them. In the upside-down, 24/7 world of the Obama Era, to be successful means I need your differences. And you need mine. ᗡ

The cappuccino effect

In an in-depth interview for this book, Dr. Milton Bennett shared the following observation with me in his inimitable style:

"One of my earlier experiences in Italy was to do what is commonly done here in the United States, which is to order a cappuccino after dinner. Following my normal procedure of always asking first, I was assured by my host that it was a perfectly fine thing, although strange, but certainly okay in this very international restaurant.

"And so I said, 'I'll have a cappuccino,' to the waiter who looked at me rather ironically and said, 'Would you like a brioche with that?' A brioche is breakfast bread and I realized that I had been skewered.

"As I spend more time in Italy, an interesting thing has happened. I have developed an antipathy to ordering cappuccino after dinner. In fact, the very thought of a cappuccino that late in the day is now more or less *disgusting* to me. I'm thinking, 'Why would *anybody* do that?' Yet I remember that at the time, I felt perfectly fine about ordering that cappuccino. And I also felt surprised at being taken to task.

"Since then, when trying to behave appropriately in an unfamiliar culture, I've started paying attention to 'How do I *feel* about that?' Although this is about a very small thing, it is a very big change. It's a change in how one makes an assessment about what the right thing to do is.

"And this is the point: How is it that we know what is correct behavior? In our own society we're socialized into a whole constellation of correct behaviors, which mostly we don't have in our head. Mostly we just do them. You ask somebody, 'Why do you do that?' and they say, 'Because it's the right thing to do.' And if you ask them even more deeply, 'Well tell me how do you *know* that's the right thing to do.' Usually they'll come to the point of saying, 'Well, it just *feels* right.' It just feels right, whether it's ordering cappuccino or approaching your boss for a promotion. It can be a very serious matter or it can be a very superficial matter, but it still just feels right or not.

"I call it 'the feeling of appropriateness.' Or using intercultural terms, it's a case of embodied ethnocentrism. The feeling is in our body. The feeling of wanting that cappuccino is a physical feeling and the feeling of not wanting it is a physical feeling, too. The difficulty in moving out of one set of feelings and into another set of feelings is the essence of ethnocentrism.

"We have our feelings that are centralized in one cultural context. So it seems to me that another cutting-edge issue is, how do we get the feeling of appropriateness in another culture? Say we are going to go do business in China; it's one thing to have the minimal and, by the way, not very useful thing of the wallet card that says when in China do this/don't do that—but it's unclear how to go to China and feel what the appropriate thing to do is there.

"Yet for us to operate competently and effectively in that context, that's what we need to be able to do. But how do we get there? How do we *feel* what is right?

"This is what I call the cappuccino effect."

SUMMARY POINTS

- Every minute in the corporate world, someone who is different from the mainstream is feeling excluded—even in companies that are committed to diversity.

- The Inclusion Paradox requires that we not only acknowledge the differences among us, but learn to navigate those differences as well.

- The current paradigm for diversity and inclusion training, which relies on sensitivity and tolerance, is inadequate for meeting the next phase of diversity and inclusion.

- Crosscultural agility is the ability to discern and take into account one's own and others' worldviews, to be able to solve problems, make decisions, and resolve conflicts in ways that optimize cultural differences for better, longer-lasting, and more creative solutions.

SHAPING YOUR STRATEGY

- How well do diversity champions in your organization understand that crosscultural competency is foundational in order to be able to move the work forward? How can you tap into those who do understand in order to deepen your organization's crosscultural competency? What things can you do to help those who don't make the paradigm shift from tolerance and sensitivity to crosscultural agility?

- Crosscultural agility is a learnable skill that everyone needs. Once acquired, it leads to the understanding that we all need each other's differences.

- Authors Fons Trompenaars and Charles Hampden-Turner explain Seven Cultural Dimensions that describe various cultural worldviews:
  - Universalism vs. Particularism
  - Task vs. Relationship
  - Achievement vs. Ascription
  - Individualism vs. Communitarianism
  - Neutral vs. Affective
  - Sequential Time vs. Synchronous Time
  - Internal Control vs. External Control

- *Archetype* and *stereotype* are not interchangeable terms. An archetype is the tendency of a group of people to behave in a certain way, while a stereotype is the belief that all members of a cultural group behave according to a specific archetype.

- How would you describe your organizational culture using the Seven Cultural Dimensions?

- Pick any minority cultural group in your organization. How does that group's archetype compare and contrast to the description of your company's preferred cultural dimensions?

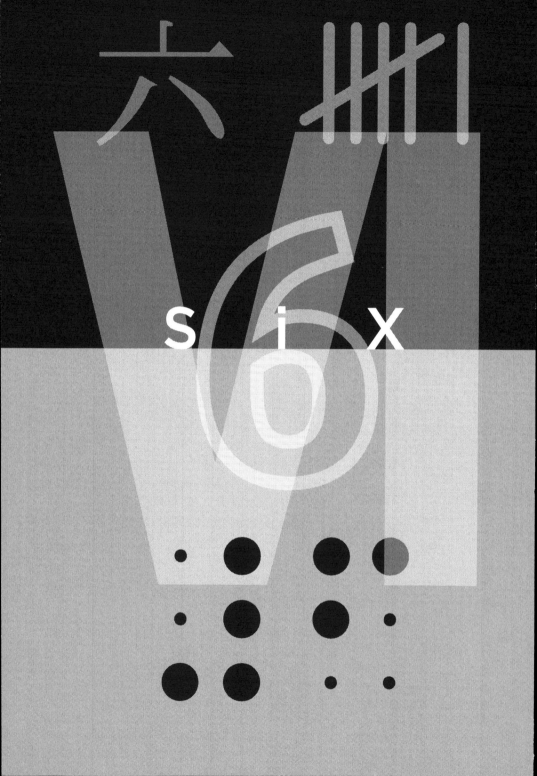

Chapter 6

Are you evil, clueless, or just plain incompetent?

Lori and I had been married only a short time when we decided to throw a party. In her German-American Midwestern way, Lori pulled out a note pad and said, "Okay, let's make an invite list." Quickly, we came up with about 25 friends and coworkers.

After we completed that task, Lori went on to handle the specific details for party planning—menu selection, music and entertainment, house preparation, and so on. Plans for the party were well underway. The following week, as I ran into friends and colleagues on the train, at work, or in the neighborhood, I would inevitably say, "Hey, Mark—we're having a party two weeks from Saturday. Here's my address. Be sure to come. And pass the word on!" When I mentioned to Lori that I'd invited Mark, Melinda, and Fareed, I got the look. "Are they on the invitation list?" she asked frostily. "Well, no. But hey, that was just to get us started." "Oh, *really*?" was her reply.

In Lori's way of thinking, the 25 names on the list represented the sum total of people who would attend our celebration. To *my* way of thinking, the invitation list was only the starting point for all the people who could possibly attend. *Todo el mundo* ("the whole world") is a phrase that frequently comes up in communal Latin America when discussing who's invited to a party or other social event. Rather than limiting an invitation list—as would be customary in the more individualistic United States—in Latin America, it's about expanding it. What Lori and I had was one invitation list, 25 names, and two culturally different ways of interpreting that list. What started as a party for 25 turned into a whirlwind celebration of more than 100.

And so it has gone—navigating the deep waters of cultural differences, running aground in the shoals of cultural friction. As we found out quickly and painfully, cultural differences can seriously derail personal relationships, not only with one's spouse, but also with friends and coworkers.

Here's where it all begins either to fall apart or to begin anew: When someone behaves differently from what we've been trained to believe is "normal," we can only assume that person is either incompetent or inept. Why else would he or she do it that way? When we think about cultural misunderstandings with those close to us, don't we often end up being furious at their insensitivity? Steamed about their moronic behavior? Outraged at their selfishness?

Dianne Hofner Saphiere, a crosscultural consultant with vast global experience, explains, "The most challenging thing is to get people to understand that their common sense *isn't common*. Common sense is really cultural sense. It's what you're expecting."

I discovered my Latin soul in Washington's wheat fields

My dad, Fernando Andrés Tapia Mendieta—the son of two schoolteachers from the fishing town of Pisco in Peru—earned his doctorate of medicine at San Marcos University in Lima. He came to the Cleveland Clinic to do his first residency as a cardiologist. My mom came from the small town of Harrington, Washington, 50 miles west of Spokane. She had always dreamed of getting out of small-town America, so she enrolled herself in an electrocardiogram technician certification program, also in Cleveland. So, between heartbeats, the cardiologist and the EKG technician met, married, and moved to Chicago, where my father completed his second residency at Edgewater Hospital, and where I was born.

When I was one year old, my parents got into their green Mercury Comet, drove to the port of San Francisco, hopped on a cargo ship, and sailed to the port of Callao off the coast of Lima, where I grew up.

Spanish was our first language at home, with English a close second. This bilingualism was interwoven with biculturalism. One night, we'd have arroz con pollo, the next, meat loaf and potatoes. We celebrated Peruvian Independence Day *and* American Thanksgiving, complete with turkey and stuffing (though cranberry sauce was impossible to get since no one knew what my mom was talking about when she asked for it at the store). She taught us about Halloween, so my siblings and I dressed up as goblins and cowboys and knocked on people's doors and called out, *"Treekohtree!"* (our butchered version of "trick or treat"). People had no idea why there were goblins and cowboys at their doorstep, but since we looked so cute, they gave us money. We learned quickly that the bigger the house, the more money we got. We pulled in quite a haul—my first inkling that becoming crossculturally adept could be profitable!

I first discovered differences when, as a third grader, I went to visit my American grandparents in my mom's hometown of Harrington over summer break. Coming from Peru to the United States was a major culture shock, which was compounded by the contrast between Lima, a city of 6 million at the time, and Harrington, population 500—not to mention the urban vs. rural differences of pace, noise, animals, and occupations—just to name a few.

I stood out immediately. Though I'm not that dark-skinned, I was the darkest person there. I spoke with a heavy Spanish accent, and when they threw a ball at me, I would kick it. During this visit, I experienced both the underside and the upside of being different: People hurled taunts and mean-spirited jests about my foreignness, but they were also genuinely interested in the son of a native daughter—Jackie Kay Graham, my mom. And so I was invited to ride on the combine during wheat harvest season, to give a slide show on Peru at the Methodist church potluck, and to play Little League baseball for the first time.

It was in Washington's Lincoln County wheat fields that I discovered my Latinness. Until I was out of the culture I had grown up in and immersed in another, I had little appreciation for the many ways in which my identity was outlined by the absence of the familiar cultural icons and customs of my upbringing. Surrounded by people who didn't look or speak like I did made me aware of the unique ways I looked and spoke. Here is where I realized I was a Latin American from Peru and began to develop an understanding of what that meant.

Returning to Lima, I continued my education in a parochial school run by North American nuns. I then prepared to go to college by pursuing both Peruvian and American high school diplomas at the American School of Lima I referred to earlier. In Roosevelt's classrooms, I discovered the life-sustaining literature of Poe, Faulkner, and Melville along with that of Borges, Vargas Llosa, and Neruda. I learned about George Washington's defiance of the British in his Christmas crossing of the Delaware in one class period, and about Tupac Amaru's rebellion in Cusco against the Spaniards in the next.

Every few years, I went back to Harrington, this time with my three younger sisters, to visit my grandparents, Brownie and Frieda. I played flag football, earned five bucks an hour pulling rye from a wheat field for a farmer who had mixed up his seeds, and watched the *Sha Na Na* show with my grandpa while munching on M&Ms. In turn, I showed my classmates where Peru was located on a map, how to get by with a few choice Spanish phrases, and that when I threw a ball at them—to kick it. I also told them stories of bullfights, professional soccer games, and political demonstrations.

By the time I arrived at Northwestern University to study journalism, I believed I was ready. I had even worked on my accent using my mom's voice as my internalized language tape. I would hear myself speak in an accented way and then repeat the same word ten times to match how she would say it.

But I was far from ready. So much of my preparation was tip-of-the-iceberg stuff—necessary, but only a beginning. I was soon to discover that most of my cultural differences were below the waterline—existent, but not obvious. With icebergs, the portion below the waterline sinks *ships*. With culture, the differences below the waterline sink *relationships*.

I've already shared my story of the differences between the Latin-American and European-American interpretation of time, but there were many other profound differences. As I relate these other stories, some of you may sheepishly recognize yourself in them because you've tripped the crosscultural wire yourselves in similar ways. Or you may end up scratching your head, asking, "Why would he do *that*?" And that is the point. We must come to appreciate the power of our differences and, as crazy (asinine, dumb, rude, weird) as they may sound to us, understand that our traditions can seem just as strange to others as theirs do to us. By sharing our stories, we can begin to forge new understandings to relate in more inclusive ways with one another.

Yeah, right

As a student at Northwestern University, I had a problem paying my tuition every month. Although I received financial aid, my dad still had to pay a portion of the cost. Now, keep in mind that my dad was in Peru. At the time, the country was undergoing hyperinflation and terrorism, and the country had implemented restrictions on transferring money abroad. To get around these multiple issues, Dad had to send cash with people he trusted who were flying from Peru to the States. I was depending on these flights to receive the money Dad sent in order to pay my tuition. But these flights weren't always headed to Chicago—they might be headed to Miami or Los Angeles. So though the money eventually arrived, at times it was two, four, even eight weeks late.

Tuition was due on the 15th of the month, with a $50 late fee applied on the 16th. So, on the 15th, I'd go to the Bursar's office and say, "My money isn't in yet." Every month, the clerk would say, "There's a $50 fine for being late." I would explain, "The money is on its way. It's coming from Peru. There's inflation, terrorism, restrictions on dollars. Can't you make an exception?" The university's response, from a universalist point of view, was always the same: "If we make an exception for *you*, we'd have to make an exception for *everyone*." Exasperated, I would retort in true particularistic fashion, "How many students do you have who come from a country 6,000 kilometers away where there is a 15,000 percent cumulative hyperinflation rate, a growing terrorist movement igniting car bombs in the Capitol, and restrictions for getting dollars out of the country?!?"

So, which was fair—one rule that applied equally to everyone, or a rule that considered each individual's unique experiences? Every month, I fought with the administrator at the Bursar's office, and every month, I lost. The universalist university system had no way to accommodate me. And so round and round we went as the Bursar and I drove each other crazy.

My parents sure had not prepared me for *this*.

Yours, mine, and ours

In the meantime, I was also driving my roommate, Leroy, crazy.

As someone coming from a communal culture, I had no problem borrowing people's things. My operating assumption was that it was okay for me to borrow from others without asking, even if they weren't around.

I had come to school quite unprepared. Having not visited the campus beforehand due to cost and distance, I hadn't known what to bring. So I borrowed a slew of things like staplers, scissors, shampoo, and tennis rackets. Through various awkward moments, I eventually figured out I should not borrow without asking. It was important in American culture to ask permission. *Ah!* Okay, I got it. But there was Part One of The Borrowing Rule that I was clueless about: Now I was asking, but I was doing it *too often*. It took me a while to figure out that one should only borrow sparingly and apologetically. "Why don't you have your own things? Get your own!" I started to hear in response as I applied Part One of The Borrowing Rule. I was so puzzled. "Why should I get my own if you're not using it? And this goes both ways. You can use anything I own—it actually would make me happy." But it didn't work that way. Coming from a developing country, I had a lot less that he would want to borrow—and he simply did not feel comfortable doing it.

When I became a homeowner many years later, I had to relearn The Borrowing Rule. One neighbor had a lawnmower, another had an extension ladder, and a third had a snow blower. I had stuff too, like an oil change drip pan, a shovel, and a rake. It took some time to figure out that even though I kept borrowing things from them, no one was borrowing anything me. I just couldn't figure out why each household should have one of everything when these tools sat idle 95 percent of the time.

Since college, my crosscultural experiences have continued unabated, whether in the publishing and corporate worlds or on working trips to Kenya, India, Canada, the United Kingdom, and throughout Latin America. Each time, I discovered new and surprising things about myself, my friends, and my colleagues in our Close Encounters of a Cultural Kind. Each time, there is a lesson to be gleaned to smooth out crosscultural interpersonal clashes. Such encounters also sharpen our insights into how cultural differences affect relationships and organizations—from working together to designing human resource programs to marketing and delivering products and services.

I'm not okay. You're not okay.

My first job was at a magazine called *U. Magazine*, a publication geared toward college students of the Intervarsity Christian Fellowship, in Downers Grove, Illinois. I was one of only two minorities in an office of about 55 people.

They were a caring group. I learned a lot during that time and made some lifelong friends. But boy, did I feel the differences. I was a communal, particularistic, synchronous, expressive, externally controlled Latino guy in the midst of an individualistic, universalist, sequential, emotionally neutral, internally controlled culture. To those who are familiar with the Myers-Briggs Type Indicator® personality tool, I was an ENFP in an ISTJ milieu.[1] To compound the differences, I had grown up in a non-air-conditioned world and loved the heat, so I often felt cold in US office buildings. Every summer, I would close my office door, open my window, and create a tropical oasis in my workspace. No one could stand being in my office. Even my packed lunch with the previous night's leftovers was problematic with its strong aromatic smells wafting in the small lunchroom as I heated it in the microwave.

The very things that worked for the majority didn't work for me and vice versa. They got the benefit of richer reporting due to a greater diversity of sources and an alternative way of looking at things. I had to learn to create a detailed project plan. But in the end, we all compromised. I perfected my English grammar syntax and adopted more of a storytelling approach. I changed to peanut butter and jelly sandwiches for the office lunchroom, and my colleagues came with me to ethnic restaurants.

Crosscultural interpersonal lesson: It's all about mutual adaptation. To trigger a good reciprocal and virtuous cycle, the one in the minority often needs to be the first mover—whether an American in Lima or a Peruvian in Downers Grove—not just through assimilation but also through adaptation. In response, those from the majority culture need to be welcoming of those who are different, show genuine interest in who they are and what they have to offer, and adapt in return.

Out of Africa

This mutual adaptation often comes about through a process of trial and error. As we get to know one another and our different cultural norms and practices, we begin to understand where the other person is coming from. Through this process, we tailor our respective approaches and eventually come together.

I experienced this shortly after college during my first trip to Africa with my wife, Lori, who was doing field study in ethnomusicology. As if dealing with crosscultural issues in the United States weren't tough enough, they were exponentially harder in Kenya, yet I credit this experience for contributing to the growth of my own crosscultural agility.

That summer, Lori and I spent time in Nairobi, Mombasa, and Malindi. But for most of our stay, we were with the Sabaot people in Mount Elgon on the Kenya-Uganda border, where people lived in mud huts insulated with cow dung and covered with thatch roofs.

As a passionate soccer fan and player, I always brought my soccer ball with me. Through my many travels, I had often been able to make connections by kicking the ball with people who spoke different languages and had different customs—whether with Cape Verdeans in Boston, Quechuas in the Peruvian Andes, or kindergarten children in Highland Park.

The day we caught the train to Mount Elgon from Nairobi, I forgot my soccer ball. Given how much emotional investment I had in my making-cultural-bridges-through-my-soccer-ball plan, I was devastated. Not only had I counted on using it as my lifeline to bridge cultural gaps, but also as my cultural prop. I only knew a smattering of words in Swahili, and those didn't go much further than *Asante* and even fewer in Sabaot. I had no family links in Kenya, and I'd never been this far from home. I felt very vulnerable.

The Land Rover picked us up at the train station and made steep climbs up the mountain around gigantic craters and through lush vegetation teeming with baboons, cows, donkeys, and elephants. I felt exhilaration and dread at the same time. Shortly thereafter, Lori began receiving invitations to various ceremonies to record the music of milestone events such as birth, coming of age, marriage, and death.

Wherever we went, the Sabaot were hospitable and welcoming—not to mention complimentary of my gumboots and jeans, to which I always said, "Thank you." I quickly discovered their culture was more communal than my Latin one. I was perceived as rude and materialistic—apparently, when others complimented something of mine, I was supposed to give it to them. And here I thought they were just being nice! The community was poor, and even though we were only three years out of college, we were viewed as wealthy. But it was not just an income difference at play. Communally, I was expected to reciprocate their appreciation for my gumboots with a gift of that very footwear. I came to understand all this, thanks to the help of one of my Sabaot friends, Christopher. When we left the mountain and were done slogging through the mud, I gave him my gumboots and jeans.

Another time, a large group of our newfound friends took us on a two-day hike to the top of a mountain, which was really a dormant volcano. On the way up, we stopped to meet one of our Sabaot friend's nearly 100-year-old grandmother. The greetings were formal, hierarchical, and full of symbolic meaning. The Sabaot subsisted on farming, and rain was both essential and capricious. When offering one's hand in greeting, the elder person spits on it as a blessing. One responds in kind. Since we were a large delegation of visitors, our friend's elderly grandmother worked her way through blessing each one of us. I was the last one. By the time she got to me, my salivary glands were so worked up and ready that, well, let's just say I *really* blessed her.

Halfway through our time there, Lori was recording a children's song with some girls near where the just-harvested corn was being husked. Suddenly, a small, round object rolled by my feet. It was about eight inches in diameter and made of balled-up plastic bags held together by twine. I looked in the direction of where it had come from. There, I saw a group of boys and men playing a game I knew very well. I picked up their soccer ball and dropkicked it over to them. They waved me over to join them. *Yes!*

Interpersonal lesson: No matter how much you prepare ahead of time, there is no way to avoid mistakes. You will embarrass yourself, but your good intentions go a long way. It's all in the recovery, as you work it through the necessary, trusted cultural informant. To call out differences constructively, find points of commonality—though they will likely be on *their* terms, not yours.

India: My polite is impolite

Prasheel and I had a great day together in the crosscultural train-the-trainer in Hewitt's offices in Gurgaon. Along with 25 of our colleagues, we had experienced exhilaration—of facing perplexing cultural dilemmas, discovering the breakthrough insights of what was going on, and having that understanding enable our ability to work together. To celebrate that successful first day, Prasheel took a group of us to an Indian restaurant for dinner. I worked my way through plates of this, that, and the other. We shared many laughs and learned much from each other that day and over dinner.

When it came time to say good night, Prasheel walked me to the outside of the restaurant so we could hail a taxi. As one was pulling up, I reached out my hand, and he took it. But when I said, "Thank you, Prasheel," I could see him visibly pull back. The smile on his face disappeared, and a grave formality descended between the two of us. I knew something had gone amiss, but I didn't know what.

"Anything the matter?" I asked him.

"Um…"

Sensing the awkwardness, I decided to lean in to our crosscultural work of the day. "No need to answer now if you don't know. But given how we talked today about calling out differences and how we need to do that as they come up, rather than assuming similarity, this may be one of those times."

By now, the cab had pulled up and the door was open, waiting for me to get in. I did, and a lively day came to a close in a less-than-ideal way.

The next morning, Prasheel jovially came up to me as soon he saw me.

"Good morning, Andrés. I hope you had a good night's sleep. And by the way, I think I know what transpired last night."

"Yes?"

"It was the moment you said, 'Thank you.'"

"'Thank you?' What's wrong with that?"

"Well, it can be seen as rude or inconsiderate."

"Yikes! Back in the United States, it would be rude and inconsiderate not to say it! Please explain."

"For us, 'Thank you' implies that someone did something for you that they would not have wanted to do. It is said in response to someone doing something out of an obligation. When you said, 'Thank you,' to my Indian ears, it sounded like a dismissal of our newly evolving professional relationship and friendship. Taking you out to dinner was something I wanted to do for you in appreciation. You made me feel like it was done out of duty, a must-do."

"Ayayay!" I replied. After explaining the Spanish meaning of this expression— "Wow and my God" rolled into one—I said, "This is so helpful. Now I understand why Americans often think Indians are rude because they don't say 'please' and 'thank you.' But I still need more help. Because gratitude is clearly something you value here in India, as you have clearly stated that your taking me out to dinner was a way of showing that, how do I demonstrate my gratitude in return if I can't say 'thank you'"?

"When I'm up in Chicago next month, take me out to dinner."

Which, you can bet, I did!

Interpersonal lesson: We often have the same value, but a different interpretation. Gratitude was the shared value, but we clearly had different interpretations of how to show it. Our ways of showing gratitude were considered ungrateful, the very opposite in our respective cultures! If we had not established a protocol and assumption of the need to call out differences, that awkward exchange outside the restaurant would have remained unspoken for the rest of our relationship.

This is just one example of awkward, unexplainable, can't-put-your-finger-on-it-but-it-didn't-feel-right kinds of comments that infest crosscultural relationships. By being able to acknowledge our differences, we were able to discover where our relationship veered off the path of trust and get back on it.

In the corporate world: The power of teamwork using differences

As you become more crossculturally competent as an individual, the next challenge is to create and nurture a crossculturally competent team with healthy interpersonal relationships. However, this does not mean these relationships won't be without friction. In fact, the more diverse the team, the more *guaranteed* the friction.

As has been an underlying premise of the Inclusion Paradox, diversity is more complex to manage than homogeneity. That said, diversity is not only a demographic inevitability, but also a requirement for innovation. The innovative, creative combustion of a diverse team can either lead to destructive explosions or generative bursts. As in one-on-one interactions, team relationships across cultural divides require shared knowledge and understanding of crosscultural issues. Also needed are skills to manage these differences and a commitment to doing so. This intentionality channels the friction in ways that move the work forward.

Here's a panoramic snapshot of what happened on my diversity and inclusion team while at Hewitt:

Tyronne Stoudemire, Global Diversity and Inclusion Director, and Susan McCuistion, Global Diversity and Inclusion Operational Leader, are diverse in more ways than gender. Tyronne is an African American from Detroit and Susan is a biracial White/Native American (Oneida tribe) from Las Vegas. Beyond that, the differences only get magnified.

When Tyronne and Susan worked on my team, they were both responsible for operationalizing strategies, though in different spheres of responsibility. Susan was very task-oriented, while Tyronne was very relationship-oriented. Our project-related interactions sound something like this:

"Hey, Susan! I have an idea for a new strategic initiative. I want to get your thoughts on whether we can get it done by mid-June."

After I would explain it, Susan would start immediately sketching out the tasks, sub-tasks and sub-sub-tasks. She would figure out how many days each one would take, factoring in holidays, workloads, slippage, vacations, *and* the probability of sick days. Then, Susan would map out the timeline, along with project details, and say:

"Andrés, I know that you want it mid-June, but because of these other issues, I'll need an extra two weeks. So let's plan on the first week of July for a final completion date."

Contrast Susan's response with Tyronne's:

"Hey, Tyronne! I have an idea for a new strategic initiative. I want to get your thoughts on whether we can get it done by mid-June."

After I explained it, Tyronne would start immediately brainstorming out loud:

"I know so-and-so is going to be in town at a conference ... maybe I can bring him in. I don't know anybody in this other area, but I know someone who knows someone in that particular area. I know that you want to have this done by mid-June, but if we plan on doing it early in July, we can piggyback on another conference when one of the speakers will already be in town."

Same end date, but approached in an entirely different way.

Given these two disparate approaches, Tyronne and Susan sometimes drove each other a little crazy. Both were very effective, but their processes differed in nuanced ways. They operated on completely different systems. Susan's anxiety rose when she didn't see a written plan. Tyronne's anxiety rose when he didn't see a list of the right people who would be contacted and drawn into the process.

Tyronne's cell phone was his baton for directing his project orchestra. Susan's project plan was hers. Each made music in his or her own way. Check out the table below for the harmonic and discordant notes of their styles as they worked together:

	Tyronne	Susan
Focus is getting the job done through	Relationships	Tasks
Mantra	Seize the day!	Plan ahead!
Highest priority	Front stage	Back stage
Leads work team's symphony with	His cell phone	Her project plan
Shortcuts	Know the right people	Cut back scope
Sounds the alarm	We don't know the right people!	We don't have enough time or resources!
Source of anxiety in working with the other	Her structure	His spontaneity
Source of learning in working with the other #1	Her structure	His spontaneity
Source of learning in working with the other #2	Leverage project tools to structure fluid working relationships	Leverage relationships to lubricate rigid tasks

The power of diversity is that every worldview offers something someone needs. When it comes to turning strategy into tangible projects and programs, I need diverse talents and perspectives on my team. Having both Tyronne's and Susan's widely divergent approaches broadened and deepened our group's reach and impact. And yes, I had them focus on doing things that played to their strengths. The diversity and crosscultural curriculum that ended up being rolled out to more than 15,000 associates and clients worldwide lends itself better to a task orientation. Creating a strategic networking alliance of high-powered corporate, not-for-profit, and government leaders who can have much impact in the global diversity field lends itself better to a relational approach.

As the Diversity and Inclusion "Center of Expertise" we were, we had better practice what we preached, right? Sure, piece of cake. No hay problema. Hakuna matata. *Right*.

You bet it's not easy. We have to work hard to make this work or our differences could undo us. So we're intentional in talking through the impact of our differences in our interpersonal and working relationships. We have to remind ourselves to assume positive intent on the part of the other, to be self-aware of how our worldview may lead to subjective interpretations, to listen intently to our colleague's side, and finally, to navigate toward resolution. The waters can be rough, but like white-water rafters, we need to expertly navigate the rapids through the myriad rocks and bends.

You bet it pays off. When worked right, it leads to richer relationships that pave the way for more innovative and memorable results.

Leaders learning through relationships

The most transformative experience I've witnessed in developing interpersonal crosscultural agility at work came about through the development of a program by Mary-Frances Winters of the Winters Group and myself. Initially developed for Hewitt leaders, the program was dubbed Crosscultural Learning Partners, to Hewitt's clients.

Here's how it works. Twenty-five senior Hewitt leaders were partnered with someone culturally different from themselves for a year. After an initial group kickoff—including a personalized and confidential IDI debrief (explained in Appendix B)—they received monthly assignments via email of an article or book chapter to read, or a movie to watch, that touched on a diversity/crosscultural issue. The senior leaders also received a set of reflection questions that touched on their individual worldviews—to help process with their partner what they read or watched—along with a set of application questions of how to apply what they learned to Hewitt's day-to-day realities. They shared each other's cultural identity stories and points of view in the context of these assignments and were often surprised by unexpected similarities and differences in how they interpreted the very same thing.

At the end of the experience, all participants retook the IDI. As a group, they had all progressed in their crosscultural agility. Their testimonials sounded like this:

A Human Resources leader speaking about the Gen X African-American trainer with whom he was partnered: "Charles [not his real name] helped me see around corners I would not have ever been able to see around. I especially realized this when he took me to the Chicago Theater for an evening debate between Tavis Smiley, host of the late-night PBS television talk show *Tavis Smiley*, Cornel West, author and professor at Princeton University, and Michael Eric Dyson, radio host and University Professor of Sociology at Georgetown University. I must've been one of only two or three Whites there in an audience of hundreds. I heard a perspective from these three prominent African-American intellectuals in front of a Black audience on the current issues of our day that I had felt pretty well versed on, yet that I did not even know existed."

An African-American Boomer learning and development manager speaking about the White male business executive with whom she was partnered: "Until I had the chance to hear my learning partner's story, I had never had an in-depth conversation with a White male. I realized that as much as I was providing him with new understandings of the Black experience, I had my own deep misconceptions of the White male experience. I was surprised to find out that this well-respected leader had come from a tough family situation, had faced many challenges in his professional life, and even today, did not have it all figured out. I honestly did not know that White males could also struggle in life."

A White, lesbian Human Resources leader speaking about the overall learning experience: "I will never look at an HR issue the same ever again." Despite her many years of experience as a highly regarded HR professional known for her effectiveness and wisdom, her experience with her learning partner busted open new ways of looking at familiar dilemmas in addressing breakdowns between associates and their managers. Given her own personal experience as an outsider who did not come out to her coworkers until she had been at the company for ten years, her self-perception was that she really had an insider's view of diversity. "In many ways that was true, yet my African-American partner helped me see how I did not know about the Black experience intimately and how it shows up in the workplace."

Initially, we worked with US-based groups who were dealing with American diversity and inclusion topics. After that, we launched programs partnering Indian and American employees who were working on the same project. Here, in addition to using the IDI to measure the program's impact, we also looked at a handful of the operational metrics that we were already using for measuring the team's efficiency and effectiveness. In comparing the pre- and post-experience results, they were markedly better at the end the program 90 percent of the time.

The watch phrase

Constructively calling out differences in relationships is pivotal. Once we can manage these, we can start to be more effective in calling them out among groups and developing savvy strategies around this ability, to which we will turn our attention in Part 3, "Calling out differences in groups."

Before we do, I realize that some of you may be wondering what happened with our *todo el mundo* party. We ended up having a blast, but it was not without its interpersonal costs. The crosscultural interpersonal lesson? "Don't do that again!" That's not to say one *can't* have a party for 100, just negotiate it up front. Rather than starting the list at 25 and allowing it to bloat to 100, simply start at 100 or even 200, as we did a few years ago for our daughter's *Quinceañera*. Yup, that's big. But this synchronous, externally controlled, relationship-based, communal guy has found a way to make it possible for my German-American, internally controlled, sequential, task-oriented wife to go grand. It requires willing, mutual adaptation to work.

The watch phrase for those in crosscultural relationships? Challenge me, yes. Opportunities to grow, yes. Just no surprises, please. Thank you. ○

SUMMARY POINTS

- Cultural differences and worldviews can derail relationships among coworkers, friends, family, and neighbors.

- Most significant cultural differences exist below the waterline and resist the easy-to-describe differences of language, mannerisms, and other diversity descriptors.

- When encountering an unexplainable behavior that makes you feel the other party is evil, incompetent, or a moron, it's always helpful to assume positive intent. With that as your starting point, begin to navigate what lies below the waterline between what you believe and what that other person believes.

- Good intentions go a long way, particularly when it comes to the inevitable inadvertent cultural missteps.

- Across cultures (societies, people, and geography), similar values may be expressed differently and lead to different interpretations.

SHAPING YOUR STRATEGY

- Think about relationships, offices, and locations where you have particular challenges in being able to relate to and understand your coworkers.

- What is it that's below the waterline in terms of how you and members of that group interpret conflict, seize opportunity, or approach negotiation?

- What are some steps you can take to navigate the difference?

- Think of a personal relationship and apply the same principle.

PART 3:
CALLING OUT
DIFFERENCES IN
GROUPS

Part 3: Calling out differences in groups

"What color is the sky in your universe?"

I've been asked that question many times—through spoken words or, silently, through raised eyebrows. Once I figured out the sarcastic meaning of the phrase, I began to wonder the same about others. But it's one thing to call out differences in personal relationships with your spouse, partner, children, family, friends, and associates. It's quite another to do so in groups. The dynamics quickly change when calling out differences at work or school, in religious communities or neighborhood associations, or as you perform civic or community service efforts.

Groups can be as small as two people or as large as an entire country. Even two people with similar backgrounds will share some cultural norms. Should a third individual enter the picture, they may not understand or be understood—even if they are speaking the same language and dressed in similar clothing—because they happen to come from a different upbringing. Our racial/ethnic background, gender, nationality, sexual orientation, disability, generation, faith practices, or other identity dimensions all come into play as we move through different environments—at work, at home, and in our community.

While self-awareness of what has shaped our own worldviews is an important first step in becoming crossculturally competent, we must move on to understand what has shaped the worldviews of others. What dynamics are inherent in the many ways in which we're different? What biases and misperceptions do African Americans, Latinos, and other ethnic groups share when it comes to their European-American male coworkers? How do White males view diversity and inclusion and the part they play in these efforts? What unique experiences have affected female professionals? How did the Great Depression shape the Silent Generation? How did the '60s form the Boomers? How did the space shuttle Challenger's midair explosion mark the Gen Xers? How has global terrorism influenced Millennials? Does life really look different from wheelchair height? How does the workplace experience differ for gays and lesbians who have to decide every day whether to be out or not? How can the performing arts help us further explore the differences among us?

To make the Inclusion Paradox come to life constructively, we must know how to call out these differences. It's the only way to find out where we share a common worldview and where we diverge from those who differ from what we're used to. What is their truth and what is yours? Only then can we move to the third and vital step (It's all about us) of being crossculturally agile, navigating the differences to a mutually satisfying solution.

The color of the sky in our universes may indeed be different. We may even have different interpretations of a "blue sky." For me, a blue sky means a nice, warm day, but in the middle of a January deep freeze in Chicago, a blue-sky day could appear on the coldest of days. A blue sky can represent a threat for a farmer hoping for rain to ease parched crops. Or it can bring elation to a tourist on a cruise to the Bahamas. A blue sky might be wishful thinking in a high-pollution city like Beijing or Mexico City. Such vastly different interpretations arise from our own personal experiences of our culture.

In Part 3, we examine in greater detail differing cultural dimensions and their impact on various diversity issues. At the G-20 Summit meeting early in his administration, President Obama said, "Each country has its own quirks."[1] Obama's assertion easily could be expanded. Whether defined by race/ ethnicity, gender, sexual orientation, disability, generation, faith, or other, each *group* has its quirks. By understanding each other's quirks, we can more fully live out the paradox of inclusion.

In the following chapters, we'll apply the Inclusion Paradox to dimensions of identity and examine areas where conflict can and does occur—despite everyone's best intentions. We'll examine specific areas where calling out differences can encourage greater diversity and inclusion. Whether the sky in our universe is blue or not, we still can co-exist on the same planet. ⌕

I SEE

7

WHITE

PEOPLE

Chapter 7
I see White people

An American story

Yup.

The White, heterosexual Boomer male is sick and tired of being the target of all those tolerance and sensitivity messages—fed up with feeling blamed for others' lack of progress, worried that diversity and inclusion advances will be made at his expense.

Many White males are also bewildered by the changing culture around them. And who wouldn't be, having grown up in a society where 90 percent of people looked like them, only to find just two generations later that only half did? By 2040, the United States will be well on its way to becoming a country where minorities are the majority, with non-Whites *today* making up 52 percent of those under the age of 18, according to the US Census Bureau.[1] And as of 2014, the US officially reached the tipping point where babies of color (age one to four) reached the majority at 50.2 percent.[2] Not only has the White male become a minority in the 50 largest US cities and a minority among all new entrants into the workforce, even an American president may not necessarily look like him anymore.[3]

To complicate matters further, the meteoric rise of emerging economies means growing numbers of White males are reporting to Indian, Chinese, and Middle Eastern bosses.

Let's make one thing perfectly clear: the White male *must* be part of the diversity story, not just for his own sake, but also for the sake of true inclusion. If in inclusion work we *exclude* an important part of the community, we might as well hang it up.

That's not to say the White male doesn't have work to do. The Inclusion Paradox means none of us are off the hook. We may be on that hook for different reasons, leading to different outcomes, but we're all on the hook, nonetheless. If we are to avoid diversity's mutually assured destruction—where White males feel that diversity is advancing at their expense—we must see in one another the keys to collective and individual success.

"Affirmative action has created a stigma in the workplace that has resulted in us having politically correct conversations about diversity rather than the ones we need to be having," said Candi Castleberry-Singleton, former Chief Inclusion and Diversity Officer of UPMC. Political correctness, while it certainly has its place within the diversity/inclusion discussion, has led to a sense of burnout, particularly among the White male to whom many politically correct related initiatives have been directed. Candi went on to say, "There's burnout on both sides, from those who have been carrying the torch of diversity, to those that feel burned by that very same torch. On one hand, burnout comes from constantly redefining, readjusting, rebranding, and remarketing diversity to try to engage people. On the other hand, if you're trying to adjust to diversity's ever-changing landscape, you get tired." And when you're tired—as White males are—you tend to tune out of constructive dialogue.

So let's say the political correctness posse backs off a bit. What would it take to get White males engaged in a constructive dialogue resulting in new conversations and actions? The Obama Era created new opportunities for changing how these unfold. While there still remains within American society deep racial issues that did not disappear on November 4, 2008, many have still raised the question of whether Barack Obama's election proves the United States has entered a post-racial era. The answer is yes...and no.

But before tackling *this* debate, I want to set the stage for changing how we talk about racial differences. Much has been written about the power issue, and vigorous debates have surrounded matters such as equal representation, access, and opportunity. Fierce and touchy discussions still take place around "racism" and "White privilege." Even the question of whether we're now in a post-racial society gravitates around power dynamics. This conversation occurs within a zero-sum-game mindset, where one group's gain is the other's loss. And in politics and business—competitive realms by nature—it's particularly difficult to get beyond the scoreboard of winners and losers.

While we must still urgently address dynamics of power, we must also add the dynamics of cultural difference to the mix. Adding the cultural difference dimension to the still relevant and vital dynamic of power opens a new avenue for getting past polarized debates. At the same time, it creates greater opportunities for what Dr. Michael Broom, author of *Power: The Infinite Game*, refers to as the "infinite game."[4]

To shift the discussion from power toward cultural differences within relationships invites the following provocative question: "What is White or European-American culture?" There's actually an emerging field of study of White culture in schools such as Princeton, UCLA, the University of New Mexico, and over 30 other colleges and universities. In some ways, they're comparable to that of African-American or Latino/Chicano studies. However, the thrust of several of these programs is to address the rise of racism and White privilege, rather than to celebrate and chronicle the emergence of White culture within the United States. That's indicative of the challenge we face.

Understanding the archetypes of White male culture is just as important as understanding those of other cultures. What are the historical, economic, political, and religious forces that shaped White culture? How do those who are from different cultures react and interpret the behavior of those with a European-American worldview? Without good answers, members of the majority culture will not be able to constructively call out their own differences or engage others in theirs.

The film *Undercover Brother* satirically explores the theme of White culture. In one scene, Undercover Brother, a secret agent played by comedian Eddie Griffin, plans to infiltrate a White-male-controlled corporation and save the world from domination by "The Man." To become a White-man-expert, Undercover Brother undergoes vigorous training, viewing a rapid montage of mainstream movie and TV clips, including *Leave It to Beaver, Murder She Wrote,* polka dancing, stock car racing, and Irish step dancing.[5] He begins screaming at the visual onslaught, whereby his colleague Smart Brother asks, "Are you alright?"

Undercover Brother responds in a whisper, "I ... see ... WHITE ... people."

Whether White males recognize it or not, the pervasiveness of White culture in mainstream publishing and media is recognized by people of color. Yet it's not uncommon to hear White males respond, "But we don't *have* a culture." When White culture *is* the mainstream culture, it's hard to see it as being anything other than "just the way things *are*."

But people of color quickly recognize *Seinfeld*, *Friends*, *The Daily Show*, Led Zeppelin, Aerosmith, and Nirvana as examples of pop culture that cater more to White sensibilities and aesthetics than to their own. While these are tip-of-the-iceberg preferences (which don't represent *all* members of the group), discovering what's below the waterline is the prize.

White males have a story, too

Both Whites and people of color would be more successful at making the mix work if they understood European-American culture in the same way White males are increasingly expected to understand the cultures and histories of various other groups. True, European-American history is better known because it has been taught in schools as de facto American history—which then cloaks the history, heroes, and writers of other American ethnic groups. But we rarely explore the cultural preferences of the descendants of those who came through Plymouth Rock and Ellis Island.

Under the umbrella of "White," European-American culture has its own diversity, equivalent to that which encompasses African Americans, Afro-Caribbeans, and Africans among Blacks. It's also equivalent to the diversity among Latinos, which encompasses first, second, and third generations, in addition to Guatemalan, Colombian, Mexican, Puerto Rican, and 24 other nationalities.

There *are* differences in worldviews shaped by the various historical and religious influences of White Americans of Italian, German, Irish, Greek, Polish, Slavic, and Anglo descent. When their ancestors emigrated to the United States, they found their way to ethnic enclaves—New York's Little Italy or Chicago's Greektown, for example. To this day, several generations removed from their arrival, these groups' cultural distinctiveness survives. It emerges particularly strongly at christenings, weddings, and funerals, as captured in movies such as *My Big Fat Greek Wedding*.

As monolithic as White culture seems today, each European ethnic group that came through Ellis Island faced discrimination from those who had preceded them. The colonizing Anglos found ways to discriminate against the immigrant Germans, Italians, Irish, Poles, and Slavs. And every group discriminated against the Jews, even when they shared the same country of origin.

The prejudice was deep and vile. Consider how the Irish were viewed in the second half of the 1800s when they fled the ravages of the Irish potato famine and arrived in the United States. In *American Pharaoh*, a biography of Chicago Mayor Richard J. Daley (son of Irish immigrants and father of the former 22-year tenured Chicago Mayor Richard M. Daley), authors Adam Cohen and Elizabeth Taylor write:

 'Who does not know that the most depraved, debased, worthless, and irredeemable drunkards and sots which curse the community are Irish-Catholics?' the *Chicago Tribune* asked in 1855. The Irish were regarded as particularly disposed to crime. 'Scratch a convict or pauper,' the *Chicago Post* declared in 1898 and 'the chances are that you tickle the skin of an Irish-Catholic at the same time … an Irish-Catholic made a criminal or a pauper by the priest and politicians who have deceived him and kept him in ignorance, in a word, a savage, as he was born.

"America reserved some of the lowest rungs on the economic and social ladder for the new Irish immigrants. Signs proclaiming 'No Irish Need Apply' were common. Advertisements for housekeepers often specified 'Protestant girls' only, because young Irish-Catholic women, as one account had it, were 'the daughters of laborers, or needy tradesmen, or persecuted, rack-rented cotters, they're ignorant of the common duties of servants in respectable positions.' Irish men, for their part, were largely relegated to the jobs native-born Whites would not take. They were the laborers who carved out the canals, laid the railroad tracks, and dug the ditches often at great personal cost.[6]

We cannot have a fair and healthy conversation unless we acknowledge the trials endured by European-Americans' ancestors. At the same time, we cannot merely expunge the legacy of racism in White culture and US society in general. We must recognize the legacy of racism in a matter-of-fact, unflinching way so that we can move on to the deeper, more constructive work of crosscultural understanding and collaboration.

With the massacre and forced removal of Native Americans from their lands and the entrenchment of slavery in the emerging US economy of the 1800s, race became a powerful societal construct. Eventually, White European groups found common causes and created boundary lines based on skin color rather than national heritage. After the Civil War, therefore, the European Americans already living there viewed freed slaves migrating to Northern cities as a common threat.

The same groups that had been persecuted turned their prejudice against people of color. Even in Richard J. Daley's own neighborhood of Bridgeport, where Irish immigrants had endured the ignominy and degradation of discrimination, Whites aimed their prejudices against Blacks. It was the era of Jim Crow laws and lynchings in the South—and segregation, White flight, and race riots in the North. The power of racism created common cause among White ethnic groups.

Over time, the construct of race and White superiority became so powerful that Whites piggy-backed on the issue of race, hopscotching over their own ethnic origin to gain acceptance and, with it, greater opportunity in society.

In the United States, race relations have been marred by points of progress and regress. Dr. King's march on Washington, President Lyndon Johnson's signing of the Civil Rights Act, and Barack Obama's election and reelection could all be deemed steps forward, while the Watts riots of 1965, the L. A. riots of 1992, the O. J. Simpson trial, and the death of unarmed young Black men in the era of #BlackLivesMatter mark steps backward. Together, they form an arc of lurching racial progress and regress[7]—and demonstrate that there's still a long way to go.

There are still gaps in educational attainment, infant mortality, and the financial well-being of Blacks and Latinos compared to those of Whites. African-American infants experience mortality rates twice that of the national average.[8] White households boast incomes 13 times the median wealth of Black households and 10 times the wealth of Hispanic households.[9] Seventy-three percent of Whites own their homes, compared to 47 percent of Blacks and 45 percent of Hispanics.[10] And while 41 percent of Whites have a Bachelor's degree or greater, just 22 percent of Blacks and 15 percent of Hispanics do.[11] In the 2015 US Senate, just seven of 100 senators belonged to a racial or ethnic minority group: three African Americans, one Asian American, and three Latinos.[12] In 2015, only 24 of all Fortune 500 CEOs were executives of color.[13]

But one cannot tell the story of White culture through the lens of racial disparities alone. We must integrate cultural worldviews born not out of prejudice but out of religious, political, economic, and social experiences. It's not enough to simply equate whiteness with racism. While racism is and was a reality with many consequences, European Americans are made up of communities, driven first to survive and then thrive. Along the way, they developed particular idiosyncratic interpretations of how to do just that.

This is why it's not enough merely to address power and law, but culture as well. Even as racism is legislated and socialized away, cultural preferences remain—not usually out of malice or intent—but in response to the primal need to seek similarity and equilibrium. These forces are at play in all cultures. Yet the group in power often institutionalizes their own preferences due to their numerical majority.

The institutionalizing of European-American preferences cannot be underestimated. To create true inclusion, we must first grasp how this deep enculturation may inadvertently create barriers for those who grew up with different cultural preferences, leading them to navigate the system with less savvy and effectiveness.

There's a key distinction between conscious barriers—which are designed to keep out people who are different (power issue)—and subconscious barriers that emerge out of a group's preference for how to survive and thrive (crosscultural issue). To identify and reduce or remove these barriers, we must first understand the conscious and subconscious choices being made. Since so much has already been said about conscious choices, I will focus on the impact of subconscious choices. This requires a more intimate understanding of the worldview of the culture in question.

European-American male worldview

"So what makes up this male European-American—or White—worldview?" Whenever I pose this question, a discomfort descends on the crowd attending the seminar. Some eyes avoid mine; others lock in. Some heads shake no, while some begin to nod yes.

Usually it's the White and African-American women who make the first pass at the answer. They tend to focus on tip-of-the-iceberg descriptions verging on stereotyping, such as a passion for golf, sports on TV, and steaks. Several of the White men look up and nod their heads as if to say, "Well, yeah."

I then lead the class on an exercise where they capture their life values and how these values were interpreted in their families of origin. For White males, self-sufficiency, hard work, fairness, and honesty typically surface at the top of their lists.[14]

In the context of European-American history, these answers make sense. The opportunity to remake themselves in America propelled millions of Europeans to pull up roots and travel through vast churning oceans, scorching deserts, and suffocating wilderness. Out of this arose the mythology of the

United States of America being the land of opportunity where anyone willing to work hard and create his or her own way could achieve his or her dreams. "Pull yourself up by your bootstraps." "From rags to riches." "God helps those who help themselves." These became the mantras of a people driven to succeed. Even happiness was to be pursued rather than realized from within.

As definable contours of European-American male culture begin to take shape, the men nod in recognition and then add more details. They own the description. "Yes, this is how we view the world. And it has served us well. It's how things work. It's what we learned from our fathers and what we are passing on to our children."

And so, not by design, but rather by their inherent norms and values, European Americans collectively created a supra-White culture. Once they had immigrated to the United States, normalizing experiences of European Americans blurred the deep cultural differences between them. The unifying value of democracy and its accompanying symbols of the Star-Spangled Banner and the Pledge of Allegiance took root. Acculturation forces of education, government policies, and mass media reinforced this self-image. And for European newcomers, an assimilationist invitation was made to become part of that great Melting Pot. Many European immigrants gave up their native language and traditional dress in order to fit in.

The White majority ran the institutions of power, commerce, and entertainment. As a result, the worldview preferences of European Americans were systematically reinforced and standards set for what was acceptable and superlative behavior in the corridors of success and power. White culture became the norm. Thus, the archetypical behaviors from other cultures became deviations from that norm.

What values consistently emerge from other cultural groups? In that same seminar exercise I conduct, almost all of the racial and ethnic groups also frequently list values such as Education and Respect. However, the greatest interest lies in looking at which values do *not* show up. Perhaps not surprisingly, others do not share the values most often cited by White men. On the African American list of values, we see Giving Back and Justice. For Latinos, we see Commitment to Family.

So *now* we have something to compare and contrast between the intriguingly different worldviews of European Americans and others. Why is it that some cultural groups don't place Fairness or Self-Sufficiency at the top of their lists? "Because this is not how it has played out for us," an African-American woman explained to her White male colleagues at a client session I facilitated. "I saw my father get good grades and was told he should only apply to a Black school to get his M.D. I heard about his repeatedly missing the IQ threshold by one point, which prevented him from getting on the officer track when he was in the military. Life is *not* fair. Hard work is not automatically rewarded."

So what's needed?

"Justice."

For many successful White men, the operating belief has been that hard work leads to success. For others, an outside intervention—justice—is required to achieve what is due.

No one list of values is more right than another—but they are different. Even when the same value is shared, it can have different interpretations. Two Baby Boomers—one Southern White male and one Northern African-American female—were paired to discuss their family's values in a course we designed titled, "The Power of Worldviews: Understanding Yourself and Others." Both agreed that they valued Respect. But listen for the differences in their interpretation:

White male: "For me, it was saying 'Yes sir, no ma'am.'"

African-American female: "Oh noooo. For me, it was quite the opposite! To say 'Yes sir, no ma'am' meant subservience. It was not the way to respect others or myself and my family."

At the tip of the iceberg, we may have shared values. But below the surface, differing interpretations often materialize. It's at this juncture that workplace dynamics begin to go awry. White males who see themselves as open-minded and fair assume a level playing field where meritocracy rewards hard work and ambition. Self-sufficiency is a good thing. Meanwhile people of color, scrambling to keep from sliding off this tilted playing field, ask for support programs that provide compensatory boosts to their efforts.

Over the years, we have conducted a workshop entitled "Why Don't They Get Me? Understanding Black and White Cultural Differences" at the National Black MBA Association annual conference. We present Trompenaars and Hampden-Turner's Seven Cultural Dimensions (defined specifically in Chapter 5, "I need your differences ... and you need mine), then ask the group to identify which ones seem more manifest in the European-American versus the African-American cultures. Their list looks like this:

White	African American
Universalist	Particularist
Task	Relationship
Individualist	Communal
Sequential	Synchronous
Internal Control	External Control
Neutral	Affective

In six of the seven cultural dimensions, Black audiences have put Whites and Blacks on opposite interpretive sides! The only cultural dimension where the answer was not dichotomized between the two groups was Achievement vs. Ascription.* No wonder the gaps in the workplace continue to be deep and perplexing: it's not just about power dynamics—it's also about cultural differences.

When conducting this exercise with predominantly European-American audiences, they are reluctant to venture into what may be African-American archetypes. Instead, they make distinctions among different European-American ethnicities. The following dialogue with a group of leaders in Georgia is typical of my experience:

"As an Italian American, I actually see myself and my family as more Communal in that family is one of our most important values. We're Affective in that we're much more expressive than Northern Europeans and we've got that Latin Catholic fatalism External Control thing going on."

....

* On the surface, the European-American celebration of accomplishment over title (admiring Bill Gates for his success despite not having graduated from college) and the high importance African Americans give to titles ("I attend Second Baptist Church, Hycel B. Williams, Pastor"), make clear the archetypical preferences of both groups—Whites seem to be more Achievement oriented, while Blacks seem to be more Ascription oriented. But dig a little deeper and you'll find that Blacks feel Whites put a lot of emphasis on titles, paying attention to who is VP, President, CEO, etc. For successful African Americans from no-status families, status is conferred on the basis of overcoming all odds. Because of these complexities, a clear distinction between the worldviews of both groups was not evident.

Fair enough. But remember that this model is best used when comparing one's own culture with another, however granular one defines it ("Calabrese Italian American," for instance). And by saying "European American," we're not saying "European" only. The "American" part is vital as well. Consider the case of Anglo-Saxon Whites who emigrated from England to escape an ascription (hierarchical) society epitomized by the monarchy. For them, America became a place of reinvention of one's identity. Regardless of the family one was born into, if one worked hard enough, one could shape one's own destiny. Even today, England remains far more class-oriented than the United States. The term "rags to riches" is not part of the British cultural values vocabulary. But it definitely is in that of their Anglo-American descendants.

Initially, European-American audiences become defensive when I ask if there's something that can be called European-American culture. Quickly, however, it becomes clear that their initial reaction is partly a means of deflecting what they assume will be negative characteristics, such as domineering, racist, sexist, etc. But as they start to describe the positive values instilled in them by the families they love and the heritage they're proud of, they begin to see that they have a distinct culture with certain values and interpretations that can consciously be described, compared, and contrasted with the increasing number of cultures they're interacting with at home and abroad.

White men have feelings, too

From this exploration of cultural worldview, let's return to the realm of power. Clearly, the White male dominates in positions of leadership, but this masks the struggles of many White males whom minorities may see as invulnerable. Much has been said about *White privilege*—the unearned societal benefits afforded to White people. In fact, much of the work of diversity is about weakening and dismantling the dynamics that inadvertently strengthen White privilege. While a valid endeavor, focusing only on this concept only perpetuates the mythology of White male invulnerability.

In a training video used during "The Power of Worldviews" course, a White male engages in a frank conversation with a couple of African Americans and an Asian American. On hearing how he's perceived as invulnerable, he replies, "On the contrary. I feel quite vulnerable. I feel that when I reach out, I won't be able to touch anyone."

Diversity and inclusion work focuses a great deal of attention on those who have been traditionally marginalized. However, White men have their own workplace issues, too. Often, their issues are overlooked because they rarely feel their experiences fit into a specific culture worthy of attention, given diversity's traditional emphasis on their privileged position.

The Winters Group, a diversity consulting firm founded and led by Mary-Frances Winters, an African-American woman, has identified the following recurring themes as unresolved issues among White male employees in many corporate environments:

- Feeling undervalued and unrecognized for expertise.
- Concern with lack of succession planning for their own aspirations.
- Concern with work-life balance and flexibility.
- Frustration with the addition of non-technical responsibilities, such as diversity training, inclusion programs, representations targets, etc.
- Believing that diversity equals quotas and that minorities are given privileges.

Winters' research[15] also found that "Both women and men have become more conscious of the personal trade-offs they need to make to advance in their careers, and that an increasing number are instead choosing to stay at the same levels, rather than continue to move up the career ladder." Work-life balance also has become increasingly important. Note the following comments from several of the study's respondents:

"The hours and goals today are bigger than they were in the past. It takes more of a toll on my family time."

"I'm on call 24/7."

"I miss a lot of family events because I work so many days."

"The time needed to complete daily paperwork comes off my family time."

Hearing the White male voice, both as a cultural group in a multicultural environment and as a group in which individuals face their own share of challenges, can open up a new space where minorities see White males in a new light.

Without understanding, we have judgment. This is why one of the most powerful ways to develop crosscultural competency is to do so within the context of relationships. To facilitate this, Mary-Frances Winters and I developed the

Crosscultural Learning Partners Program described in Chapter 6, "Are you evil, clueless, or just plain incompetent," where senior leaders and managers (many of whom are White males) are matched with someone culturally different for a yearlong learning program through personal dialogue.

Not only did we observe the expected *Aha!* moments among White males, but minorities also experienced an awareness of their biases toward White males. At the end of the yearlong program, we sat in a circle sharing what everyone had learned. Referring to the White male colleague with whom she had been partnered, one African-American woman confessed, "I had no idea White men could feel vulnerable and not have all the answers. But my learning partner was so honest with me about his own challenges of growing up in a single-parent household and his learning disability that I had to face my own stereotyping of White men. It was eye-opening." A White male in the circle responded, "This process was liberating. For the first time, I could see the potential that really addressing diversity can have for our business without all the baggage of being the bad guy."

White men as partners in diversity

What, then, are the possibilities when White men are more fully engaged in creating diverse and inclusive environments? Bill Proudman, founder of the White Men As Full Diversity Partners consulting firm, says that successful diversity and inclusion efforts must ensure we're addressing all employees, including White males. "It's vital that they become engaged partners," he says. "In fact, the real diversity goal for White males is to foster an environment where they feel part of the diversity and inclusion story and have options to get personally involved. Many White men have never examined the notion that they have self-interest in diversity and inclusion efforts. To explore this is new terrain for them, as they mostly view diversity and inclusion efforts as about everyone else."

While White males are significantly more likely to say their company is actively working to support diversity, they're also significantly less likely to feel that they're personally included in a company's diversity efforts, according to engagement survey data[16] from various companies.[17] Their engagement scores are consistently lower than for other groups at the companies surveyed.

As long as White men feel left out of the discussion, inclusion—making the mix work—cannot be achieved. As Proudman explains, diversity initiatives that ignore the potential contributions of White males only help foster the misconception that these efforts are nothing but a "chore" or a nuisance. "Most diversity work fails to fully engage White men," he says. "This leads people to view diversity as a win/lose proposition rather than a win/win. It's one reason why so many White men feel threatened or blamed by the topic." Because many White men don't view themselves as having a culture, they often think of themselves primarily as individuals, rather than members of a White male group. This mindset makes White men feel personally threatened and marginalized by their company's diversity efforts. They see it as only about changing representation (the mix), rather than including White men in the effort to make the mix work.

If White males are not engaged, they won't move proactively toward progress. And since they make up the overwhelming majority of corporate America's middle managers (the very group essential for enacting cultural change), they can by sheer inertia choke progress. Due to their size—plus their mandate to keep a company's essential services humming and product going out the door—middle managers are the most resistant to changing the status quo, regardless of the initiative. Usually, they are not required or rewarded for thinking and acting innovatively or strategically.

The reverse is also true. "Ironically, while this group can squash change by inertia, it can, if motivated right, make things happen," Georgia Power's then Vice President of Diversity Frank McCloskey (a White male) told me at a diversity conference we both attended. "Action, not reflection, is their bias. And when the action is clear and compelling and they're held accountable for results, big changes can happen. In order for this management and culture shift to occur, it must be seen as improving management effectiveness and employee performance. It can't be seen as 'adding to my pile of work.'"

What could this look like? Howard Ross, Co-founder and Chief Learning Officer of Diversity Consultancy at Cook Ross Inc., advises that White male employees become more actively involved in their organization's diverse culture, participating in a diversity-strategy group, mentoring and coaching, or being the person who directs the minority development programs and minority recruitment efforts. Even more ideas are featured in Chuck Shelton's book, *Leadership 101 for White Men: How to Work Successfully with Black Colleagues and Customers.*[18]

We will see an even greater impact when White men see for themselves how diversity and inclusion can help them achieve the day-to-day business goals for which they're accountable—by finding and penetrating emerging markets both within the United States (nearly $3 trillion purchasing power by people of color and another $1 trillion by women business owners) and globally. When they start to see that what worked for them when dealing with people who looked and thought like them will not necessarily work when dealing with those from other cultures, the more these White males are going to diversify their teams and build the kind of crosscultural competence that will enable them to bridge gaps and close deals.

Post-racial? Yes and no

In the Obama Era, perhaps the hotly debated question is whether his historic election in 2008 and reelection in 2012 marks the beginning of a post-racial USA. The answer is both yes and no. Speaking at the February 17, 2009 Chicago Dream Dinner honoring Dr. Martin Luther King Jr.,[19] the Reverend Jesse Jackson Sr. reached new rhetorical heights when dissecting how we see evidence of King's dream both achieved and deferred at this defining time in American history. Reverend Jackson said we cannot take lightly the fact that Obama's election is evidence of a dream achieved in a nation that outlawed slavery just over 100 years ago and gave Blacks the right to vote less than 50 years ago. At the same time, African Americans are the largest demographic group in jail, in infant mortality, in poor academic performance, and in debt. In that sense, the dream is still deferred. Post-racial? Yes and no.

This color line doesn't just show up across the socioeconomic spectrum. It also runs right through racially diverse middle-class groups.

Consider this scenario: It is 2015, and a group of about 40 people are holding 8 ½ x 11 sheets of paper, each containing a large handwritten number. They jostle to line up in numerical order, based on a self-scored questionnaire about their racial experiences. At the beginning of the line are those with the most negative experiences. At the end are the ones with the most positive. The visual is unambiguous: those with the worst experiences are Black and the ones with the best are White—and in between are the Latinos and Asians. How did this happen?

First, let's consider the makeup of the participants in the survey: a progressive group of Chicago area leaders from business, civic government, the legal profession, and non-profit organizations. They are White, African American, Latino, and Asian American. All are college-educated, mid-career, successful leaders. They share a passion and commitment to community development. Age-wise, they are all post-Civil Rights era babies. They are an elite group selected through a rigorous process for a yearlong program called Leadership Greater Chicago. Over the course of the program, they will build deep bonds with each other.

Despite the post-racial ethos of the group, a stark color line emerges. But what defines the line? The answer may lie in Dr. Peggy McIntosh's[20] seminal work "White Privilege: Unpacking the Invisible Knapsack."[21] In it, she makes 50 statements about her racial experiences in society that reflect "my own unearned advantages as a White person relative to African-American colleagues with whom I work."[22] As it turns out, her *personal story* resonates with many others who share her cultural and racial heritage—so much so that I felt it relevant to develop an exercise for the Chicago group based on Dr. McIntosh's list of "unearned advantages." Participants were asked to compare their experiences in housing, education, shopping, walking down the street, driving, and so on with those of Dr. McIntosh. Typical statements from her work include:

- I can go shopping alone most of the time, pretty well assured that I will not be followed or harassed.

- If I should need to move, I can be pretty sure of renting or purchasing housing in an area which I can afford and in which I would want to live.

- I can choose blemish cover or bandages in "flesh" color and have them more or less match my skin.

- Whether I use checks, credit cards, or cash, I can count on my skin color not to work against my appearance of financial reliability.

- I am never asked to speak for all the people of my racial group.

- If a traffic cop pulls me over or if the IRS audits my tax return, I can be sure I haven't been singled out because of my race.

An "Always" answer got a score of 5, a "Sometimes" 3, and "Never" 0. Participants added up their scores and then lined up from high to low across the room. That's how the stark color line materialized, with Whites scoring the highest with numbers above 100 (meaning, to their surprise, that their experience of having racial privilege was strong) and Blacks having the most negative scores—in the 20s and below. Asians and Latinos scored in between the first two groups, with their numbers ranging between the 20s and 60s. Regardless of when or where this exercise is conducted, the results are essentially the same.[23]

Let's return to my question from before: Are we now in a post-racial society? Unfortunately, the answer is no. And not for some time to come. Despite signs of racial progress, there remain potent signs of racial distress with new dimensions. Take, for instance, the arrest of Harvard tenured professor Henry Louis Gates in front of his own home when Boston police thought he was a burglar trying to break in.

Or take the 2012 Trayvon Martin shooting, when a 17-year-old African-American youth was shot and killed by George Zimmerman, who has been described as a multi-racial Latino male. Race shaped that public outburst around the case: from the presumption that racist motivations were behind Zimmerman's shooting of Martin, to accusations that race colored the police's initial decision to release Zimmerman instead of arresting and formally charging him to a legislative review of Florida's Stand Your Ground law.[24]

In 2014 and 2015, race continued to spur more disturbing discord than unity in American cities. Ferguson, Baltimore, Staten Island, Charleston, Cleveland, and Chicago saw unarmed Black Americans killed by police or civilians.

These events are dramatic flash points that there continues to be a stark racial divide in how Blacks and Whites view the world. In September 2105, a PBS NewsHour/Marist Poll asked respondents if there was equal opportunity for getting hired for a job. As reported by NPR, while 52 percent of Whites said they feel the opportunity to get a job was equal among Whites and Blacks, more than two-thirds of African-American respondents (76 percent) said it was not equal.

And when it comes to legal justice, half of Whites said African Americans and Whites had the opportunity for equal justice under the law. Among African Americans, only 11 percent said the opportunity for equal justice is shared by Blacks and Whites, while 87 percent said it was not. As for the question of police brutality, responses were even more stark, with 42 percent of Whites believing that police give equal treatment to people of both races, while 90 percent of Black respondents disagreed.[25]

It's as if these two groups live in two different countries. And to some degree, they do.

There's hope, however, in that we're having dialogues, making relationships, and finding new ways to collaborate across racial lines as never before. This is definitely true in the Obama Era. The election and reelection of President Obama pointed the way for a possible post-racial America and represented an opportunity to transform—not transcend or eliminate—our racial differences. As Obama said, his elections were a chance "to continue the long march of those who came before us, a march for a more just, more equal, more free, more caring, and more prosperous America."[26]

The President recognized the nation's complex racial reality and always had to tread carefully in discussing race. He showed a hyper-awareness of the sensitivities, often to the chagrin of many of his supporters who had been hoping the nation's first Black president would more explicitly and often address race. Only in his final two years in office did he begin forthrightly to address race, likely feeling much less hindered due to not being up for reelection anymore. While the debate continues about how he handled race throughout his tenure, he clearly made deliberate choices throughout on how he was going to negotiate this political and social third rail.

He explained, in a 2012 interview for *Rolling Stone* magazine,[27] *"My view on race has always been that it's complicated. It's not just a matter of head—it's a matter of heart. It's about interactions. What happens in the workplace, in schools, on sports fields, and through music and culture shapes racial attitudes as much as any legislation that is passed. I do believe that we are making slow and steady progress."*

Slow it has been, indeed. During this time, we have seen some of the most uplifting evidence of racial progress as well as some of the ugliest expressions of racism. Compare many of the pictures of violence and unrest in US city streets on CNN.com with those of *Life* magazine in the 1960s, and it's as if nothing has changed.

From his Beer Summit with Professor Henry Louis Gates Jr. and Sergeant James Crowley when he carefully addressed the race issue, to his commenting on the Trayvon Martin case that "You know, if I had a son, he'd look like Trayvon," to his exhortation to racial reconciliation and socioeconomic equality in his deeply personal eulogy for the Reverend Clementa Pinckney after the Charleston church shooting, President Obama has moved from hesitant supporter to vocal participant in his efforts to transform race in America.

Moreover, his addressing inequity was not just confined to what he said in speeches. Some of his most sweeping legislation has the potential to have an enormous impact on people of color in the United States. Consider some of the following likely benefits:

- Healthcare reform that will now insure nearly 32 million people, disproportionately (about a third) of whom are people of color.

- Education reform in which the Obama Administration has invested more than $100 billion,[28] most of it is going to "failing schools" where 50 percent of Black and Latino kids are not graduating.

- The Consumer Protection Act that benefits all Americans from potential abuses from credit card companies, but here again, disproportionately those falling prey to unsavory practices have been people of color.

Given his firsthand experience of being a person of color in America, President Obama has charted a highly nuanced approach to race. Some say it has not been enough; others say it's best for him to remain low-key on the issue. Still others have celebrated his being more open in addressing racial issues in the end of this administration. Whether one agrees or disagrees with the statements he has made on race issues, several of his actions, while not framed under the banner of racial inequality, have been aimed toward promoting racial equality.

When it comes to race in America, is the glass half-full or half-empty? Americas are making their own judgments, with 56 percent of Black respondents and 60 percent of Whites saying that race relations have gotten worse in 2015, according to the earlier-mentioned PBS NewsHour/Marist Poll.

Though it has gotten more difficult recently to hold on to this view, I still consider it half-full. From tip-of-the-iceberg European-American cultural contributions, such as Rice Krispies®, Halloween, Rock 'n' Roll, hamburgers, hot dogs, baseball, and Yahtzee to a worldview that believes in reinvention and perseverance, there's plenty to celebrate in White culture. American culture has also been heavily influenced by African-American culture when it comes to music, dance, and fashion, as well as the underlying contributions of the higher value of expression, more direct communication, and a commitment to community. Then there are the Asian contributions—from the calming spirit of yoga to a more holistic view of health. Latino tip-of-the-iceberg contributions include salsa—both for chips and for dancing—and expressive architecture and interior design, in addition to societal contributions of *familia,* community, and work strategies that embed relationships at a deeper level.

Even as we redouble efforts to erase the racial legacies of socioeconomic inequality, do we really want to erase the unique and rich contributions that each culture, including that of the White male, contributes to the whole?

If post-racial means a place where we've erased legalized forms of inequality and a justification for lack of opportunity based on the color of people's skin, then we're surely post-racial. If post-racial means a land where our children are more likely than us to grow up with kids who don't look like them as their classmates, best friends, and later as their lovers and intimate companions, then we can call that post-racial.

But if post-racial means erasing all those ways in which our uniqueness enriches one another, we may want to answer in the negative that we don't want to be post-racial. Or maybe it's time for a new term. "Maybe the desired state is *trans*racial," wonders Mary-Frances Winters. "A national culture where race does not divide, but rather enriches."

We see White people. We see Blacks and Latinos and Asians and Native Americans. True to the American Way, we see Americans reinventing who they are every day, both as individuals and as a society of people. Americans are in the midst of an era of reinventing their new racial relationships with one another—it's just too soon to declare what the "new" is. ⌐

SUMMARY POINTS

- It's important for European Americans to understand the American White male archetype in order to compare and contrast their cultural values and expressions with those of others.

- European-American culture has various nuances and its own intracultural diversity.

- White males need to feel included and involved in the diversity and inclusion effort. If they are left out of such initiatives, true inclusion will not be achieved.

- In the same way that there's African-American, Asian-American and Hispanic-American cultural history, there's also a European-American one.

SHAPING YOUR STRATEGY

- Are White males in your organization engaged in supporting and moving forward diversity and inclusion work? Do they feel included? If not, why? What actions can be implemented to include them? If they already feel included, how can you harness this sense of inclusion for greater impact?

- How knowledgeable and understanding are your non-White cultural groups about the White male experience?

- If there's a gap of understanding, how can you bridge this gap?

8

IN LEADERSHIP

WHY CURRENT BEST PRACTICES WILL NOT BE ENOUGH TO SHATTER THE GLASS CEILING WOMEN IN LEADERSHIP: WHY CURRENT BEST PRACTICES WILL NOT BE ENOUGH TO SHATTER THE GLASS CEILING WOMEN IN LEADERSHIP: WHY CURRENT BEST PRACTICES WILL N

Chapter 8

Women in leadership: Why current best practices will not be enough to shatter the glass ceiling

It is one of the corporate world's greatest anticlimactic moments: Throughout the world, women now represent nearly half the world's three billion strong labor force[1]—in Latin America, Europe, the United States, Canada, Asia, Australia, and a host of other places.[2] Yet, despite this watershed statistic, women only hold 24 percent of senior management positions and barely 2 percent of executive positions.[3]

But leadership representation is not the only dismaying issue. Highly educated and skilled women are leaving corporations altogether. And while, yes, some are choosing full-time family ambitions, this only explains part of the story. Many women, tired of fighting against conscious and unconscious sexism, are taking their talents and starting their own entrepreneurial enterprises. In fact, along with Latinos, women are the fastest-growing segment of sole proprietorships. According to the *2014 State of Women-Owned Businesses Report* between 1997 and 2014, when the number of businesses in the United States increased by 47 percent, the number of women-owned firms increased by 68 percent—a rate 1-1/2 times the national average.[4]

Despite these setbacks, women have revolutionized the workplace, not only by their presence, but also through their perspectives, skills, and demands. They've introduced new approaches to managing people and working in teams and led the way to new benefit concepts that support work-life balance, including alternative work programs and onsite childcare. Their true impact, however, is even more profound.

During the Obama Era, President Obama often spoke emotively about the strong women in his life. During the 2008 presidential campaign, he penned a white paper titled *Barack Obama's Plan to Support Working Women and Families*. In it, he cites the women in his own family as a testament to the contributions of women toward the advancement of female empowerment, not just in the home, but also in business. *"My mother was a single mom who put herself through school, followed her passion for helping others, and raised my sister and me to believe that in America, there are no barriers to success if you're willing to work for it."* He goes on to say, *"My grandmother worked on a bomber assembly line during World War II—she was Rosie the Riveter. After the war, even though she never got more than a high school diploma, she worked her way up from her start as a secretary at a bank, and shouldered most of the financial responsibility for our entire family when I was growing up. My wife Michelle, the rock of the Obama family, has worked her way up from modest roots on the South Side of Chicago, and has juggled jobs and parenting with...skill and grace.... My accomplishments are only possible because of these women."*

It's not much of a stretch to think that Obama's personal experiences with a working mother and grandmother—and later, a high-powered professional wife—were behind the reasons for his support of the Lilly Ledbetter Fair Pay Act, or to make it the very first piece of legislation he signed as president. In the spirit of equal pay for equal work, the act extends the time period that women can sue employers for paying them less than their male colleagues for the same job responsibilities. At the bill signing ceremony, Obama spoke of the impact the legislation would have on his daughters and future young women. He said, *"I sign this bill for my daughters, and all those who will come after us, because I want them to grow up in a nation that values their contributions, where there are no limits to their dreams and they have opportunities their mothers and grandmothers never could have imagined."* [5]

While Obama attributes his personal success to the women in his life, women also have brought increased wealth to organizations and nations. According to a 2011 report by Catalyst, companies with the most women board directors had higher returns: those with three or more directors outperformed those with none by 84 percent for return on sales and 46 percent for return on equity. Even in the financial sector, the presence of women makes a distinct difference. In the wild world of hedge fund management, between January 2007 and May 2013, women-managed hedge funds yielded a 6 percent return compared to the men-managed funds, which returned 5.8 percent. And during the 2008 crisis, women-run funds lost just 9.6 percent compared to men's 19 percent loss. At a nation-state level, the United Nations published a report that demonstrates a strong positive correlation between the education levels and income of women and the GNP of countries.[6]

The bottom line: The more educated and highly paid women are, the richer entire countries and companies are.[7]

Considering this degree of impact, women around the world are starting to say, *"Now, just wait a minute!"* They are enriching the overall working environment and making companies wealthier, but what do they have to show for it? In Japan, women hold just 8 percent of all management jobs.[8] In Mexico, male employees outnumber female employees three to one.[9] In Europe, women represent only 25 percent of senior managers.[10] In the United States, among Fortune 500 companies, women held only 8.1 percent of executive officer top earner slots:[11] 25 percent are corporate officers, 19 percent are corporate board members, and 4.6 percent serve as CEOs.[12] The robust pipeline of women in various industries has not yielded the expected results at the most senior levels. At this rate of change, it will be 40 years before women enjoy parity with men at the corporate officer level.[13]

In light of the past 10 to 15 years of heightened diversity work, women had hope that the ubiquitous glass ceiling would finally be shattered. Yet, the first five years of "patience, we've only just begun" evolved into the next five years of "patience, we're making some progress" to the past three to five years of "we're really stuck."

And it's true. Women are *really* stuck, despite having similar levels of ambition as men, and sometimes more education. In the United States, women now earn 57 percent of bachelor's degrees and 52 percent of doctorates.[14] Increased education levels align with greater ambition, which can be considered a birthright of today's young women whose mothers struggled with these same issues.

According to research by Ellen Galinsky, President and Co-founder of the Families and Work Institute, Millennial women and men are equally likely to be ambitious and desire positions with greater responsibilities. And this holds true whether these younger women are mothers or not. But the robust pipeline of women in various industries has not yet yielded the expected results at the most senior levels.

In certain countries, the dashing of rising expectations is making a growing number of women rethink the corporate deal. This shift in attitude could mean quite a loss for corporations. In the United States and Australia, for example, a growing number of senior women professionals have gained enough economic, personal, and professional power to abandon the corporate world entirely, opting to start their own businesses instead. In the United States, women and African Americans are leading the way as the fastest-growing segments for start-up companies. Every 60 seconds, a woman—often a self-exile from the corporate ranks—starts her own business.[15]

The argument could be made that for women of color, the rise in business ownership is related to the lower rate of advancement up the management ranks. According to the Working Mother Research Institute, in 2012, less than half of the women surveyed said they are satisfied with their ability to move to a better position at their respective companies. According to the 2012 Diversity Best Practices benchmarking study, participating companies promoted women of color into rising levels of management at much lower rates than White women or men of any race and ethnicity. In fact, women of color had the lowest promotion rate, implying there is an insidious double glass ceiling for women of color.

In this chapter, I explore the requirements for breakthrough change in the advancement of women leaders. In the process, I examine some implications for corporations if women are to make the desired gains. It won't be enough simply to retool their diversity efforts. Corporate leadership will have to address the different perspectives and cultural behaviors women bring to the workplace and begin to discuss these differences openly and honestly, both with the women themselves and with their male colleagues, at all levels.

This exploration will also touch on some of the gains women have made since the first printing of this book. The Obama Era aligned with the growing prominence of women and girls in the political, social, educational, and economic spheres all across the globe. The twenty-first century is witnessing an emergence of female power. Despite the current statistics that point to stagnation in women's advancement in leadership, the glass ceiling holds massive pressures that cannot be contained any longer.

As Hillary Clinton mentioned at the end of the 2008 primary elections in her hard-fought campaign versus candidate Obama, "Although we were not able to shatter that highest and hardest glass ceiling this time, thanks to you it has 18 million cracks in it, and the light is shining through like never before, filling us all with the hope and the sure knowledge that the path will be a little easier next time, and we are going to keep working to make it so."[16]

The impact of this female power is shaking the status quo in workplaces, homes, communities, schools and universities, legislative bodies, organizations, and informal and formal networks. Women are not only changing who is making decisions and doing work, but also how decisions are made, how work is accomplished, and the reasons underlying those changes.

In the past few years, the intervention most frequently requested in diversity today is for the advancement of women around the world. Current corporate best practices will have to adapt to this surge in female power and this growing acceptance that companies need to enable women to reach their potential, both for their sake and the sake of their organizations. Those that can't or won't adapt will be swept out to sea by this rising tide of women.

Best practices

Yes, there are best practices to live by, and I will summarize what many have already deemed necessary for women to rise in corporate ranks. Diversity practitioners, think tanks, and women executive councils generally agree about what needs to be done, but they are unsure how to resolve the limitations of existing approaches to the issue. Shattering the glass ceiling requires more than mere diversity—inclusion must be embedded into leadership development and succession plans, requiring that women's skills be separated into "ready now" and "ready in three years" categories. Inclusive environments must be fostered where all manner of differences, including gender, are welcomed and embraced. Women must be mentored, and they must take part in open and honest discussions concerning their current skills and development needs. And, yes, there must be pay equity.

These practices, *well executed*, will yield results—but only incrementally. Today's corporate structure and assumptions inherently prevent women from taking their rightful seats at the leaders' table. Thus, we must look beyond best practices to new paradigms.

Just what is it about being female that makes rising to the top so challenging? How can companies make room at the leaders' table for the archetypical female traits that now impede their advancement? Let's look at some new thinking on what needs to happen.

Beyond best practices

Corporations need to rethink their current paradigms to begin shattering the glass ceiling. It's time to:

- Rethink what strong leadership and strong management looks like.
- Rethink the value of tenure.
- Rethink compensation models.
- Rethink whether competencies developed elsewhere are transferable to the workplace.
- Rethink how unspoken rules about alternative work arrangements may be detrimental to women's advancement and their full inclusion into organizational life.

Let's break down each of these points individually.

Rethink what strong leadership and strong management looks like

Quick! What attributes come to mind when you hear the words "leader" and "manager"? If you're like most respondents, chances are you thought of characteristics such as self-reliant, forceful, independent, analytical, assertive, willing to take risks, ambitious, makes decisions.

Now consider this: When both sexes are asked to list attributes that come to mind when they hear the words "man" and "woman," there's a strong correlation between those cited for "leader," "manager," and "man" and a very weak overlap with those cited for "woman." In fact, the attributes most often associated with "woman" are loyal, compassionate, sensitive to the needs of others, and understanding—adjectives that are conspicuously absent from the leader and manager lists.

Women find themselves in a Catch-22. If they don't act like men, they don't get recognized as leadership material. If they do, other types of derogatory adjectives that rhyme with that of Halloween characters begin to surface. *This is the double standard women face at the glass ceiling fault line.*[17]

"I simply got tired of having to act like a man," declare women who left their corporate jobs to start their own businesses. Others who choose to stay are pressing for the freedom to be more authentic. According to Kathy Flanagan, an executive coach on issues of women and leadership, 82 percent of female leaders say that remaining true to themselves in their leadership role without losing credibility is a top issue. "Books with titles such as *Games Your Mother*

Never Taught You, Hardball for Women, and *Why Good Girls Don't Get Ahead but Gutsy Girls Do* are being challenged by new titles such as *Success on Our Own Terms*, *Swim with the Dolphins*, and *Pitch like a Girl*," says Flanagan.

Ironically, it turns out that what corporations need more than ever is more archetypically female traits. New leadership requirements differ greatly from the traditional male military model of command and control. In today's upside-down world, the upper echelons of organizations (and really, throughout enterprises) need leaders who are team-building, multitasking, consensus-building, stress-resisting, and employee-developing dynamos. In a March 2011 *Harvard Business Review* piece titled "The New Path to the C-suite," authors Boris Groysberg, L. Kevin Kelly, and Bryan MacDonald wrote that, "Today, technical and functional expertise matters less at the top than business acumen and soft leadership skills."[18]

In several performance management studies, female managers outperform their male counterparts on a variety of criteria.[19] In her article, "Women Leaders: Strategic Yet Invisible Assets," Kira Porter makes the case for what she refers to as the "Post-heroic Model" of leadership that includes communication, emotional intelligence, collaboration, negotiation, entrepreneurship, coaching, and mentoring.[20] All of these are traits that tend to show up more consistently among women.

The competencies that differentiate high-performing executives are also well documented. Key areas include: strategic skills such as business and financial acumen; operating skills such as strategy execution and setting priorities; and personal and interpersonal skills such as demonstrating integrity and communicating a compelling vision. Data from Korn Ferry leadership assessments show that female executives outperform male executives in 17 out of the 67 leadership skills rated. In contrast, male executives outperform female executives in 4 leadership skills. While women scored higher in the areas of building talent, engaging employees, collaboration, and customer focus, men were rated higher in the areas of strategic skills and financial acumen.[21]

The need for female influence is even more urgent, given the increased complexity and surging globalization of the marketplace. Rethinking leadership models would not only multiply opportunities for women, it would actually strengthen the effectiveness of multinationals. The punch-in-the-gut barrier is the immediate, intuitive, pre-programmed response that Malcolm Gladwell talks about in his book *Blink*. These knee-jerk assumptions and decisions about people who are female, of color, older, younger, with disabilities, etc., made without thinking, often sabotage our best inclusive intentions. *To shatter the glass ceiling, therefore, it is imperative that corporations develop crosscultural competence to acknowledge and act on gender issues—call it gender intelligence.*

Throughout this book, I make the case for crosscultural competence, a concept that can also be applied to traversing gender differences. Until males come to understand that their concept of what makes a strong leader or manager is culturally determined by their experience as *males*, they will never see they are inadvertently stifling the upward arc of ambitious and talented women. Until then, they'll continue to perpetuate an assessment of leadership and management that creates more and more *people like them*. Not only do they need to recognize the subjectivity of their leadership model preference, they must develop the capacity to value leadership styles different from their own—*even when they don't understand them*. The global economy creates a new opening for this type of approach, since the same unlearning of familiar assumptions is required to excel globally.

Now comes the gutsy part: What might leaders begin to hear as they open themselves to new voices and approaches?

Rethink the value of tenure

The correlation between tenure and assumptions creates a dilemma for women who choose to leave the workforce in the early years of child raising. When they return, an employer will often welcome them back. Yet they fail to acknowledge the perils of being out of the workforce for a few years, causing them to fall behind their peers. In one of the most comprehensive writings on this issue, "Hidden Brain Drain: Off-Ramps and On-Ramps in Women's Careers," the authors lay out what they refer to as the "penalties" for taking time out.[22] While off-ramping only lasts an average of two years, women lost an average of 18 percent of their earning power. (When they off-ramp for three or more years, the figure rises to 37 percent.) So here's the brain-drain impact: 93 percent of the women currently off-ramped want to get back to work. But only 74 percent succeed in obtaining jobs and *only 5 percent* of women who on-ramp want to return to the company they used to work for.

While the Talent War for specialized skills is still hot even in a downturned economy, experienced female professionals are waiting on the sidelines ready to get back in the game, but for a different team. Yet the Talent War is only part of the challenge. Calling out differences among various groups—in this case, women—enables all employees to feel valued enough to give their best efforts. Corporations have a prime opportunity to strengthen their talent pipeline by staying in touch with their female alumnae and enticing them back. Let's keep looking at some of the things that could do just that.

Rethink compensation models

"Several studies have shown that women are not motivated by the same competitive compensation structures as those that have traditionally appealed to men," says Flanagan. "They prefer to measure themselves against their own Personal Best standard." The securities industry bemoaned for years that they could not recruit or retain female brokers because many women didn't like the competitive, transaction-based reward system, she explains. Yet the industry did not adapt to this difference until external customer pressures drove it toward fee-based (relationship-centered) compensation. Only then did the industry begin to see significant advances in the recruitment, retention, and advancement of female financial advisors. And the industry profited. The adoption of innovative strategies enabled the financial services industry to forge robust relationships with both new and current customers, enriching its financial standing in the overall economy. Navigating the gap among cultural worldviews—including gender-based perspectives—made this all possible.

Across industries, similar questioning must take the place of deep-seated assumptions about what types of rewards will resonate deeply with women professionals. In studies and focus groups, women have made a number of things clear:

- Pay is not the greatest motivator.
- Competitive compensation models don't attract.
- Meaningful work pulls.
- A sense of belonging is prized.
- Long hours disengage.

According to Korn Ferry's research, women at the executive level are motivated by many of the same things as men, but there are also some differences. Men favor a broader scope of responsibility, influence, and performance more often, whereas women value stimulating work that gives a sense of personal accomplishment in a friendly environment.[23]

Somewhere in these declarations lies the path to new ways of rewarding women (and we shouldn't be surprised if a good number of men ride these coattails). We should also beware the dangerous assumption that women are not as driven by high pay as men—this could lead to a subconscious rationalization for not focusing on closing the wage gap.

Rethink whether competencies developed elsewhere are transferable to the workplace

What lies behind the whopping drop in earnings for women who off-ramped, but now want to get back on track? The assumption is that none of the experience gained during their time off the corporate track is of value to the business. The corporate world is quick to make correlations between sports leadership accomplishments and business leadership—why not do the same for family-raising accomplishments?

Consider the competencies required to raise a family. The ability to manage multiple responsibilities is a must, especially for the sandwich generation, who cares not only for small children but aging parents as well. In our complex modern life, each home is an economic profit-and-loss center. Everyone is burdened with multilayered responsibilities in carefully planning for one's retirement or managing one's health. In addition, today's increasingly multiracial/international families require complex problem-solving, project-planning, and crosscultural skills.

It's a mistake to assume that a woman's skills will get rusty during her off-ramp time. Instead, we should imagine a development planning session that takes place right before she goes on maternity leave. The goal would be to itemize some of the experiences during her corporate time off that will result in new—and needed—skills. Can corporations assign an economic value to those skills that would then be factored into the woman's compensation once she returns to the workforce?

Maybe we should raise the ante by saying we need to measure not only *women's* advancement, but also *mothers'* advancement. In looking at women in top roles, how many of them are mothers? The answer to this question could go a long way toward supporting the notion—and convincing corporate leaders—that being a mother is no more of a disadvantage than being a father.

"In fact, being a mother can be a big advantage in growing professionally," says Linda Mateja, formerly Senior Corporate Human Resources Leader at Hewitt. "People who stay home with kids still develop competencies that are applicable in the workplace. Examples could be negotiation skills, time management, project planning, even presentation skills if they are active in community or school activities."

Women who become mothers are confronted with a variety of issues and situations that require them to become experts at time management and prioritization, not to mention compassion. Don't these skills translate accordingly into a workplace environment? Don't managers need to be able to manage their time effectively, prioritize tasks and responsibilities, and show empathy, support, and understanding to their colleagues and partners both inside and outside of the organization? These maternal skills translate perfectly in a corporate environment. In fact, many men—if they're able to adjust their traditional male-oriented perspective—could stand to learn a lot from working mothers.

In 2012, Yahoo's board was able to overcome their discomfort with the hiring of its new CEO Marissa Mayer, who was brought on board while she was pregnant—a first for this type of situation. The public scrutiny of Yahoo's selection at this stage of Mayer's life belies the often non-discussed yet underlying belief that pregnant women are a hire risk. Despite blogosphere howls about Mayer's short maternity leave, her willingness to accept the post and return quickly to work speaks volumes about her confidence and ability to handle multiple responsibilities. And she did it again when she gave birth to twins at the end of 2015 and came back to work two weeks later. Her example is more than 20 years in time and mindset from the 1992 speech by then Ceridian CEO Lawrence Perlman that asked, "A Pregnant CEO: In Whose Lifetime?"[24] Clearly in his.

Rethink how unspoken rules about alternative work arrangements may be detrimental to women's advancement and their full inclusion into organizational life

Much has been written on alternative work patterns, such as reduced-hour jobs, flex hours, job shares, and so on. Companies that provide these benefits rightly pride themselves on their progressiveness. Yet we must ask: Is there a hidden "penalty" career- and income-wise for those who take this route? Sure, there's a logical implication that "time equals money." But plenty of studies demonstrate that the *quality* of the time and *commitment* of the employee may actually mean more money than merely looking at total time.

Study after study has shown that flexibility is one of the most valued benefits for a workforce dealing with greater complexity and greater opportunities in the various facets of their lives. In the "Off-Ramps, On-Ramps" report, 64 percent of women cite flexible work arrangements as being extremely or very important to them. Just 43 percent say earning a lot of money is an important motivating force. Then there's the cultural stigma many experience when taking advantage of corporate-approved job flexibility programs.

Often, managers are not supportive, and coworkers are judgmental. While the economic equation of the value of time away from the corporation may be difficult to calculate, it's clear that addressing the stigma can go a long way toward retaining female talent.

Unprecedented opportunity

The outlook may sound gloomy, but the situation is far from bleak—particularly if corporations play to their strengths. *Multinational companies are one of the most significant change agents for the advancement of women around the world.* After so much pummeling for their mediocre advancement of women leaders, let's take a moment to praise multinationals for their transformative impact on women's roles both inside and outside the corporation. While it's true that corporations have a long way to go in furthering the advancement of women, there's no denying that multinationals have been an accelerating force in the overall advancement of women.

Multinationals, particularly those rooted in American and European contexts, come from a worldview of meritocracy—those who perform the best tend to reap the greatest rewards. Of course, when we look at the dearth of minorities and women in top leadership, it's clear that these very corporations have fallen far short of living up to their value of meritocracy. Nevertheless, that value is there and it's the epicenter on which we base our diversity case. However imperfectly this value is lived, it's still a force to reckon with.

As discussed in Chapter 4, "This thing is global!", women in India and China have seen their fortunes change tremendously in recent years. The opportunity to acquire a job with a multinational and earn her own wages has given her significantly greater power. She can choose where she lives and whom she marries—if she chooses to marry at all. Of course, glass-ceiling issues are sprouting up in these emerging powerhouse economies, as women are still in that first phase of entering professional workplaces. Nevertheless, women's standing in these traditional societies is changing, fueled by a multinational appetite for talent.

Though corporations don't like to think of themselves as social change agents, their impact is undeniable in the new capitalist economies of India and China. By finding new ways to attract and retain female talent, corporations contribute not only to the enterprise's bottom line, but also to the health of greater society. Isobel Coleman, former Director of the Council on Foreign Relations and founder of the Women and Foreign Policy program, makes the case in an article in *Foreign Affairs*. Companies that adopt practices and policies that empower women can expect to see "their labor forces become more productive, the quality of their global supply chains improves, and their customer bases expand."[25] She predicts that this movement could be "the greatest cultural shift of the twenty-first century."

But here's the rub: As national policies and practices attempt to harness this undeniable female energy, nations and societies face significant challenges in balancing their economic desires while remaining true to their particular societies' cultural traditions. Let's look at just a few of these countries.

Latin America

In Latin America, appreciating diversity and preventing workplace discrimination are nascent concepts that in the past five years have gathered quite a bit of force. Creating awareness of the importance of diversity is critical. Although many countries have legislation about workplace discrimination, these policies have not been strictly enforced.

Worldwide, women make up about 40 percent of the managerial ranks, but in Latin America, that number falls to 30 percent. In addition, there are significant gender gaps in pay and leadership positions, with some statistics showing a 17 percent pay differential[26] and a 1:17 female-to-male ratio in top leadership positions.[27] In Colombia and Venezuela, women make up 40 percent of the workforce or university student bodies, but earn roughly 40 percent less than men.[28] In addition to these barriers, women also must deal with the pressure to assume the traditional roles of wife, mother, and family caregiver—a challenge that many see as incompatible with a high-powered career. To make things worse, pregnancy-based sex discrimination often is an issue for women in lower socioeconomic groups. For example, companies that operate in free zones in the Dominican Republic routinely screen women for pregnancy, and the results are used in hiring and firing decisions. The fact that this practice is illegal—and prohibited by many international human rights treaties—has done very little to change actual practices.[29]

Despite these significant barriers, there are ways around these work-life dilemmas. Companies that are willing to hold difficult discussions and challenge traditional executive mindsets can find ways to resolve those challenges. Consider a Fortune 500 global engineering firm with a growing Latin American presence that wants to promote its female employees. The challenge: such promotions require relocation of these employees—many of whom are married with children—who resist or refuse the promotion due to the need to relocate.

The company assumed initially that women's reluctance to move was because of their husbands. But rather than going with that assumption, they tested it. Turns out that what was holding these women back was not primarily their husbands, but their obligation to their parents and parents-in-law—a twist on the traditional relocation challenge for companies and families. In response, the company considered the issue from a fresh perspective: What if relocation also included moving the women's parents? Companies could revisit the costs of relocation, since families throughout Latin America are decreasing in size from four to two children. Why not use that demographic reality to redefine the traditional family to include elderly parents? This win-win scenario would allow these women to maintain their caregiving roles while enabling companies to retain and advance top female talent.

Asia

While women make up 19 percent of US Fortune 500 board positions,[30] this number is only 11.1 percent in Hong Kong Hang Seng Index companies.[31] In 2015, about a third of all complaints to Hong Kong's Equal Opportunities Commission involved sexual discrimination, with about 80 percent being pregnancy-related.[32] This may have to do with stronger traditional values, including women's role in the family.

In Japan, a law was passed in 1986 to ensure equal opportunities for men and women, but it was not binding and faced fierce opposition from employers. The law was amended in 1999 to become binding, but many women still encounter strong discrimination because of Japan's rigid gender roles and the belief that women should retire upon marriage. Systems to enforce the law have not been put in place, and women find themselves relegated to clerical work or assisting their male counterparts. In 2014, Japanese women held only 10 percent of managerial positions[33] compared to 43 percent in the United States.[34] In addition, they receive lower salaries and fewer perks. As a result, more Japanese women are choosing to work for foreign companies where they encounter less discrimination.

To address this brain drain, Prime Minister Shinzō Abe has proposed some bold goals via legislative bills dubbed "womenomics" that require all public sector institutions and companies with more than 301 employees to develop concrete action plans to increase the representation and participation of women. To support working parents, Japan also will champion a number of key initiatives, including increasing the capacity of nursery schools and enhancing childcare leave policies.[35]

In 2015, at our Korn Ferry offices in Chicago, I hosted a Japanese delegation of 35 executives on a tour of the United States for the express purpose of gleaning best practices for the advancement of women. Though promising that the delegates were excited to begin initiating changes, I reluctantly informed them that change was not going to happen as fast as they would like, given the impact of so many legacy practices and attitudes that have held women back throughout the years.

Despite these ongoing challenges, today's young women in Asia, and particularly in China, are pressing to break out of their traditionally defined gender roles. I witnessed this phenomenon at a November 2011 forum on the advancement of women held in Shanghai, China, which was hosted by *Working Mother* magazine and Diversity Best Practices. Forum participants were women who are on the forefront of a social and economic revolution. These women are changing China's social and economic gender script. "It's our time to rise up to the fullness of our potential," a participant said. "It's what women have always wanted to do—our great grandmothers, our grandmothers, our mothers—but for the first time not only do we have the actual economic opportunity due to China's growth, but we also have the social opportunity due to China's opening up to the West."

These corporate and entrepreneurial women are sprinting to make up for lost time. They are devouring leadership development, women's conferences, mentorships, and sponsorships to find answers to questions their elders never faced. For them, work-life balance is one of their most pressing issues, and they apply the same tenacity to addressing it as they do toward corporate politics and opportunities. In the process, their power in intimate relationships with men is also changing. Asian women are assertively transforming their nation's economies and social structure.

The Middle East

Perhaps the greatest culture clash between traditional gender roles and the rising tide of female ambitions occurs in the Middle East. The Arab Spring focus on toppling oppressive dictators can't help but be accompanied by the rise of a new modern order that redefines the place of Arab women. Young men and women are seeking opportunities for education, economic advancement, and freedom of expression. The logical offspring of that movement is a secular fatwa—an Islamic religious ruling—against the oppression of women.

Westerners are often confused by the images displayed through the media from that part of the world. Veiled women demanding freedoms—not from wearing the veil, but to be licensed to drive, to attend school, and to be gainfully employed—creates a kind of cognitive dissonance for Western mindsets. Is this revolution political, economic, or social? In fact, it's all three. By willingly wearing their veils, many of these women say they are embracing their cultural identity, while sloughing off other oppressions and declaring their freedom of personhood and global citizenship.

In 2012, a fourteen-year-old girl from Pakistan, Malala Yousafzai, shook up the region when she was shot by the Taliban after she blogged in defiance to the group's prohibition to girls being educated. "Where in the Quran does it say that girls should not be educated? I have the right to play. I have the right to sing. I have the right to go to market. I have the right to speak up."[36]

Malala's brave words may have initiated a shift in the region's cultural landscape. As the Taliban looks to the future of Afghanistan and their role there as the United States winds down the war, they have hinted that they may grudgingly support Malala's point. This reluctance demonstrates two main points: that much work lies ahead on women's rights in the Middle East, and that beneath their veils, women are becoming increasingly assertive and beginning to swell their voices in the Arab uprisings.

Women's rights as human rights

As women make increasing demands for social freedoms, educational access, job opportunities, and control of their minds and bodies around the world, their calls represent nothing short of national and international security issues. As US Secretary of State from 2009 to early 2013, Hillary Clinton said, "What we are learning around the world is that if women are healthy and educated, their families will flourish.... If women have a chance to work and earn as full and equal partners in society, their families will flourish. And when families flourish, communities and nations will flourish."

Too many women and their communities and nations are not taking advantage of the female energy within their borders. Even in the female-friendly twenty-first century, women around the globe still are denied full human rights. Secretary Clinton made advocating a women's agenda one of her touchstones in every one of the dozens of countries she visited during her tenure. Whether she was in Burma, the Congo, Iraq, Afghanistan, China, India, or Haiti, Clinton talked about economic trade, terrorism threats, missile deployments, and, always, the advancement of women.

During her trips to these regions, Secretary Clinton was bolstered in these discussions by cold enduring facts. The lack of full human rights for women has economic consequences. Though women perform 66 percent of the world's work and produce 50 percent of the food, they earn 10 percent of the income and own 1 percent of the property.[37] The best investment for the developing world is educating girls. Educating girls yields a higher rate of return than any other investment—social or economic. Socially, educating girls leads to a host of positive results, from delayed marriage and childbearing to healthier pregnancies, families, and decreased infant mortality rates. Economically, giving girls access to education increases their future earnings from 10 to 25 percent. Just as in the developed world, educated mothers tend to ensure that their daughters attend school, which boosts their life circumstances and leads to these girls pushing their own daughters into better life situations as well.

Secretary Clinton punctuates her messages to world leaders this way: "Human rights are women's rights, and women's rights are human rights." These rights, which men take for granted, extend from the geopolitical realm to the shop floor, cubicle farm, and the executive suite.

A woman's place...

...is in leadership and valuable jobs contributing valuable work. From the onset of women's migration into the workforce, they've been transforming it in several stages, or waves. The first wave could be called *accommodation*—it resulted in anti-sexual harassment policies, childcare, family leave, and flex time. The next phase is about *empowerment*. The voices from focus groups, surveys, statistics, speeches, and writings can be summarized this way: "Either we're more empowered within the corporation's structures or we'll channel our empowerment into running our own businesses."

We must also consider the marketplace impact of women executives leading organizations whose products cater specifically to women. "What we have seen is the evolution of the value of women," *Working Mother* magazine's former CEO Carol Evans observed. "In the past, companies like Avon or Procter & Gamble had men in most executive and management roles, even though more than 80 percent of their customers were women. Leaders like A. G. Lafley of P&G and Jim Preston of Avon changed that equation, bringing women into all levels of leadership. Companies with predominantly female customers have often been in the forefront of the advancement of career women. Today, Avon and Xerox have had two back-to-back female CEOs— at Avon, Andrea Jung and Sheri McCoy, and at Xerox, Anne Mulcahy and Ursula Burns. Procter & Gamble has had a powerful cadre of women general managers and presidents. All three of these companies have been named to the NAFE list of Top 50 Companies for Executive Women many times.

Still, companies need to make transformational changes to attract, develop, and retain female talent in order to break the glass ceiling. Managing consulting firm Deloitte stands tall as one of the pioneers in moving beyond best practices that were only achieving gradual change. Through the leadership of Cathy Benko, Vice Chairman and Chief Talent Officer and Anne Weisberg, Director of Talent Organization at the time, the company changed many of its practices and ways. As a result, their representation of women partners climbed from 10 percent in 1997 to 18 percent in 2010. And in 2015, Deloitte was the first of the Big 4 firms to name a female CEO.[38]

Despite advancements, companies still need to make transformational changes to attract, develop, and retain female talent in order to break the glass ceiling. PepsiCo, a multinational company with over 270,000 employees and led by Indra Nooyi, one of the most powerful women in business, recognized that to capitalize fully on top talent, it needed to implement a strategic initiative that focused on women of color. Women of color experienced significantly lower job satisfaction with higher "intention to leave," slower time to promotion, and lower trust scores. To address this, with the help of Korn Ferry, PepsiCo implemented a key initiative, Women of Color Multicultural Alliance—a strategic initiative that focused on attracting, retaining, and developing women of color in middle and senior management ranks. The Alliance's impact was significant—there was a 75 percent increase in advancement for women of color and a 100 percent reduction in attrition among program participants. For more on this effort, see the sidebar below, "PepsiCo case study: Women of Color Multicultural Alliance."

PepsiCo case study: Women of Color Multicultural Alliance

Do innovative programs truly bring about change? If done right, they sure do.

Korn Ferry partnered with client PepsiCo to improve the morale, engagement, and retention of women of color. First we will discuss the outcomes, and then how we got there:

- 75 percent increase in advancement for women of color; representation of women of color rose from 4 to 6.8 percent at the Senior Manager/Director/VP level in two years; accelerated time to promotion by six to ten months.

- 100 percent reduction in attrition among participants; decline in turnover from 42 percent to less than 2 percent in three years; average onboarding time for new reporting relationships decreased 25 to 40 percent.

- Turnover for women of color who participated in the program was one-half the rate of those who had not.

- Significantly higher ratings on organizational health survey among women of color.

- External recognition: PepsiCo won the 2007 Catalyst Award.

What was the program that led to such strong outcomes? It was PepsiCo's award-winning initiative, the Women of Color Multicultural Alliance, a business imperative focused on the attraction, retention, and development of women of color in middle and senior management ranks. Major Alliance activities and components included a national leadership development conference, regional networking events, and robust career development tools and resources.

But the heart of it was Power Pairs®, a program developed in partnership with Korn Ferry that built authentic relationships and advancement opportunities for women of color through facilitated dialogues with immediate and skip-level managers. The objectives were to build personal and professional networks; help participants better understand others' work styles, professional interests, and career goals; and foster more authentic and honest relationships.

Conversations conveyed mutual expectations, identified gaps, and helped participants collaboratively develop action plans for working together more effectively. Power Pairs® at PepsiCo helped bridge the many gulfs between managers and women of color, including those between gender and race. This rare quality time spent with managers gave participants the chance to voice their career plans and goals while receiving direct feedback.

All of this deliberate, ongoing dialogue, built on a foundation of trust and understanding, yielded breakthrough results. In effect, the glass ceiling can be broken, but it can't be left to chance. It requires focused effort.

Source: Korn Ferry Institute Proofpoint, October 22, 2014 [39]

Advancement of Women virtual roundtable with Korn Ferry thought leaders on gender

At Korn Ferry, we have an Advancement of Women Worldwide set of solutions driven by vastly experienced consultants and thought leaders in this area. The following sidebars by four deep experts in this topic address various dimensions that often get overlooked or are misunderstood in what it takes to address the advancement of women.

••

The common pitfalls

By Peggy Hazard, Korn Ferry Managing Principal, Co-Lead Advancing Women Worldwide

Here are four key pitfalls I see organizations often fall into when it comes to implementing strategies and programs for the advancement of women:

Wrong focus. Most organizations focus on and measure only representation of women. But just having "more women" is not in and of itself a business case. In fact, without addressing the "how"— using inclusion skills to value, manage, and leverage differences—just having more diversity can lead to lower performance and resentment. There is lack of understanding of what it will really take.

Ready. Fire. Aim. Many organizations begin their women's initiatives by implementing activities targeted at women (events, groups, broad training) before they pinpoint the real issues that impede women's performance and advancement and prioritize the levers that will drive the change.

False expectations. Most efforts are designed to assimilate women to the male norm, to 'lean into' the system that favors masculine life patterns and styles. This may work for some, but it is unlikely to work for the majority of women.

It's all about the women. Shared responsibility is essential to moving the needle. It is the responsibility of top leaders and every manager to work to bring out the very best in each individual and team, and that includes acknowledging and leveraging differences and removing diversity-related headwinds to optimize the full range of talent— women, generations, international teams, etc.

Overlooking the power of networks

*By Wendy Beecham, Korn Ferry Managing Principal and former
CEO of Watermark, an organization for senior women leaders in the
San Francisco Bay Area*

It has been thoroughly documented that the three key areas affecting the potential for women to advance in the workforce include:

- Access to experiences that will develop the strategic and financial skills and influential reputation at higher levels of the organization.

- The lack of access to the networks that support women being invited to these experiences.

- The unconscious bias that exists at all levels and held by both genders.[40]

I'd like to focus on the area of developing networks. There have been documented differences in the way women and men connect to pillars of influence both within and outside their organizations. Korn Ferry's research on the Four Stages® of Contribution that describes the expectations of how one's contributions change over time shows that many women get stuck in the Independent Contributor Stage 2 and become unable to transition to the Leveraged Contributor Stage 3.

Why is this? Turns out that the very skills required to succeed at Stage 2 can get in the way of succeeding at Stage 3. And there are documented gendered differences in how women and men navigate the challenges. As they are making their way in a Stage 2 role, more women than men are very focused on getting things done on their own and believe their competence will speak for itself, leading to them being tapped for their next promotion. And they wait and they wait.

What more men than women do at this transition point is to focus not on being heads-down "doing," but on spending more time strategically influencing.

In my many years or observing and coaching women in the workplace, I've noticed a classic example of gender differences when it comes to preparing for a major presentation that involves getting a major project improved: Many women tend to focus on gathering as much data to support their case as possible and making the best presentation they can to ensure they are representing themselves well. In the meantime, many of the men tend to spend time meeting with key stakeholders to pre-sell their idea and remove any barriers to success before the meeting. And this is what leads to better win rates for their ideas.

Women need to be aware of these dynamics and make different choices. And their organizations need to be vigilant of how the lack of awareness on the part of male leaders and managers is perpetuating the existence of the glass ceiling.

Rethink career progressions

By Audra Bohannon, Korn Ferry Senior Partner, Co-Lead Advancing Women Worldwide

The work offered can often be more tactical and not strategic and tied to key business outcomes.

At the same time, organizations seem stuck in figuring out how to optimize effectively the contributions of a major part of the workforce currently being underutilized—a conundrum indeed. Given that the world of work is so different today, the way organizations approach career progression needs to be different too. Organizations that understand the need to embrace the differences associated with a diverse workforce are unleashing creative and innovative ways to build cultures of inclusion, and therefore high engagement. Here are a few effective approaches:

Rethink what success looks like. Today, the time horizon is way too short in assessing success. Companies need a more expansive approach that is inclusive to women at different stages of their career journey, which can—without mixed messages—take into account the real life choices many women face as they seek to integrate their professional and personal goals and needs. This in turn should trigger a rethinking of an alternative career path that is more of a zigzag than a ladder and that has cadences that alternate between fast and measured. With many organizations becoming more matrixed, it has become important for companies to create opportunities for all employees to offer high value and contribution. For some, it may mean an aggressive career track to the highest levels of organizations; for others, it could mean engaging in challenging and meaningful work that is rewarding and contributes to the business objectives.

Women are mentored and sponsored. Yes, women who are mentored on the unspoken rules of how to succeed do benefit from these insights. But without active sponsorship—a leader who actively advocates for and creates opportunities for up-and-coming female talent—they will not be able to perform. For example, women need more than just "more work." Women need to receive VIC assignments (visible, important, and complex). These VIC assignments are most often doled out in an arbitrary way that tends to benefit the same type of talent—mostly white and male.

Leaders and managers are equipped to understand gender differences. There are many reasons why the experiences of women and men in the workplace and society are different. While clearly women succeed in every walk of life, there are many more who would be even more successful if more managers appreciated their differences and used more effective ways to value the unique perspectives they bring to the workplace. They should also value the particular challenges women face.

· ·

Stop trying to make women more like men

By Leslie Little, former Korn Ferry Senior Partner, specialized in delivering transformational change for CEOs and top executive teams

Women are not problems to be solved. Yet when you scratch below the surface at the various approaches many companies are taking to help advance women, it sure looks like they are attempts to assimilate women into the white male workplace. "Lean in—to the white, male hierarchical system," women are told.

The result is that the needle has not moved much for women, and indeed, in many areas we are regressing. "Fixing" the women to create a one-size-fits-all leadership model is completely counter to why we need diversity in the first place.

Women will never be like men, nor should we want them to be. We need to reframe our thinking to design cultures and leadership behaviors that capture the diverse and value-additive points of view women bring into the decision-making process and into corporate leadership.

The corporate white male cultural definition of success is highly driven by competition, aggression, and an overreliance on independence.

Those with the most aggressive behavior climb the ladder to the top where the prize of the most money sits. Those with the most money individually "win" at this game of corporate life.

The underlying mindset in this mad dash and siloed focus on financial success at all costs is a win-lose zero-sum game that fails to take into consideration the many interdependencies with which all teams operate. This zero-sum game is exactly why so many women have chosen to opt out of corporate cultures.

We need a mindset shift to redefine the cultural norms and, in this, shift our definitions of leadership and success away from win-lose competition to win-win collaborative, team problem solving—something cognitive science has proven women excel at.

This win-win approach fosters the collaboration, agility, and innovation—and the subsequent growth—companies so desperately need. Instead of trying to fix women to fit in, organizations need to value women as drivers of new ideas and innovation, and to let them do what they already know how to do best.

• •

It's not only women who stand to gain if corporations heed this call. Communities, men, and children will benefit as well. If corporations can unleash women's power, they'll unleash greater corporate profits. In addition, men need to acknowledge how men have benefited from women taking a stand on work-life balance. Because women took the heat, it's become more acceptable for men to take time off to watch their daughter's soccer game or visit their son's classroom. Thanks to women campaigning for family-friendly benefits, working men are spending a great deal more time with their children than their fathers did. So fathers and their children are benefiting as well. Whether seeing Mom work, seeing home life valued more, or just seeing more of Dad, today's generation of children has stronger role models of holistic success.

Before corporate leaders can rethink current practices and assumptions, before they can take advantage of the unprecedented opportunity in front of them, before they can truly open up women's place in leadership, they will have to acknowledge the very real and sometimes uncomfortable differences women bring to the workplace—differences that go beyond biology, but that could form some of the basis for women's alternative perspectives on goals, behaviors, and motivations. Corporate leaders may have to encourage some culture-altering discussions about defining and meeting organizational needs. In other words, they will have to learn how to recognize these differences and act on them.

While at Hewitt, Linda Mateja saw additional advantages to creating greater inclusion for women managers and leaders. "In light of the economy and emerging labor retention strategies, this may be a labor force where the cost management strategies of reduced and flexible hours, sabbaticals, job shares, etc., may actually lead to win-win results for both employees and companies. This could have the outcome of retaining a broader pool of labor into the future that may be seeking freedom to more flexibly manage their time plus be more open to trade-offs for flexibility (for example, modified pay for more flexible hours, working fewer hours to help balance the corporate budget and provide work-life balance, etc.). Taking these approaches now may be key in bringing many back to the same company as the economy turns up as a payoff for having done relationship-building with their female talent."

In the Obama Era, more opportunities for women opened up as women have started demanding more for themselves and greater recognition for their contributions—not just as working mothers and care providers at home, but also as leaders in the competitive world of business and in the political arena. The 2012 elections swept a groundbreaking historic number of women into national office, with 20 in the Senate and more than 75 elected to the House. New Hampshire—with its all-female delegation—stands as a testament to the growing recognition of the issues women face and their willingness to flex their growing political clout with their votes.[41]

President Obama was vocal about the need to help women break through that glass ceiling and celebrating their contributions. In his white paper on working women cited at the beginning of this chapter, Obama wrote, "We have a chance to move America in a fundamentally different direction, and that starts with empowering women and strengthening families."[42] (More on what has happened since in Chapter 15, "Work-life flexibility: The Mother of all battles.")

Corporate authenticity, connection, contribution, and flexibility—these attributes are what many female leaders want in the workplace. Such components will be key to creating the conditions that will lead to the greater advancement of women. For too long, contribution has come at the expense of authenticity. But no more.

Women are asking pointed questions like, "Why are the traits that have gotten me to a certain point in my career now the very things that are preventing me from advancing?" And they're saying, loud and clear, through both words and deeds, "I refuse to compromise who I am for preconceived notions of what I should be. Accept me as I am or I'll walk out the door." ♀

SUMMARY POINTS

- Women have revolutionized the workplace by their presence and perspective, skills, and demands. Yet, for the most part, their contributions have not resulted in representation at the highest levels of organizations.

- Since well-executed strategies for moving women into leadership roles have proven inadequate for the task, we must move beyond best practices by adopting new paradigms to shatter the glass ceiling.

- Organizations need archetypal female characteristics and gender differences. Others—including men, communities, and societies—have benefited from women's efforts to make the workplace adapt to their needs.

- Multinational organizations are one of the most significant change agents on the planet.

- The Obama Era coincided with a female-friendly twenty-first century that needs more of the core skills and competencies that women have.

- As synthesized by Hillary Clinton, "Women's rights are human rights, and human rights are women's rights."

- Workplace flexibility benefits companies. It enables women, men, and their families to meet their responsibilities at home and at work.

SHAPING YOUR STRATEGY

- What is the actual representation of women at the executive and senior management ranks in your organization? How will you assess the pipeline of female talent to feed these roles? How much resistance do you think you'll encounter in trying to go beyond best practices in addressing some of these structural barriers to the full advancement of women?

- What can women do to increase their visibility and opportunities for advancement?

- What can men do to increase women's visibility and opportunities for advancement?

- How can you move beyond best practices to rethink:
  - what strong leadership and strong management look like.
  - the value of tenure.
  - compensation models.
  - whether competencies developed elsewhere are transferable to the workplace.
  - how unspoken rules about alternative work arrangements may be detrimental to women's advancement and their full inclusion into organizational life.

Chapter 9

The Millennials: Why this generation is challenging the workplace like no other

We are not ready for our children to go to work.

I don't mean this in a protective sense, but rather in a "my-God-what-have-we-here" sense, as the children of Boomers—the Millennials—are becoming half of the workforce and starting to move into positions of leadership. In some fundamental ways, their worldviews and those of the older generations before them are in creative tension with one another in ways that have been disrupting the status quo for talent management.

Unlike the Boomer flower children, the iPod kids are not about the counterculture. They *are* the culture. It is our workplaces that are out of sync with the new 24/7, global, plugged-in, downloaded, computer-interfaced rhythms of the digital society.

A few years ago, as I watched my then 16-year-old do her homework, I realized the future was already here. Here's what my blog entry then captured: "She taps away on her wireless laptop, linking to assignments from the teacher's website. Researching on Google, she copies and pastes quotes and stats into Word. 'Yes,' I think approvingly, 'this is what the wise use of technology should look like.' But, of course, there's more. She's got six IM chats open. A couple, thankfully, are about the homework and an upcoming dance recital. But others are about weekend plans, a hot movie, a cute boy. It's all topped off by a flaming session among the girls. At the same time, she's updating her profile on Facebook, downloading music, burning CDs—*and* talking on the phone.

"Marisela, are you doing your work?" I ask with that father-knows-best tone.

"Yes, Papi, don't worry."

"But what is the *quality* of that work?" I continue with furrowed brow.

"Papi, don't worry. It'll be fine."

And sure enough, it is, as that quintessential scorecard, the report card, shows.

I can just see her and her classmates at their first job. They're outside catching some rays, using their high-definition wireless laptops that they've slipped out of their purses. They're shaping a client report while planning their service vacation to Costa Rica, doing their holiday shopping, updating their résumé on Jobs.com, and catching up on the latest outrage on YouTube—always with ever-present, instant communication with coworkers, family, and friends around the world to the beat of background music by their favorite artists.

Sure enough, the judgments about this generation are flying:

"Not serious about hard work."

"Distracted."

"Self-centered."

"Not interested in learning from how things were done in the past."

"Don't want to pay their dues."

"They spend too much time online."

"They want to be CEO in just five years."

And so on.

As a diversity leader, I know that a telltale sign of inclusion breakdown is when judgments pop up unchallenged and groupthink sets in about newcomers. When others' behaviors are different from those we are accustomed to, we assume these people are incompetent or bad. We are seeing this attitude now in reaction to Millennials, and we will likely see it with members of Generation Z. As in other forms of diversity, this kind of stance is not just exclusionary, it's also unhelpful in addressing the real issues.

Generational diversity has become just as much an issue as gender and racial diversity. In fact, along with gender, it has become the most common diversity topic globally. We must seek to resolve this divide—not only in order to nurture inclusive environments that enhance corporate culture and optimize results, but also to adapt our workforce to the Millennials' way of doing things. Just by nature of who they are, this generation will transform the workplace. Already they're transforming the US political landscape: the 25-and-under generation voted in very large numbers, making them a key factor in Obama's 2008 election.[1] Not only did they vote in large numbers for Obama (giving him a 34 percentage point advantage in 2008 and 23 percentage points in 2012), they also had an impact on nearly every social issue—women's equality, LGBT rights, immigration, the environment, role of government—and they voted overwhelmingly in opposition to the older Boomer generation.[2] More than just one-hit wonders, both the 2008 and 2012 elections illustrated the stark contrast of the generational divide between this generation and the Baby Boomers. But it wasn't just their values and idealism: Gen Y's technological savvy allowed them to build a digital grassroots movement that advocated their beliefs. This group has significantly shaped the Obama Era. And their impact is felt not only in the United States but also around the globe. Their effect on the global landscape will only increase as more Millennials become supervisors, managers, and leaders.

Just as today's world is virtual, round-the-clock, global, diverse, networked, and digital, so are Millennials. Their generation and the Obama Era have been one and the same. For them, the upside-down world is right-side-up because it's what they grew up with. As candidate and president, in both the 2008 and 2012 elections, Obama fully tapped into Millennials' energy and worldview—through his strategies and polices and his operational plan that heavily utilized Web 2.0 social networking. Obama even inserted Millennial slang into his political observations when he referred to one of his opponent's positions as "sketchy" and offered interviews on social media—including comedian Marc Maron on podcast "WTF," YouTube personalities GloZell, Bethany Mota and Hank Green, an online sit-down with comedian Zach Galifianakis on *Between Two Ferns*,[3] and seven appearances on that most trusted of news shows among Millennials, Jon Stewart's *The Daily Show*.

Obama's social contract with Millennials helped mobilize the most effective and far-reaching presidential election grassroots effort, hitting record numbers of volunteers, donations, calls made, and doors knocked on.

Culturally, this is not just an election phenomenon. It is a way of life. What we saw in terms of bottom-up mobilization and the ability to influence a major outcome is indicative of the kind of transformation Millennials will have on the workplace and the workforce.

Who are the Millennials?

Not only is there a lack of agreement on what they should be called (Millennials, Generation Y, Nexters, and Un-Baby Boomers, to name but a few), but there are also discrepancies as to the actual size of the population and the birth years that categorize them.

Is it 1978–1995, 1981–1993, or 1980–2000? Depending on the date ranges, the cohort number ranges from 70 to 80 million. Either way, they are anywhere from their late teens to early thirties. Regardless of the exact dates and ages, this is a very large group. In the United States, it is just as large as the Boomers and slightly larger than Xers (75 million vs. 66 million).[4]

The life events that have shaped this generation include 9/11, Oklahoma City, Columbine, global warming, AIDS, Katrina, Enron, the Iraq War, ISIS, globalization, the digital revolution, a wildly fluctuating stock market, the rise of India and China, and an overall decline in the United States' stature. In the workplace, the Millennials have come of age in an era when job tenure is not a given due to layoffs driven by constant restructuring due to globalization, mergers and acquisitions, the pressure of quarterly earnings, and hyper-competition. Millennials have responded in kind by eschewing loyalty for job-hopping at an average of every two to three years.

These headlines of death, destruction, and increased competition make Millennials very present about today, intent on enjoying every moment. They are a pragmatic bunch; they know their work arrangements are transactional and they must be prepared to move on when the situation no longer works for them—or their employer. In addition, they are more socially and environmentally conscious. Given the uncertainty both in the workplace and in the world, many Millennials place friends, family, and community ahead of work.

A special relationship with parents

Many Millennials grew up in hectic, dual-career households that tended to be more child-centric, with both mothers and fathers heavily involved with the kids. The relationship between Millennials and their parents is unprecedented: according to research compiled by Tamara Erickson, former president of the Concours Institute, 90 percent of Millennials report being very close to their parents. Compare that to 40 percent of Boomers who said back in the 1970s they would be better off *without* their parents! Millennials see their parents as role models, which translates into them trusting authority (parents 86 percent, teachers 86 percent, police 83 percent). With this closeness, many have become equal partners in family decisions, such as where to go on vacation or where to make major purchases like the new flat-screen TV, hybrid car, or dog.[5] Working Mother Media's former CEO Carol Evans said, "We Boomers rebelled against our parents. Now, as parents ourselves, we have vowed not to let social change become a barrier between us and our children."[6]

Millennial children are reciprocating by reaching out to their parents for help with their own major decisions. Parents get extremely involved in college applications and even in their child's job searches, earning the moniker of "helicopter parents" for overprotectiveness. Nevertheless, Millennials expect to stay close. To the chagrin of many parents, they often move back home after college. Marrying later and being saddled with debt make living at home more appealing to Millennials, as they struggle to pay down both credit cards and tuition. As of 2013, about 70 percent of graduates left college with an average of $28,000 in debt.[7]

Diverse and global

Millennials are highly diverse. Forty-two percent report being racial or ethnic minorities—around twice the share of the Baby Boomer generation when they were the same age.[8] For Millennial women, college is not just an option, it's an expectation. So, too, are they expected to compete equally with men for jobs. And homosexuality is not a big deal for Millennials—regardless of their political party affiliation. Not only are teens more comfortable coming out, most find they're accepted by their peers. My daughter, for example, assuaged my boy wariness by telling me of certain guys, "Don't worry, Papi; he's *gay*!"

Among my daughter's peers, global experience is common. Marisela spent six months in Lima, Peru, during her high school sophomore year, and her friend Rebecca spent a summer with her Argentinean relatives in Buenos Aires. Anna went on a multi-week service trip to Ecuador. Paulina traveled with her grandma to the Czech Republic and participated in a ceremony in which she carried a Holocaust Torah back to its original synagogue.

Our kids' global network extends through their digital network. Text messages fly between a café in Miraflores, Peru, and our car, as we drive along I-80 on our way to visit relatives in Kansas. Webcam chats not only allow for keeping in touch, but also for introducing friends to one another. Skype calls simultaneously connect family and friends in Guadalajara, Simi Valley, Miami, Chicago, San Diego, and Lima.

Millennials are emerging as the first truly global generational cohort. Globalization supported by technology means a shared experience through world events like the rise of global terrorism, the acceleration of global warning, and the hyperlinking of the global economy. Meanwhile, the latest technology—such as iTunes and smartphones—has played a role in shaping Millennials' worldviews and how they think, play, and work.

How Millennials are challenging the workplace

The identities and personalities of Millennials affect what they're looking for in an employer. It's fair to say that Millennials have different expectations, priorities, and career ambitions than previous generations. A 2015 Allstate/ National Journal Heartland Monitor poll[9] found a difference in respondents who were labeled as members of the Millennial generation vs. the Boomer generation. When asked what their primary concern was during their first job, about 64 percent of Boomers talked about making as much money as possible or learning new skills. When asked the same question, Millennials were much more likely to say that their top priority was doing something that they found enjoyable or making a difference in society, with 57 percent choosing one of these options.

For organizations that traditionally attract and/or rely on a younger workforce, getting it right with Millennials is a matter of economic life and death.

Millennials are already challenging the workplace in many ways:

They challenge the tenure paradigm. Experience and knowledge are no longer correlated with age, they argue, as they show up, globally traveled, socially networked, and multi-tasked while carrying their iPads and smartphones. For the older generation, this is not just about being current on what kids are up to nowadays, but about the very competencies and technical skills demanded by today's marketplace. Which begs the question: Who is better equipped?

They challenge best practices mentality. Globalization and the technology that enables it have been paradigm-busters that are not yet finished in changing the rules of the game. The power of Millennials rides on the speed at which knowledge doubles. What used to take centuries now takes months. The Boomer approach of "Let me show you how best practices forged over time" is doomed to obsolescence, simply because those practices worked in the past—and the past is now defined as recently as the previous season of *Modern Family*. Millennials operate in a just-in-time mode in which a "best practice" lasts only as long as the project.

They challenge traditional planning. Millennials live synchronous lives where inputs come from all over at all times and decisions are made accordingly. They coordinate; they don't plan. In a multitasking, hyper-connected, 24/7 world, *plans* don't hold up. I watched my daughter and friends coordinate where to meet on a Saturday night. When I was growing up it was, "Meet you at 7 p.m. in front of the bakery next to the movie theater. I'll wait for you for 15 minutes. If we don't meet up, then plan B is..." For her, it's:

"See you around 7 p.m. downtown."

And then, at around 7 o'clock, "I'm downtown—where are you?"

"Walking up the side street with the crazy mannequins."

"Okay, I'll start walking there. Call me when you get to the fountain."

Moments later, "Hey, we just ran into Ricardo before we got to the fountain. We are now by the ice cream place, meet us there..."

This is how they're going to manage their projects in the workplace. Are you ready?

They challenge directions. They want to be empowered: "Give us a problem to be solved and the right tools," they say, "and we'll figure it out." Paradoxically—and this may be due to better relationships with parents—they want to be coached and mentored when needed. They want to be both autonomous and connected at the same time. Command-and-control management is out. Coaching and collaborative management are in.

They challenge rigidity in time, space, job, and career. "Where and when we work should not matter, as long as the work gets done," they declare. "Connecting, even thousands of miles away, is as easy as connecting face-to-face. In fact, it's even better because we can all be in more places at once. Who I am, what I do, and the jobs and careers around me need to evolve iteratively and continuously, like software version releases." How will MyJob 1.0 evolve into MyJob 2.0? 5.3? 7.9?

They challenge traditional recruiting strategies. This younger generation comes through the door more restless than ever. They want to be valued, put to work, rewarded, and affirmed from the get-go.

A 2015 Korn Ferry executive study asked Millennials what matters most, and the greatest number of respondents (23 percent) said it was "the ability to make an impact on the business," followed by "a clear path for advancement" (20 percent) and "development and ongoing feedback" (16 percent).

Income came in at fourth place at 13 percent. When questioning what makes Millennials choose one job over another, more than a third (38 percent) said "visibility and buy-in to the vision of the organization" while 28 percent said "a clear path for advancement." "Job title and pay" came in third place at 18 percent. "This research demonstrates the changing priorities of today's young workforce. Where traditionally we might have expected salary to be the number one differentiator for talent choosing their next employer, Millennials are now placing greater value on understanding for the company's mission and how, as employees, they can play a role in growing the organization into a better, stronger brand," said Trish Healy, Futurestep Vice President of RPO Operations in North America. "As part of the recruiting and onboarding process, organizations need to clearly communicate the paths for advancement and create ongoing dialogue about development opportunities."[10]

How corporations can prepare and change

Given these urgent challenges, current corporate philosophies, practices, and policies will not suffice when it comes to attracting, engaging, and retaining this generation. Gen Y will challenge the workforce like no other. Current people practices were designed during a very different era, and much of what compromises reality presently did not exist when today's people practices were designed. Benefits, performance management systems, and corporate cultures were designed to solve a different set of needs and problems for a very different workforce.

Corporations need to start making some fundamental changes.

However, when making these changes, corporations must never lose sight of the contributions of the Boomers and Gen Xers. If the concerns of these older generations are not validated and addressed, corporations run the risk of alienating them, which could lead to disharmony and a lack of willingness to work constructively with the incoming flux of Millennials. Millennials, in turn, must be open to the ideas of their predecessors and willing to work with them accordingly.

Boomers tend to approach their work like an assembly line approach, handling a specific task or project sequentially, perfecting each piece as it goes along and then only adding to it once each module is in tip-top form. To a Boomer, quality is a product of several sequential pieces that is not to be shared with anyone—let alone managers—until the very end. Given their familiarity with the World Wide Web, Millennials don't work sequentially, but rather synchronously. To a Millennial, quality is iterative. They demand feedback on each piece along the way; a little bit of encouragement so they know they're on the right path rather than waiting till the end to be told that more needs to be done.

If they're willing to listen, Boomers can greatly benefit from Millennials' technological prowess. But, in turn, Millennials can also learn from the experiences Boomers have acquired over the years.

While much has been written about the potential conflicts between Boomers and Millennials, little has been said about what Gen Xers can do to bridge this disparity or what all three generations can learn from each other. Given their close proximity in age to the Millennials, Gen Xers are in a unique position to gain their trust and serve as mediators in this discussion. Gen Xers came of age during the rise of the post-modern world that has been the Millennials' only experience. Thus, they exist at the crossroads between the traditional "This is the right way to go about doing things because this is how it's always been done" viewpoint of the Boomer and the more task-oriented "Give me feedback now," multitasking, technologically savvy approach of the Millennial.

Millennials bring much energy and idealism to the corporate environment. However, they mustn't mistake their technical competence for experience. Indeed, their greatest weakness *is* their lack of experience. But what perhaps makes them even more vulnerable is their reliance on multitasking. They pride themselves on their ability to work on different projects simultaneously, but in doing so, they run the risk of not delving as deeply or completely into a project as may be required. In addition, a growing number of research studies show that our brains really can't handle true simultaneous multitasking, as evidenced by the high number of accidents due to texting and driving. They also show that our productivity may actually go down.[11]

Each generation needs to listen to and respect the differing perspectives and experiences each brings to the table. If Boomers learn to appreciate that Millennials' contributions can benefit them and vice versa, then the overall effectiveness and output of an organization can increase tenfold: a win-win situation for everyone, regardless of age or work experience.

Let's take a look at some of these win-win benefits.

Create designer benefits, jobs, careers

Millennials don't understand *standard*. All their lives, they've been able to design everything—from travel experiences (extreme mountain biking in the Andes during the day, white tablecloth dinner at night) to tennis shoes (color, shapes, favorite saying stamped on the heel) to musical setlists (Shakira, Tony Bennett, Lady Gaga, Snoop Dogg, all on one custom-burned CD).

This is fueled by three trends: technology, rapid change, and diversity. *Technology* enables a cost-effective way to customize products and services. *Rapid change* makes yesterday's standard antiquated. *Diversity* generates demand for multiple types of solutions—not only from the perspective of race/ethnicity, gender, and nationality, but also in terms of personality, thinking styles, and even hobbies. MySpace, MyYahoo, MyObama were only the beginning. Now we have MyJob, MyCareer, MyBenefits. In this universe, time and place are not fixed. They bend, flex, blur into different dimensions that dislocate fixed structures.

Designer benefits

Much like the Millennials busted up the paradigm that an artist or producer determines the music setlist through a mass-produced CD, they are pushing back against corporations that seek to determine their "setlist" of benefits. What would be value-added for the programmer, financial analyst, or communicator who also happens to be a marathon runner, social services volunteer, or community thespian? To provide value to Millennials, benefits must address the needs of a culturally, racially/ethnically diverse generation that is virtual, autonomous, empowered, and continually digitally connected as well as a generation that possesses a variety of worldviews regarding money, health, and success.[12]

Fixed benefits plans (even those with limited flexibility provided by "cafeteria-style" design that allows for some choices) will not be able to withstand these pressures and demands. Corporations must give up trying to figure out what's best for their employees within the fixed categories of health, wealth, and paid time off. Indeed, they would do well to emulate the new iTunes paradigm, which shattered the model of buying fixed setlists and reduced music purchasing to the basic unit of a song.

"Give us a budget and diverse options and we will decide what best enables our multifaceted lives," Millennials are saying. Think of the possibilities. Instead of a free physical, the 20-something may opt to take credits for solar-powering their homes or buying a hybrid car. Others may prefer to subscribe to short-term paid sabbaticals every six months. Still others may take a $500 credit at a camping retailer to fund their adventure travel or a paid community service day twice a month.

Corporations still have fiduciary responsibility, of course. Companies may want to require that at least 20 percent of employees' MyBenefits goes to catastrophic health insurance. Or, they might employ automatic enrollment in their 401(k) plans, and then leave it up to employees to opt out if they wish.

Organizations must pay close attention to the interface necessary to enable these options. Content is important, but for Millennials, the interface is everything. If it doesn't sing, they will abandon it. The iTunes $1.29-per-song paradigm is brilliant, but it's the clean, attractive, easy-to-use interface that enables the revolution. As people make more and more complex decisions, Millennials will value smart-decision support tools, particularly when they're offered in the spirit of coaching and mentoring.

When I was at Hewitt, we began to move in this direction via a benefits delivery interface called People Like Me™. It provides decision support about choices that may work best for individual users by providing example stories of people in similar circumstances with comparable backgrounds.

Designer jobs and careers

The job is dead!

Long live the job!

Jobs that look the same day after day, fixed in their definitions of roles and responsibilities, must go.

For Millennials, the job experience must match the fast-moving, connected, iterative world in which they live. In fact, project-based work may better suit their restlessness. Millennials seek employers who have designed jobs to be broken into pieces or modules that can be easily manipulated into non-standard work arrangements. What's more, they expect to choose whom they work with across functions, geographies, and organizations.

Consider the type of job Leah Campbell, a colleague's college-aged daughter, looked for. At Wesleyan University, she created her own major, *Embodiment Studies*. In order to understand interpersonal and intercultural dynamics, she explored "how people move through the sociophysical environment, between individuals and among groups, in ways that distinguish, excite, blur, and uphold their conceptions of self-identity." Her course work included cultural studies, dance, architecture, psychology, philosophy, and anthropology.[13] Surely she, and many of her peers, have carried this drive for self-expression and meaningful relational thinking into their job expectations.

Organizations must create a process *and* interface for making individuals aware of available projects for which they can compete. Granted, job candidates will need to meet criteria for competencies and technical skills. But rather than living in a fixed job description, their competencies will be seen as portable from project to project. Clearly, some jobs are more conducive to this portability than others. But organizations must be careful not to get stuck in assumptions about what may or may not work.

These designer jobs should be shaped to offer meaning, as Millennials pursue a portfolio of diverse concerns: career, family, planet. In their commitment to a greener, safer, more progressive world, Millennials desire employers who share their philosophy of balancing hard work with having fun and giving back. This is not just about flexibility to take time off and pursue interests outside of work. It's about finding ways for the work itself to be more meaningful.

This flexibility can come in two different flavors: jobs that are advertised as contributing something tangible for the betterment of the world (developing medical devices for improving quality of life or green solutions that improve the environment) and jobs in which the core skills and competencies can be devoted to improving humanity. Give engineers a percentage of time during which they can work on pro bono side projects, for example.

But how does one fund such programs? In focus groups I've conducted, Millennials have indicated they're willing to make trade-offs, such as a reduction in pay, in order to live their values.

Designer jobs, of course, take us to designer careers for many of the same reasons. Wanting to save the planet, conquer Machu Picchu, or just do something different will take Millennials on what could seem like circuitous career paths. Corporations will not only have to offer greater flexibility for them to do this, but also not view these pursuits as detours but as opportunities for developing leadership skills and job competencies. And beware: Millennials are not the only people pushing this button. Already a growing number of working mothers and fathers want to off-ramp for a few months or years to raise their children, and then ramp back on without the feeling that they're stuck forever in the corporate slow lane.

Can career maps be embedded with the developmental and experiential value of stepping out into a great new adventure—whether it is parenting, community development, or trekking in the Andes? In the midst of a Talent War, wouldn't companies want to find ways to nurture their growing alumni network as an already-developed talent pool that they can tap?

Create a culture of continuous coaching, support, and collaboration

Provide continuous feedback

Accustomed to instant metrics on the web (YouTube views, Amazon rankings, instant poll questions—"Who will win the election?" "Should paparazzi stop hounding Miley Cyrus?"), Millennials expect to know at every moment how they're performing—but without too much analysis. Thumbs up/thumbs down will suffice, as they glance up from texting on their smartphones. And don't wait until the yearly review to tell them how they're doing!

A legacy of constant parental praise means Millennials expect attention. Mentors and managers who coach, rather than give directives, are welcome. Managers who give Millennials ownership of projects (whole or in part), along with the freedom to decide how to do their work, all the while staying constantly in touch (albeit unobtrusively) will motivate and get the best out of their young workers.

This is not an idealistic or cynical crowd. Above all, they are pragmatic. They are task-based rather than process-oriented. Instead of explaining best practices or spending too much time on up-front training, give them the opportunity to make important contributions from Day One. Get them started right away, with objectives to achieve and great technological tools to use. In their horizontal, flat world, they will find each other, share lines of code, URLs, emails, videos, photos, and websites to find solutions and accelerate goal achievement dramatically.

Employers will also do well by giving Millennials markers of achievement—frequently attainable goals and milestones, titles, new responsibilities, and small but frequent promotions. The days of pay broadbanding structures—that have workers slogging through vast expanses of time before a promotion is attained—are over.

Create ultra-collaborative environments

In the Millennial social nerve center, all team members are connected to one another through texting, cell phones, email, social networking pages, and mass media. Problem solving is a group effort, particularly since today's technology makes instant collaboration possible. In helping a friend from Peru find colleges to attend in the United States, my daughter and her friend were connected via Skype and webcam. They surfed the web together and sent each other links. They downloaded media players and java scripts and watched campus orientation videos, while filling out forms and emailing them to each other. The thousands of miles between them were irrelevant. This kind of ultra-collaboration need not take place between just a few individuals or even many individuals within an organization; it's also possible with competitors, customers, and academics—even with avatars, virtual entities created by real people, but who have their own names and identities.

In *Wikinomics: How mass collaboration changes everything*, authors Don Tapscott and Anthony Williams show how masses of people are creating TV news stories, sequencing the human genome, remixing their favorite music, designing software, finding cures for diseases, editing school texts, inventing new cosmetics, and writing the global encyclopedia, Wikipedia.[14] The blogosphere is teeming with voices bouncing ideas, criticism, and opinions off each other in an ever-present, hyperkinetic fashion that accelerates the development of new ideas, products, and services, which are then instantly disseminated globally.

Among its hundreds of case studies, *Wikinomics* shares the story of the Geek Squad, Best Buy's electronics and computer support service. One Geek Squad manager uses multiplayer games, such as Battlefield 2, for members to exchange best practices and solve problems. While inside the game, Geek Squad members intersperse fights with quick exchanges to solving clients' problems. They play, talk, and demo their solutions to each another, networking simultaneously—sometimes with as many as nearly 400 members at a time. This mass collaboration has improved on-the-job performance by keeping members connected. In the process, it helped deliver $280 million to the bottom line.[15]

Mass collaboration requires greater transparency and less spin. After all, things can't be hidden when thousands are connected. Hierarchy and control are no longer tenable in the same way as before. It may not be long before we see thousands of employees writing policies, co-creating with customers, and defining a company's best practices.

Develop intergenerational crosscultural competence

In researching this chapter, I conducted separate focus groups with Millennials, Xers, and Boomers. As predicted, judgments fly when people are not crosscculturally competent—in this case, about differences in generational worldviews. One participant commented, "As an Xer myself, I find many of the Millennials I've encountered kind of repellent—rude, bossy, disrespectful, etc.—which I think a lot of people my age and older feel about the emergent generation." She went on to say that she needed tools to "help me better interact with these kids."

Among Boomers, there was clearly a deep divide between those who seemed to share this sentiment and those who were adapting their styles to get the most of their Millennials by engaging and learning from them.

Some of these opinions go beyond the well-worn "Well, they can teach us about technology."

Give me feedback. "These Millennials want feedback all the time!" a Boomer manager complained. "We have a hard enough time doing it once a year, what with the 360-degree feedback requests, compiling the inputs, and pulling it all into a well-written assessment form." When I shared this sentiment with the Millennial group, they respond, "Oh, they don't understand! We're asking for feedback in the lunch line!" Millennials said all they want is a 30-second, thumbs up or thumbs down, checklist-type assessment done on the fly while going through the salad bar or on the way to the elevator or via an IM. Managers who master this type of feedback often get strong reviews from Millennials.

You call that quality? Then there were the clashing worldviews about the interpretation of quality. Boomers were brought up with the technological paradigm of the assembly line—a sequential process in which each step is an additive improvement and the product is not presented for evaluation until it comes out perfect at the other end of the line. "We learned to dot our i's and cross our t's," one Boomer remarked as she went on to describe the state of the output she received from the Millennials reporting to her: "It's incomplete. With typos. Half thought-out. I don't get why the work is so shoddy!"

In talking through this opinion with Millennials, I discovered that their worldview is shaped by a different technological paradigm, the Internet—a non-sequential, synchronous process in which multiple points lead to one point, and one point can lead to multiple points. The creation process is iterative and continuous. With three clicks on Facebook, one *publishes* a timeline that invites friends to like with a click and comment with a few taps of the keys. The work is far from complete, but ready for interaction as the members of the network comment, send links to their favorite songs, pictures, or YouTube videos. From one participant: "Our point of view is that in order to achieve quality, you have to show things as you're building them. Otherwise, you're going to spend a lot of time on a product that may turn out not to meet the need. Better to get the input early on throughout the process rather than after it's completed."

Reciprocal learning. Of course, Millennials have plenty to learn from Boomers and Gen Xers as well. In our upside-down world, youth may actually mean more experience in certain things, but life and work experience distills wisdom and softens one's bravado. Millennials need that. As a Millennial male focus group member explained, "At some point, we need to face reality ... no one is going to put me in charge on my first day, nor should they." There was acknowledgment that the newest approach to an issue is not always the best one. Group members understood there are benefits to doing things in established ways.

"The thought of clocking in with face time at the office is my kryptonite," said one female Millennial focus group member. "But there has to be a balance between what we're looking for in autonomy and micromanagement. We don't want to be micromanaged, but at the same time, we're looking for someone to provide coaching and advice and serve as a mentor." Another explained that their generation wants to make their own mistakes and learn from them.

Not content simply to throw stones at older generations, the majority sentiment in the Millennial focus groups was of wanting to work with them. They seemed to understand the diversity and inclusion imperative of needing each other's differences and the synergy that kind of collaboration offers. And Millennials remain optimistically pragmatic about the need for all generations to work together. "The company that can master that synergy could really use it as a competitive advantage in the marketplace," said one. The global medical technology firm Becton, Dickinson and Company is explicitly seeking to achieve this through an intergenerational affinity group called Network XYZ.

Sidelined Xers? In this discussion, Xers have felt somewhat on the sidelines. Some felt the Millennials were getting too much attention or that too much was being made of their differences. The challenge for Xers is twofold. Demographically, they're a significantly smaller cohort compared to Millennials and Boomers.[16] But they also are experiencing the very real dynamics of being the transitional generation. Xers were brought up by Boomer parents and became digital in their teens and 20s. Millennials, on the other hand, grew up in a digital, global, terrorism-threat environment that fully shaped their experiences, making their worldviews stand in stark contrast with their Boomer managers.

But rather than a detriment, Xers can lean into these realities to enhance their influence. Because they are indeed the generation in the middle, they, more than anyone else, understand what it's like to navigate through a major historical paradigm shift. They have straddled the transition from modernism to postmodernism. They can talk both Boomer and Millennial language. The challenge for them is whether they get stuck in resentment or move on to being influential brokers.

A final word

To create collaborative environments, organizations must focus attention on diversity and inclusion, equipping individuals and organizations to navigate differences. Building crosscultural competence across all workers is vital. In my crosscultural work, I advocate for reciprocal adaptation. The trick for Boomers, Xers, and Millennials is to stop judging each other and start valuing what each brings to the table. Creating a productive and winning enterprise means moving from "I tolerate your differences" to "I need your differences... and you need mine. Together, let's solve the world's problems."

With every new wave—whether within the worlds of art, business, technology, or politics—there is resistance. Newcomers with new ideas invite skepticism and balking. This time it's the youth who are crashing the party. The Millennials are in the building.

RUUP4IT?[17] ⍝

SUMMARY POINTS

- While some Millennial characteristics have to do with the common dynamics of youth, others are the result of unique, cultural, historic, political, and economic realities that have shaped their worldviews.

- The younger generation comes through the door more restless than ever. They want to be valued, put to work, rewarded, and affirmed from the get-go.

- Jobs that look the same day after day—fixed in their definitions of roles and responsibilities—must go. Millennials desire job experiences that match the fast-moving, connected, iterative world in which they live. They seek employers who have designed jobs to be broken into pieces or modules that can be easily manipulated into non-standard work arrangements.

- Millennials expect to know how they're performing at every moment, but without too much analysis.

- Rather than judging each other for particular ways of doing things, Millennials, Xers, and Boomers should recognize that each group has unique perspectives from which to draw upon and benefit one another.

SHAPING YOUR STRATEGY

- How are Millennials behaving in your work environment? How much acceptance or resistance are they finding on the part of Boomers and Xers?

- Are your corporate policies and philosophies in alignment with or in opposition to the Millennial way of operating?

- If there are barriers, how can you begin to initiate change?

- What guidance and perspective can you offer Boomer managers about how to get the most out of their Millennial workforce?

- How is your Xer population feeling about intergenerational dynamics, and how can you tap into their unique perspectives to generate greater intergenerational inclusion?

- Has anyone started talking about Gen Z, the ones coming up right behind GenY? What is their worldview?

dis +

10

THE DIVERSITY ISSUE WE FEAR THE MOST

ability

Chapter 10

Disability: The diversity issue we fear the most

It took only four seconds for John Vcelka's life to change forever. The five-foot-ten, athletic, rock-climbing, river-rafting, volleyball-playing 34-year-old skied into a tree going 40 miles per hour. His skull cracked, his left shoulder shattered, and his spine fractured. Airlifted by helicopter off Breckenridge Mountain and flown to Swedish Hospital in Englewood, Colorado, his battered body clung to life, breath by labored breath. By the time he was wheeled out of the operating room 12 hours later, John was alive, but with a bed-ridden, never-walk-or-talk-again prognosis. At the apex of his youthful vigor, John was disabled. Life as he knew it was over.

Or was it?

Stories like John's scare us. Like many, I thrive on intellectual challenges and work, but the pleasure of dancing with my wife, kicking a soccer ball with friends, or catching a wave on an emerald blue sea are how I experience living with vitality and joy. The fear of losing the ability to physically do the things we love is common. So are the myriad misconceptions that tag along with this fear.

Not only is this fear prevalent in society and workplaces, it's something even diversity practitioners struggle to address. Is it any coincidence that disability is the most neglected diversity issue in our organizations? Although we often include the concept in our one-word definition of diversity *(raceethnicitygendersexualorientationdisability)*, the issue of disability rarely shows up, even in a token way, when we design diversity and inclusion conferences, invite speakers, and develop enterprise-wide inclusion strategies.

As diversity professionals, we're good at converting dismay over long-neglected issues into passionate advocacy and effective programs. But when it comes to disability, we've been passive. "If I'm in a diversity conference and someone even mentions disability, it catches my ear because it so seldom happens," says Deb Dagit, President of Deb Dagit Diversity LLC and formerly Vice President, Diversity and Chief Diversity Officer at Merck. This is our collective shame.

Dagit goes back to the early days of diversity efforts in the '70s and '80s, when it was extremely difficult to talk about race. "You couldn't be a good diversity leader if you had not crawled through the broken glass of all the programming you were subjected to, from the time you were a child, about people from different races. We've also had to face our fears in terms of gender, faith, and sexual orientation. To do so, we attended hundreds of workshops, read multiple books, and entered into one-on-one mentoring, courageous conversations, and just painful self-examinations. But we've yet to do this with disability." Dagit is disheartened by the many master diversity trainers who have told her how proud they were to be able to look at a person with a disability and not run away. "That's how bad it is...that they feel they've made great strides if they can just stay in the presence of someone with a disability."

Our inaction stems from our fear—fueled by the unknown, usually marked by misinformation about those who are different. As always, naming and facing the fear must be our starting point. Much of our work, then, is to confront this fear by deflating negative stereotypes and smashing common misconceptions about disability. Misguided views diminish us all.

Before going further, let's not assume we even have a common understanding of what we mean by "disability." What is disability? Is disability a handicap recognized by law? Is it something you are born with? The result of an illness or accident? Is it physical, mental, or both? Are aging or obesity disabilities? The answer is important because using all of these definitions, one in five Americans (57 million) has some form of disability, making this the largest minority group.[1] Globally the number is 1.1 billion.[2]

Various demographic issues will increase this number significantly, making it one of the most important emerging diversity issues in the workplace. For one, a majority of aging Baby Boomers (49 percent) say they don't plan to retire until they are 66 or older, either because they simply want to keep busy or they can't afford to stop working.[3] That's significant because 30 percent of the US population between the ages of 55 and 64 is disabled.[4] Then there are the Veterans who have returned from the Iraq and Afghanistan wars. Nearly 45 percent of the 1.6 million Veterans from those two wars have filed for disability benefits.[5] All told, 3.5 million[6] of the 21.8 million[7] US Veterans have a disability.

Disability also intersects with other diversity issues. The cumulative effects of racism, sexism, and able-ism (also known as *intersectionality*) compound the challenge. Around 20 percent of African Americans have a disability, making them the group with the highest incidence.[8]

Some other statistics to consider: Fewer than half (41 percent) of people with a disability between the ages of 21 and 64 are employed. People with a non-severe disability are less likely to be employed than those with no disability—75 percent to 83.5 percent, respectively. Not surprisingly, individuals reporting a severe disability are the least likely to be employed (28 percent).[9] Only 15.5 percent of those with a severe disability work full-time, compared to 63 percent of people with no disability and 48 percent of those with a non-severe disability. More than two-thirds (69.5 percent) of people with a severe disability are not employed at all, compared with 25 percent of people with a non-severe disability and 16.5 percent of people with no disability.[10] In the midst of a war for talent, we must keep in mind that 65 to 70 percent of people with disabilities of working age (16–64) are either unemployed or underemployed.[11] Workers with disabilities are also earning 37 percent less than their peers. They took in 63 cents for every dollar paid to workers without disabilities.[12]

In this chapter, I explore the roots of our underlying fear of disability and the disabled, address common misconceptions, answer questions many have been hesitant to ask, and share ways we can proactively address disability diversity.

Roots of the fear

Why the fear? I believe it's because disability is the one diversity category that any of us, if not already in it, can join, either through an accident or by merely getting older—the former a possibility and the latter an eventuality few wish to discuss.

"It's not like it's possible for me to one day wake up as a person of color," says Marca Bristo, President and CEO of Access Living, a disability civil rights and empowerment organization in Chicago. Bristo herself is in a wheelchair due to a diving accident. As happened to John Vcelka, just four seconds could separate any of us from becoming part of a group that before was completely unrelatable to us.

Vcelka explains the discomfort expressed by able-bodied people: "I've found that there are three types of reactions to me being in a wheelchair. There are those who simply can't bear it and avoid acknowledging the disability, often by avoiding me. There are those who call out my condition, 'Oh, my gosh! How are you doing…is there anything you need?' And then there are the people who will say 'Hi' or whatever and interact with me as they would with anyone else."

He explains that after the accident, most of his able-bodied friends, the ones that he spent time with regularly, drifted away. "It was not from a lack of attempts on their part, but as they visited me, they would say, 'I can't see you in a wheelchair.' What I came to realize was that it was true—it wasn't me they were seeing in the wheelchair. They were seeing *themselves*. They kept imagining that if they had gone through a similar injury, they wouldn't be able to cope with it." So, with excuses of being too busy, his friends stopped visiting and long-standing relationships withered.

Dagit, who is short-statured and uses a cane due to a genetic fragile bone condition, brings up another dimension to the disability issue. "In my global diversity work, it's remarkable how consistently, across cultures, disability is viewed as some kind of punishment for an individual or a family due to past sins. Paradoxically, it's often also seen as evidence [the disabled] are special, here to teach us things about miracles, about the meaning of life. But in that specialness, they're set apart and not mainstreamed. Regardless of language, culture, or climate, it's amazing how consistent these beliefs are."

Corporate barriers

Along with peoples' personal hang-ups regarding disability are corporate barriers, embedded in our systems and processes. These barriers reinforce our fears and ignorance and ultimately prevent successful sourcing, attraction, and retention of people with disabilities. Too few people with disabilities succeed in the workplace due to the spoken and unspoken beliefs that they can't do their jobs effectively. Businesses worry, too, about the possibility of increased costs, safety, legal liability—and how employees and customers will react. To lower and dismantle these barriers, we must first explore how and where they show up in our organizations.

The hidden nature of many disabilities

Some people have visible disabilities, the most iconic of them being a person in a wheelchair, the *de rigueur* picture of disability as diversity. Yet those with visible disabilities make up less than 29 percent of people with disabilities.[13]

Many disabilities are essentially invisible by their very nature (e.g., chronic pain, mental health disorders, or malfunctioning internal organs). That is, you may not be able to tell simply by looking at the person that he or she is disabled.

Others seek to hide their disability (or disabilities) to fend off discrimination. Just as the first women and people of color broke through the glass ceiling by minimizing their differences (women who adapted by "behaving like men" and people of color who tried to "act" White through their speech and body language), disability pioneers did the same. US President Franklin Delano Roosevelt went to extraordinary lengths to keep his wheelchair out of sight. Consequently, millions of Americans didn't even know he had polio.[14] In my work in diversity, I have come across various examples such as an administrative assistant with an increasingly worsening hearing loss who secretly recorded conversations and played them back at the end of the workday to get all the information she needed, as well as meeting a salesperson with diabetes who worked as a diabetes technician because that made it easier for him to check his blood glucose levels and administer his insulin medication without anyone detecting his condition.

Once women and people of color had entered the workforce in numbers beyond tokenism (someone hired just to have "at least" one from a group but where there are no other efforts to hire on a critical mass), they began changing workplace culture by their very presence. The same must now happen for people with disabilities. Companies try to excuse their dearth of women or minorities at certain levels by saying, "We can't find any." The same is true with disability—but employers won't be able to use that same old excuse much longer. A growing number of people with disabilities are aggressively pursuing education and training. Currently, 2.2 million college students in the United States (11 percent of the total student population) have disabilities,[15] with 25 percent of those majoring in computer science, engineering, and science,[16] key areas in which the talent shortage is especially acute.

Assumptions about what people with disabilities can and cannot do

While everyone knows it's inappropriate and illegal to discriminate on the basis of disability, there is plenty of evidence that it still occurs. The Bureau of Labor Statistics reports that the unemployment rate for people with disabilities is twice as high than the United States as a whole at around 12 percent.[17] Globally, 44 percent of people with disabilities are unemployed.[18]

It is misunderstanding, calcified attitudes, and outright prejudice that keep so many people with disabilities un- or under-employed. The following story, told by a paraplegic we'll call David, is typical. Listen to the debilitating emotional thought process he goes through:

"A lot of the jobs that I'm applying for are online, and they always have the EEO (Equal Employment Opportunity) thing on there. And on just about every one of them, they ask if you have a disability. I am so afraid to fill that part out. I know it says that they don't use any of the answers that you put on there for consideration for the job. I know that I have to answer truthfully if I answer it at all. Sometimes they give you an option of not answering, and I feel like if I don't answer they will think I'm trying to hide something."

This agony is compounded in the first face-to-face interaction. "I went on an interview the other day. When I showed up for the scheduled time, I asked for the hiring manager and when he came out, I said, 'Hi, I'm David. I'm here for my 5 p.m. interview.' He looked at me in my wheelchair, perplexed. 'We have a meeting at 5 o'clock? How can I help you? Uh...oh, yeah, right, okay!' But it was immediately clear I had no chance, despite my 24 years of retail experience."

Those with a visible disability must contend with pervasive assumptions about what people with disabilities can and can't do. "There is a societal belief that having a disability means you can't work," says Bristo. She goes on to explain that this assumption is codified right into our Social Security system, shaping the beliefs of both the able-bodied and those with disabilities. The benefits provided assume the person will not be able to earn a wage. For children, the assumption is they will not have access to a competitive education, skills training, or equal access to academic preparation. "That whole system is based on a model that people with disabilities have to be taken care of because they can't take care of themselves," Bristo says. "And while no one is going to argue that some people may need it, for many people it becomes a trap from which they can't get out. The system needs to be more flexible."

So if disability does not equal inability, we must rethink what's required for the job in terms of physical ability. Progressive companies are pretty good at answering the "what does the role require?" question when faced with a disabled employee and the need to respond to Americans with Disabilities Act (ADA) requirements. But this approach severely limits the opportunities available for people with disabilities.

Able-bodied people's beliefs about the requirements for performing a job are riddled with assumptions that must be questioned. For example, a person who uses a wheelchair applied for a store manager's job at a video rental store, where the hiring manager's immediate reaction was, "You can't do this." The applicant responded by saying, "Give me a day-to-day listing of a store manager's responsibilities, and let's walk through them and see what a person in a wheelchair can't do." As they went through the list, the only thing that came up would be reaching the top shelf. The applicant said, "Okay, that's fair. But is that something I need to do, an absolute?" The manager answered, "No, it's not."

Myriad stories circulate of disabled people advancing against all odds. *DiversityInc* magazine captured the story of Melodi King, who has cerebral palsy, a neurological disorder that attacks the body's musculature. The condition mostly affects her right side, which causes her hand to curl into a fist.[19] In college, her keyboarding teacher told her she would have to quit the class because she couldn't type like the other students. She responded by teaching herself to type 60 words per minute with only her left hand. Cerebral palsy "has actually forced me to have stronger problem-solving skills and makes me prepared to deal with situations that other people can't handle well," this former manufacturing development program analyst at Merck told the magazine. "It forces you to be adaptable."[20]

Glass ceiling pioneers have had to "work twice as hard to get half as far." Many became super-achievers in ways that are not realistic for the bulk of the bell curve to exhibit. To be truly inclusive, "organizations need to meet us halfway to give us a basic level playing field—hence the concept of reasonable accommodations," says Bristo.

Further complicating things are common misperceptions that one disability implies another. If someone can't hear, for example, people wonder if they can read. And if someone is in a wheelchair or has a speech impairment, people automatically assume he or she also has an intellectual disability. Some assume people with disabilities don't have a mind of their own. Says Vcelka, "I'll be at a restaurant with my girlfriend and the waitress will ask her what *I'll* have to eat." Some misguidedly jump to conclusions about what a person with a disability will need to be able to do his or her job—without even asking the person. In one case, a manager insisted that a new hire, who is blind, have a guide dog, even though the employee had never used one and didn't need to.

Workplace implications

If fear is the core barrier to creating true inclusion for people with disabilities, we must first work to dismantle it.

Disability advocates stress that we must recognize disability as a normal part of the human condition and acknowledge that it affects us all to some extent. When disability is present, we can accept it—not as an aberration or something gone terribly wrong, but rather as how life can be. As Bristo says, "When you're smack in the middle of dealing with a disability, most people find resources they didn't know they had. And what you thought you feared is not often what the experience ends up being." The simplest and most straightforward way to get comfortable with disability is to spend more time with people who have disabilities, she says. Once we do, "the mystique and mystery disappear, and then the person is seen for what he or she can do rather than what he or she can't."

Personal relationships are a powerful source in lowering barriers between able-bodied folks and those with disabilities. But if we are going to keep dismantling the barriers, we must be ready to *redefine* ability. The embedded assumption that to be disabled means to be unable must be undone. This is the key to making the mix work.

Redefining ability

John Vcelka sits in his wheelchair at a white board in front of a group of two dozen able-bodied students. "Which of these do you believe I've not been able to do since my accident?" he asks, pointing to the names of 36 different sports, including water skiing, rock climbing, and rugby. The students respond eagerly, calling out activity after activity. With the red marker in his hand, Vcelka circles one—canoeing. "This is the only one I've not done," he says as he taps the board, "and not because I've not been able to, but I just haven't gotten to it yet!"

People with disabilities are redefining what it means to be disabled and able-bodied. Check out Olympic-caliber athletes like South African open water swimmer Natalie du Toit and her compatriot, sprinter Oscar Pistorius, both of whom are amputees. In competing—not in the Paralympics, but rather for Du Toit in the mainstream 2008 Beijing Olympics and Pistorius in the 2012 London Olympics—they declared they didn't want their disability to put them in a different category. They wanted to compete with the best. Du Toit says, "In the water, I'm just like everybody else. [In competition, other swimmers] wouldn't hold back, saying, 'there's a disabled athlete, I'll go slower.'"[21] Pistorius had a tougher time as he sought to qualify for the team going to London. Was it his qualifying time or his Flex-Foot, a sharply designed prosthetic, that track and field officials suspected might give him an unfair advantage?[22] In Pistorius' case, some even said having the disability meant greater advantage.

Lais Kari is a blind proofreader. With the help of a digital replayer (with software that reads computer screen text aloud), Lais has become a top proofreader at Serasa Experian in São Paulo, Brazil, a leading global information services company. She sets the replayer to read back text one letter, comma, and period at a time at 10 times the normal speed and zips through documents, correcting grammatical errors as she goes. Her job allows her to work with one of her great passions—the Portuguese language—and she loves it. Disability isn't the problem, Lais explains. "What's a problem is convincing others that it's *not* a problem."

In the 2005 documentary film *Murderball*, quadriplegic men play quad-rugby. It is one of the more aggressively physical sports played by athletes who have, arguably, some of the most significant disabilities. They use "Stick-Ems" so the ball sticks to their hand, and they bang their wheelchairs into each other in hopes of knocking the ball out of the other person's hands or knocking the person over.

Vcelka climbs rocks by shifting rock-climbing's basic premise that it's mainly about leg use to making it mainly about arm use.

And the stories continue: the paraplegic roofer; the hearing-impaired team manager of a joint US-India technology team; the blind former governor of New York, David Paterson; and autistic mathematics genius, Daniel Tammet. His memoir, *Born on a Blue Day: Inside the Extraordinary Mind of an Autistic Savant* (Free Press, 2007), is the remarkable story of the author's experiences, beginning with being perceived as a useless drain on society and then describing how he went to school, got a degree and a job, sustained a long-distance relationship, learned how to speak Icelandic in a week, and even taught in Lithuania. Tammet's story is of particular interest to researchers because he is one of only 50 people today living with synesthesia (in which the stimulation of one sense causes sensation in another—like when a sound produces a sensation of color) and autism. We all have a lot to learn from Tammet's life story, and from others whose disabilities may not be outwardly noticeable.

The growing number of "defying the odds" stories challenge the *unable* tag society has placed on those with disabilities. These stories are changing the way people with disabilities think about themselves. The Office of Disability Employment Policy (ODEP) at the US Department of Labor has found that more young people with disabilities are graduating from high school and college. And according to the Job Accommodation Network (JAN), workers with disabilities have performance and retention ratings comparable to those without disabilities.[23]

Often, the disability conversation segues into questioning whether people with disabilities have more powerful abilities than the able-bodied—moving from the extreme of "they can't do anything" to "they're superhuman." Dagit reflects on this phenomenon. "Yes, when you have a disability, it forces you to see the world in a different way and not to be afraid of things—not to be afraid of public speaking, or be intimidated by an executive, or negotiate through conflict that others see as impossible to solve because the muscles you have or the skills that you learn as a person who is differently-abled—are things difficult to acquire for anyone if you're not forced to. And I don't mean if you're blind you can hear better. I mean, if you're forced to rely on things other than the ableness of your body, you'll develop adaptive strategies that serve you well in a variety of circumstances. What you notice about people's tone and their body language, what you notice about human dynamics—it's just transformed."

Disability diversity parallels historical diversity issues as well. "When African Americans excelled at sports, society tried to make it like there was some innate biological difference. Couldn't it just be possible that they tried harder?" asks Dagit. "Or with women, society starts to go down this path: 'Women are better at multitasking because they're able to use more parts of their brain, but they're not as good at science and math.' We're trying to look for scientific proof, rather than see that there are adaptive behaviors where people apply more time, energy, and effort."

Wounded warriors: Skills intact

The face of disability today is partly, and movingly, defined by the United States' *wounded warriors*, those soldiers who have returned from Iraq and Afghanistan. Thanks to the advanced technology of contemporary warfare and battlefield medicine that lead to higher survivor rates, many more Vets, compared to wars before, are returning with prostheses rather than in body bags. Despite their injuries, for most, their skill sets are intact and they're eager to work.[24]

In Dan Senor and Saul Singer's book *Start-Up Nation: The Story of Israel's Economic Miracle*, the authors write about US soldiers' ability to transition from the battlefield to the boardroom. They state, "Given all this battlefield entrepreneurial experience, the Vets coming out of the Iraq and Afghanistan wars are better prepared than ever for the business world, whether building start-ups or helping lead larger companies through current turbulent periods... Vets bring things to the table that their business peers could only dream about, including a sense of proportionality—what is truly a life-or-death situation and what is less than that; what it takes to motivate a workforce; how to achieve consensus under duress; and a solid ethical base that has been tested in the crucible of battle."[25]

The success of our Veterans has never been more apparent than in 2011 when Obama's White House challenged private industries to hire or train more than 100,000 Veterans by 2013. The call to rally around Veterans and support them with employment opportunities was quickly met. In 2011, the unemployment rate for 9/11-generation Veterans was more than 12 percent, and as of 2015, the unemployment rate for post-9/11 Veterans has fallen by almost five points. With this success came another private sector commitment to hire 90,000 Veterans and military spouses.[26]

This transition, however, requires a cultural change in these organizations— from an able-bodied workforce to one that easily incorporates those with disabilities. This also requires a cultural change for those old enough to remember that those who became disabled in previous wars did not have the same technological and social support that exists for Veterans today to help them demonstrate they can still perform at the highest levels.

JPMorgan Chase is one of the companies taking up the Obama Era challenge. In a recent initiative, JPMorgan Chase employees partnered with the Wall Street Warfighters Foundation, an organization that helps service-disabled Veterans transition from active duty to new careers. The company provides ongoing support to Veterans pursuing careers in the financial services industry. Wall Street Warfighters alumni have moved into financial services positions at Goldman Sachs, JPMorgan Chase, Citigroup, and Drexel Hamilton.[27]

Reassessing ability

The other way to redefine ability is to see disability in new ways. Dagit described a conference in Washington, D.C. attended by more than 700 people with a brittle-bones condition. It results in frequent bone fractures, which can be caused by something as seemingly harmless as going over a bump or sneezing. They have heart valve and colon challenges, significant hearing loss, joint laxity that leads to chronic tendonitis, and severe spinal curvature. "And yet, this is not a group of unhappy sad sacks," she said. "These are people who are leaders in government, who are actors in the theater, who are holding all kinds of important and meaningful jobs, who have full lives that include family and community."

"But able-bodied people would walk into this conference and see something that is tragic, that needs to be cured, that we need to research. Ironically, those with a disability often look at the 'poor able-bodied people' who don't get to experience their unique perspective because they've not had to struggle with some dimension of disability." This is illustrated by a conversation Dagit recently had with her 13-year-old son, Van, who has the same brittle-bones condition. A homework assignment at the beginning of the school year asked seventh graders to answer questions about themselves, including the one thing they would most like to change about themselves. After giving the question some thought, Van asked, "Mom, what if there isn't anything I want to change?" "Just write that down if that is how you feel," she replied. As he was packing up his folders after finishing the assignment, Dagit asked, "Van, what about your bones breaking easily and you being smaller than the other kids...is that something you would like to change?" "No. I like me the way I am," he replied.

Let's get practical

The conversation starts deep, by looking at others' fear and discomfort with people with disabilities. Yet, moving into action on disability is about mundane, practical solutions.

Physical space – It's more than just parking spaces and restroom stalls

While ramps and designated parking spaces are good to have, they're just a start. Moving within the building is equally as important as being able to get into it. To walk through Access Living's four-story building in downtown Chicago and view their unique design is to realize just how much we've built the world for able-bodied people.

Using a design principle called *Universal Design*, Access Living contains elevators that open on both sides to eliminate jostling for wheelchairs, voice commands that announce the floors, and light sensors that automatically adjust as the sun moves across the sky, keeping levels constant. All desks and chairs are easily adjustable, restroom entrances are set up with curved long entrances without external doors so people in wheelchairs can easily enter and exit. Low-emitting carpet material (that doesn't require detergents to clean it) eliminates air contaminants that may be harmful to people with chemical sensitivities. And low-pile carpeted floors provide the right balance between traction and gliding for wheelchairs and walking aids.

Simply put, the building has been designed for all. Advocates for Universal Design say it only makes sense, given how Baby Boomers will, as they age, be the beneficiaries of the principle.

disabilityworks works

"What businesses don't know is what's keeping them from hiring people with disabilities," says Karen McCulloh, former Executive Director of *disabilityworks*, a statewide initiative located at the Chicagoland Chamber of Commerce. "One of our objectives is to reach out to businesses that don't realize that the community of people with disabilities is an untapped resource of qualified workers."

Disabilityworks partners with businesses through the Chicagoland Business Leadership Network (CBLN) and with service providers through the Chicagoland Provider Leadership Network to improve employment opportunities for people with disabilities. The initiative grew out of a task force focused on disability and employment started by former Chicago Mayor Richard M. Daley. The task force was in session for three years before *disabilityworks* was founded in 2005. "It's all about moving people with disabilities into the workforce," said McCulloh. In less than a year, nearly 200 people secured jobs from the leads distributed by *disabilityworks* via the Internet and email blasts to people with disabilities, service providers, and job placement specialists."

Adopting a business-oriented focus that balances labor supply and demand, *disabilityworks* seeks to make systemic changes in the attitudes and behaviors of the business community and the community of support for people with disabilities. Several times a year, *disabilityworks* CBLN holds special workshops on the Americans with Disabilities Act (ADA). These closed-door sessions, facilitated by an attorney well versed in the topic, address the perceptions and issues that appear to hinder a company from hiring people with disabilities. Included is a discussion about employers' concerns regarding the cost of reasonable accommodations. Several studies have found these costs to be, on average, $500 or less. "No question is going to sound stupid; no question is going to sound discriminatory, because if you don't know, you don't know, and lack of information and education will keep businesses from hiring people with disabilities," says McCulloh.

> *Disabilityworks*' public-private partnership approach and its successes have been so distinctive that it has been awarded the Department of Labor's New Freedom Initiative Award, an honor given to companies and individuals who work to make work environments more inclusive to people with disabilities.[28] The initiative also has shared its message and methods with international delegations from Russia, the Ukraine, Great Britain, and Armenia, as well as various states across the country. As *disabilityworks* continues working on incorporating people with disabilities into all aspects of the workforce, McCulloh sums up the ongoing effort: "The employer outreach area is where the work needs to be done and, as lots of research shows, whatever helps people with disabilities helps customers as well."

At this point, you might be wondering how much it costs to implement services for the disabled. Aren't such accommodations just for a handful of people? If so, why should we spend thousands of dollars on programs and facilities that are only going to benefit a few?

Well, first of all, there are more people with disabilities than you probably realize. And even if these services are only for a handful, there are compliance reasons for responding to their needs. From an ethics and philosophy perspective, it's all about inclusion for everyone—whether for thousands or for a few.

Dos and don'ts

I usually avoid providing this kind of list, given the reductive implication that inclusion simply requires checking boxes off a checklist. But of all the diversity issues we face, this is one where people are most often confused about what to say and do. Able-bodied people end up either not giving help when it's needed or offering it when it's not, creating an awkward and sometimes hurtful cycle that we need to break.

That said, here's some simple—yet often ignored—advice from the people with disabilities I spoke with for this book:

- Don't assume that you, as an able-bodied person, know best what someone with a disability needs. Ask. This applies even when you see someone who may be struggling (pushing up an incline, for example). Ask first. They may indeed need the help and welcome it. But if they answer, "No, I'm fine," accept it.

- If someone with a disability offers you a cup of coffee or a piece of pie and starts getting it for you, let him or her. The last thing you should do is say, "What are you doing that for? You don't need to do that; let me."

- Given how prevalent this problem is, I have added this reminder: Don't use the stall for those with disabilities unless all other stalls are occupied.

Wheelchair dynamics

You may have noticed that some people use wheelchairs that do not have push handles on them. This didn't come about by chance. Those who use such wheelchairs chose this option on purpose. When able-bodied people see the push handles, they have an instinctual response to grab them and push the person in the wheelchair. "It is one of the worst things you could do," says Vcelka. "It really makes one feel like less of a person when someone grabs ahold of your chair and starts pushing you even when I'm saying, 'Please don't push my chair; I'm fine. If I need help, I'll ask for it.'"

A female employee at a large Fortune 500 company uses an old, heavy manual wheelchair. She is constantly urged by her manager and coworkers to get a newer, sleeker version that's lighter and easier to push. Her response: "My wheelchair, the way that it is now, is also something that surrounds me, and if somebody bumps into me, they're not going to hurt me. I can sit on the armrest to reach things. I can climb down on the footrest to pick up something off the floor. If I get a different type of wheelchair, I forfeit all the other things that this chair does for me."

Like most diversity issues, we need to find the right stance between being proactive and being paternalistic. Most importantly, we must respect the individual.

Mental health and cognitive disability dynamics

Admittedly, in this chapter, I've put my emphasis on physical disability rather than mental health disorders (such as depression and panic disorder) and cognitive disability. But just as we need to rethink the realities of physical disability and what it does and does not mean, we need to rethink the dynamics of cognitive disability—such as, for example, Down syndrome, spina bifida, and autism. While we may have made some progress in addressing physical disabilities, society remains further behind in addressing its biases and misconceptions about people with cognitive disabilities.

Proving the ability in disability is especially difficult for people with cognitive disabilities. But increased research into autism spectrum disorders (ASD) is increasing our understanding of the unique abilities of this group. This is particularly true of those with Asperger's Syndrome, sometimes referred to as high-functioning autism. Although people with Asperger's Syndrome share with classically autistic people some of the same difficulties with social interaction, sensory processing, and repetitive behavior, they possess unique skills, such as synthesizing information in novel and complex ways. High-functioning people with an ASD pay precise attention to detail and routine processes; their minds are geared to order, complex systems, and mathematics. In other words, they have exactly the qualities valued in the sciences or computer lab. With 730,000 Americans under the age of 21 having an ASD, according to the Centers for Disease Control and Prevention, there is a pressing need to begin to channel their talents into appropriate jobs in areas such as science, technology, engineering, and mathematics.

Companies such as Danish software-testing firm Specialisterne have been seeking out and hiring from this highly capable group. And there's growing recognition that in science and technology, some of the most brilliant people (Albert Einstein and Thomas Edison, for example) lived with learning disabilities or autism. Yet, their minds roamed the outer fields of thought and brought back ideas no one had yet considered. With so many critical twenty-first century problems to be solved the world over, it's time people pay attention to these outliers.

Little by little, more acceptance

Bristo talks about freeing people with disabilities from the imprisonment of their homes and opening up more workplace opportunities for them. Legislative changes, the push for diversity and inclusion, and technological advantages are lowering the barriers, albeit slowly.

Unlike building designers, who have been slow to get onboard, techies love the challenge of programming their software to meet the needs of people with different levels of ability. Virtual and remote work creates more opportunities for workers needing flexibility, as well as for those who have difficulty getting around.

We've not yet hit the tipping point in terms of society's attitudes toward those with disabilities, but things are inching that way. "It used to be that if I saw another person in a wheelchair at O'Hare Airport coming toward me in a terminal, by the time we got up to each other, I knew the person. There were that few of us really flying," says Bristo. "Now, the airlines can't keep up with us because there are so many people with disabilities flying."

Approaches to cognitive disabilities lag further behind, but here, too, we see signs of progress. In many public schools, kids with Down syndrome, spina bifida, and autism have been integrated into mainstream classes.[29] Both research and practical experience show that those with cognitive disabilities are more able in thought and skills than previously believed. This leads to better post-school preparation, whether going into college, a vocational trade, or a service job. When the first edition of this book was completed, my goddaughter, Jennifer, who has Down syndrome, was a senior in high school. She's had an active social life filled with friends, dancing, and movies that she balanced between school and her public library job, where she sorted and reshelved books. Since then, she's worked at the local chapter of the American Cancer Society, and currently volunteers several days a week at Misericordia, a residential community for people with developmental disabilities.

As we address the inclusiveness requests of those who have been on the margins, benefits flow to the full community. I don't mean this in a *feel good* way, but in a practical, helpful way. The working mother's battle cry for work-life balance ended up also benefiting working fathers, near-retirees, and Millennials. In the past, the clamor for mentors by people of color has also benefited up-and-coming majority talent. And now, disabled individuals' urging for user-friendly workplaces will bring benefits for all—curb cuts and wider aisles help parents with strollers, carts, and luggage. Accessible doorknobs make it easier for people with packages to open doors. And voice recognition technology (originally created to allow people with disabilities to write text on a computer without typing) is now the basis for the technology many of us use when making smartphone calls.

In addition to the medical and social models we use to understand the lives of people with disabilities, we should also consider the Emerging Market model. This model sees people with disabilities as a large and growing group of employees and consumers. In other words: significant marketplace opportunities.

If the workplace potential of people with disabilities is just beginning to be recognized, their massive purchasing power has yet to be capitalized. The global disability market has mushroomed to the size of China. Its 1.1 billion people control $4 trillion dollars in spending power. If you include family and friends who have a direct and emotional connection to people with disabilities, the numbers nearly double to a staggering 2 billion people who control $8.1 trillion dollars.[30]

Take the ubiquitous Baby Boomers. The first legion of their huge demographic has already turned 65, and they are redefining what it means to grow older. Despite the inevitability that aging will render them increasingly disabled, they want to stay involved in their lives and in society. New products and services that help both able-bodied and disabled Baby Boomers stay independent have been blossoming in the economic landscape, from walk-in therapeutic baths to retirement communities that reinterpret the communes of the 1960s as a mutually supportive way for seniors to share housing.

In recognizing a customer service need, airlines are offering gate-to-gate transportation for people with less visible constraints, like respiratory ailments, though it first started the practice to help those in wheelchairs. Universal Design dovetails nicely into green design and the potential economic benefits that it brings. Making necessary ergonomic adjustments for those with disabilities will make ergonomic furniture even more ubiquitous, meeting everyone's needs for healthy keyboard work in an era with a sharp climb in repetitive stress and carpal tunnel injuries.

We have been looking at how people with disabilities are beginning to strengthen the workplace and invigorate the marketplace. However, these advances are not sufficient to effect a fundamental shift in attitudes toward and opportunities for people with disabilities. We must develop cultural change strategies to undermine long-held beliefs and attitudes that continue to create barriers to disability inclusion.

The ambivalence of many in the diversity field toward—and even the neglect of—disability is a reflection of larger societal attitudes. After the globally historic passage of the ADA in 1990, which put the United States ahead of other countries in pioneering disability issues by the early 2000s, the United States had lost its leadership in dealing with disability issues. However, in the Obama Era, we've seen a renewed emphasis on bridging the gap between the able-bodied and those with disabilities. Though, as with other legislation in the Obama Era, the emphasis has not been without controversy.

Within months of taking office, President Obama announced that the United States would join the more than 150 other nations in signing the unprecedented United Nations Convention on the Rights of Persons with Disabilities. The President acknowledged this was merely a starting point. "And even as we extend our commitment to persons with disabilities around the world, we're working to deepen that commitment here at home," he said in remarks marking the 19th anniversary of the Americans with Disabilities Act (ADA) and the signing of the treaty. "We must consider what can be done to eliminate anti-disabled prejudices that exist—both consciously and subconsciously—within our society."[31] But as a reflection of the ambivalence toward addressing disability, along with the polarized politics of our times, this Obama-Era intent has met resistance—in a vote taken late in 2012, the US Senate rejected confirmation of the treaty.[32]

Similarly, the US Department of Labor has issued a directive that many see as too onerous: that anyone doing contracting with the federal government employ at least 7 percent of their workforce with people with disabilities.[33] This is a heated debate but there's no question that it's President Obama's inclusive policies triggering the debate.

Despite many advancements with disability and inclusion efforts, the resistance by politicians and businesses and the lingering indifference on the part of diversity practitioners signifies that we still have a long way to go.

To address this seriously lagging diversity issue, we need to take a stand. Says Dagit, "Until we come to the realization that every single one of us is temporarily able-bodied, we're not going to make significant progress on this. It is enlightened self-interest that will drive us to solutions. If we create a world where people with disabilities can fully participate, then we'll have created an insurance policy for ourselves and anyone we care about. It's not an 'other' issue. It's a self issue." ♀

SUMMARY POINTS

- Misconceptions about disability are based on fear, which is prevalent both in society and in our workplaces. Even diversity practitioners continue to struggle with this issue.

- Disability is a normal part of the human condition, and it affects all of us to some extent. Sooner or later, we will face our own disabilities, making it an issue of self-interest.

- Accessibility issues are about more than parking spaces and restroom stalls. When accessibility is based on the concept of Universal Design, buildings and environments will become accessible and welcoming to all— disabled and able-bodied people alike.

- Veterans with disabilities, with all their skills learned in combat, possess multiple competencies that benefit businesses.

SHAPING YOUR STRATEGY

- How proactive is your organization in addressing disability issues?

- What are the biggest barriers among individuals and within your organization to attract, hire, engage, and develop those with disabilities?

- Where would you assess your own comfort with disability in others? In yourself?

GAY 11

GAY

HOW MY GAY FRIENDS UPENDED MY
UNDERSTANDING ABOUT MOST EVERYTHING

Chapter 11

How my gay friends upended my understanding about most everything

While working as a senior leader at Hewitt, Jocelyn Purcell also served as the business leader sponsor of the Lesbian, Gay, Bisexual, and Transgender (LGBT) affinity group. In that capacity, she was asked to speak at a Pride celebration. To prepare for the event, she decided to see what it would be like not to be able to talk about the people you love in everyday workplace conversation. Here's how she described the experience:

"It was not uncommon for LGBT colleagues to tell me how difficult it was not to be out. One person called it 'putting on the cloak.' She explained the constant decision about whether to put on the cloak or feel safe keeping it off. Many coworkers still wear that cloak because they don't trust that they can take it off. Imagine how much more the work world could gain if the energy spent putting on the cloak was spent instead on the team and the client.

"So the idea was to try to put myself in the shoes of someone who was not out in the workplace and how that would feel. I have had the privilege of being able to be 100 percent who I am—in all aspects of my life—at work. And those of you who know me well, know that I like to talk about my family, my activities outside of work, and like to talk with others and find out about their families and their activities.

"So, I decided that for one week, I would not talk about anything outside of work. I would pretend that I was afraid to because it could lead to questions I did not want to answer. And because I couldn't talk about it, I would not ask others about it—because that

would inevitably lead back to questions about me. As I thought about other implications, I realized I would need to take down all my pictures in my office of my family—because I wouldn't be able to have to answer questions like 'Who is this in the picture?'

"Every time I thought about entering into a week of shutting down part of myself, the energy that would take was overwhelming to me. The tremendous amount of restraint to be someone other than who I am would affect the focus and attention on my work I usually have. And the thought that in the middle of a stressful day, I couldn't look at pictures of my family and take some strength from their smiling faces and remind myself about what is important—the way I do every day—was too much.

"So, I didn't do it. I couldn't do it. And the truth is, I didn't have to do it. I have that choice. But many of our associates who are gay—but are not out—do not have that same choice."

Jocelyn's story comes from the perspective of someone who is an ally of those who are LGBTQA+. (To sort out the variously used acronyms see endnote.[1] In this chapter, I will use the shorter and most common, LGBT.) We also had the opportunity to hear from coworkers who, on a daily basis, do not have the choice Jocelyn has long taken for granted. Let me share how this happened during Gay Pride Month not too long ago.

My name is Diana.
I am 39 years old. I love the work I do...
and I consistently perform above expectations.
I am a lesbian.
I am the same person I was before you read the previous sentence.

– Affirmations Exhibit during Gay Pride Month

Forty LGBT associates—and their allies—joined Diana in telling their stories through a 130-foot photographic Affirmations Exhibit, nestled in the main reception areas of Hewitt's largest four US offices. A virtual version of the exhibit was posted on the company's intranet.

Some gay associates took the opportunity to come out through the stories they shared in the exhibit. Others told of the anguish of having to watch their pronouns when talking about their weekend on a Monday morning. The impact was earth-shattering. After viewing the exhibit, a 20-something daughter chose to come out to her mom. And parents of LGBT children opened up about how the affirmation of gay employees as members of the Hewitt community felt like an affirmation of themselves as parents. This, in turn, freed them to be more open with coworkers about their own families.

The more people felt free to engage in conversation, the more it encouraged others. Given how divisive LGBT issues can be in society, in politics, and in corporations, the mood shift from polarized polemic to constructive dialogue made the event the most influential I have ever witnessed in shifting the discourse on LGBT issues within a community of people.

The Obama Era has created an opportunity to create an alternative to either/or polarization. Obama's 2009 Inauguration Day was marred with controversy when it was announced that two guests with diametrically opposed views on LGBT issues were asked to offer invocations at Inaugural events. This created great discomfort, even outrage, on all sides of the issue.[2] But it was clearly a deliberate attempt to include diverse, even opposing voices, and in that attempt, create a both/and opportunity to engage in a different kind of conversation. This is a manifestation of the Inclusion Paradox. In order to have inclusion, we must constructively call out the differences among us.

It's not just about forging a better understanding of something that previously seemed foreign or elusive. Within the dialogue itself, insights emerge and shed new light on common conundrums. Hearing the stories of my LGBT friends and colleagues not only helped me understand them and their contributions better, it also helped me discover new pathways to gender issues in general.

Before we delve into further insights, let's go back to the impact of the exhibit itself. We learned that charged conversations on LGBT issues had lost some of their edge. This impact was measured through the engagement scores of LGBT associates, which we tracked by allowing participants to self-identify themselves. As one of the premier experts on employee engagement—how likely workers are to stay, say good things about the organization, and give their best—Hewitt has incontrovertible data that proves lifting the engagement of groups of employees results in greater productivity and, ultimately, greater profitability.[3]

"Raising and maintaining engagement even a few percentage points can have a substantial impact on results for most organizations, so lifting engagement for what could be 5 to 10 percent of the population would surely provide significant returns," said Ray Baumruk, Aon Hewitt Partner, Employee Research & Insights, Engagement, and Human Capital Measurement.

The Stories
From the Affirmations Exhibit

My Question

Every morning I praise I thank You for blessing me with another day.
Throughout the day, I thank You for your grace and mercy.
And every night before I close my eyes,
I thank God for bringing me through another day.
Every day I live, I strive to be more like You.
More loving. More understanding. More forgiving. More patient.
As I am praising Your name, others condemn me.
They judge me.
They label me.
They outcast me and those I associate with.
My question:
Lord, why can't they see me as Your child and love me as You love me?

– Fatima

When we initially approached members of the LGBT affinity group with this idea, we were met with uncertainty. Steve Wasik, one of the leaders of the affinity group, told me, "I've had to deal with coming out to parents whose love, I learned, was conditional. I've spent years trying to find acceptance during a time when AIDS and gay hate crimes were in full bloom. Am I ready to share this pain, this very deep part of me, here at work? Why did I have to come out over and over again, each time bracing for whatever the reaction might be?"

But the more they thought about it, the more a growing number of members embraced the idea. As Steve explained, "I've been searching for a way I could help make my workplace more LGBT friendly without damaging the fragile existence I thought I had created. I didn't want to expend any more energy wondering if people knew, or what the response would be if they found out."

Eventually he agreed to tell his story, and others followed. We received more stories than we could use. The exhibit went up with 40 stories and accompanying photographs. Here's what my fellow associates read as they weaved their way through the exhibit:

"I am proud that I am Chinese and I am proud that I am gay. I have fought back and I will continue to fight back. How I am on the outside will be who I am on the inside...once again" – Jimmy

"ADJECTIVES: Methodist. Politically Conservative. Gay. HIV-positive. Employed. VERBS: Prays. Thinks. Loves. Hurts. Works. I've found that actions really do speak louder than words. Have you?" – Doug

"Did I just slip and say 'she' when I was talking with my coworker about what I did this weekend? For a year and a half of working at Hewitt and not being out, I struggled almost daily with racing thoughts as I worried about my pronouns, or hoped that a coworker hadn't realized that I was with my girlfriend when I saw him at the restaurant the night before." – Andrea

"The hardest thing is explaining to my 8-year-old why some people might give him a hard time because he has two moms. He doesn't understand why some people would think there was anything wrong with that. He also doesn't understand why having a different color skin, or being a different shape or size, or speaking a different language, or having a disability causes some people discomfort. He keeps asking, 'But why, Mom? It just doesn't make sense to me!'" – Kaleen

*"Hewitt is the only place where I have ever worked that allows me to be myself, and for the first time I can have pictures of **MY FAMILY** on my desk and my coworkers will come by and look at **MY PICTURES** of **MY LIFE.** I don't have to hide who I am for fear of being ridiculed or being fired."* – Cynthia

"Hewitt is a place where for the first time in my entire life I have been able to be completely honest, feel acceptance, live my faith in my work, and openly love my non-traditional family." – Bill

"When my clients glance at the ring on my ring finger and ask, "What does your husband do?" I am faced with that inevitable moment of decision—do I gray the lines and boundaries of the truth or am I honest in my response and risk alienating my customer? The firm I work for requires honesty and integrity, but my truth at times risks alienating me from critical connections—my clients and my team. Do I dance around with the words that hide her identity by saying 'us,' 'we,' or 'they'? This 'pronoun game' distracts when trying to build trusted partnerships." – Cara

Straight allies spoke of their coming out as well:

"My friend Steve is gay. I knew this before I received a note from him inviting me to attend a GALAA [Gay and Lesbian and Allied Associates] meeting, but I wasn't sure how, or even if, I should talk to him about his being gay. I was nervous, because I didn't know how open he was or if he was even out. I knew that sending that meeting invite took courage. He put his life out there for me to accept or reject, just as my sister had 14 years ago with my mom. I'm so glad that Steve opened this new door to our friendship, because I was too afraid to do it."

Then there's Steve's response:

"My friend Allison is straight. When I came out to her shortly after joining Hewitt, I was afraid I would lose our newly forming friendship, and I wasn't sure I could handle that. I had come out to my parents when I was 18. I couldn't understand why my mother was down on her knees, sobbing in front of the shelves that held all my high school pictures, after I told her I was gay. Tearing down the walls is what I thought of as I emailed Allison about becoming a GALAA ally. I loved her and myself enough to take the chance. My whole life, personal and work, is better because of Allison."

The outpouring of emotion was a cultural balm that brought LGBT and straight employees together. At the exhibit, associates wrote notes and placed them in a Comments box. To be sure, not all embraced the spirit of the exhibit. Overwhelmingly, however, those who took the time to write a comment were moved:

"I was on the verge of tears after reading the stories. They really brought to light what those in my family who are gay go through every day."

"Awesome! The strength, openness, and honesty in each and every affirmation made me proud to be a fellow associate."

"It's time for me to get involved as an ally in GALAA. No one should ever have to live his or her life in hiding."

"Thank you, Affirmations participants: I found myself on an emotional roller coaster as I read the stories. Everything from sadness for the obstacles many of you have dealt with, happiness for the weight I hope that has been lifted from your shoulders, anger with myself for times when I didn't have an open mind, and privileged to work with truly amazing people."

We went a step further the following year and created "Family Affirmations" for LGBT associates to share with their peers about their partners, children, and even pets. Even for those who have different beliefs about LGBT issues, the stories were humanizing.

"For me and the rest of us at Hewitt, it was a great turning point," said Steve. "For those who participated, it was a courageous step into the unknown, yet we knew we weren't out there alone. We had the support of our CEO and CDO, business leaders, and allies. We had our own personal strength, which had brought us to this point in our lives. And, we had the strength of our stories, banded together, saying with one voice, 'We survived. And today, we work hard for the company and search for joy, happiness, and love—just like you.'"

Why did it work?

Debates grounded in religious and political beliefs are inherently contentious when different belief systems are at play. But conversations grounded in relationships can foster a dramatically different dynamic. The inclusion goal in LGBT issues should not be about reaching agreement, but rather about creating a workplace environment in which anyone who wanted to be out could do so without worrying about real or imagined repercussions. Once we reached that realization, we came upon the idea of sharing stories.

This idea was influenced by my own journey. It was my best friend's story that obliterated my machista-influenced understanding of gays and lesbians. Married, with two children, a man of impeccable integrity and commitment, he told me one day over coffee that he was gay. It had taken him more than 35 years to say those words and to accept his own story—a story he had fought against since he was eight years old; a story he tried denying in countless ways, including choosing to live a heterosexual lifestyle, when his orientation was homosexual. He had arrived at a point where the years of denial were increasingly asphyxiating him. Letting the story of his true self come out was his liberation.

It was mine, too. I went from a culturally biased view of gays, lesbians, bisexuals, and transgendered people to one grounded in the reality of their identities and experiences. My assumptions about LGBT people—based on religious, political, and psychological beliefs—withered in the crucible of my friend's story. It had been easy to hold certain beliefs with conviction when the issue was abstract and not a part of my life. But once it became about my best friend of ten years, I came to realize that my beliefs about LGBT folks did not fit *any* dimension of who he was. He told me his story; I listened. And it changed me.

Authentic, engaging stories spur us to action. One person who saw the Affirmations Exhibit wrote, "How do I respond, live, and behave at work to support colleagues in similar situations? Where can I learn more and ask questions?"

Yes! This was exactly the kind of dialogue we intended to elicit. In his introduction to the exhibit, Hewitt's CEO at the time, Dale Gifford, wrote, "These stories are also about courage, often in the face of rejection, fear, and distrust in overall society. Yet, each of them found the strength to overcome the barriers that stood in the way of being the best they could be. When we have an environment in which this is possible, we can focus our energy on our talents and our work."

A new era for LGBT

The Obama Era left a lasting legacy on LGBT issues. Whether it's the President's declaration that he supported gay marriage (making him the first US president to do so), the appointment to the Commerce Department of Amanda Simpson (making her the first-ever presidential transgender appointee), the repeal of the US military's Don't Ask, Don't Tell policy, or the Supreme Court 2015 landmark decision requiring all states to recognize same-sex marriage, we have entered a new era in how mainstream culture views lesbian, gay, bisexual, and transgender issues.

How did we get here? For one, I believe that the repeal of the Don't Ask, Don't Tell (DADT) policy in the US military was a key watershed moment in US LGBT history. The US Department of Defense—one of the most conservative institutions in the United States government and one of the largest employers in the world—changed a long-standing policy regarding gays and lesbians when it declared gays and lesbians could serve openly as military personnel.

Since its inception in 1993, DADT had been an awkward, convoluted, and ultimately dehumanizing compromise. As is true with most cultural change, organizations and societies often have to take an interim, contrived step to move toward true change. DADT was particularly *"sin querer, queriendo"* (without wanting, wanting) in terms of accepting the reality of same-sex orientation. It required that military personnel refrain from requesting information about someone's sexual orientation, yet officials who admitted to being homosexual or bisexual in identity or behavior be discharged from the military. Gay and lesbian servicemen and women were forced to choose between never discussing an essential aspect of their identity or leaving military service, while the sharp edge of suspicion remained hanging over their military careers.[4]

This dehumanizing policy, despite its inherent contradictions, lingered way too long. But in December of 2010—in the midst of political wrangling about everything from the economy to nuclear treaties with the Russians—DADT was repealed by Congress and signed into law by the President soon thereafter.[5] In June 2012, the Department of Defense celebrated its first-ever Gay Pride Month with then-Secretary of Defense Leon Panetta kicking off the day via live videoconference message to the entire DOD.

The bottom-line message could be summarized this way: One can be brave, loyal, strong, willing to die for one's country, *and* gay.

This, indeed, is cultural change. A series of dominos proceeded to fall, leading to over half of the states in the US to allow same-sex marriage through one-at-a-time electoral referenda or court challenges. The June 2015 Supreme Court decision was the culmination of that process. The US became the twenty-first country to permit same-sex couples the same legal rights and benefits as heterosexual couples.[6]

Highlights of key LGBT events during the Obama Era

- President Barack Obama is the first US president to declare support for marriage equality.

- December 2011 – LGBT rights is used as a criteria for whether a country will receive US foreign aid.[7]

- The high court in New Delhi, India, rules that the law making same-sex sexual activity illegal is unconstitutional and discriminates against gays and lesbians.[8]

- In 2013, 20 percent of same-sex couples had minor-aged children in their homes.[9]

- About 4 percent of adoptive parents are same-sex couples.[10]

- 65,000 adopted children and 14,000 foster children live in households headed by gays or lesbians.[11]

- 2015 – 366 companies participating in the Human Rights Campaign's (HRC) Corporate Equality Index received a score of 100 percent.[12]

- Between 2004 and June 2015, 37 US states and the District of Columbia legalized gay marriage.[13]

- June 2015 – US Supreme Court declares same-sex marriage a constitutional right.

LGBT in the workplace and marketplace

As we witnessed the changes that took place in the Department of Defense, the more included LGBT employees felt in their working environments, the more organizations learned about this often invisible and misunderstood group. According to the San Francisco-based LGBT workplace advocacy group Out & Equal, there is no precise count of the total number of workers in corporate America who identify as LGBT. However, even back in 2006, seven out of ten heterosexual respondents to an Out & Equal survey said they knew someone who is gay.[14]

Despite progress, there are still myriad workplaces in which talented employees are leaving behind a part of who they are in order to get ahead. This is no surprise, given that it's still legal in 28 states to fire employees because they identify as lesbian, gay, or bisexual.[15] In 32 states, it's still legal to fire someone for being transgender.[16]

Many of these workers are forced to stay closeted at work in order to keep their jobs or avoid harassment. In 2013, crimes against LGBT individuals ranked second among all hate crimes, accounting for more than 20 percent.[17] No surprise then that according to a 2014 study by the Human Rights Campaign, 53 percent of LGBT workers in the US hide their sexual identity at work and 35 percent feel compelled to lie about their personal lives while at the office.[18]

LGBT people face other challenges, too. Most are not able to benefit from inheritance laws, have a guarantee that their healthcare proxy wishes will be honored, nor can they marry their partners, buy life insurance for them, or put them in their wills. They must anxiously wonder whether long-term care facilities will accept them when they can no longer take care of themselves. Choosing doctors is fraught with difficulty since they don't know which physicians will be both accepting of them and knowledgeable about particular LGBT health issues.

However, this lack of rights will eventually be addressed as the full implications of the Supreme Court decision take hold.

Other dilemmas remain unresolved. While many companies now provide domestic partner benefits, LGBT employees typically get taxed for the portion of insurance premiums that cover their partner, incurring a financial burden that does not apply to married heterosexual couples.

An increasing number of companies are rethinking common assumptions about LGBT employees, the issues they face, and what they're looking for in the workplace. Nearly 1,400 people—representing 22 countries and 118 corporate and organization sponsors—attended the Out & Equal Workplace Summit*, a conference for the LGBT community held in Baltimore, Maryland, in October/November 2012.[19] This growing awareness has led to more inclusive policies. In 1992, only three Fortune 500 companies offered domestic partner health benefits. Within five years, that number jumped to 46. By 2006, it was 249.[20] A 2013 HRC report indicated a record of 90 percent of all companies and 67 percent of Fortune 500 companies offer health benefits for same-sex couples.[21]

The Human Rights Campaign (HRC) rates large US businesses on how they treat LGBT stakeholders. Conducted annually, the Corporate Equality Index (CEI) ranks companies on a scale of 0 to 100 percent, based on a checklist

....

*Initially, 2,500 participants were expected to attend the 2012 Out & Equal Summit. However, attendance was affected by Hurricane Sandy, which caused massive East Coast disruptions.

of about a dozen LGBT-inclusive practices. The first report, issued in 2002, found 13 out of 319 companies achieving a 100 percent score.[22] In 2009, an astounding 260 major US businesses received a 100 percent score, an increase of one-third over just the year before. Increases in the number of companies reaching this rating continued in 2010 with 306 until 2011 with 337 companies achieving a score of 100 percent.[23] (See "Highlights of key LGBT events during the Obama Era" sidebar for more information.)

Seeing this high-water mark in 2011, the HRC, as part of their methodology, raised the bar of what it took to reach 100 percent by inserting harder-to-achieve standards, now that certain things such as domestic partner benefits—so revolutionary a few years ago—had become standard in many Fortune 500 companies. Predictably, the number of companies achieving 100 percent dropped in 2012 to 252. But the gambit is working in that it is spurring those who had previously achieved 100 percent, but who had slipped due to the new standards, to enact the polices that will get them back to the coveted designation of 100 percent once again.[24] By 2015, 366 major businesses spanning nearly every industry earned a top score of 100 percent.[25] A record number of major businesses implemented transgender-inclusive healthcare coverage and partner benefits. To continue to promote progress toward LGBT inclusion, the HRC announced in 2014, and will implement in 2016, new criteria on their scorecard. The changes stemmed from the guiding principle that discrimination has no place in a top-rated CEI business. In the 2016 CEI, a business must have sexual orientation and gender identity non-discrimination protections included in both US and global operations, require US contractors to abide by companies' existing inclusive non-discrimination policy, and implement internal requirements regarding philanthropic giving to non-religious organizations that have a written policy of discrimination on the basis of sexual orientation and/or gender identity.

Companies are also starting to see the marketplace through LGBT eyes—and with good reason. The purchasing power of the LGBT population reached $690 billion in 2007,[26] and estimated to reach $884 billion in 2014.[27] This surpasses US Asian 2014 buying power by nearly $60 billion.[28] In addition, the average household income for married or partnered gay men is $115,500, compared with $101,100 for married heterosexual men; for married or partnered lesbians, the average household income is $88,500, compared to $100,800 for married heterosexual women, according to the 2013 LGBT Demographic Report by Experian Simmons.[29]

In light of these figures, advertisers are beginning to wise up the enormity of the LGBT market, which is, by far, one of the fastest-growing and largest in the world.

Adding to the vast purchasing power of the LGBT population is strong brand loyalty and willingness to support brands that back LGBT issues. Eighty-seven percent of LGBT adults say they would choose a brand that offers equal benefits for their LGBT employees over ones that don't. Notably, 75 percent of heterosexuals also consider whether a company provides equal workplace benefits as part of their criteria when making buying decisions.[30]

Who could foresee this unprecedented change?

IBM, for one. In 1994, they launched a small business initiative aimed at LGBT business owners.[31] Responding to management's challenge that they offer ideas to help strengthen IBM's business, the LGBT Diversity Committee mapped out a market analysis that demonstrated a significant untapped market of LGBT business owners who needed computers and networks. This led to a deliberate strategy on Big Blue's part to go after the LGBT market, which they eventually grew into a multimillion-dollar business.

Checklist for an LGBT-inclusive workplace environment

The HRC's Corporate Equality Index rates Fortune 500 and other large US businesses on how they treat LGBT stakeholders. In 2016, the HRC updated its criteria. Conducted annually, the Corporate Equality Index rates companies on a scale of 0 to 100 percent based on the basis of the following criteria (for fully detailed list go to HRC document sourced at this endnote[32]):

Criteria 1: Equal employment opportunity policy includes:

   a. Sexual orientation for all operations
   b. Gender identity for all operations
   c. Contractor/vendor standards include sexual orientation and gender identity

Criteria 2: Employment benefits

   a. Equivalent spousal and partner benefits (Includes parity between employees with different-sex spouses and same-sex partners or spouses in the provision of the following benefits: COBRA; dental; vision; legal dependent coverage)

b. Other "soft" benefits – includes parity between employees with different-sex spouses and same-sex partners or spouses in the provision of the following benefits: bereavement leave; employer-provided supplemental life insurance for a partner; relocation/travel assistance; adoption assistance; qualified joint and survivor annuity for partners; qualified pre-retirement survivor annuity for partners; cash balance; rollover and hardship options; retiree healthcare benefits; and employee discounts

c. Transgender-inclusive health insurance coverage (Equal health coverage for transgender individuals without exclusions for medically necessary care)

Criteria 3: Organizational LGBT competency

a. Competency training, resources or accountability measures (in at least three of the following):

- New hire training clearly states that the non-discrimination policy includes sexual orientation and gender identity and provides definitions or scenarios illustrating the policy for each

- Supervisors undergo training that includes sexual orientation and gender identity as discrete topics (may be part of a broader training), and provides definitions or scenarios illustrating the policy for each

- Integration of sexual orientation and gender identity in professional development, skills-based or other leadership training that includes elements of diversity and/or cultural competency

- Senior management/executive performance measures include LGBT diversity metrics

- Gender transition guidelines with supportive restroom/facilities, dress code and documentation guidance

- Anonymous employee engagement or climate surveys conducted on an annual or biennial basis allow employees the option to identify as LGBT

- Data collection forms that include employee race, ethnicity, gender, military and disability status—typically recorded as part of employee records—include optional questions on sexual orientation and gender identity

b. Employee group or Diversity council

Criteria 4: Public commitment

c. LGBT-specific efforts, including at least three of the following: recruiting, supplier diversity, marketing or advertising, philanthropy or public support for LGBT equality under the law, and have internal guidelines that prohibit philanthropic giving to non-religious organizations with an explicit policy of discrimination against LGBT people

Criteria 5: Employers will have 25 points deducted from their score for a large-scale official or public anti-LGBT blemish on their recent records

When Wendell became Breanna

Through each L, G, and B story, my assumptions about identity, sexuality, gender, and the workplace implications of what it meant *not* to be out have frayed, ripped, and torn. But it was the T that ultimately dissolved so many things I thought to be true.

In mainstream culture, Olympic decathlete champion Bruce Jenner came out as transgender in 2015 and completely upended the conversation. She announced via Twitter: "I'm so happy after such a long struggle to be living my true self. Welcome to the world Caitlyn. Can't wait for you to get to know her/me." Among the millions of responses was one from President Obama: "It takes courage to share your story." Later, the White House encouraged others to share their stories via http://ofa.bo/s6mA.

My own personal opportunity to learn about transgender inclusion came when I was leading diversity at Hewitt. The first time I met Wendell Speed, I was having lunch with about 25 members of Hewitt's LGBT affinity group. Out of the corner of my eye, I saw someone pass by the meeting room's open door once, twice, and finally a third time before he walked in and took a seat at the far end of the room. In between bites of pizza and salad, associates introduced themselves with their coming-out stories. And then it was Wendell's turn.

He looked around the room, uncertain for a beat, and then gathering his courage, he shared. "I work in Information Services, and when my manager assigned me a pager, it precipitated a crisis for me. 'If I come in right away, you won't recognize me,' I told him. 'What do you mean?' my manager asked. I explained that even though he knew me as a man, I dressed as a woman when not at work. And in responding to an urgent page, I would not have time to change."

Wendell was a charismatic and respected IT database administrator for Oracle/SQL servers. He also happened to be African American, plus a gifted musician who eventually ended up directing Hewitt's diversity chorus, a multiethnic singing group. This was the first time he had told a group of coworkers he was transgender.

Transgenderism is a little understood dimension of sexuality and identity, not just among the straight population, but also in the L, G, and B communities. Transgender is an umbrella term used to refer to individuals whose biological sex is not congruent with their gender identity. This encompasses a full range—from the occasional, recreational crossdresser to the person who identifies as transsexual.

Crossdressers typically dress in clothing traditionally associated with the opposite sex. They change back and forth between presenting themselves as a man and woman. Transsexuals are people who desire to live permanently as the opposite of their birth sex. Some choose to have sex reassignment surgery—something that Wendell intended to do.

Over the next 18 months, we supported Wendell, his manager, and his peers, as he became Breanna. While Breanna was relieved that she experienced more acceptance than she had anticipated, some of her peers were relieved for an altogether different reason. "I finally had an answer to the great mystery: Why were Wendell's nails so perfect?" exclaimed a fellow colleague.

While all of us—Breanna included—found joy, relief, and even humor in the situation, these were tricky waters to navigate. Hewitt's non-discrimination policy at the time covered sexual orientation, but this was different than transgenderism. In consultation with the HRC, we recommended that Hewitt revise its policy to state that the company did not discriminate on the basis of "gender identity and expression." The CEO endorsed our recommendation and policy was set.

As usual, principle is one thing, implementation quite another. How and when do we introduce Breanna to Wendell's coworkers? What's the process for legally changing a person's gender and what implications does it have for benefits coverage? How do we deal with the very practical, yet sensitive issue of restroom use? The very real story in front of us jarred our ingrained presuppositions about decorum.

But navigate we did. Wendell started to show up at certain after-hours events as Breanna. He began taking hormones and his body began to change. Eventually, Wendell transitioned to remaining as Breanna all day at work. We had a carefully choreographed change management process that included emails and face-to-face meetings with managers and peers. *New York Times* writer Lisa Belkin interviewed Breanna and wrote, "The workplace piece of her transgender puzzle, the part she had worried about most, 'turned out to be the simplest,' she said. 'That was a surprise.'"[33]

Along the way, we not only got educated on transgender issues, but also—as often happens when we learn constructively to call out differences—we suddenly gained new insights into other issues, such as gender. What does it mean, when you really think about it, to be male or female? Is gender a binary either/or identity, or is it more of a continuum? What does masculinity and femininity mean after all? Right now, picture in your mind what masculine and feminine look like to you. Now, think about all the men and women you know. How much do they overlap in their gender expression in terms of what it means to be a man or a woman?

The transgender issue got me thinking about male/female workplace team interaction in ways that go beyond the Venus/Mars dichotomies or even some of the excellent social linguistic work by the renowned Dr. Deborah Tannen, who has written extensively on male and female differences in the workplace and elsewhere.

Today, 66 percent[34] of the Fortune 500 include "gender identity" in their non-discrimination policies, compared with only 3 percent in 2002, according to the HRC.[35]

The day after Breanna was introduced to her colleagues, she sent me an email: "Today I could finally be me."

In the cacophony of contentious debates, what can we learn from the LGBT individuals in our midst?

Shh. Listen. ⌒

Glossary of terms

Bisexual

A person who is emotionally, romantically, sexually, and relationally attracted to both men and women, though not necessarily simultaneously. A bisexual person may not be equally attracted to both sexes, and the degree of attraction may vary as sexual identity develops over time.

Coming out

The process in which a person first acknowledges, accepts, and appreciates his or her sexual orientation or gender identity and begins to share that with others.

Crossdresser

A person who sometimes dresses in clothing and/or accouterments (such as makeup and accessories) traditionally associated with the opposite sex.

Gay

A man or woman who is emotionally, romantically, sexually, and relationally attracted to members of the same sex.

Gender

An internal sense of self and the role a person takes in social interactions, as in "man" or "woman," "masculine" or "feminine," "he" or "she." Gender involves a person's internal feelings of "gender identity," as well as external "gender role" or "gender expression." Gender is not a synonym for biological sex, although the sex and gender of most people are congruent (a concept referred to as *cisgender*).

Gender expression

All of the external characteristics and behaviors that are socially defined as either masculine or feminine, such as dress, grooming, mannerisms, speech patterns, and social interactions. Social or cultural norms vary widely and some characteristics that may be accepted as masculine, feminine, or neutral in one culture may not be assessed similarly in another culture.

Gender identity

A person's innate, deeply felt psychological identification as masculine or feminine, which may or may not correspond to the person's body or the biological sex originally listed on his or her birth certificate.

Gender Identity Disorder

Gender Identity Disorder is a psychological diagnosis previously recognized by the American Psychiatric Association. In order to eliminate stigma and ensure treatment for individuals experiencing distress, the term was changed to *gender dysphoria* in the new edition of Diagnostic and Statistical Manual of Mental Disorders (DSM-5®).[36] This disorder is marked by severe distress and discomfort caused by the conflict between one's gender identity and one's designated sex at birth. Not all transgender people experience gender dysphoria or are diagnosed with Gender Identity Disorder.

Gender roles

Societal expectations of how we are supposed to appear and behave depending on our assigned biological sex. Among the most explicit social rules is that one is expected to present oneself in public in a manner consistent with one's sex, and that presentation is to be unambiguous.

Gender transition

The term "transitioning" refers to the process through which a person modifies his or her physical characteristics and/or manner of gender expression to be consistent with his or her gender identity. This transition may include hormone therapy, gender reassignment surgery and/or other components, and is generally conducted under medical supervision based on a set of standards developed by medical professionals. The transition process typically includes a one-year "real-life experience" in which the individual lives and presents consistently with their gender identity under medical supervision.

Gender variance

The degree to which a person's gender identity or gender expression is different from cultural expectations. A gender variant person is one whose gender variance is high enough for the person to be harassed or discriminated against.

Homophobia

The fear and hatred of—or discomfort with—people who love and are sexually attracted to members of the same sex.

LGBT

An acronym for "Lesbian, Gay, Bisexual, and Transgender" (also written as GLBT, LGBTQ, and LGBTQ+).

Lesbian

A woman who is emotionally, romantically, sexually, and relationally attracted to other women.

Living openly

A state in which LGBT people are open with others about being LGBT.

Outing

Exposing someone's sexual orientation as gay, lesbian, bisexual or transgender to others, usually without their permission—in essence "outing" them from the closet.

Queer

A term that is inclusive of people who are not heterosexual. For many LGBT people, the word has a negative connotation. However, younger LGBT people are often comfortable using it and have reclaimed it as a symbol of pride.

Sexual orientation

An individual's physical and/or emotional attraction to the same and/or opposite gender.

Sexual preference

What a person likes or prefers to do sexually—a conscious recognition or choice, not to be confused with sexual orientation.

Straight supporter/ally

A person who supports and honors sexual diversity, acts accordingly to challenge homophobic remarks and behaviors, and explores and understands these forms of bias within himself or herself.

Sex

Categorization as female or male based on anatomic features or other biological markers such as chromosomes or hormones.

Sex reassignment surgery (SRS)

Surgical transformation of the genital area from the appearance characteristic of one sex to that of the other sex; may also include breast reduction in transsexual men.

Target sex

The sex toward which an individual is transitioning.

Transgender

A term describing a broad range of people who experience and/or express their gender differently from what most people expect. It is an umbrella term that includes people who are transsexual, crossdressers, or otherwise gender non-conforming.

Transsexual

A medical term describing people whose gender and sex do not match, and who often seek medical treatment to bring their body and gender identity into alignment.

Sources: Human Rights Campaign (HRC), other LGBTQA+ advocates

SUMMARY POINTS

- Many LGBT employees are forced to remain in the closet at work in order to keep their jobs.

- A growing number of companies offer benefits and have adopted inclusive practices directed toward LGBT employees and consumers.

- Companies are starting to see the marketplace through LGBT eyes. Consumers from emerging markets, particularly LGBT, are actively considering an organization's internal diversity policies when selecting a company for purchasing decisions.

- Conversations grounded in relationships can foster dramatically different dynamics than those grounded in religion, politics, or other belief systems. Knowing someone on a personal level matters.

- In addressing many diversity issues—particularly those that deal with transgender employees—principles, practices, and policies may be easier to manage than actual implementation. Calling out differences and navigating the gap between assumptions and reality can make the constructive difference.

SHAPING YOUR STRATEGY

- On a scale of 1 to 10, where 10 is full acceptance, openness, and supportive policies of LGBT, and 1 is a place where LGBT employees are afraid to be out, where would you rate your company in terms of LGBT diversity?

- How would your LGBT employees answer the previous question? How would the rest of your work population answer it?

- Do you know your company's HRC Corporate Equality score? Do you know what you need to do to improve that score? If you have not participated, would you consider doing so? To find out more, please visit www.hrc.org/issues/workplace/cei_criteria.htm

- Is there a way to use the strategy of focusing on relationship versus debate to create a more participatory and inclusive conversation around LGBT issues?

PART 4:
CALLING OUT
DIFFERENCES IN
ORGANIZATIONS

Part 4: Calling out differences in organizations

Organizations are living organisms. In many ways, they act like people. They're equally as culturally complex as the humans who comprise them. So, while we are bulking up our own crosscultural strengths, we must remember to develop this competency within our organizations as well.

Beyond essential strategies and techniques for creating organizational change—such as rewards, training, leadership, and engagement—this section of the book focuses on the actual cultural dynamics that take place in increasingly diverse organizations. In essence, these are the worldviews that shape organizational culture and, in turn, suggest approaches for defining good work, fair policies, and engaging environments.

As with people and groups, what seems "right and true" in an organization may simply be, as Dr. R. Roosevelt Thomas Jr. says, "a preference, tradition, or convenience," but not necessarily a "requirement" for getting the job done.[1] To create true inclusion—an environment where the mix of people is working creatively and efficiently—we must call out our differences within the organization. For example, do the needs of Millennials, Gen Xers, women, and racial minorities within an organization vary significantly from the needs of the mainstream workforce? Are leaders adequately equipped to lead diverse and multicultural teams in the global marketplace? How do organizations adequately prepare for the Talent War, especially one that's already being lost in junior highs and high schools, where students of color are graduating in decreasing numbers and without relevant skills?

We must consider the unexpected places in organizations where exclusion may inadvertently occur—within benefits offerings, for example. It may be surprising to learn the different perspectives African Americans, Latinos, women, and White men bring to retirement investing or maximizing their healthcare benefits. What works for one does not automatically work for another. Organizations must take special care to develop benefits plans and marketing tools tailored to each community's specific worldview.

It's hard enough to manage individual change but, in the end, will, strength, skill, and motivation can be enough. When it comes to organizations, change is even more difficult to achieve, and these four dimensions are simply not enough. The inertia of "how things have always been," the Herculean task of changing people's minds, and the ability to create a new path where one previously did not exist all create barriers to delivering organizational change. This is why many companies often fail to round the bend when dangerous curves lie ahead, instead plunging off the precipice because they cannot control their momentum.

In spite of these obstacles, a number of organizations have managed to navigate the curve of change successfully. Their leaders sounded the clarion call for change just in time to make the hairpin turn, allowing them to make the necessary adjustments and investments. These organizations grasped the depth of the challenges posed to systems and structures created for another era and were courageous enough to engage in what Joseph Schumpeter referred to as "creative destruction."[2]

In the Obama Era, entire nations are facing this type of transformational challenge. If ever there was a time to begin an honest evaluation of our programs, policies, and processes—the very ones that contributed to past successes—that time is now. ⌇

the Inclusive Leader

Competencies
Experiences

12

Traits
Drivers

**GLOBAL
LEADER**

**GROWTH
LEADER**

**INNOVATION
LEADER**

**CHANGE
LEADER**

Chapter 12
Must have: The Inclusive Leader

Throughout our journey together in this book, we have been applying the Inclusion Paradox to the unprecedented demographic shifts of this era by identifying new ways of thinking and new approaches. But there are two factors that could make all our efforts obsolete: 1) Leaders with a lack of conviction that diversity and inclusion is vital to their organizations' success, and 2) Leaders without the skill to manage diversity's tensions and assets.

Leaders who can address both of these limitations are must-haves for organizations that want to move to next-generation diversity—clearly, we need Inclusive Leaders.

Sounds appealing, but what exactly is an Inclusive Leader?

At Korn Ferry, we have developed a comprehensive answer. But first, let's start by defining the twenty-first century leader. Doing so will help us to see how this path will take us right to the heart of inclusive leadership.

Twenty-first century executives have prioritized seizing mind-blowing opportunities and thwarting hair-raising threats. Given that current legacies, traditions, and best practices are not working in providing guidance like they did in the past, today's leaders face unprecedented obstacles that leave them feeling unprepared in handling diversity and inclusion challenges.

Korn Ferry research, mining over 2.5 million leadership assessments, has defined the success profile of this twenty-first century leader. Let's begin by discussing this profile and its implications for leading inclusively.

A successful twenty-first century leader must be four things at once: a global leader, a growth leader, a change leader, and an innovation leader.

As you can see in the figure below, each type of leader embodies a certain set of behaviors.

Korn Ferry research: 21st century leaders needed today

Global leaders

- Attract global talent, operate across boundaries, meet diverse customer needs
- Require global perspective, **cultural agility,** self-awareness, openness, and flexibility
- Depend on their capable, self-directed teams

Innovation leaders

- View problems as challenges to be overcome
- Use technology for new products/ services
- Work hard to stay in front of trends by creating new markets
- **Open to diverse points of view**

Change leaders

- Pivot the organization in anticipation of or in response to market changes
- Swiftly change the business model and lead competitors because of adaptability and foresight
- **Master the ability to inspire and motivate people in a dynamic environment with unprecedented diverse teams**

Growth leaders

- Thrive in new, complex, and crowded business environment
- See and understand how to reach, design for, and **serve traditionally underrepresented consumers and clients**
- Grow business under difficult circumstances that may involve a lack of resources, fierce competition, or razor-thin margins

If we look closely at this table, we see that all four of these critical dimensions of being a twenty-first century leader requires the skills of diversity, inclusion, and crosscultural agility (in the bolded text).

Let's explore this connection to diversity and inclusion for each of the four dimensions:

- *Global leaders* need to exhibit crosscultural agility, a competency composite that requires self-awareness of one's own cultural influences, the ability to see workplace situations from the perspective of others, and the wherewithal to accept different types of beliefs and behaviors for addressing business challenges.

- *Innovation leaders* must not only know how to attract talent from diverse backgrounds, perspectives, experiences, and thinking styles, but also be able to activate this diversity through inclusive environments that invite innovative perspectives as well as give permission to those who don't adhere to the status quo in order to have their voices be heard as catalysts to innovation.

- *Growth leaders* need to pursue unprecedented diverse consumers whose aspirations, needs, wants, and desires can vary widely from traditional and legacy consumers and customers. This demands truly understanding people very different than oneself.

- *Change leaders* must be able to quickly hire skilled talent from all talent pools, master the ability to inspire and motivate people in a dynamic environment with unprecedented diverse teams, manage organizational cultural differences in the midst of complex mergers and acquisitions, lead leadership teams with multiple nationalities in the midst of launching brand-new organizational global structures, and be able to navigate the brand's positioning in the midst of touchy social diversity issues and complex national country politics.

Therefore, by definition, *the twenty-first century leader must be an Inclusive Leader.*

These requirements often instill a sense of anxiety and perplexity in leaders when confronted with the charge for them to lead inclusively. At first, they show excitement and demonstrate conviction, laying out the following business case:

- Today's world does look completely different demographically and is only going to continue to change.

- If we are going to attract more than our fair share of the best and scarcest talent, we need diversity.

- Markets are growing in the diverse, previously untapped emerging areas of the world and among a broader set of demographics in our own regions.

- Diversity is required to achieve innovation.

But inevitably, they change course and confide that they are mostly unprepared to be inclusive in the ways these business challenges require, acknowledging that they don't have an understanding of what to do and how to do it.

And, in fact, research confirms their hesitations. As companies have gotten better at recruiting diversity (after all, we have greater diversity today than we did five or ten years ago at both the entry and supervisor levels), they have struggled to retain that talent and advance it into positions of leadership and influence.

Further, leadership has not yet been able to fully achieve the promise that greater diversity is good for the organization. A study by N. J. Adler demonstrated that while diverse teams do indeed outperform and out-innovate homogenous teams, they can also be significantly less effective.[1]

Impact of diversity on team performance

Reference: Adler, N.J., International Dimensions of Organizational Behavior (4th ed.). Cincinnati, Ohio, South-Western. 2002 | © Milton J. Bennett, 2008

Why? Because diversity by itself is not enough. Rather, it has to be skillfully managed in an inclusive way. Without inclusion, diversity has a high chance of becoming chaotic, leading to lower productivity and engagement, higher turnover, and litigation.

This speaks to the attractiveness of homogeneity. It is indeed easier to manage a group of people with similar backgrounds and experiences. However, it is significantly more difficult to convince teams made up of individuals of varying differences to understand their thought patterns and behaviors and value them at a deep and personal level.

But Inclusive Leaders who are skilled at navigating these differences are able to optimize their performance to the point that the differences, rather than just being obstacles to overcome, are actually leveraged assets that lead to better performance than that of homogeneous teams.

If diversity is the mix, and inclusion is making the mix work™, this research and the emerging maturity in executives' understanding of diversity has shifted the question from "How do we create a diverse workforce?" to "How do we leverage the wealth of knowledge, insights, and perspectives of our diverse workforce?" Cue The Inclusive Leader.

How Inclusive Leaders generate engagement, innovation, and marketplace penetration

In Chapter 2, "Sustainable diversity: Relevant, profitable, and game-changing," I described how sustainable diversity requires us to go beyond the best talent in the midst of the Talent War imperative and explore how diversity and inclusion can help organizations achieve their broader business goals.

So, while not forgetting the need for greater diversity to meet talent needs, let's synthesize the connections from key business needs to inclusive leadership:

The business case for inclusive leadership

Inclusive Leaders drive organizational growth in the 21st century

Biggest challenge:
Create growth

To have growth, you need to differentiate

To differentiate, you need to innovate

To innovate, you need diversity

To activate the diversity, you need inclusion

To manage all this, you need inclusive leadership

As we can see, for the twenty-first century leader, inclusiveness is the new currency of power, influence, and effectiveness. It is the catalyst for unleashing talent to the fullness of its potential, which in turn provides the jet fuel that companies require to seize the world's opportunities by storm.

According to a study by Shapiro Consulting and Opportunity Now, the uplift of an Inclusive Leader on the workforce is palpable and has a multiplier effect. Organizations with Inclusive Leaders experience the following high-impact benefits in employee outcomes:

- 79% improved collaboration
- 81% improved performance and productivity
- 84% greater engagement and loyalty
- 84% increased motivation
- 86% increased innovation and creativity[2]

Another report, *Innovation, Diversity and Market Growth,* also determines that organizations with Inclusive Leaders are:

- 70% more likely to have captured a new market in the past 12 months
- 45% more likely to increase market share[3]

Further, a 2014 McKinsey study, *Diversity Matters*, of 366 companies in the United States, Canada, Latin America, and the United Kingdom show correlations between diversity in leadership positions—a key metric of inclusion—and financial performance. Companies that were in the top quartile in terms of women in leadership were also in the top quartile of financial performance, outperforming those who did not have strong gender diversity by 15%. Even more stunning is that those in the top quartile in terms of leaders of color outperformed less diverse companies by 30%.[4]

But despite the clear correlations between inclusion and positive business impact found in the McKinsey and the Opportunity Now studies, most companies lack truly Inclusive Leaders. In the Opportunity Now survey, 66 percent of employees said that less than half of the managers in their organization were Inclusive Leaders.

So, paradoxically, while many companies see the value in recruiting and developing a diverse workforce, they fall short at optimizing the value of that diversity through inclusive practices and behaviors.

The qualities of the Inclusive Leader

What, then, are these qualities that Inclusive Leaders need to master and demonstrate and which are in short supply at organizations?

At Korn Ferry, we explored this question in the same systemic and holistic way we look at integrated performance qualities, using Korn Ferry's Four Dimensions of Leadership and Talent (KF4D). The KF4D is used to assess and develop people's talent by looking at their competencies, experiences, traits, and drivers. What does an Inclusive Leader look like through this lens when forged from our 2.5 million assessments over the last forty years?

First, there are these key questions that must be answered within each of the four dimensions:

- **Competencies** – Does the leader have the skills required to lead in a vastly global and diverse world and market?

- **Experiences** – Does the leader have the variety of experiences that prepare them to get the best out of *all* their people in a global and diverse world?

- **Traits** – What is the leader's disposition toward cultural differences and commonalities?

- **Drivers** – What are the leader's cultural preferences that influence how they engage, collaborate, innovate, and lead?[5]

The Inclusive Leader

Competencies
Does leader have the skills required to lead in a vastly global and diverse world and market?

Experiences
Does the leader have the variety of experiences that prepare them to get the best out of *all* their people in a global and diverse world?

WHAT YOU DO
WHO YOU ARE

Traits
What is the leader's disposition toward cultural differences and commonalities?

Drivers
What are the leader's cultural preferences that influence how they engage, collaborate, innovate, and lead?

Let's look at each of these dimensions in turn:

Competencies

First, we identified just over a dozen competencies from our Korn Ferry Leadership Architect™ (KFLA) that tied to inclusive behaviors in one way or another.[6] These are grouped around the following six competency clusters:

- Building collaborative relationships
- Optimizing diverse talent
- Influencing people
- Being flexible and adaptable
- Being open
- Being authentic

The Inclusive Leader Competencies (developmental view)

Open and aware
- Self-aware
- Develops self
- Nimble learner
- Global mindset
- Resilient

Actively promotes difference
- Values differences
- Attracts diverse top talent
- Develops all talent
- Communicates the value of D&I effectively
- Drives engagement

Optimizes organizational performance
- Drives vision and purpose
- Builds effective diverse teams
- Builds trusting networks
- Cultivates innovation
- Drives results

Builds a trusting and open culture
- Manages ambiguity
- Manages conflict
- Interpersonally savvy
- Courageous
- Instills trust

Influences effectively
- Organizationally savvy
- Situationally adaptable
- Persuasive
- Collaborates
- Balances stakeholders

"Inclusive Leaders that exercise the behaviors within these competency clusters," says Korn Ferry Senior Partner David Lange, "have learning and crosscultural agility, are curious about the unknown, possess the humility necessary to ask the naïve questions, are self-aware about their own beliefs and preferences, and are students of how others from other cultures can be different and similar to themselves while simultaneously using this very friction to ignite new and unexpected answers. They also show up as authentic and transparent, inspiring others to be and do the same."

···

Inclusive leadership from the inside out

By Kevin Cashman, Korn Ferry Senior Partner and bestselling author of Leadership from the inside out *and* The Pause principle

For nearly thirty years of work in our research laboratories in leadership development, our Executive Institutes and Chief Executive Institutes, we have extracted deep insight into what is really essential for leadership as we work as a team with one leader at a time to facilitate his or her accelerated development and breakthroughs.

One of the characteristics of effective leadership is the ability to lead from the inside out and the outside in. Leading from inside out means that the person can tap into the depths of their person and have it flow outward to influence others. Leading from the outside in means they are able to serve a variety of constituencies and, for each one, they have to be aware of how they are receiving them.

Diversity and inclusion, to be effective and sustainable, is also about both outside in and inside out. I have seen organizations that think about it too narrowly as just outside in. They focus solely on how can they tap organizational systems and processes such as hiring and rewards to be more inclusive with what is outside the system.

However, in deep inclusive leadership, the development work is about inside out. How is the person limiting others or limiting possibilities by their own biases, their own belief systems, their own behaviors, or their own self-awareness or lack thereof?

For diversity and inclusion to be sustainable, we have to transform key leaders from the inside out as well as transform systems from the outside in.

Turns out that what is required from Inclusive Leaders from the inside out is essentially an extension of the three qualities we have found is required of exceptionally effective leaders: authenticity, influence, and value creation.

- **Authenticity.** Self-awareness is the developmental breakthrough underneath the characteristic of authenticity. The most effective leaders tend to be the most self-aware of their strengths, development areas, biases, influences, and their impact on others. They understand where they are in their journey of understanding their unique and authentic selves, and, in that, are able to both be true to themselves and help others be as well. This is why emotional intelligence is at the core of inclusiveness and diversity because it's at that intersection of self-awareness and awareness of others that authentic connection between people takes place.

- **Influence.** It's possible to be authentic but maybe one is not able to move people. Effective leaders are able to take their self-awareness to move and activate others and they do that by reminding themselves and others of what's really important. This is how purpose-driven value systems lived authentically inspire people to get aligned around mission, strategy, and execution. And from a diversity perspective, these leaders are able to tune into and address the unique needs, wants, and aspirations of people from a vast spectrum of differences.

- **Value creation.** These leaders not only create a great amount of financial value, but they do so by affecting multiple bottom lines as they bring value to multiple constituencies: their teams, the organization, customers, and in some cases, the environment and other societal needs.

You put these three leadership outcomes together and we see that inclusive leadership is not so much about a role in the hierarchy, but rather about being an authentic influence that creates enduring value.

Experiences

"Does the leader have the variety of experiences that prepare her or him to get the best out of all their people in a global and diverse world?" asks Senior Partner Kevin Cashman, author of numerous groundbreaking books on leadership, including *Leadership from the inside out: Becoming a leader for life.* "This is no small matter. Inclusiveness is one of those qualities that is forged in the crucible of having been exposed to a vast diversity of people and contexts that challenge our preconceived notions of how the world works. Without these perception-challenging experiences, it is nearly impossible to shake the grip of the unconscious biases we all have about who others are and how we evaluate their performance while also finding ways to motivate them to optimize their contributions."

David Lange shares examples of grounding experiences:

- Crosscultural experiences in professional and personal life. Has the leader had an extended stay within a different culture whether inside his or her country or outside of it? This could be for a slew of reasons such as growing up in a family with parents carrying out overseas assignments in business, not-for-profit, government, military, or missionary organizations; or firsthand as a student studying abroad or doing a service program during high school or college and later on in expatriate assignments of his or her own.

- Job assignments across a variety of contexts that are cross-functional, cross-divisional, cross-market. Comparable to the displacement from the familiar that is elicited by the examples in the first bullet, these kinds of experiences force individuals not to operate from their traditional comfort zone and where their go-to assumptions are challenged every which way. These kinds of experiences, if approached with humility and in a spirit of learning agility, are always transformative in leaders being able to develop a sensibility to see things from other perspectives they would not have been able to had they not been put in these alternative situations.

- Playing a key role in the integration of two corporate cultures in a merger and acquisition event. An Aon Hewitt study shows that respondents from 96 companies said that 71% of M&A transactions fail to achieve their financial synergies due to the inability to constructively resolve corporate culture differences.[7] Inclusive leadership is a must to navigate the deeply felt understandings of the values and behaviors for how best to succeed that permeate the two organizations and which have for the most part worked for them. But now they must reconcile the way forward when the expected behaviors are in conflict with one another. The failures and successes in doing this are formative experiences for shaping Inclusive Leaders.

Traits

What is a leader's disposition toward cultural differences and commonalities? Much research over time has mapped out reactions to difference across a spectrum. Dr. Milton Bennett developed a very useful construct in this area, within a framework he calls the Developmental Model of Intercultural Sensitivity.[8] Bennett's DMIS model maps the range of dispositions, with some competencies embedded throughout, moving from Denial to Polarization to Minimization to Acceptance to Adaptation.

When compared to our Korn Ferry research on traits, we have mapped and re-worded these as dispositions toward difference in the following sequence:

- Avoidance
- Indifference
- Judgment
- Non-Exploratory acceptance
- Exploratory curiosity

Let's explore why understanding a leader's disposition toward difference is important to operating inclusively.

The limitations of Avoidance, Indifference, and Judgment should be self-evident. One can imagine how the Avoidance and Indifference traits will lead to a lack of engaging the reality of differences that, as we have seen so far, are necessary to mitigate the inevitable conflicts that arise in diverse environments. And, conversely, not engaging these differences will lead to decreased leverage of power for greater creativity and innovation. And Judgment, well, we can easily see so much evidence of its lack of constructiveness both in society and in the workplace as this turns into racism, sexism, homophobia, Islamophobia, and other forms of prejudices and discrimination.

The concept that leaders have the most trouble understanding is why Exploratory curiosity would be more inclusive than Non-Exploratory acceptance. Dr. Bennett calls this latter disposition "Minimization," which he defines as a mindset in which the individual focuses more on commonalities and less on differences. This, of course, is the legacy of a generation of diversity work that stressed being color-blind and gender-blind—a place where, in Dr. Martin Luther King's words, people would be "judged not by the color of their skin, but by the content of their character."

Why is this uplifting message and its accompanying trait characterized by a lack of curiosity in how our differences could make us non-inclusive? It's because this assumption of similarity can mask ways in which we are different, and thus, ignore each individual's diverse life experiences. And if key gaps are not recognized by acknowledging differences, it can lead to a form of bias: When we assume that everyone is the same, we assume that everyone is "just like me."

The Inclusive Leader is cognizant of this trap and not only demonstrates active curiosity in how others' differences can make a difference in their experience with the organization, but also nurtures an organizational environment in which others are encouraged to do the same.

Drivers

Drivers are often thought of as the sources of motivation, energy, and purpose in leaders. In the KF4D model, at the macro level, an example of performance drivers include making a lot of money, achieving recognition, striking balance between work and personal, inspiring people, and making a difference in the world. In the Inclusive Leader set of drivers, however, the focus is on the culture drivers that influence how leaders engage, collaborate, innovate, and lead as they encounter differences. This is critical information to consider, because leaders' work-style preferences are indeed influenced by their cultural worldviews.

Over the last 50 years, interculturalists such as Milton Bennett, Fons Trompenaars, and Geert Hofstede have in one way or another codified various continua or spectra of how people from different cultures are influenced by the experiences and influences that make up the culture(s) they identify with. In a business context, some examples include the following:

- *Communication preference*: Direct or indirect?
- *Ascribing status*: Hierarchically or participative?
- *Getting things done*: Through tasks or through people?
- *Managing risk*: Seeking flexibility or seeking stability?
- *Locus of control*: Within oneself or outside oneself?
- *Decision-making timeframe*: Short-term or long-term?
- *Managing time*: Managed by the clock or managed by the dynamics of the experience?
- *Managing emotions*: Showing emotion or restraining from showing emotion?

Cultural self-awareness on the part of a leader is essential to understanding how one's preferred style may or may not be helpful and productive when working with team members from different cultures and experiences.

"Inclusive Leaders are skilled at identifying their own and others' cultural drivers and are then able to exercise the necessary curiosity to compare and contrast how others may be similar to or different from them," explains Lange. "With this insight, they can shape their individual interactions for optimal connection with others and sharpen their inclusiveness by ensuring the organization's strategic priorities are crossculturally adept in addressing unconscious bias. They can do this while also adjusting to the different needs, aspirations, and wants of an increasing number of people whose cultural drivers can be very different from leaders forged in previous years."

The inclusive organization

Inclusive Leaders lead to Inclusive Organizations. Leaders need to be inclusive in order to help their organizations be more effective, innovative, and differentiated through highly engaged, high-performing diverse teams.

The Inclusive Organization can be measured in a few ways. The simplest method is to develop a summary report of all the Inclusive Leader assessments. This report would provide an aggregate of the collective strengths and vulnerabilities of the organization's leaders in their efforts to lead inclusively.

For deeper analysis of the Inclusive Organization, a D&I audit can be created to measure the organization's maturity along the various phases of diversity and inclusion. As is evident in the diagram below, the elements of maturity include not only the classic vertical dimensions of D&I (awareness, training, affinity groups, councils), but also the more systemic and embedded dimensions such as reputation, alignment to business performance, and marketplace growth.

Definitions: Where is your company on organizational D&I maturity?

Where is your organization now and where do you want to be?

STAGE 1
FOUNDATION

Compliance
driven

- Regulatory
  requirements
- Representation is
  measured
- Diversity only
  about race and
  gender

No:
  - Business case
  - Dedicated
    resources
  - Leader
    involvement
  - Strategy

STAGE 2
AWARENESS

Talent/values
driven

- Diverse talent
  seen as benefit
  to org
- Inclusive culture
  acknowledged as
  asset
- Leaders
  accept some
  responsibility for
  D&I
- Definition
  of diversity
  broadened
- Diversity hiring
  based on targets
- Some D&I
  initiatives
  implemented
- D&I seen as
  enhancing brand
- Training focused
  on awareness
- Efforts are
  programmatic

STAGE 3
APPLICATION

Performance
driven

- Leadership
  applies D&I to
  business priorities
- Strategies
  designed to
  create inclusive
  work environment
- Leaders have D&I
  accountabilities
- Impact of D&I
  begins to get
  measured
- Training focused
  on interpersonal
  capability
- Efforts begin to
  be systemic

STAGE 4
INTEGRATION

Business
focused/
operationally
driven

- Management
  supports diversity
  by role modeling
- D&I integrated
  into all talent
  management
  processes
- D&I recognized
  as contributing to
  business success
- D&I seen as
  an essential
  leadership
  competency
- Training focused
  on business
  application

STAGE 5
SUSTAINABLE

Market/strategy
driven

- D&I is systemic
  enabler for
  growing and
  managing the
  business
- D&I enhances
  business
  performance
  and competitive
  advantage
- Leaders are D&I
  change agents
- Organization's
  reputation for D&I
  makes it employer
  of choice
- Workforce reflects
  the market

The results of the audit will determine where the organization falls in their D&I maturity and how the leaders rank in the Inclusive Leader assessment. Regardless of where the organization falls, the leaders now have an opportunity to apply their inclusive leadership skills to move the organization up the maturity scale.

Regardless of which assessment is used, the payoffs will be exponentially profitable.

Interweaving inclusive leadership with leadership development

*By Noah Rabinowitz, former Leadership Development
Global Practice Leader, Korn Ferry*

A 2015 Korn Ferry study[9] with over 7,500 responses worldwide uncovered four critical leadership development challenges—and each one has direct diversity and inclusion implications:

1. **Driving a changing business strategy.** Leadership development has the potential to build and activate the new capabilities—including the new ideas and innovations essential for growth—that will drive a changing strategy into the future. But, currently 55 percent of leadership development programs are judged as fair, poor, or very poor. Clearly, there's a lot of room for improvement.

   Diversity implication: So much of the marketplace is being upended by the changing demographics of unprecedented diversity. Leaders who are untrained in inclusion and crosscultural agility skills will fall short of addressing this major dimension in driving changing business strategy. Further, the workforce makeup must resemble the changing customer profile—not only to match how it looks, but also to infuse the organization with the diversity of thought required for innovation.

2. **Building the talent pipeline.** Organizations are struggling to find the right talent for the jobs of today and tomorrow. Only 17 percent of executives are confident that their organization has the leadership capabilities it needs. Leadership development has always and will always be about developing the bench, preparing leaders, and creating flow through the talent pipeline. But, development has not yet fulfilled its promise of creating strong bench strength that prepares the organization for its next chapter.

   Diversity implication: The statistics of the diminished talent pipeline add to the urgency in training leaders to understand how their organizations inspire, source, attract, retain, engage, develop, and promote talent from traditionally underrepresented groups, which is where the growing volume of talent lies. Much more can be done to accelerate the development of talent pools that are currently underrepresented. Doing so will increase bench strength and create more readiness and opportunities.

3. **Aligning culture to strategy.** Leadership development is just as much about shaping culture as it is about shaping leaders. By developing the next generation of leaders toward a new cultural mindset, we push the organization forward and align behaviors and attitudes to the culture we need and want. However, studies show nearly 62 percent of first-level leaders are neutral, somewhat inactive, or very inactive in driving strategic change. To change and align culture, we need them more engaged.

   Diversity implication: Yes, cultural change is vital for organizations to survive and thrive when it is very difficult to do. One great opportunity lies in bringing in more talent that is different in its personal and professional experiences and who bring a different worldview of how things need to be done. Leaders have to be developed not only to bring the mix in the door (diversity), but also to ensure that mix is working well (inclusion). As organizations seek to build cultures of performance, achievement, growth, and engagement, this recruitment of talent can only be accomplished by creating an environment in which all employees feel they contribute to their fullest potential.

4. **Becoming more mission-focused and socially conscious.** Leaders today are starved for meaning and purpose. In our work, we have seen over and over that organizations that align their values and culture to a higher sense of purpose achieve greater long-term results. This can be achieved by developing leaders who are self-aware, committed to change, and who believe in the power of organizations to make a difference in their community and the world. However, 52 percent of organizations ranked "becoming more purpose- and values-driven" as their lowest priority when it comes to developing leaders.

   Diversity implication: This one takes us back to where it all started: Do the right thing. It's about creating an organization that is not only driving the bottom line, but also serving some larger societal purpose. Our society is changing, and organizations should be ahead of these changes. This means greater levels of understanding, collaboration, contribution, and impact. Instilling an attitude of service to something other than self can develop this. Being a more diverse and inclusive organization—by design, attitude, and skill—lies at the heart of being mission-focused and socially conscious.

Rank the most important leadership development priorities in your organization

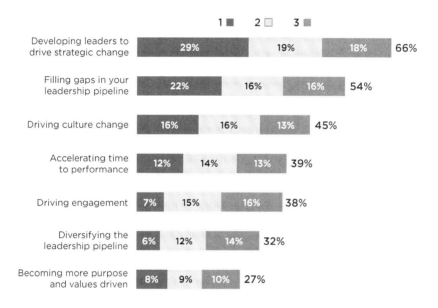

....

The Inclusive Leader in action – A Millennial perspective

By Carolyn McChesney and Caroline Crow, Associates, Korn Ferry

What types of talent issues can Inclusive Leaders tackle more effectively as they grow in and develop across all four dimensions of the KF4D for The Inclusive Leader? I asked two Millennial colleagues to share their opinions on this. Here's what they came up with.

Among the various challenges Inclusive Leaders face is understanding how to optimize Millennial engagement and performance—a group that will constitute 75 percent of the workforce by 2025.[10]

Part of doing this is understanding how Millennials view diversity differently than Boomers. Unlike their older colleagues, Millennials don't limit the definitions of diversity and inclusion to demographic differences. Millennials believe in cognitive diversity—the blending of unique perspectives within a team.[11] They see value in diverse experiences and backgrounds and believe that others' range of perspectives should be used to innovate. Sometimes known as the "Teaming Generation," Millennials can often be unconsciously inclusive and expect leaders to leverage their young workers' inclusive behavior.[12]

Here are a few ways we believe they can do this:

1. **Free others from downplaying their identities.** Much of the failure to leverage diversity comes from the fact that minorities often feel the need to downplay—or cover—who they are when they are in the office. *Covering* is a term that was first used by sociologist Erving Goffman to describe how people with "known stigmatized identities" consciously choose to "mute" those identities.[13]

   Sixty-one percent of those surveyed by Deloitte University said they cover at work.[14] This includes people of different races, ethnicities, personalities, physical and cognitive disabilities, and sexual orientations. Even 45 percent of straight white males—a group that historically hasn't been the subject of diversity and inclusion studies—reported covering.[15] The same is true for those with obvious differences, such as gender, who choose to cover by de-emphasizing particular ways of doing things. For example, a woman may not present an idea in a fashion that may be truer to her preferred style out of fear that she won't be accepted in the workplace as a result.

Inclusive Leaders help nurture environments in which employees are comfortable being their most authentic selves. This is especially true when a leader is attempting to recruit and retain Millennials. According to a study by Deloitte University's Leadership Center for Inclusion, one of the reasons Millennials change jobs about every two years is because "they are intolerant of workplaces that don't allow them to be themselves."[16]

While Millennials have grown up in diverse environments and therefore may not feel as strong a need to cover, many still do. And covering not only costs them; it costs their organizations.

2. **Foster environments of uniqueness and belonging.** Studies show that employees feel they are included when they are seen as both similar to and distinct from their coworkers.[17] The Inclusive Leader promotes these feelings of uniqueness and belonging in several important ways.

   First, he or she takes the time to get to know individuals not only in a work context, but also personally. Specifically, what drives the employee? What are his or her goals—both professionally and personally? What is his or her work style? What really makes this employee unique, as he or she would define it?

   Next, the Inclusive Leader empowers his or her employees and assigns projects and tasks that are best suited for each team member. This approach improves employee engagement and drives productivity. According to one study, employees that have worked with an Inclusive Leader felt their performance and productivity improved by approximately 81 percent.[18]

3. **Create a sense of value and provide career advancement opportunities.** When employees feel they are valued, company loyalty and levels of retention improve. This is not new knowledge; however, the link between inclusion and retention is less well known. According to a recent Korn Ferry study, 84 percent of respondents say a lack of attention to diversity and inclusion contributes to employee turnover.[19] Additionally, 44 percent of survey respondents say their organization's diversity and inclusion programs do not enhance employee retention.[20] This means that even though companies may have inclusive practices in place, the current leadership's good intentions are not enough, especially for Millennials.

Many Millennials point to a lack of leader emphasis on cognitive diversity and inclusion as a cause of their dissatisfaction in the workplace.[21] Inclusive Leaders recognize this gap and respond by investing in their employees, because they know that Millennials, more than members of any other generation, desire to see and understand the direct impact of their work.[22]

When the Inclusive Leader encourages collaboration and transparency, Millennials are more likely to be engaged and produce better results. And when employees are engaged, they are less likely to look for other employment opportunities. ♀

SUMMARY POINTS

- Moral support and even conviction of the business case for diversity are not enough to achieve breakthrough in creating diverse and inclusive environments. Leaders and managers need to be actually *skilled* at leading inclusively.

- Today's volatile world requires twenty-first century leaders with four vital characteristics: they need to be Global Leaders, Innovation Leaders, Change Leaders, and Results Leaders.

- Essential competencies within each of these four twenty-first century leader characteristics are Inclusive Leader qualities. Therefore, to be a twenty-first century leader, one must be an Inclusive Leader—not just for the sake of D&I but simply to lead effectively.

- The Inclusive Leader can be assessed in a research-validated way through Korn Ferry's Four Dimensions of Leadership and Talent. Inclusive Leaders have Competencies, Experiences, Traits, and Drivers that can be measured and also developed through capability building and other forms of learning.

- Research proves that Inclusive Leaders will be able to measurably generate and mobilize high-performing diverse teams, manage conflict, harness diversity in an inclusive way to generate more innovation, attract and retain best talent from all backgrounds, and penetrate more diverse marketplaces with their products and services.

- Inclusive leadership is an expression of the vital characteristics of a contemporary leader: transparency. In this case, it's about self-awareness and openness about one's own cultural identity and the ability to leverage one's own story to connect with the stories of other leaders, managers, and employees from all backgrounds.

- Millennials have high expectations that their leaders be inclusive. In fact, in their minds, it's not an option not to be if the leaders are to be respected and followed.

SHAPING YOUR STRATEGY

- Make it clear that for D&I to move forward, leaders must go beyond being D&I champions. They need to be skilled at it. To do this, assess your leaders against the criteria of what an Inclusive Leader looks like, how they behave, and can skillfully do.

- Create individual and group developmental plans that address the gaps in the Inclusive Leader assessments. Then provide the developmental support.

- Embed performance expectations that require inclusive leadership for them to be achieved. This can be in all forms of key performance indicators (KPIs) that span the gamut from diverse team effectiveness to reduction of quality issues to marketplace penetration. Ensure these metrics are as close as possible to each leader's areas of responsibility.

- Work with these leaders to own the advancement of D&I in the organization by their declaring what the business case is and validating the strategy for moving forward. Inclusive Leaders accept the mantle that the advancement of D&I, or the lack of it, falls on them rather than on their D&I leader, whose role is not to achieve D&I breakthrough, but rather to be the influential strategist and facilitator for inclusive leadership performance.

MENTORING 1

COMMUNITY 2

RECOGNITION 3

ADVANCEMENT 4

Chapter 13

The four pillars of what makes people of color stay and thrive

Her dismay was palpable. As chief diversity officer of a Fortune 500 company, she rightfully felt proud of the ten MBA hires they snagged at the National Black MBA Association annual conference. Yet, within a year, they were all gone.

She reviewed the massive effort it had taken to recruit them, beginning with obtaining the commitment from the CEO and senior VP of HR for the budget and resources to stage a convincing presence at the conference. Those costs were substantial—$50,000 to sponsor the event; $35,000 to transport and set up their booth; and the travel costs of more than 30 recruiters, hiring managers, and diversity practitioners, along with the costs of setting up follow-up interviews, flying candidates to corporate offices, onboarding, and then training in the company's methodologies. Now, once again, they had ten open positions to fill and all the extra time and money it would require, not to mention the economic loss in productivity. This "revolving door syndrome" is one particularly painful aspect of our ongoing two-steps-forward-one-step-back work.

Many of our companies have gotten quite good at multicultural recruiting. We show up at the marquee diversity events, such as The National Society of Hispanic MBAs (NSHMBA), Black Data Processing Associates (BDPA), State Health Insurance Assistance Program (SHIP), and the National Association of Asian American Professionals (NAAAP). We hound recruiters to maximize local diversity job fairs. We spend big bucks on four-color ads in *DiversityInc*, *Black Enterprise*, *The Advocate*, and *Hispanic Executive Magazine*, among a few dozen others. We've got our story down to a compelling, inspiring "we-want-you-because-we-believe-in-diversity" message. And the recruits buy it ...

... until they hit the hidden barriers of exclusion ... until they experience the raised eyebrows of disapproval when they apparently said something out of turn ... until they see someone from the majority who started at the same time get the plum project that's often followed by the even more plum promotion ... until the great effort with the high-impact result passes without comment or is minimized with a "that's the least we expect from you" shrug ... until they get that first performance review with the message of "you seem to be doing fine, *but* ..." And so the engagement strands that connect the employee to the organization begin to snap, one by one. This weakened connection gives way then to the third or fourth call from the headhunter that this time gets returned and soon the employee is gone. The gain for the company is then erased.

According to a Hewitt client survey a few years ago, two-thirds of companies focus on recruitment, but only one-third focus on retention.[1] In response to this gap, chief diversity officers are increasingly shifting their focus from merely finding employees to keeping them. Good work is indeed happening in the areas of mentoring, development, promotion, rotational roles, and other creative approaches—yet we still have a way to go in mastering their implementation. What is often overlooked is the elusive element of creating a culture of inclusion. Companies must ask themselves, what must be put in place so people who have traditionally been outside the mainstream feel they're truly part of the community, rather than intruders at worst and guests at best?

At this point, using the principle that cultures are different, I'd like to present what I consider the four pillars for engagement and retention:

- Community
- Recognition
- Mentoring
- Advancement

While more than a dozen best practice engagement factors are important to all majority and minority employees, this quartet of factors resonates especially deeply with multicultural employees. Together, these four pillars will create a solid foundation for the engagement and retention of multicultural talent.

Community

Let's return to the cultural studies discussed in Chapter 5, "I need your differences ... and you need mine." As you will recall, Trompenaars and Hampden-Turner identified seven cultural dimensions that manifest themselves differently in different cultures. Some cultures believe identity comes from the group they belong to. Others believe it comes through the individual. They refer to this as Communitarianism vs. Individualism. All four major racial/ethnic minority groups in the United States (Black, Latino, Asian, and Native American) are communal cultures where the sense of group identity—as expressed by *la familia*, the clan, the church, the affinity group—is deeply ingrained. This is in contrast to the majority culture of European Americans, which is more individualistic. It's no coincidence that the first-person pronoun "I" in English is the only pronoun that is capitalized in any language.

This is why affinity groups are of particular importance to multicultural employees. A minority needs a place of refuge in a majority sea. There's a primal desire to be connected to others "like me." This centering, connecting practice, which nurtures a full sense of identity, explains the allure of affinity groups. But there's another community connection that's often overlooked. Members of communitarian cultures long for a sense of connection to the larger community, which is the enterprise. If their only connection is to the demographic affinity group and not to the full corporate community, their sense of identity within the corporate walls will be incomplete, leading to disengagement and eventually turnover.

This is why it's critical to identify those elements required to have an inclusive culture. No one likes being excluded. To be excluded from the community is to have part of one's identity truncated. For multicultural employees, exclusion has not only been painfully real, its negative impact goes deeper, given their longing to be part of something larger than themselves. Corporate cultures, so dominated by the European-American individualistic culture, often overlook the higher-octane energy that could be infused into their corporations by more effectively nurturing enterprise-wide community building. They ignore the reaction of multicultural employees who never fail to notice when CEOs and other executive leaders—even middle managers—show up at heritage month events.

Nor does their absence go unnoticed. Individualistic cultures may minimize the potential impact of their presence since all they did was show up, but for the communal cultures, showing up does something vitally important: it affirms the multicultural group as part of the larger community. More importantly, it's a declaration that the leader also wants to be part of the multicultural community. Those with individualistic worldviews must evaluate the benefit of the event not in terms of how it will benefit them personally, but how their presence will benefit the community.

Another example can be found in the "default settings"—the themes, food, and entertainment that are selected for community events sponsored by the enterprise. Is there a cultural bias toward rock 'n' roll, golf, and pizza? How about some soul food, salsa dancing, and soccer? Or the inclusion of *arroz con pollo*, greens, and Filipino *pancit*?

Corporations must take these same factors into consideration when contemplating their benefits administration. Are they relying too much on an individualistic approach to preventive care ("take care of yourself, go for your physical")? Would they be better served by fostering communal on-site healthcare clinics where employees can bring their families as part of a communal event complete with free checkups, immunizations, and health risk assessments?

The idea here is not to be prescriptive, but to acknowledge that the active nurturing and building of community goes a long way toward engaging and retaining multicultural employees.

Recognition

For multicultural groups that have traditionally been oppressed and marginalized, public recognition is like water in the desert. Oppression and marginalization are acts of dehumanization. They are declarations through words and deeds that certain groups are not fully human since there are restrictions on their universal human rights. When a person of color is recognized publicly for his or her achievement, it's more than an affirming statement. It is a frontal assault on centuries of messages implying that people of color do not matter, that they cannot achieve, that they cannot excel. It is an act that bestows dignity by declaring, *You exist. You are valuable. You matter!*

Given the communal nature of multicultural groups, recognition of the one is recognition of the many. The community as a whole takes pride in the achievement of one of its own. Postings of recognition are often widely circulated by leaders of affinity groups to their membership lists. Of course, recognition can come in many forms, but for people of color, the public nature of recognition is vital. That's why corporate cultures with understated approaches to recognition may inadvertently undermine the desired payoff when recognition is done quietly rather than shouted from the rooftops. For people of color, recognition reverberates even more powerfully when it's done outside the corporate walls. This is why talented professionals of color are often the recipients of numerous awards and recognitions granted by community, not-for-profit, and volunteer organizations with an array of honorifics—such as Outstanding African American of the Year, Community Role Model Professional, Latin Pride—awarded at elegant banquets and trumpeted through press releases.

Too often, these third-party recognitions are overlooked by the corporations where these individuals work. If colleagues and leaders from the enterprise would show up more regularly at these events, the third-party recognition would be magnified exponentially. Why? Because showing up on their turf further reinforces the message that these associates matter. It declares that where they live and the communities they're a part of have value and legitimacy. They're as real and genuine as the places frequented by the enterprise leaders. Companies can also do a better job of making the community and the press aware of recognitions and promotions awarded to their multicultural talent. When these types of approaches are used, we start getting into the synergistic power of the pillars of multicultural engagement and retention. Recognition to the individual speaks. Recognition among the internal community sings. Recognition among the external community proclaims.

Mentoring

Much has been researched, quantified, qualified, and written about the role mentoring plays in the advancement of multicultural talent. Every day, conversations with multicultural talent reinforce how mentoring from senior leadership increases their possibilities for *advancement* and adds to their sense of connection to the *community*. Mentoring is also a form of *recognition* that leads to multicultural talent being more public about this pivotal relationship with members of the majority group. Mentoring, then, is a pillar with deep structural connections to the other three pillars.

That's not to suggest that mentoring is entirely without flaws. There is a problematic, potentially undermining assumption behind traditional mentoring—that it's still a one-up, one-down relationship. More often than not, it's the White male who remains in the position of authority, and it's the multicultural employee who is left to glean secrets on how to enter the inner circle.

Even here, there's still value because in all communities—whether executive-floor corporate swamis or Amazon-like tribal executives—the ushering in of the new by those who have come before is as human and ancient as the creation of hierarchy. However, we must recognize this for what it is. Receiving tips about what will or will not get you acceptance or the types of behavior that will elicit the sidelong glance of disapproval and silent gonging is priceless. But at what cost?

Traditional mentoring has the inherent contradiction of creating a vehicle for inclusion—not necessarily by dismantling the barriers of exclusion, but by revealing the paths around them. "It may indeed be an 'old boys' network, but let us teach you the ropes," is the name of this game. While unspoken, it is still understood: "Yes, deals do take place on the golf course, so we'll foster this mentoring relationship on the back nine as I help you get to know some of the company's movers and shakers."

We can't be naïve and say this is not helpful. For those on the receiving end of the mentoring, it's incredibly advantageous in terms of getting connected to leaders who can open some doors. But this is not the way to sustainable, transformative change that would positively benefit professionals of color beyond a mere handful. It perpetuates the exclusiveness of a process that continually puts those who are different at a disadvantage. It also perpetuates an asymmetrical view of mentoring.

We need to rethink this concept.

Does mentoring have to be hierarchical? What about reciprocal mentoring, where the assumption is that executives not only have something to impart, but also something to learn from the multicultural employee they're partnered with? We saw the impact of this in Chapter 6, "Are you evil, clueless, or just plain incompetent," where I described the Crosscultural Learning Partners Program.

Traditional mentoring is intended to overcome a risk aversion on the part of the power elites about whom they let into the cockpit. That anxiety is assuaged in large part through relationships. "I know who he or she is when no one is looking," is the sought-after testimonial. "She's good people." This relational dynamic can lead to the inadvertent exclusion of multicultural talent from job-advancement opportunities because they simply are not known. This then causes a greater risk aversion on the part of the majority leaders when it comes to their advancement. The bigger barrier in these cases may not necessarily be race/ethnicity or gender, but rather that majority leaders simply don't *know* their multicultural talent. Yet it's that very diverse background that has inadvertently created social barriers for getting to know them.

Reciprocal mentoring addresses this need for leaders to get to know these individuals up close and personal, without falling into the hierarchical form of mentoring. At the same time, it provides a learning environment for the corporate executive to personally and professionally benefit from one of the basic premises behind diversity—diverse talent brings new and fresh perspectives to age-old as well as cutting-edge business issues.

Mentoring programs that are not reciprocal—where the burden of guiding the other is carried by the senior leader—are well-intentioned, but have inherent limitations. They assume the minority or woman being mentored has little to offer the senior leader in return. Reciprocal mentoring programs, on the other hand, help break through cultural assumptions about what is good and strong leadership.

One of the finest examples of the blossoming of reciprocal mentoring that my colleague Julia Sweeney, a Managing Principal at Korn Ferry, witnessed was when working with a global energy company. While in this example the diversity was along gender and generational lines, the principles applied are very much in the vein of how organizations and people of color can mutually benefit from one another in this kind of non-hierarchically based learning.

This is how she tells it.

> **"** The president of a business had gathered his direct reports and varied players for a two-day working session to consider investments in talent planning. At the center of discussion was an essential recognition that there would soon be a mass exodus via retirement of a large group of leaders, many of these predominantly white males.
>
> "Trend data was laid out, anecdotal examples projected, and assumptions made regarding engaging and gaining commitment from a broader workforce so as not to jeopardize the future success of the business. A young woman, 30 years junior to the president, spoke up with insights about the motivations of her peer group and the environmental conditions that lend themselves to the team operating at their best. There was a notable moment of curiosity by the pedigreed executive regarding how much he had to learn from this young woman who was technically smart, interested and ambitious, yet, until now, entirely disconnected from the inside current manager and future leader.

"She came from an altogether different body of workers than those who historically rose through the ranks, with few exceptions. On the first break, rather than reconvening with the usual close inner circle, the president sought her out and the two of them engaged in an energetic exchange of ideas. This continued throughout the assembly and, in some ways, the newly united duo—with he, 'seeking to understand' and she, 'demonstrating initial courage,'—set precedent then and there for how an inclusive culture works.

"So what was the ensuing dynamic among the direct reports to the CEO who would typically be vying for time with the leader on aspects of their operations, sales, etc.? Could they see themselves stepping out of the unspoken rules and norms of these close-quarter environments and changing the side-bar and break-time behaviors and conversations?

"This sort of example does manifest in many organizations and, while several factors contribute to successful formal and informal reciprocal mentoring, when it takes hold, it seems there's an internal progression for the senior leader, including: a) a sincere belief in the value of contributions from non-traditional sources including multicultural groups, b) a visceral awareness of one's own opportunity to learn from individuals coming from these groups, and c) a senior leader's own courage to change behavior and to open up with a new curiosity. 🙶🙶

Advancement

This pillar cannot be realized without the other three, but the first three do not guarantee this final one. No advancement means there has been no progress.

In 2012, 70 percent of the US workforce became women and minorities.[2] According to the Bureau of Labor Statistics, as of 2014, women made up 47 percent of the US labor force; meanwhile, minorities are 36 percent of the workforce. Yet, the lack of meaningful representation of these key populations in leadership is one of the greatest challenges for today's corporations. The presence of role models for diverse talent across the organization is vital, and considering the accelerated globalization of the marketplace, it's clear that diverse leadership is essential to addressing the unique and complex challenges of global markets, customers, and employees.

In corporations where labor relations are healthy, where no systemic issues of discrimination exist, and where diversity is celebrated, leaders are perplexed by the slow progress of diverse representation at the executive level. For multicultural talent, there is downright frustration and even outrage. This is one of the most significant indications that it's time for the next generation of diversity and inclusion work.

Various studies, in addition to analysis at Korn Ferry on the talent management issues of minorities and women which I will elaborate on below, reveal some of the unique leadership development challenges they face. Typically, they revolve around issues of risk aversion and leadership culture.

Risk aversion

In terms of risk, a complex dance transpires between majority-dominated management and high-potential female and multicultural talent. On all sides, the different players tend to shift away from their default risk-tolerance levels when it comes to the corporate ascent of diverse talent.

One groundbreaking body of research of these differences on risk taking was conducted by Harvard-trained social psychologist Dr. Jeff Howard. Through his consulting practice as well as through his innovative "Efficacy" training that is part of the Korn Ferry suite of solutions, he saw patterns of clear differences emerge.

According to Howard's research, minorities tend to either make the lowest risk moves or the highest risk moves, while mid-level women opt for the lower risk options. By contrast, White males consistently take more calculated risks. Since leadership advancement is helped by the demonstrated ability to take calculated risks, an individual's or a group's comfort with risk can be a predictor of advancement. When it comes to risk taking, there are distinct differences between those in the majority and those in the minority—differences that put those in the minority at a disadvantage.

In an interview, Dr. Howard shared the remarkable results of a variation of the classic ring-toss game that is part of his research on risk taking that eventually evolved into a developmental training experience. In this exercise, participants are given four plastic or rope rings to try to land on a small post. Using a tape running 16 feet away from the peg, and measured off in one-foot increments, the participants decide how close or how far they stand from the post. The closer to the post they stand, the lower the risk; the farther from the post the higher the risk of missing the post. Of course, with four rings, participants have four chances at "ringers," with more points gained the farther one is able to successfully nail it.

Simple enough. Except that while initially the exercise was designed to gauge risk-tolerance levels of *individuals*, throughout thousands of training sessions, clear different patterns emerged in the behaviors of different *groups*. Participants of color, European Americans, and women within both groups showed different behaviors. The women seemed more inclined to stand within one to three feet of the post and went for the safe, almost sure bet. Many of the Black and Latino men either went for this same safe bet or for the low-probability Hail-Mary toss of nine to sixteen feet. The White men, in contrast, however, seemed more inclined to stand about four to eight feet or at a medium distance from the post. *The calculated risk*. There were clear differences within each group, of course: some women took a wild risk, some people of color went for the moderate risk, some White men went straight for the one-foot marker. Yet the overall group patterns were clear: people from different groups seemed inclined toward different levels of risk.

How does the ring toss game show up in real life? In his corporate consulting practice, Dr. Howard observed that "White males were more likely to use a moderate risk strategy to learn how to succeed. They seemed more willing to volunteer for assignments that represented a calculated risk—the kind of risk that is a stretch, yet where the chances of success are realistically within reach. This type of moderate risk taking can result in rapid development of new knowledge and skills, and is something successful organizations look for in their next generation of leaders."

But for many minorities, the story is different. Given various and multiple social psychology dynamics that include the internalization of negative assessments made by society and people in their lives toward people of one's racial/ethnic minority group, many people of color tend to avoid moderate risks, playing it safe, and therefore guaranteeing slower skill development and that they will not be noticed as emerging leadership talent. Or conversely, really having little hope for any advancement due to believing the system is stacked up against them, they will take a "what the hell" attitude and swing for the fences, hoping against all hope that they just may get lucky because of a belief that merit and effort really seem to have little to do with whether they advance or not.[3]

One of Dr. Howard's protégés, Audra Bohannon, now a Senior Partner at Korn Ferry and one of the most celebrated Efficacy facilitators in the field, has career-long experience with seeing how this shows up in organizations. She points out that management also shifts its own risk tolerance. She explains that it may be more inclined to subconsciously say, "Go for it!" in giving a chance to an up-and-coming White male leader, the belief being "we should give him a shot." Yet management is less inclined to give similar opportunities to women and minorities. Instead, risk-averse comments begin to emerge such as "she is still two jobs away," or "since it would be a very visible position, we can't afford for him to fail," and so on. Failing to address these risk-aversion actions inhibits the advancement of women and multicultural talent.

Leadership culture

The leaders of successful companies understand that they stand on the shoulders of those who came before them. They are also the beneficiaries of a culture that spotted their talent and gave them opportunities to prove themselves. While they may be sincere in their desire to diversify their representation, homogenous leadership teams often don't realize that their assessment filters can be culturally biased. Strong leadership can look very different in different cultures or among women, but a majority-dominated leadership team tends to overlook these qualities because they differ from what is considered strong leadership in their culture.

To develop more female and multicultural leaders, management teams must cultivate additional crosscultural competence for spotting alternate leadership qualities they themselves have not demonstrated. In an increasingly diverse and global environment, such qualities are vital. There are already some best practices that have yielded good results in achieving greater advancement of multicultural and female talent. Many companies make it a requirement, for example, that multicultural talent and women be included in all succession plan boxes. Yet, we need to go beyond this practice and find new ways to address the unintended barriers created by risk aversion and leadership culture.

Lifted up together, these four pillars will strengthen the foundation for the engagement and retention of multicultural talent. Under the tent that can be supported by the four pillars, we must continue to find alternate ways to address the challenges of the revolving door syndrome for multicultural talent.

The challenges of multicultural engagement and retention are multiple and vexing. Yet we have hope, because many great ideas have led to significant progress over the past couple of decades. In one chapter of the Judeo-Christian scriptures, there's a verse that reads, "We are perplexed but not in despair."[4] This certainly applies to the inclusion work of diversity practitioners and business leaders today. This half-full reality is what propels us to continue to find new ways to address the half-empty reality. ℺

SUMMARY POINTS

- All four major racial/ethnic minority groups in the United States (Black, Latino, Asian, and Native American) are communal cultures where the sense of group identity—as expressed by *la familia*, the clan, the church, the affinity group—is deeply ingrained. This is in contrast to the majority culture of European Americans, which is more individualistic. It's no coincidence that the first-person pronoun "I" in English is the only pronoun that is capitalized in any language.

- Corporate cultures, so dominated by European-American individualistic culture, often overlook the higher-octane energy that could be infused into their corporations by more effectively nurturing enterprise-wide community building.

- For multicultural groups that have traditionally been oppressed and marginalized, public recognition is like water in the desert.

- Corporations need to go beyond putting women's or multiculturals' names into their succession planning boxes and find new ways to address the unintended barriers created by risk aversion and leadership culture.

- Employers should consider reciprocal mentoring, where the assumption is that the executives not only have something to impart, but also something to learn from the multicultural employee with whom they're partnered.

- The Advancement pillar cannot be realized without the other three pillars (Community, Recognition, and Mentoring). However, the first three do not guarantee this final one, and no advancement means there has been no progress.

SHAPING YOUR STRATEGY

- What are the racial/ethnic minority groups that exist in your corporate environment? How do they interact within their own group, with other minorities, and with the majority culture? Are members of the majority culture aware that the way they interact with people from their own culture may differ from how they interact with those from other cultures?

- How well does your organization recognize the contributions of its minority employees? How can your company better publicly acknowledge their efforts and contributions?

- How risk averse are your leaders? What barriers does this risk aversion create, and how can you overcome these barriers?

- Does your organization have a reciprocal mentoring program? If so, what have been the results? If not, what steps can you take to implement such a program?

WHY NOT ACKNOWLEDG
ING DIFFERENCE$ CAN
MAKE U$ $ICKER AND
POORER WHY NOT AC
KNOW EDGING DIFFER
EN E$ CAN MAK U$ $ICK R
AND P OR R W Y NOT
A KNOWL DGING DIF
FER N E$ MAKE U$ $I K
R A ND P O   ER W Y
N T AC NOW EDGING
D FFE E   E$ MA E U$
ICK R A ND P O ER
ING I FE EN E$ MA   E
$ IC E A D OO E
W Y OT A K   L D
N   IF RE E   AE
U   IC   A D   O
I H   O   W E
I   F   N   O
Y   O   D

Chapter 14

Why not acknowledging differences can make us sicker and poorer

I

A blur of cars, multicolored microbuses, and motorcycles zoomed past us. We broke into a sweat while running up the street and frantically jumping to hail a cab—all of which passed us by. It was 20 minutes before the start of the citywide state of emergency curfew, and we were 30 minutes from home. Yet no one was stopping for us. We started making plans to walk down the middle of the avenue and wave our underwear, the only white thing we had on us (as required by martial law if you happened to be out after curfew) when we succeeded at making a VW Bug screech to a halt as we threw ourselves in its path. "Monterrico!" we cried out. "Okay, yes, that's on my way," the driver said. "Hop in!"

Growing up in a Latin-American military dictatorship shaped how I view the world. I was just 17 when I jumped into that VW Bug to avoid getting arrested, but the volatility of that era—12 years of a military dictatorship, and the economic and political aftershocks when the *generales* gave back power—permanently shaped my stance toward so much of life. How I view time, money, health, and risk were subconsciously shaped by the forces of growing up in an underdeveloped Latin-American country that alternated between populist and right wing democracies and military dictatorships.

The uncertainty of the government, the savings-devouring wildfire of hyperinflation, and the sense that so much was out of our control led to the need for creative improvisation. Whether dealing with military checkpoints on our way home from the movies or figuring out how to secure a kilo of rice and sugar in the midst of shortages, these effects linger long after the headlines have become history.

Through my upbringing, I developed insights into effective multicultural marketing. As an employee, the subconscious ghosts of that time haunt my decisions when I do something seemingly mundane, such as signing up for employee benefits. After the economic and political roller coaster of growing up in Peru, where we did not know what the state of our government would be in the next four years, projecting my nest egg for the next 40 years was quite an abstraction. After a five-year cumulative inflation rate of 15,000 percent, who wants to save their money? Inflation was so rampant that restaurants wrote their prices on a blackboard because by the time one ordered food, ate it, and received the bill, the prices had changed!

Even long after circumstances have changed—and they have changed dramatically as Peru now has a prospering economy and a stable democracy— our worldviews are wired in the past. After managing food shortages due to a bureaucratized economy and constant blackouts caused by terrorist bombs, I placed as a low priority getting my annual physical? Present circumstances often have little impact on cultural perspective—unless there is an effective intervention.

While Chief Diversity Officer at Hewitt, then as President of Diversity Best Practices, and now as the Global Practice Leader for the Workforce Performance, Inclusion and Diversity Practice at Korn Ferry, I have wrestled with determining these interventions. In my role I am responsible, along with our deeply experienced team of thought leaders and global consultants, for identifying the various ways in which exclusion may inadvertently be taking place. There are the classic issues of representation and advancement of women and minorities, but there are other areas that get overlooked. For example, are non-majority groups equally taking advantage of the benefits available to all employees?

It turns out that in many circumstances, they are not.

For instance, African Americans and Latinos both under-save in their 401(k) plans compared to Whites and Asians—even when they earn the same amount of money. Women sub-optimize their returns by investing more conservatively than men. And minorities under-participate in preventive healthcare, even when it's available to them at little or no cost.

Why is this happening? How can we bridge these gaps? The search for these answers has led to a treasure trove of information and insight. It has also led the way to some new types of solutions, including the need to communicate— or market—these benefits in ways that are inclusive of the worldviews of different diverse groups. In our research, we discovered solutions that tapped into cultural behavioral drivers—often quite divergent from mainstream assumptions—that motivated individuals into actions that were good for them and their families. The Inclusion Paradox requires that we call out differences in doing this.

Rather than comprehensively addressing the many ways in which differences show up, I will examine a case study of racial/ethnic differences. This exploration serves as a template for how we can do the same with other types of differences to uncover the best ways to motivate employees to manage their health and finances more effectively.

Multicultural marketing of employee benefits

Think of the last time you turned on your favorite TV show and one of the ads moved you—not only emotionally, but to action—to buy a product, go on a trip, or support a cause.

Marketers spend a significant amount of time and money figuring out how to reach *you*, whether you're a 20-something or a senior citizen, a Gen Xer or a Baby Boomer, a man or a woman, a Latin-American immigrant or a Texas cowboy. Not only have they figured out how to reach you, but how to move you as well.

Their approach is based on sophisticated market research data that reveals patterns in the way different demographic groups tend to move, act, and believe. Marketers understand, of course, that not all members within these demographic groups move according to the group norm, but there's enough of a pattern for them to shape messages and find channels that hit the broad mark time after time.

Take a moment to think about each of the following TV programs and consider the audiences that come to mind for each:

- Sunday afternoon NFL game
- *Sabado Gigante* (which just went off the air after 50 years) on Univision
- *The Jamie Foxx Show* on BET
- Any movie on Lifetime
- *Blue's Clues* on Nickelodeon
- *Modern Family* on ABC
- *Friends* in syndication

Clearly, each of these networks has determined how to reach their prospective audiences based on scientific market research. But just how much of this same market knowledge applies to human resources products and services? Quite a bit, actually. Cultural studies show that different demographic groups approach issues of health, wealth, and career in distinctly different ways.

Let's consider these differences with regard to healthcare. Mary Lynch is Senior Vice President of Human Resource Services for CHRISTUS Health, a Catholic healthcare organization in the southern and southwestern United States and Mexico. She speaks of the challenge to be inclusive and provide care and services to those with differing worldviews, especially when they are from a different religion: "When we talk about inclusion, growing up in the Western world and having things done a certain way challenges us today to broaden our horizons and look at other perspectives, such as the practices of Eastern medicine, because many come to the healthcare environment with very different beliefs. For example, some people believe that certain foods are healing foods. One of the hospital's lessons was that not everyone considers eggs or oatmeal to be a suitable breakfast. Hospital staff [in our organization] learned that Vietnamese patients might actually prefer chicken soup for breakfast."

If serving *oatmeal* could be a culturally insensitive thing to do, then what else could we be missing when designing benefits that touch the critical needs of physical, emotional, and financial health? The search for answers must start with determining where these differences exist, understanding *why* they exist, and then finally, identifying crossculturally savvy ways to bridge unhealthy gaps.

Employees as consumers

Employers must start to view employees not as passive recipients of benefit packages, but as consumers—consumers of jobs, career opportunities, and benefits. Doing so is not only beneficial in attracting the best talent, it's also a smart way to achieve optimal results from benefits plans that are less generous than before (more costly for less value).

Making it all more difficult, companies are finding that the one-size-fits-all approach—meant as a way to manage costs—is increasingly ineffective. Already, employers are forcing employees to make tough choices on their healthcare packages as they weigh the tradeoffs between high deductibles and lower premiums. And how about the alphabet soup choices between PPO, HMO, POS, HRA, HSA? Late at night, on the eve of the deadline for the annual benefits enrollment, with forehead in hands, employees are truly benefits *shopping*.

These are *consumer choices*, and they must be packaged and marketed as such to help employees make smart choices on behalf of themselves and their families—in ways that also help employers better manage their costs.

Choices now are more dependent than ever on the employee than on the employer. And in a multicultural, multigenerational workplace, communications that worked when audiences were more homogenous will not work today.

Today's HR programs are legacies from the philosophies and structures of more than 50 years ago—when most of the workforce was White and male. So while the workforce has changed dramatically, why is it that benefits have not changed to align with it? If benefits truly are designed to meet the needs of today's employees, benefit plan strategists must realize that programs conceived many years ago will not resonate with today's new workforce.

We must move into the *multicultural design and marketing of benefits*. In doing so, we look for archetypes without falling into stereotyping. It's important to look for patterns—where the bell curve of behavior is concentrated—because it helps us see areas in which we need to call out differences in order to create true inclusion. Like a moving impressionistic painting, what we initially perceive may not be the truth, but it invites us to peer more deeply into the messages hidden in the bold patterns. We need to discover the deeper meanings of our first impressionistic pass and—with these insights—design and market benefits in ways that mutually benefit employees and corporations.

Time warps and money binds: Having enough for the future

Let's make this practical by looking at one benefit that is increasingly important to the financial well-being of employees—the 401(k) savings plan (or 403(b), etc.). This benefit has become particularly valuable as entitlement programs, such as pensions, go away and Social Security turns into Social Insecurity.

Even when members of different racial groups earn the same amount of money, investment practices vary dramatically. The 2008 Black Investor Study (conducted by Charles Schwab and Ariel Capital Management, the largest minority-owned investment firm in the United States) revealed a 15 percent gap in savings when comparing White and Black individuals. In households earning more than $50,000 annually, only 65 percent of Black people invested in stocks or mutual funds, compared to 80 percent of White people in the same income bracket.[1] In another study, the *non*-participation rate at one Hewitt manufacturing client was 33 percent for Hispanics/Latinos, compared to 26 percent for African Americans and 9 percent for Whites.

The differences don't stop there. When we first conducted a 401(k) and diversity analysis for a client, we looked at five different behaviors in retirement savings. We saw discernable differences between Black and White individuals, as the following table indicates.

Differences in 401(k) behaviors between Blacks and Whites

Behavior	Black	White
Participation	52%	71%
Average contribution rate	2%	5%
Average percentage in equities	43%	60%
Internet usage	45%	72%
Loans outstanding	14%	5%

Hewitt Associates, analysis of 401(k) usage at a Medical Education Institution, 2005

Compared to Whites, Blacks not only under-participated, but their contribution rates were less than half that of Whites. They also invested more conservatively, were three times more likely to take loans through their 401(k) plans, and were 30 percent less likely to use the Internet to manage their retirement money.

For the next set of clients, we added Latinos/Hispanic-Americans and Asians/Asian-Americans to the mix and studied the factors most significant in determining various 401(k) behaviors. We looked at age, tenure, salary, gender, and race/ethnicity. We hypothesized that salary would be by far the largest determinant of whether people saved, how much, and the methods they used in doing so.

Again, race/ethnicity emerged as the main determinant for differences in behavior. Depending on the client, gender and income alternated as the second most prevalent factor.

In 2008, we upped the ante. In partnership with Ariel, and with funding from the Rockefeller Foundation, we looked at the 401(k) data of 57 Fortune 500 companies across a variety of different industries and sectors. In the process, we studied the patterns in investment behaviors of almost 3 million employees. The findings of this comprehensive study revealed the same pattern: race was the *most* influential factor in whether and how people saved. The findings of racial gaps from that one client showed up across the board—not only in the aggregate, but in every one of those 57 participating companies.

The table below shows the differences based on race when comparing employees within the same income bracket.

Overall results by ethnicity

Regression-adjusted comparison of 401(k) behavior: Minorities compared to Whites

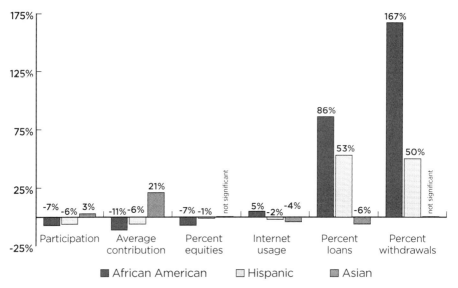

Hewitt Associates analysis, in collaboration with Ariel Capital Management, of 401(k) usage of 57 Fortune 500 companies with nearly 3 million employee records. A 2009 study funded by the Rockefeller Foundation.

These findings were a game-changer. But why would skin color affect savings behaviors? We'll get to that in a moment.

The study was repeated in 2012. This Ariel/Aon Hewitt update on the *401(k) Plans in Living Color* study[2] showed that significant gaps remained among different racial and ethnic groups. Blacks and Latinos continued to save far less for retirement than White employees; participation differences continued to exist; and different racial/ethnic groups borrow against or cashed out these accounts at significantly different rates.[3]

The 2008 economic recession aggravated the racial and ethnic differences seen in 401(k) and 403(b) accounts. More Latinos and Blacks than Whites or Asians tapped into their accounts to deal with short-term financial distress. Whether those hardship withdrawals were for unexpected emergencies, daily living expenses, or simple debt, they all had the common denominator of affecting workers' long-term financial security.

Here is just one example of how exploring the differences among various racial/ethnic groups and developing creative responses to diversity challenges can provide positive results. We have opportunities to address the gaps in remaining areas, such as contribution rates and borrowing/cash out rates. This is exceptionally important to remember since Black and Latino employees, even when they are in the plan, are still not saving enough to meet their retirement years' needs.

In addition, how Blacks and Latinos handle their retirement accounts further undermines their ability to optimize their returns. For example, their decreased Internet usage when it came to managing their retirement money raised important questions about how best to communicate to multicultural audiences. For a variety of reasons, certain demographic groups are less inclined to use the Internet. Thus, corporate employee communications that rely too much on the Internet may be inadvertently leaving some employees behind.

According to the Ariel/Schwab Black Investor Study, Black people also differ from White people in what they're saving *for*. While retirement is cited as the number one reason for the majority of Whites, Blacks tend to prioritize saving for a home and their children's college education. When it came to a preferred vehicle for investment, African Americans preferred real estate over the stock market (45 percent vs. 40 percent).[4]

Over time, the Ariel/Schwab studies have shown little change in the opinions between Blacks and Whites, with two exceptions. For the first time since the study began, the 2010 Black Investor Study showed that Blacks felt that stocks or stock mutual funds were better investment vehicles than real estate. However, the investment rate between Blacks and Whites maintains a significant gap. White investment rates remained around 80 percent even during the recession, while the investment rate for Blacks continued its downward trend to about 60 percent.[5]

We can also apply the Inclusion Paradox to other differences, such as age and gender. In comparing the retirement savings patterns of men and women, we see the effects of socialization. Women face uncertainties about how to participate—and whether to participate at all—because many of them have been less exposed to financial matters given sexist attitudes by parents and society that assumed women didn't need financial literacy in the same way as men and who have also had more interruptions in their careers. They also need to save more than men due to lower average salaries, more conservative investing, longer life expectancies, and higher retiree medical needs. In a 2008 study,[6] Hewitt found that 30 percent of women did not contribute to their 401(k) plans and another 24 percent did not contribute at a high enough level to take advantage of the company match. Given these factors, women will need to replace nearly 130 percent of their final pay at retirement, 7 percentage points more than men. Over 30 years, the average woman will need to save 2 percent more of her pay each year than the average man in order to achieve the same standard of living.[7]

Money worldviews

What's the cause of these disparities? This question must be answered in order to successfully pursue the multicultural marketing of benefits. Only then can we know how to effectively reach different audiences with messages that ring true and lead to action.

In an April 13, 2009 article, "How Obama Is Using the Science of Change," *Time* magazine declared *Nudge: Improving Decisions about Health, Wealth, and Happiness* to be among a handful of books "already shaping dozens of [Obama] administration policies." Authors Richard Thaler and Cass Sunstein make the case for tapping into the findings of behavioral economics to influence preventive healthcare and long-term savings choices that address worrisome gaps.[8] They base their arguments on hundreds of experiments, conducted over decades, which explore what shapes the choices we make. Their perspective is that our choices lead us either to good or not-so-good results, depending on the influence. Much of what we accept as truth might not be objectively true, contrary to our shared social assumptions. This work is particularly timely in light of the trend to push health and wealth decision making away from government and corporations and toward employees.

Seeking the middle ground between the government dictating what people should do and unrestrained *laissez faire* capitalism, the authors make the argument for *nudges*. These nudges are created by *decision architects* who design policies and programs that are more likely to produce desired results, based on what we know about behavior. Among the many nudges they describe include automatically enrolling employees in their 401(k) and giving them the choice to opt out.

Behaviorally, humans tend toward inertia. The *Time* article references a study in which only 36 percent of women joined a 401(k) plan when they needed to initiate enrollment. Participation jumped to 86 percent when they were automatically enrolled and then given the chance to opt out.[9]

The 2012 Ariel/Aon Hewitt updated study proved this out. The participation gap in 401(k) among the various groups has narrowed when comparing 2012 vs. 2009 results. And why? Indeed it's the growing numbers of employers automatically enrolling employees into 401(k) or 403(b) plans. By applying the human reality of inertia in reverse, they have offered them an opt-*out* rather than an opt-*in* choice. The result? The enrollment gap between Black and Latino workers on the one hand and White or Asian employees on the other practically disappears.

The *Nudge* authors focus on American mainstream culture, so they stop short of exploring how behavioral economic theory plays out in different subcultures. But here, as in the following section on health, I will offer crosscultural insights about the behaviors of different racial and ethnic communities. I encourage you to extract principles to apply to the health and wealth behaviors of other demographic groups.

Returning to 401(k) under-participation by Latinos and African Americans, cultural studies show that Latinos have a shorter time horizon than Whites. In focus group research I have conducted over the years, when asked how they define "the future," Latinos tend to answer, "The next three to five years." Whites tend to say, "The next generation." Asians tend to say, "The next century."

Why is this? Latinos like myself have come from a part of the world and during a time in which we've been unsure what our government was going to be like in four years. So the concept of projecting a nest egg over the next 40 years has been a complete abstraction. Whether experienced firsthand by a parent or grandparent, or delivered by institutions such as churches, cultural worldviews get passed on subconsciously.

For African Americans, the reasons may be different, but the under-saving behavior is the same. According to Mellody Hobson, Ariel's president and a frequent guest financial analyst on *Good Morning America*, there are various socio-historical factors at work. When you've been marginalized from participating in diversified investment vehicles by the now-outlawed practice of redlining (the practice of denying services, either directly or through selectively raising prices, to residents of certain areas based on the racial or ethnic makeups of those areas)[10], what viable savings choices remain? African Americans either turned to mom-and-pop savings institutions in their communities that offered only basic savings vehicles, or they stashed their money under the mattress. Making matters worse, recent corporate scandals and the global economic meltdown resulted in many employees losing their jobs and their long-term savings, while unethical corporate leaders were led out in handcuffs or faced Congressional scrutiny. These scandals further undermined an already existing wariness on the part of African Americans regarding the financial system. The people being hauled out of gleaming corporate offices in handcuffs or sitting in front of Congressional hearings don't look like them. Given these legacies, it's not unusual to meet African-American millionaires who still use low-interest savings accounts as their primary investment tool.

How about the differences between Whites and Blacks with regard to what they save for? African American emphasis on saving for college is understandable, given the role of higher education in building a Black middle class. Given long-standing systemic discrimination, for many African-American families, a college education may still be a first- or second-generation phenomenon. Coupled with uncertainties about financial aid, African Americans may save more than will actually be needed for college at the expense of their retirement savings.

While these answers provide the *why* for low participation, they don't tell us how to close the gap. The low participation rate of Latinos and African Americans is worrisome, given the wholesale shift from guaranteed pensions to greater employee responsibility in preparing for retirement through 401(k) plans. If employees don't make good choices along the way over a long period of time, they will be in jeopardy of not being able to take care of themselves and their families when the time comes to retire.

Again, here is where the authors of *Nudge* offer help. The Ariel/Aon Hewitt[11] study suggests further changes that can "nudge" employees to prepare for retirement. It recommends upping the penalties for non-hardship withdrawals and fine-tuning contribution rates. With changes like these, it is possible to narrow the disparity gap between how different groups get ready for retirement, which can only strengthen our entire society.

Multicultural marketing of 401(k) and retirement planning

Since long-term investment can create wealth for all, how can employee communications respond to diverse attitudes and beliefs about saving? How can it motivate people of color to plan more assertively for their retirement? The answers to these questions go beyond having more diverse pictures in 401(k) materials or translating those same materials into another language.

Let's take a look at traditional communication and marketing efforts about retirement savings.

What picture comes to mind when I say "retirement planning brochure?" White audiences state the following: A white-haired couple strolling on the beach, maybe a golden retriever at their side.

So how do we make this picture more inclusive? Some say we should show a Black couple walking down the beach. But while diversity in the pictures is a start, it isn't everything. So, maybe we should translate it into a Spanish version, perhaps.

But even if we replace the couple in the picture with a couple of color and print the words in another language, we still have the wrong image. Why? *Because the whole picture is wrong to begin with for non-White groups.* In focus group research I have conducted for many African Americans, their image of retirement often includes another job, possibly one in which they are giving back to their community. Latinos often picture an elderly couple surrounded by grandchildren. They look at the White couple on the typical retirement brochure and feel sorry for them. "They are all alone! Why have they been abandoned? No wonder they need the dog."

Regarding lower web usage, the challenge is not just to recognize there is a gap or even to understand why the gap exists. Rather, we need to know what can be done, in a culturally savvy way, to motivate under-participating groups to get more comfortable with the web. This might entail providing easier access, addressing distrust of corporate websites, and making the sites more appealing by speaking directly to the audience's worldviews and preferences. It might require more in-person sessions offering hands-on demonstrations of how to manage one's money through Internet tools. For Latinos, it might mean creating family-oriented events where they can bring their children— who often are digitally proficient—so they can not only enjoy being with *Papá* or *Mamá* at work, but can be included in some of the navigation exercises.

 A few years ago, I teamed with one of Hewitt's Communications practice leaders to facilitate a Latino focus group about using the Internet to manage money. Our discussion elicited some unexpected insight into some of the mainstream messages used to motivate money management via the Internet.

Our communications consultants had created materials not only to orient employees to their 401(k) benefit, but also to encourage them to manage their money via the web, thus reducing administration costs by reducing traffic to the call center.

As communicators, they were practiced in knowing their audience and tapping behavioral drivers. Instinctively, they knew the message "Save your employer money—use the web!" would not work. Instead, they chose the motivator of "control." Throughout their materials, they wove in messages such as "Take control of your money, take control of your future." In addition, they showcased the 24/7 access of the web tool, along with color graphs showing asset allocation and the ability to move one's money as many times as one wanted.

We conducted various segmented focus groups. Not surprisingly, the message of control played very well with White employees. When challenged, one flustered participant responded, "Of course we like the message of control. *What other message could there be?"*

However, the Latino group had a defiant answer to this rhetorical question. When presented with the message of control, seven out of the nine Latinos responded negatively.

When asked why, they responded, "Because it's the removal of a benefit." The communicators responded, "But it's not. You still have the call center, but now you have the web as well."

"You don't understand," said one. "The benefit for me was that my employer took care of my money. And now you're telling me I have to take control of that."

"Don't you want to?"

"No."

"Why not?"

"Because I did not grow up with my parents ever talking about it amongst themselves, much less teaching us about it."

For this group, the "taking control" message was intimidating and daunting. The thought of managing money via the web did not offer a greater sense of control—it actually made them feel *less* in control. For us facilitators, it was an epiphany. The communicators realized they had created communication pieces based on the "traditional" workforce, which, until recently, was mostly White and mostly male.

Companies need to consider not just the message, but also the delivery. Hewitt and Ariel studies show that African Americans and Latinos have more communal and oral cultures, which respond better to face-to-face presentations and workshops. This raises the potential for higher costs. Email blasts are more cost effective than workshops. But as the workforce gets more diverse, what happens when these cost-effective measures are not effective in creating behavioral changes?

The multicultural marketing of benefits is not just about one-way adaptation on the part of corporations to account for differences among diverse populations. It's also about knowing how to move employees toward behaviors that are good for them and for their employers. Web usage for managing money, for example, reduces administration costs for companies by reducing the number of calls to the 401(k) call center.

Smartphones and other mobile devices combined with social media tools are proving to be very adept at linking consumer behavior to technology, and in some instances, changing it.[12] According to a Pew Internet study, about 88 percent of American adults own a cell phone, 57 percent have a laptop, 19 percent have an e-reader, and 19 percent own a tablet computer. About 63 percent of adults wirelessly go online by using these devices.[13]

While the racial/ethnic digital divide of Web 1.0 has been widespread and real, it is disappearing thanks to the social media of Web 2.0. The Pew Internet study says, "Groups that have traditionally been on the other side of the digital divide in basic Internet access are now using wireless connections to go online." For instance, Latinos lead all ethnic groups in the purchase of tablet computers (15 percent vs. 8 percent for Blacks and 7 percent for Whites). And Latinos are the highest users of text messaging, mobile Internet, email, downloading pictures, and uploading music to mobile devices.

Driving up minority 401(k) participation at McDonald's

Shortly after joining the McDonald's board, Ariel Investments CEO John Rogers gave a talk in honor of Martin Luther King Jr.'s birthday to members of one of the company's employee networks—the McDonald's African American Council, known as the Mac2C. *Businessweek* reporter Lauren Young described the speech in an online sidebar to her article "McDonald's Supersized Retirement Plan: The fast-food giant is persuading more African-American workers to enroll in 401(k)s. Can McDonald's keep talent by helping families save?"

"[During the talk] John Rogers focused on the plight of Black investors and why they don't save more, using data from the annual survey of Black investors Ariel conducts in conjunction with Charles Schwab. 'If people of color retire with less than half the money saved as Whites, it's a real crisis for our country,' Rogers told the crowd. Rogers didn't know that Andrés Tapia, [then] Chief Diversity Officer at Hewitt Associates, the benefits consulting giant, also was present. After the event ended, the two men clicked as they started comparing notes on the issue, along with possible solutions. 'It was the first time ever in all my public speeches or private meetings that I ran into someone who not only understood what I was saying, but also was thinking about trying to solve the same problem,' Rogers said. It also helped that James Cantalupo, who was McDonald's Chairman and Chief Executive at the time, heard Rogers speak. 'We need to think about the economic health of minority employees and vendors,' he told Rogers."

A Hewitt utilization analysis of 401(k) by racial ethnic groups revealed that gaps existed at McDonald's as well. Given their long-standing commitment to diversity, the fast-food giant decided to do something about it. Most companies won't even match a contribution until an employee puts in at least 3 percent, but McDonald's decided that employees who put just 1 percent of their salary in the plan would get $3 for every $1 they invested. McDonald's then makes a dollar-for-dollar match on the next 4 percent. This could lead to a company match of as much as 11 percent. To ease the pain of automatically deferring 1 percent of pay, the company gave managers a one-time, 1 percent salary increase. And then, to make sure employees took advantage of the program, they made enrollment automatic—with, of course, the option to opt-out if one did not want to participate.

What motivates McDonald's? "In addition to this being a tangible demonstration of our commitment to diversity," explained Richard Floersch, McDonald's Chief Human Resources Officer, "this is also about a talent retention strategy in an industry that sees a costly 36 percent turnover."

Other torchbearers are lighting the way in their own companies. Ariel president Mellody Hobson sits on the corporate boards of Starbucks, Estée Lauder, and DreamWorks, where she is advocating an analysis of the retirement savings habits of minorities at those firms. In the second half of 2009, the 57 companies participating in the Ariel/Hewitt 401(k) and diversity study had on-hand their own data, as well as information on how they compared to other Fortune 500 companies and to others in their industry. Based on the results, they focused on how they should respond. In addition to approaching this issue with design strategies such as McDonald's, some companies began to couple incentives with financial education tailored to the worldviews of the various populations in their workforce. (For a more detailed account of how a medical education institution has approached this issue, see Appendix D: "Driving up minority 401(k) participation at a medical institution.")

McDonald's I'm lovin' It™. And so are its employees. Calling out differences and addressing diverse assumptions below the waterline has the potential to create stronger financial health for all.

Qué será, será: When it comes to health, can fate be defied?

Much has happened with the nation's healthcare system since I first penned this book. The passage of healthcare reform and the judicial confirmation of its constitutionality have dominated political debates and public discussions for several years, and continue to do so. Whether it's called by its official moniker, the Patient Protection and Affordable Care Act, or more informal titles like the Affordable Care Act (ACA), healthcare reform, health insurance reform, or even Obamacare, this legislation has been a game-changer for how the nation provides and pays for healthcare.

The need for this legislation was predicated on the reality that the US healthcare system is sick and needs healing. Even with the ACA and its 2014 launch, the system faces a long recovery process that must include attitude and mindset changes by everyone. The challenges are real and daunting:

- Before the passage of the ACA, between 46–50 million Americans did not have health insurance, including a sizeable proportion of families with a working adult.[14] And for the millions who are insured, too many are limited in what their insurance covers. This situation has forced them to pay out of pocket for preventive procedures like mammograms or colonoscopies, to tackle practically incomprehensible policy documents on what is covered, and to worry about unexpected insurance price increases or medical denials. Some 45,000 people die every year because they lack access to healthcare.

- Of the uninsured, more than half (55 percent) were people of color. While only 13 percent of Whites lacked healthcare insurance, 32 percent (14.4 million) of Latinos, 21 percent (6.9 million) of Blacks, 19 percent (3.8 million) Asians, and 28 percent (700,000) American Indians were uninsured. Many of the newly insured under the ACA will be people of color, making the legislation a massive diversity and inclusion initiative.

- Within five years, national health expenditures will increase by more than $1 trillion over today's nearly $3 trillion.

- The poor health status of many American workers costs the economy about $153 billion in lost productivity.

An even more disconcerting challenge is the shortage of medical personnel. The ACA will transform the insurance standing of about 32 million Americans who now lack health insurance. But our healthcare system is nowhere near ready to accommodate the coming influx of new and *diverse* consumers. The capacity to handle that number of patients is simply not there, and the severe shortage of doctors, nurses, and other medical professionals is critical. By 2020, the nation will face a physician shortage estimated to be about 91,000.

A look at the healthcare system through a diversity lens indicates a need for additional worry. It already falls short of providing quality care to people of color, even when they have insurance. Racial health disparities are deep, pervasive, and well documented.

Compared to Whites, African Americans and Latinos under-participate in preventive healthcare, even when it's available to them at little or no cost. What's more, they use the emergency room—the most expensive form of medical intervention—at a higher rate than other groups. By contrast, Asians tend to over-insure, paying for more health coverage than they actually need. These patterns not only lead to greater health and/or cost risks for the members of these groups, but they can also lead to greater healthcare costs for employers and governments.

Some worldviews, such as Catholic Latino fatalism, create resistance to taking proactive measures to reduce their health risk. Dr. Thomas Fisher, former Vice President of Health Care Service Corporation and also at the University of Chicago, who leads efforts on addressing healthcare disparities, explains another variable: "It's about establishing trust and having conversations. If physicians can't establish the type of relationship where trust is central, where patients can feel confident that this is in their own best interest, then patients are unlikely to be motivated to adhere to uncomfortable, costly, or inconvenient recommendations."

But companies need not be fatalistic, believing there's nothing they can do to encourage Latinos or African Americans to seek preventive care. It is not enough to understand why certain groups don't respond to mainstream messages. By calling out differences, it's possible to find overlooked enablers *within* a cultural worldview that can motivate members of that culture to engage in preventive care.

With that in mind, let's look at diversity disconnections throughout the healthcare system that lead to disparities. These are not only detrimental to diverse groups, but also contribute to higher healthcare costs.

Disparities in disease prevalence. According to the Centers for Disease Control and Prevention (CDC), racial and ethnic disparities are clearly evident in the incidences of fatal diseases and in other medical areas. A few:

- The African-American death rate from cardiovascular disease is *40 percent higher* than it is for Whites.
- The African-American death rate around all forms of cancer is *30 percent higher* than for Whites.
- The African-American death rate from HIV/AIDS is seven times that of Whites.
- The Latino death rate from diabetes is twice that of Whites.
- When comparing African-American and White women who get regular mammograms, Black women still die from breast cancer at a higher rate than White women.[15]

- Black and Latino teens are three times as likely to be diagnosed with schizophrenia instead of a mood disorder, the more common diagnosis for White teens.[16]

- Racial and ethnic minorities are less likely to be treated for pain, and they find their pain is underestimated compared to White patients.[17]

- Blacks and Latinos are treated through amputation at a higher rate than Whites, a statistic that suggests interventions that are too little or too late.[18]

- Fear of discrimination and stigma keep many in the LGBT community from seeking care for themselves or their families or from disclosing relevant personal information once in care.[19]

Just what are the cost implications of such disparities? If we break down one data point, Latinos not only suffer a higher incidence of diabetes, but are also more likely to die from the disease than diabetic Whites. And with Latinos expected to comprise almost one-third of the United States by July 1, 2050,[20] a costly situation will get exponentially worse. We need ways to call out differences, so we can develop workable solutions.

Disease prevalence is not the only place differences surface in healthcare. Here are a few more examples:

Disparities in communication. When it comes to reliance on corporate-provided communications to help make healthcare decisions, a Hewitt study found it is 31 percent for Whites (a low number to begin with), 24 percent for African Americans, 11 percent for Asians, and 6 percent for Hispanics. Companies spend millions of dollars communicating their health benefits to employees, but the more diverse the population, the lesser the effect.[21]

So where do minorities go for their information? Instead of print materials, they rely on personal communication, talking with family members, and the *amigo* around the corner. Of course, friends and family members are not healthcare experts, so Latinos look to their doctor to be the primary disseminator of medical information. Although a doctor is an expert, studies show significant communication breakdowns between physicians and their ethnic patients. Nearly half of non-English-speaking US patients say they have a hard time communicating with a doctor, nurse, or health provider who speaks a different language. In other words, there's a breakdown at the very point where they seek the most authoritative information about health. But it gets worse: even when they get good advice, they don't follow it. In one survey, 24 percent of

Whites, 30 percent of African Americans, and 40 percent of Hispanics said they did not follow the doctor's advice because it was too costly.[22]

Worldviews at play. Classic issues of racism and discrimination are at play in many of these disparities. According to Dr. Fisher, other breakdowns result from obvious, yet important, gaps in "in-language" communications. He tells of how medical literature describes cardiac episodes as "crushing or pressure more like an elephant sitting on a chest." Yet older African Americans often describe cardiac pain as "sharp," which can lead doctors to another diagnosis. "If physicians don't ask some follow-up questions, or describe it more carefully, that sharp chest pain may, in fact, be the type of pressure/crushing that leads to a cardiac diagnosis."

But the more profound differences show up at the level of worldviews.

Think about traditional communication about preventive care. Typical messages are: "Take care of yourself," "You've only got one life to live," "Enjoy your life." These messages are inadvertently based on an *individualistic* European-American worldview. Not surprisingly, these messages usually resonate well with the traditional European-American audience.

By contrast, communities of color in the United States often possess a more *communal* worldview. Individualistic messages usually do not strike a familiar chord, and they are less influential in increasing their health prevention behaviors. Among Latinos, our communal perspective shows up in our language, as we pepper our conversations with *nosotros* (us), *la familia* (the family), *el equipo* (the team).

We must then factor in different cultural beliefs about our ability to manage what happens to us today and tomorrow. Interculturalists Fons Trompenaars and Charles Hampden-Turner refer to these as the *internal* and *external control* dimensions of culture. Those cultures that believe there is something one can do to avoid fate are referred to as having a strong sense of internal control. European-American culture has a strong sense of internal control. This worldview is manifest in sayings such as, "Pull yourself up by your bootstraps," "Tame the wild west," and "God helps those who help themselves." By contrast, other cultures have a sense of external control, believing there is little they can do to make their present or future better or less dangerous. Hispanic culture, influenced by Latin Catholic fatalism, operates within this external control worldview. The Spanish language reveals this worldview in sayings such as *"Dios quiere,"* (God willing), *"Qué será, será,"* (What will be, will be), or when showing up late to the airport, *"El avión nos dejó"* (The plane left us).

This plays out in healthcare. Why do Whites engage in more preventive healthcare than minorities? In part, it is connected to the worldview of internal control that says, "There's something I can do today to minimize the risk of something bad happening tomorrow." Preventive healthcare presupposes this very worldview. For those who have an external sense of control, governed by fatalism, the worldview manifests itself in beliefs such as, "There is nothing I can do today to prevent something that is going to happen to me tomorrow."

These different worldviews are evident in surveys as well. When asked, "Is your good health a matter of luck?" in a Commonwealth survey, a quarter of Latinos and African Americans said yes, compared to only half as many Whites.[23]

No wonder those individualistic, internal control messages work for one group but not others.

With the Affordable Care Act, the future of healthcare moves from an implied contract between employer and employee to a basic constitutional right. And with rights come responsibilities—including the duty for everyone to take care of his or her health as much as possible. So preventive health behaviors become not just a private issue, but a public one as well. The ACA promotes prevention in health matters, and incents health providers to take a more active role in motivating patients toward preventive care. This is where the different healthcare worldviews play out on the national stage. And it's why calling out our differences on prevention messages and behaviors becomes more of a national priority, less of a commercial one.

The case of the dehydrated, Vietnamese women in labor

Do these worldview differences make a difference in life-and-death situations? They sure do. Consider this story told to me by intercultural diversity consultant Howard Ross:

"A strange phenomenon occurred at a hospital that served a diverse patient population. No one could explain why, but most of the Vietnamese women coming in for delivery became dehydrated as they went through labor. While not always life-threatening, this affected the health of these women as well as the connection between mother and baby because it delayed lactation. It was also more costly to the hospital due to the resulting lengthened hospital stay. It took a professional willing to call out differences to unlock the answer. While knowing nothing about Vietnamese culture, he knew enough about the differences in worldviews to ask the right questions: What was it about how

Vietnamese women experienced labor that was different from other cultures? What was the hospital doing that failed to consider these differences?

"The world of medical anthropology yielded this finding: Vietnamese culture sees the world as having hot and cold events. During these events, people need to consume the *opposite*. Labor and delivery are seen as cold times. Therefore, patients should not consume cold foods or liquids. This discovery yielded a *Eureka!* moment. How did the hospital keep women hydrated during labor? By giving them ice chips to suck on. The breakthrough was in getting the nurses to ask the patients what temperature water they wanted. This resulted in patients requesting and drinking plenty of warm water, thereby avoiding dehydration."

Other gaps exist that are related to language, culture, and leadership. Many states mandate interpreters for patients whose primary language is other than English. However, access or quality of these interpreters is patchy at best, which can lead to tragic consequences. A paper titled "The Legal Framework for Language Access in Healthcare Settings: Title VI and Beyond," tells of 13-year-old Gricelda Zamora. Like many children of immigrants, Gricelda served as the family's interpreter. This arrangement worked for a while, until she developed severe abdominal pain. Her parents took her to the hospital. But Gricelda was too sick to interpret for herself and the hospital failed to provide the family with one. Thus, her parents did not understand the doctor's direction to see the doctor in three days or return to the emergency room should her symptoms worsen. Two days later, with Gricelda's condition rapidly deteriorating, her parents rushed back to the emergency room. Doctors discovered she had a ruptured appendix and airlifted the gravely ill teen to a nearby medical facility. Gricelda died a few hours later.

As evidenced by this sad and highly preventable anecdote, addressing some of the cultural gaps that exist will require the skill of cultural competence in order to treat patients effectively.

And the gaps show up in practically every aspect of the medical experience— consider the visiting hours that don't allow for night and double-shift workers to visit their hospitalized family members. Or how about the story shared by former Surgeon General Antonia Coello Novello at the 2012 Hispanic Association on Corporate Responsibility National Conference:

"A Spanish-speaking patient read a prescription and interpreted the instructions of 'Take a pill once per day' as 'Take eleven pills once per day' because in Spanish the letters o-n-c-e means *eleven*. Further, the very concept of westernized medicine can be a cultural mismatch for some. Certain groups prefer the wisdom and treatments from centuries-old traditions of *curanderas* (female faith healers) and shamans."

These cultural and language gaps are further exacerbated by the lack of diversity in the medical profession, particularly in its upper echelons. Fewer than 12 percent of physicians, speech and language pathologists, and physical therapists and only 15 percent of registered nurses are Black or Latino, even though these two groups represent about 25 percent of the working population—twice the number that is represented in healthcare provider roles.

And the numbers get worse as we advance in levels of leadership: fewer than 16 percent of medical and healthcare managers are Black or Latino, and Asians represent less than 5 percent of these managers. Additionally, people of color constitute only 9 percent of all healthcare CEOs.[24]

These gaps and disparities in health outcomes, healthcare access, preventive care participation, care quality, and others require a holistic revamp of the entire healthcare landscape. One skillset that can serve as an antidote to the many ills that exist within our healthcare system is crosscultural competence—which, as I have shared throughout this book, is the ability to recognize, value, and navigate through cultures other than one's own. This skill must exist throughout the healthcare supply chain. At the hospital, this ranges from the front desk greeter to the orderly, to the person taking vitals, to the person managing the waiting room, to the nurses, doctors, executives, and board members.

Aside from offering insurance coverage as an employee benefit, healthcare has not traditionally been the purview of most of corporate America. That is changing as more and more companies are getting involved in the well-being of their employees through a variety of initiatives, which positively affects a company's healthcare costs. This is happening for good reason. Employees of color are carrying a disproportionately greater burden of having to show up to work with more health problems, more aches and pains, and greater depression. This situation not only affects their work performance, but also their engagement, stamina, and, indirectly, their advancement opportunities.

Organizations must play a part in restoring our healthcare system. Companies can support wellness initiatives for employees, and taking diversity into account can help increase the effectiveness of these programs. For instance, Health Care Service Corporation—commonly known as the operator of Blue Cross Blue Shield of Illinois, Texas, Oklahoma, and New Mexico—embarked on a weight loss campaign for employees. Collectively, employees lost 53,000 pounds in 2011.

Linking what we now know about how multicultural audiences are using social networking and digital devices, such as smartphones, can lead to positive changes in employee behavior. The San Francisco-based health and wellness company, Keas, uses an online, interactive game that helps clients' employees to adopt healthier habits. Employees can take quizzes, set goals for exercising, eating right, and other healthy habits—all through the use of a web-based gaming program. Team members cheer each other on and earn financial rewards for meeting health goals. Two companies that have contracted with Keas found that 50–80 percent of employees participate in the games and programs.[25] Since Blacks and Latinos are already frequent users of social media, how responsive might they be using this type of "gamification" to address issues of health and wealth?

Here's another instance in which interactive technology and/or social media promotes health and wellness: the American Diabetes Association in Washington State has teamed up with Facebook to create a mobile application that enables the diabetes community to manage the disease.[26] Given the greater incidence of diabetes among Blacks and Latinos, how effective might this effort be in helping to keep this disease under control?

Cultural competence plays a role by providing insights about the types of messages and incentives that resonate with specific employee populations. Healthcare is the ultimate work-life issue because it affects employees at work, at home, and within their communities.

Corporate communications that partner with community

We need to think about corporate communications that go beyond company walls.

According to a poll commissioned by New American Media, ethnic—not mainstream—media is the primary and secondary news source for 50 million Americans. Considering current demographic trends, this number is only going to grow.

Many minority groups do not look to the corporation as the primary influencer in their lifestyle decisions. According to one Hewitt poll a few years ago, Whites are more likely to seek out and trust medical information provided by their employer. Minority groups look to their community leaders—the priest, pastor, imam, alderman—as the voice of authority. In this era of multiculturalism and diverse workforces, corporate communicators could benefit from developing strategies that partner with these channels to get messages across to employees.

According to the May 2007 issue of *Hypertension* magazine, Black men's barbers could help test their clients for high blood pressure.[27] In one study, a group of men receiving standard hypertension care was compared to a group that received enhanced intervention via their barbershop. The proportion of men in the enhanced intervention group that received hypertension treatment increased from 45 percent to 92 percent, while those who successfully managed their condition rose from 19 percent to 58 percent. Barbers were then trained to check blood pressure, provide health education, and make medical referrals.

Imagine a diabetes management campaign initiated by a large company employing people from various ethnic communities. Equipped with the messages they want to provide and the know-how to deliver them most effectively to non-White employees, these corporations could enlist the help of community leaders. Maybe ask to do a benefits workshop for employees in the community center, rather than in the corporate offices? Perhaps a community leader would be willing to lend her or his voice to the message? These corporations could then partner with ethnic media to cover the topic. They could buy ads in community and ethnic papers in return for the publisher agreeing to print editorials reinforcing messages on health or retirement savings.

Companies doing health benefits inclusively

On location pharmacies and health clinics

Employers like Walmart, Pitney Bowes, and Disney are experimenting with onsite health clinics for their employees. The premise: With their large employee base, they can help clinics manage costs and make a checkup less time-intensive and more accessible for employees. This model is likely to appeal to the worldviews of various minority groups, including Latinos, who represent an ever-increasing percentage of the workforce.

These at-work clinics are bound to be attractive for cultures with communitarian and paternalistic worldviews, particularly Latinos, who have a higher expectation that "My employer will take care of me and my family's needs." And since the clinic is at work, it's a chance for Mamá and Papá to integrate work and family by bringing the whole family to the workplace for a medical checkup.

What if employers sponsored healthcare fairs for the whole family? Nurses could take blood pressure and draw blood samples for cholesterol and diabetes screening, while HR staff at PC workstations show employees how to use the intranet to access benefits information. Make it a party. Kids walk away with lollipops and balloons, and their parents learn their cholesterol levels.

Finding the levers that tap into minority worldviews

An individualistic, internal-control message of "Take care of yourself" may not be enough to motivate a communal, fatalistic Latino male to get an annual physical. But what if you showed him a picture of his 15-year-old daughter at her *Quinceañera* (coming-of-age 15th birthday), and then made your case:

¿Si algo te pasará a tí?

(If something happened to you.)

¿Quién cuidaría a tu hija?

(Who would take care of her?)

Cuídala.

(Take care of her.)

Cuidándote.

(By taking care of yourself.)

De una vez, chequea tu salud.

(Once and for all, get a checkup.)

¿Si algo te pasará a tí?
¿Quién cuidaría a tu hija?

Cuídala, Cuidándote.
De una vez, chequea tu salud.

Several sizes fit most

I'm not suggesting organizations adopt a multitude of approaches to address every possible demographic. But we need to get past the one-size-fits-all mentality that's grounded in the views and preferences of the majority group. As Hewitt research reveals, there are overlaps in behavioral drivers between different groups, sometimes surprisingly so. For example, there is a key similarity in 401(k) behavior between older Baby Boomers, low-income European Americans, and African Americans. They all have less experience with financial literacy, leading to non-participation, tentativeness, and over-conservative behaviors that bring down their investment returns.

By identifying these overlaps, we can develop marketing campaigns that address the needs of a variety of demographic groups. This is accomplished by shaping the campaigns around a handful of behavioral drivers (e.g., "Inexperienced with investing" and "Very experienced with investing") rather than a given demographic group. So while "one size fits all" is not effective and "all sizes fit everyone" would be cost prohibitive, the new approach could be called "several sizes fit most."

Providing flexible programs that meet individual needs is only half the battle. If employees don't use them, it doesn't matter how suitable the programs. Success only occurs when workers understand what is available to them *and* use what best meets their needs. They must become educated consumers. All employees must be empowered to make decisions that personally optimize the effectiveness, financial efficiency, and appreciation of programs.

Targeted communication may be required for various groups so that each is motivated to take the desired action. These are the "nudges" authors Thaler and Sunstein argue for in their book. Granted, some employers already use different, specific messages for younger and older employees when it comes to retirement savings. This same type of specialized communication can inform and then motivate a wide variety of diverse employee segments to take action.

Employers should not aim to have separate communication initiatives for each demographic group, however. It's illegal to target specific employee segments—for example, sending pieces of communication to only one demographic group. What's more, effectiveness would be compromised, as the over-reliance on archetypes leads to stereotypes.

It's not only the choice of message that's important, but also the medium. Studies have found, for example, that older workers, those without high school diplomas, and employees without broadband access at home are less inclined to use the Internet.[28] By being aware of cultural tendencies, communication campaigns can be shaped with more of a marketing approach to help get individuals more comfortable with using the web or other communication channels.

From the beginning of the diversity movement, the underlying premise is that a diverse workforce would be beneficial to the enterprise. It would bring more creativity and innovation—and a workforce that could better recognize the needs, wants, and desires of an increasingly diverse marketplace. A diverse workforce offers a communal benefit as well. As we call out differences to create, communicate, and market health and wealth benefits, something unexpected emerges: by developing alternative ways to meet the needs of diverse groups, we discover new ways of reaching the *majority* as well.

When describing a Latino-oriented, communal, family-focused pitch for preventive care, I've had European-American audience members say, "Hey, that's appealing to me, too." I've had White audiences tell me, "That example you pointed out for Latinos and the 15-year-old daughter taps something deep within me—and I'm not Latino. Or maybe I am and I don't know it! Those traditional forms of communication don't move me either."

This is diversity at work. While we need a handle on broad-based archetypes to assess our communication strategies and benefit plan designs, there are plenty of people in other cultural groups that, for various reasons— personality, income level, geographic location, spiritual beliefs—also need different ways of being reached. Taking into account the mix and how to make it work creates new forms of outreach whose benefits go beyond the minority groups. Diversity enriches us all.

Think about how Latino culture already has enriched mainstream US culture— salsa has surpassed ketchup as the number one condiment. *Dulce de leche* is the second-best-selling ice cream flavor, right after vanilla. And the popular TV show *Ugly Betty* (now available online) came directly from the Spanish telenovela, *La Fea Betty*. Cristina Benitez's book, *Latinization: How Latino Culture Is Transforming the US* dedicates 125 pages to this phenomenon.

La Fea Betty   **Ugly Betty**

There is also a long, rich history of how Black and White cultures have influenced each other. Merely by tracing the gospel roots of rock 'n' roll, one can embark on a socio-cultural-historical journey of cross-influences encompassing hairstyles, clothing, expressiveness, and more. Likewise, as women entered the workplace in large numbers, they transformed male culture, both inside the corporation and at home. In addition, Americans have influenced cultures worldwide through the export of values like democracy and free trade, as well as through pop culture flowing from Hollywood and MTV.

Multicultural marketing is built into the Inclusion Paradox. To create true inclusion, we must call out differences. In so doing, not only do we broaden our own outreach to include diverse workforces in the organization's mainstream culture, but we also create ways for these different groups to influence and enrich the mainstream culture. This is 3-D inclusion: Influences that flow every which way for the enrichment of all.

This is the next frontier of true diversity and inclusion. In the Obama Era, long-held assumptions around corporate and governmental benefits are being deeply questioned and made more relevant for today's multicultural workforce.

If done right, employees and citizens—from the minority to the majority—and their organizations and nations will be the winners. ◌

Cultural immersion

Corporate communicators must steep themselves in the iconography of different demographic groups. The whole marketing piece needs to work—not just through the substitution of diverse images, a different language, or even the appropriate worldview levers. The feel of the entire piece—from font to colors to images—needs to appeal to different demographic groups, while still meeting corporate branding guidelines, of course.

For example, here are some images that may appeal to Latinos. Keep in mind that some may appeal to middle-class Latinos, and others may appeal to low-income Latinos. Also, some country-of-origin differences may work with one group of Latinos and not another.

Illustrated soap operas called *fotonovelas* are popular. Latino Health Care Solutions, owned by UnitedHealthcare®, uses this form to create storylines in which a father and his two daughters talk about the dangers of untreated diabetes.

For Mexican migrants to the United States, *lucha libre* (wrestling) superheroes are players in morality dramas. *Super Amigos* is a documentary of four men in Mexico City who have taken on different causes using the *lucha libre* art form. Super Barrio (Super Neighborhood) fights against people being evicted through gentrification. Super Gay fights for homosexual rights. Ecologista Universal fights against global warming and contamination, and Super Animal dons his mask to protest bullfighting. Could any of these superheroes be recruited to put on a cape and fight heart disease or diabetes?

 Soap operas on primetime, with all their taboo topics, are a typical form of family entertainment. For Latino culture, where family issues can be hard to talk about, telenovelas provide an acceptable, albeit somewhat sensationalized, outlet to broach difficult subjects. One Latino public relations firm inserted a story line dealing with alcoholism into one of the more popular telenovelas showing in the United States.

A Pedro, un amigo de trabajo, le diagnosticaron diabetes. Él está muy asustado porque su papá también tuvo diabetes y murió a consecuencia de ella.

Los hispanos tenemos más posibilidades de sufrir de diabetes.

Pero no debería de asustarse. Lo que tiene que hacer Pedro es tomar responsabilidad por su salud.

¿Cómo?

A mi tía le diagnosticaron diabetes hace ya 10 años, pero ella tomó la decisión de que quería vivir. Cambió su forma de comer. Ahora come frutas y vegetales, pollo y pescado, y cocina con aceite de canola o de oliva.

Además, camina media hora cada día cuando el tiempo lo permite, o si no, usa la máquina caminadora, revisa sus niveles de azúcar con regularidad, y toma sus medicinas a la hora que le tocan.

La gente que tiene diabetes puede vivir una vida larga y sin complicaciones, si se cuidan, comen una dieta apropiada y se mantienen físicamente activos.

Mi tía visita al médico con regularidad para la revisión de sus ojos y sus pies, y para controlar el colesterol y la presión arterial.

Es importante que la gente que tiene diabetes cumpla con todas sus visitas médicas, para poder controlar la enfermedad.

Mi tía dice que tiene muchas razones para vivir, especialmente por su familia, y que la diabetes es una enfermedad que se puede controlar. Dice que se va a morir CON diabetes, pero no se va a morir DE diabetes.

Y su premio ha sido que no ha tenido complicaciones por la diabetes.

Si es miembro de UnitedHealthcare, y usted o algún miembro de su familia necesita información acerca de la diabetes, llame al número en su tarjeta de membresía de UnitedHealthcare o visite www.uhclatino.com.

SUMMARY POINTS

- Inadvertent exclusion may determine whether minority employees take advantage of company benefits and how they go about doing so.

- Compared to White Americans, African Americans and Latinos tend to under-save in 401(k) plans and under-participate in preventive healthcare programs. Meanwhile, women are more conservative in their investments than men.

- Employers must start viewing employees as consumers, not passive recipients, of company benefit packages.

- When it comes to health and other company benefits, one size does not fit all. Such an approach can be both cost-prohibitive and ineffective.

- In an increasingly diverse workforce, the "average employee" no longer applies, and company benefits designed for that fading paradigm do not resonate with today's emerging workforce.

- We must move to multicultural design and marketing of benefits. This entails much more than translating words and changing pictures—it means considering the differing worldviews of multicultural constituencies.

- Crosscultural agility and understanding the existence of different worldviews helps companies find motivators within cultural contexts that encourage employees to participate in various corporate benefit offerings.

- Calling out differences in employee behavior may uncover common behaviors across different groups. Instead of developing different approaches for each demographic group, companies can look at the behavior drivers shared by these constituencies.

- Employee health status economically affects company performance.

- The Affordable Care Act will add about 32 million currently uninsured Americans to the current healthcare system.

- Societal trends affect an organization's employee healthcare coverage.

- Diversity and inclusion strategies that are well known in the corporate world can be used in the healthcare system to improve patient outcomes and increase cost savings.

SHAPING YOUR STRATEGY

- Has your organization experienced differences in the utilization of benefits based on demographic characteristics? If you don't know, how can you convince key stakeholders that it's worth their efforts to find out?

- How successful is your organization at designing and marketing multicultural benefits packages? What can it do to change the way these packages are created to make them more inclusive of different cultural worldviews?

- What motivators can your organization tap into to encourage employees to participate in preventive care and save more for retirement?

WORK

LIFE

15

THE MOTHER OF ALL BATTLES

Chapter 15

Work-life flexibility: The mother of all battles

The imaginary work-life camera slowly pans out to reveal Mom and Dad both working. A nursery is available on-site, and older children are welcome in the workplace. There's no commute, and home-style breakfasts and lunches are served daily. A progressive twenty-first century Best Company for work-life balance? Perhaps.

But I was actually describing a typical life working on the family farm before the Industrial Revolution. Since coal-based energy technology changed all that two centuries ago, workers and their families have had to toil within an economic model that violently cleaved home and work into completely separate spheres.

This split resulted in irreconcilable parental, spousal, community, and workplace responsibility dilemmas. Until recently, it was simply understood that individuals had to solve their dilemma by choosing one sphere over the other. "You can't have it all!" was the message to angst-filled female employees. The work-life balance movement, led by the first modern-age working moms, counterpunched. Propelled by the flagship publication of the movement, *Working Mother* magazine, women challenged detrimental workplace and career assumptions. Taking the retort and remaking it, the working moms' battle cry became, "We *can* have it all!"

Baby Boomer women launched the powerful archetype of the Super Woman who worked a fulfilling career; had a satisfying, intimate relationship with her husband; stayed in shape; and tended expertly and lovingly to her children's emotional, developmental, and practical needs. Rising to the challenge, millions of women strived to live balanced lives. In the first decade of the twenty-first century, 55 percent of first-time mothers returned to work within six months of giving birth, compared to 14 percent in the early 1960s.[1] But they struggled against a Category 1 headwind of inflexible structures—not only those related to the office, but also school schedules, store hours, doctors' appointments, and traffic-clogged commutes, to name just a few.

The women at the forefront of this movement made demands: more flexible office hours, onsite childcare, and paid-time-off (PTO) banks that allowed workers to care for runny noses and fevers. Not wanting to lose this newfound talent pool, corporations slowly, reluctantly, responded. Today, PTO banks exist in about 30 percent of companies.[2] And arriving a little late due to a sick child or leaving a little early for a day care pickup is tolerated, for white-collar workers anyway. But only a handful of truly progressive companies have tried to bridge the home-office gulf by providing on-site day care and fitness centers.

While generally helpful, these accommodations worked around the edges, rather than yielding transformational changes that could resolve the home-office split. Balance remained elusive. As long as office and home and standard work hours remained in place, this artificial dichotomy kept the ideal of work-life balance out of reach.

These systemic barriers didn't stop other demographic groups from jumping on the work-life bandwagon, however. Working fathers, singles, near-retirees, and Millennials *all* want it. "Moms' requirements for flexibility have opened this up to others who didn't even realize they wanted it too or were too afraid to ask," says Kristin Slavish, an HR Vice President at Aon Hewitt.

As more women worked, they had less time for housework and childcare. Dishes stacked up; diapers needed to be changed; deadlines loomed. Men had to take up the housework slack. While imbalances still exist, the trend is toward housework equity. According to the Council on Contemporary Families, men's contribution to housework doubled—from 15 percent to 30 percent[3]—between the 1960s and the first decade of the twenty-first century. Men are now increasingly expected to contribute equally to the functioning of the household as well as to succeed at work.[4] Meanwhile, something profound and inherently human happened as fathers spent more time with their kids—they discovered the joy of parenthood, just as they came to realize how much they had missed from their own fathers' deficit of time with them. What started as an imposition to accommodate their partners' job aspirations became, for many, a personal desire. Suddenly, fathers were demanding their own work-life balance so they could coach their kids' 4 o'clock soccer practice or attend a late-afternoon kindergarten recital.

WORK-LIFE FLEXIBILITY: THE MOTHER OF ALL BATTLES

As these parents broadened the demand for work-life balance, singles began to make their voices heard as well. Parenthood, they argued, should not be the only argument for honoring a request for balance. They, too, had other priorities they wanted to tend to—church, synagogue, and mosque commitments; serving as a Big Brother or Big Sister to a neighborhood kid; taking care of aging parents; preparing for a marathon.

Next in line were near-retirees who, feeling healthy and intellectually alert, did not want to retire altogether. Some did not feel economically ready—either they hadn't saved enough for their post-work years or they discovered they were going to live much longer than the actuaries had anticipated. Next came the Millennials, the And Generation, for whom nanosecond technology means there are no trade-offs. For them, the divide between personal and work has shrunk along with the size of their laptops.

The good news: This congruence is accelerating debates about the next generation of work-life balance. The bad news: In a 24/7 global economy, Americans, Canadians, and Western Europeans compete with Indian, Chinese, Filipino, Eastern European, and Central American talent located *anywhere* in the world. And where G7 developed nation wages have gone stagnant and health and retirement benefits have been curtailed, most individuals have to work harder than ever.

Still, few want to go back to sacrificing family, community service, and other pursuits at the altar of work and career success. We cling to the aspiration to be more than our work. Yet, the increasingly competitive marketplace and the quest for a more holistic life are careening down a collision course with each other. The pioneering working mothers freed the genie from the bottle, and there's no stuffing it back in. It is shaping up to be the Mother of All Battles. Which will yield to the other? Or is there another way?

Work-life balance is dead! Long live work-life flexibility!

There is a battle being waged *within* the work-life movement. The original clarion cry had been all about balance between work and everything else. But given the rush of life—the expectation that we manage our own tech support, retirement savings, health management, learning, and career planning; the increased load on our personal lives as we manage children's complex schedules and care for aging parents; and ubiquitous access to *all* information *all* the time—the quest for balance has yielded little but frustration. Is balance even possible? In clamoring and longing for it, we and progressive companies have inadvertently made both spheres larger—making the elusive Holy Grail of work-life balance even more out of reach.

When I describe this to audiences, they ruefully connect with this realization. "But if balance is out of reach, how about flexibility?" I ask. "Yes!" they respond. "That's what it is." They elaborate: "We need the flexibility to manage the competing priorities in our whole lives—flexibility to move in and out of being a worker, boss, parent, partner, sibling, son, daughter, volunteer, community organizer, athlete, arts lover, friend, camper, dreamer."

We've surrendered to the faster, more complex pace of life and thus tempered our quest for balance. At any one time, something will be out of balance in our lives, as family emergencies, client deadlines, an upcoming competition, or vacation consume a greater share of our collective moments. But we won't surrender to inflexible structures. Flexibility is the currency we need to survive and thrive.

Even First Lady Michelle Obama came out in support of greater work-life flexibility. At a women's economic roundtable in Pontiac, Michigan, on July 9, 2009, she said, "As we all know, our country is in the midst of a major economic crisis. And we're all feeling the effects.... And folks are feeling it at the workplace. Because right now, thousands of women across the country don't have family leave at their jobs. And those who do can't afford to take it because it's not paid. And 22 million working women don't have a single paid sick day. That's just unacceptable. Families shouldn't be punished because someone gets sick or has an emergency."[5]

In the Obama Era, an increasing number of employers are offering flextime in lieu of higher salaries, raises, or the traditional end-of-year bonus. As Michelle Obama alluded, companies simply cannot afford to increase salaries during tough economic times. But they *can* offer greater flexibility in exchange for high productivity, loyalty, and a decrease in turnover.

As long as we were tethered to offices and desks, bound by 9-to-5 rhythms, we faced a dead end in our ability to help workers balance their work and home loads. Limited by time and space, corporate equations could not yield different answers. Accommodations were made through an either/or equation. Part-time or flextime assumed that time away from the physical workplace meant work did not get done. While many working mothers got what they asked for—more time with their kids—it came at the cost of their long-term career advancement. The preeminent career advancement equation became: Strong Performance + Time = Advancement. High-performing women who chose to take time off simply fell behind.[6] No matter how good they were, most would never be able to make up for the lost work time.

To accommodate this conundrum, Ellen Galinsky, President of the Families and Work Institute, suggests, "Employers need to think of career flexibility, not just flextime and flex place, so that there is an understanding that there are times where you move in and out of the workforce. Think about the irony: flexibility *can't* be a rigid flexible work arrangement!"

But now, technology—the culprit responsible for creating the work-home split in the first place—is saving the day by enabling flexibility.

The pivotal tool was the Internet, which offered employees a platform on which they could share their work with colleagues in Mumbai, London, and Chicago or with team members at their kitchen tables. The Internet made a new equation possible, driving a wedge into the concept of workplace. With *work* and *place* no longer inexorably connected, alternate possibilities emerged.

Still, one more structural equation remained to reconfigure: Work From Home + Slow Connectivity = Diminished Productivity. Along came broadband wireless, which toppled the final vestiges of structural limitations. For knowledge workers, work can now happen anyplace, anytime, with instant connectivity to anyone and any content.

We have reached the tipping point in the Mother of All Workplace Battles. Full work-life flexibility is now structurally possible. The next battlefront has become policy.

The resistance – trapped in twentieth-century thinking

Many leaders and managers are busy spray painting over the "Long Live Flexibility!" graffiti on figurative corporate walls. The rigid structures of the modern corporation made sense in the workplace era. But the emerging work/place shift runs smack into long-held assumptions of how, where, and when work gets done. How does one manage by walking around if there's no one in the office? And how can you raise productivity if there's a fear of "out of sight, out of mind"?

"Most senior leaders and middle managers in organizations today are still operating in a 'time card' mentality," says Carol Sladek, Work-Life Consulting Leader at Aon Hewitt. "They can't get past measuring productivity in hours and the number of hours an employee's car is in the office parking lot."

Managers are not getting much support from the organization when it comes to managing this complexity. While a third of companies offer flexibility at manager discretion, nearly two-thirds provide no training for managers on how to go about doing this.[7] Further, in many places where work-life flexibility benefits exist, it is understood unfairly that those who sign up for them have removed themselves from the career advancement track.

Leaders and managers may resist making way for work-life flexibility. Understanding why requires a short philosophical conversation. *Modernism*, the worldview that believes reality is fixed and determined by those in authority, is being challenged by *postmodernism*, a worldview that believes reality is based on each individual's interpretation. This philosophy first emerged in literature: the story doesn't necessarily mean what the writer intended, but rather what the reader understands it to mean. Soon, postmodernism infiltrated multiple arenas. It has influenced new interpretations of history,[8] the creation of alternative curricula—from Montessori to African-American and Women's Studies—and the emergence of New Age and "The Secret" spirituality.

This postmodernist worldview has also made the diversity movement possible. Modernism accepts how things are—including the dominance of White males in leadership—because there can be only one reality and that is the one we live in. Postmodernist thinking allowed the deconstruction of assigned roles, which led organizations to question the lack of diversity in leadership roles. The key to inclusion—making the mix work—lies in understanding the varying interpretations of the workplace experience by diverse constituencies.

This takes us to work-life flexibility. Different constituencies, for different reasons, want to redefine what "work" looks like, and when and where it gets done. This postmodern view triggers conflict with the modernist view of many leaders and managers. The battle lines manifest mostly along generational lines (Baby Boomers, disciples of modernism, on the one hand, and Gen Xers and Millennials, the children of postmodernism, on the other), though individuals of all ages are lining up on either side.

Diffusing backlash

As the established worldview clashes with the emerging one, a backlash occurs. The forces of culture change move according to the laws of physics: as the new worldview begins making inroads, it invites an equal reaction of resistance.

With work-life, the resistance comes from multiple fronts. It's not just managers who resist loosening the structures to allow more flexibility for working mothers, for example. According to Carol Evans, former CEO of Working Mother Media, it also happens among women themselves as they wrestle with the implications about their own identities. "We see one wave of the backlash against working mothers come from other women who have staked their positions as stay-at-home moms," she says. "Not all stay-at-home moms, of course, but a vocal minority of them who may resent the lifestyle choices that working mothers have made."

She goes on to explain that another wave of backlash comes from other women—those first glass-ceiling crashers who chose not to have children in order to move up the corporate ladder. And even more backlash comes from White men who feel women in the workplace are being granted special privileges. Then there's the inevitable backlash from singles, who feel that people with children are allowed work schedule freedoms that they themselves should also receive. "These bands of resistance then go up against family-friendly company programs," says Evans.[9] The shock waves of debate reverberate throughout the corporation.

The Inclusion Paradox requires solutions that break the *zero-sum game* mindset and instead get into what Dr. Michael Broom refers to as an *infinite game* mindset.[10] In a zero-sum game mindset, one's gain is another's loss. In an infinite game, one's gain triggers gains for others as well. It goes beyond the 1 + 1 = 2 of win-win to 1 + 1 = 3 or more. The challenge lies in discovering how *all* constituents—including managers and leaders—can win in the quest for true work-life flexibility.

When we constructively call out the differences of traditionally marginalized groups in order to understand what they need, we get new answers for other groups as well.

Let's look at how this works. Addressing working moms' need for maternity leave leads to the realization that new fathers need time off as well in order to bond with their new child and support their partner. In addressing the architectural needs of those with physical disabilities, we discover an overlap between what they need and the desire to make our buildings greener. And in rethinking the subconscious bias toward a White male style of leadership, we create new possibilities for introverts.

"This is one of the reasons why, in all the work that we do at *Working Mother*," Evans explains, "whether we are working on behalf of women of color, diversity in general, or working mothers, we always emphasize the benefit to all employees for any gains that any one group makes. Because if I have never had a child but now my mother needs elder care, I can take advantage of the same flextime a working mother gets to take care of her children." Young, healthy men and women are now using flexibility to train for marathons. Millennial singles can more easily volunteer in a political campaign. Near-retirees can take off mid-afternoon to hang out with their grandchildren. "Any progress that we make, we can apply to other groups," concludes Evans.

Candi Castleberry-Singleton mentions her own experience creating workplace flexibility programs at Motorola and UPMC, where she served as Chief Diversity Officer, emphasizing the benefits these programs ultimately provide to a wide range of employees, not just working mothers: "Flexible work programs get traction when people can see how they personally benefit from them. Because people tend to mentally associate flexible work programs with female employees, I never use the term 'working mothers' or 'working parent' to sell them. Instead, I present the programs as inclusion initiatives—meaning they're available to everyone—so that both women and men see the personal advantages of flexible work, whether for reasons related to parenting or something entirely different, such as going back to school to get an MBA."

Such programs gain greater traction when managers and leaders see that they win as well. Employees are dealing with ever-longer commutes, made even more unattractive by heightened concern about reducing our carbon footprint. Productivity suffers when employees arrive at the office stressed even before the workday begins. Settling in at their desk, their minds may wander to their 2-year-old's ear infection or the need to get home in time to make dinner for a frail, aging parent, or their 6 p.m. physical trainer session, or their desire to finish a painting in time for an upcoming art exhibit.

Some managers think they've put boundaries in place to keep "the rest of life" at bay by demanding their workers be seen. However, such restrictions are breeched right under their noses through a digital sieve called the Internet. They may appear to be busily working on a new marketing campaign or drafting the white paper that will unveil the firm's revolutionary thought leadership to the world, but in reality, workers are webcamming into their doggie day care to see how their schnauzer is doing, scheduling immunizations for their kids, planning their next vacation, and monitoring highway backups on their Waze app.

Ironically, many studies show that those out-of-sight workers tucked away in their home offices are actually more engaged with their employers, more productive, and more satisfied with the ability to manage their work and their life responsibilities.[11]

Virtual, telecommuting workers deconstruct their workdays. Rather than dedicating large chunks of time to specific things—9 to 5 for work, 6 to 9 for family—they chunk work into productivity modules that are interspersed with childcare, fitness, artistic expression, socializing, and personal planning modules. They may go offline from work at 3 p.m., but they're back online at 9 p.m. after the kids have gone to bed and the clothes are in the washer. This arrangement, by happy coincidence, helps move the work forward in a global economy: now, managers have workers who can take calls from ten time zones away in India, without those calls intruding too much into their lives.

There are still more benefits for businesses. In the quest for reducing costs, having virtual workers enables a game-changing reduction in the real estate footprint. This means not only less office space, but also less furniture, fewer coffee stations, lower energy costs, reduced security costs, and so on. In addition, a mobile, flexible workforce will no longer need to ask for flextime to meet home demands. Flex is built in.

Maria Awilda Quintana is a Gen X executive at Banco Popular in San Juan, Puerto Rico, whom I met at a conference for financial advisors where I was giving a workshop on Millennials. In the conservative environment of the banking industry, Quintana breaks with conventional wisdom to get the highest productivity from her employees. "At five o'clock, I send anyone who is still in the office home. 'Go take care of your kids, go work out, go volunteer,' I tell them. And they can't believe that their manager is telling them to stop working when there is so much work to do." In a hierarchical, communal Latino culture, this directive has a powerful, positive effect. And guess what? At 9 p.m., after the kids have gone to bed and the dishes are done, they're all logging in from home. "I never set that up as an expectation," she says. "But they do it because in my helping them with meeting their multiple life demands, they flex in return to help the bank meet its multiple demands." This not only means a more engaged workforce, it also translates into business results. Quintana's team's client satisfaction scores are over 86 percent.

This, then, is the quid pro quo—the employment contract of what gets offered in exchange. Flexibility begets flexibility. Zero-sum game capitulates to infinite game.

The postmodern twenty-first century workplace

So in this flex world, where exactly *is* the office? It's in the home den, at the Starbucks, or the neighborhood park. It's wherever one can take an Android or a laptop with a broadband wireless card. It does not mean the end of the traditional office, but rather, its redefinition. Instead of the workplace being *the* place where work gets done, it becomes a place where a *certain* type of work gets done.

There are still plenty of reasons to maintain the workplace. Virtual workers need face time for relationship building, certain types of creative brainstorming, and production, among other activities.[12] Clearly, there are plenty of customer-facing businesses that must have personnel on-site. Also, the traditional office is an option for the type of employee who can focus better away from home or is energized by working in the presence of colleagues. But even here, the office moves with the worker. He or she may not have a fixed desk. And as they move around the building from meeting to water fountain to boss's office, they can stay in constant touch with colleagues in and out of the office. "Walking down the hall" can be literal or virtual, as colleagues available for a quick visit show up in an online chat tool and ping, "R U there?"

While cube farms signaled an end of sorts to the hierarchy of job title and experience based on the size and position of one's office, they still demarked boundaries. Broadband wireless enabled through pocket-sized devices now supports a less restricted and contained workplace, as the office goes mobile even within the building. At the same time, acute cost pressures and the push to reduce their contribution to global warming are heightening corporations' appetites to shed costly real estate. "They still want the quality and the performance, but they don't want to pay for workspace that's occupied less than half the time," says Tom Vecchione, the workplace leader for Gensler, one of the top global workplace design organizations.[13]

As flexible work-life trends create a new paradigm for working arrangements, a new office design becomes a necessity. In a recent workplace survey, Gensler discovered that "Today's office workers spend less time at their desks [alone]. Instead they're collaborating, learning, and socializing with their peers."[14] The workspace needs to be redesigned to accommodate these preferred styles. At one media company, Gensler designed bench-style desks for print reporters, bullpens for Internet reporters, and dog-bone-shaped workstations for broadcast teams. It's the postmodern workplace, where deciding how to use the space is up to the users. The top financially and innovatively ranked companies already are seizing these issues—and reaping the rewards. At these companies, 82 percent of workers expressed satisfaction with their physical workplace, versus 49 percent of workers from average-performing companies. Why does this matter? In their survey, Gensler validated a high correlation between workplace design and multiple business measures, such as productivity, business competitiveness, job performance, and worker satisfaction.[15]

The "green imperative" dovetails into this. With greenhouse gas emissions from all buildings accounting for almost half of the US total, new flex buildings must open up to natural sunlight and enable more efficient heating and cooling. Meanwhile, from a disability perspective, we need to move from a compliance-driven "Americans with disabilities" approach to true, inclusive flex buildings that are holistically user-friendly to people of different sizes, mobility, and light and noise sensitivities.[16]

The Inclusion Paradox is at play here as well—more open spaces facilitate the inclusive collaboration of people with diverse skills and approaches. When it comes to the evolving workplace, Chris Sullivan, former editor of *Architecture* magazine, writes, "One-size-fits-all standardization is history."[17]

Uber-flexibility – Diversity of one

Clearly, work-life flexibility is about time and space. But it's even more profound than that. Work-life flexibility is about a state of mind. If we can bend and twist where and when we work—and concepts like 9-to-5 and "the office" start to feel anachronistic—then what other givens of "how things work" can be challenged?

Galinsky sees even greater challenge to work and advancement: "We ought not to assume that workers will get on a track and stay on that track, and there are on-ramps and off-ramps. Instead, we ought to think of career lattices. You just can't think about careers as linear ladders that we're climbing, and if we move, we fall off into the abyss. That's just not reality, and we are losing huge talent when we think that way."

Diverse workers from different perspectives are challenging assumptions about the rigid structures regarding paid time off, career progression, the definition of a job, and of the desired types of healthcare coverage, retirement savings, and other benefits.

It is a call for uber-flexibility.

In Chapter 9 on Millennials, I laid out some specific ways in which the twenty-something uber-flexible worldview is forcing new and urgent conversations in corporations. Here, I want to explore the implications of uber-flexibility to diversity.

The diversity movement has established the need to create different approaches for attracting, engaging, and advancing groups of employees, such as women, LGBT, and people of color. Mentoring, affinity groups, and affinity job fairs are a few ways this has been tackled. Given the continued presence of glass, concrete, bamboo, tortilla, and rainbow ceilings, strategies and best practices for *diversity of groups* are needed.

In the end, we are multidimensional people who can't neatly be defined by one diversity category. I am a fifty-something, able-bodied Peruvian male in a mixed marriage with one adult daughter. I describe my faith as Catholic Evangelical Afro Baptist New Age Pentecostal. My passions include soccer, dancing, the beach, world music and food, and reading and writing. Yes, I do have several archetypical ways of being, doing, and thinking that correlate with being Latino and a guy. I believe these archetypes are helpful in crafting diversity strategy for addressing group needs and wants. This is evident in how I approach different diversity topics in my writing and work. A natural extension of uber-flexibility is the concept of *diversity of one*.

But uber-flexibility doesn't just challenge the one-size-fits-all mentality. It also challenges the updated response that several sizes fit most. Uber-flexibility demands that we address the multidimensional needs and wants of individuals—the African-American Millennial female IT engineer marathon runner; the wheelchair-using actuary and extreme sports athlete; the gay doctor who seeks to volunteer in Africa with Doctors Without Borders; the passionate fifty-something human resources executive running for a local political office. The variations are infinite!

At first, this kind of talk seems costly in the eyes of business folks. On twentieth-century technology platforms, the ability to customize corporate responses to the individual was, indeed, cost-prohibitive. But early twenty-first century technology has dramatically driven that cost down. Remember when cell phones passed the tipping point from being a luxury item to a mass-market product? We are at the same type of tipping point for corporate individualization. Online magazines provide content at a fraction of the cost of print magazines. Services such as iTunes distribute music to millions every day without any postage costs. We are on the verge of learning how to tailor corporate experiences and employee benefits in cost-effective ways that address individual wants and needs. We just need creative souls to design the programs and delivery systems.

A few years ago, Best Buy experimented with what they called Results-Only Work Environment (ROWE) where there would not be any formal work schedule. Hours worked were set by the employee. Best Buy then measured employee performance solely on output, not hours. According to the company, productivity increased 35 percent, engagement increased, and voluntary turnover declined for those on ROWE.[18]

Why should other companies take this kind of approach? Despite the tough economic climate, we still are in a fierce fight for skilled talent. But wages are rising slowly and will remain under pressures due to global labor competition. Subsidies for health and retirement are declining, meaning employees have to pay more out-of-pocket for less. Companies can't really compete on salary and traditional benefits anymore. The new competitive benefit will be uber-flexibility, in all its forms.

Why work-life flexibility will drive high-performance work cultures and strong business results

In business, the bottom line is always the bottom line. What impact will work-life flexibility have on financial measures? In addition to the cost savings that come by reducing turnover, a more flexible workforce can contribute directly to higher revenues and improved margins. According to Hewitt's 2008 Timely Topic Survey, "About Flexible Work Arrangements," two-thirds of employers said flexibility increases engagement; nearly two-thirds said it improves retention; and nearly half said it enhances recruiting. In the 2012 poll by the National Partnership for Women and Families, 86 percent of respondents wanted Congress to work on family-friendly policies like paid family leave and paid sick leave for employees.[19]

Given these stories and statistics, Carol Evans says—half-jokingly at first, before she makes it a statement of conviction: "We developed a theory at *Working Mother* that flexibility is the answer to every problem. It's the answer to high rent and environmental pollution, family time, engagement, boredom with our jobs and careers, access for those with disability, cost management in an age of margin squeezes, staffing in a 24/7 global world, to mention a few."

President Obama seems to agree. At a 2010 White House Forum on Workplace Flexibility, which was hosted by Michelle Obama, the President encouraged businesses to think about flexibility in the workplace as more than a women's issue, but an economic imperative. He cited a report by the White House Council of Economic Advisers that found companies with flexible work arrangements have lower turnover and absenteeism, higher productivity, and healthier workers.

"This disconnect between the needs of our families and the demands of our workplace also reflects a broader problem, that today, we as a society still see workplace flexibility policies as a special perk for women rather than a critical part of a workplace that can help all of us," Obama said. *"Workplace flexibility isn't just a women's issue. It's an issue that affects the well-being of our families and the success of our businesses. It affects the strength of our economy—whether we'll create the workplaces and jobs of the future we need to compete in today's global economy."*[20]

The push for greater flexibility became a policy goal of President Obama and has been a key part of Hilary Clinton's 2016 campaign platform. Organizations such as *Working Mother* magazine and the National Partnership for Women and Families have driven petition drives to Congress asking for the instituting of a paid family leave insurance program for new parents. This would broaden the impact of the current Family and Medical Leave Act and bring US employers and workers in line with the rest of the industrialized world where the United States has been *the only nation in this group without paid parental leave*. In fact, only 16 percent of US companies offer paid family leave.[21]

Carol Evans sees flexibility not just as a women's or family concern, but as a business issue. She explained, "It's also critical to the economic health of our companies and our nation. Our ability to compete in the global marketplace depends upon the energy, intelligence, and commitment our mothers and fathers bring to the workplace every day—qualities that are built on a strong family foundation."

Flexibility makes managing by objective more critical than ever. What matters is delivering results. The how and where become much less relevant. So, how to manage this uber-flexibility? Managers focus on ensuring results. Objectives, targets, and goals become the new boundaries, replacing physical walls, desks and chairs, and employees being within a manager's line of sight. And as companies are flexible, workers are flexible in return. Flexibility begets flexibility. It is both a worker and manager currency that both can use with each other. In the mother of all workplace battles, flexibility means everyone wins. ♀

SUMMARY POINTS

- Women were instrumental in pushing for work-life balance. Corporations slowly responded with more flexible office hours, on-site day care, and PTO banks instead of rigid vacation or sick time allotments. Yet traditional structures stayed intact and balance remained elusive.

- Women's push for work-life balance encouraged others— fathers, singles, near-retirees, and Millennials—to request the same consideration.

- Work-life flexibility is a more attainable goal than work-life balance.

- Work-life flexibility represents more than merely revising our traditional views on space and time. It is a profound reworking of a state of mind. It is *uber*-flexibility.

- Uber-flexibility rejects the one-size-fits-all or the one-size-fits-most paradigm, recognizing we are multidimensional people who resist category-limiting labels.

- In addition to the cost savings that come about by reducing turnover, a more flexible workforce contributes directly to higher revenues and improved margins.

- As companies become more flexible, workers are more flexible in return. Flexibility begets flexibility and everyone wins.

- Workplace flexibility is more than a business benefit, but also strengthens our national economy.

- Paid family leave for new parents will bring the United States in line with other industrialized nations.

SHAPING YOUR STRATEGY

- How flexible is your organization? What flex benefits do you offer and what percentage of your staff takes advantage of them?

- If your organization is not flexible, what are some of the reasons given for adhering to a twentieth-century work model? What can you do to alleviate manager resistance in ways that are reassuring to them?

- How does your company's workspace reflect the trend toward a more open, flexible work environment? How can you provide a more streamlined office design?

the broken, leaking, plugged up

16

talient

pipeline

The Toughest Challenge

Chapter 16

The toughest challenge: The broken, leaking, plugged-up diverse talent pipeline

Are companies ready for the Talent War? In most cases, the answer is a resounding "No!" The pipeline is cracked; it's leaking; it's clogged up. In some places, it's connected to talent pools that are drying up, and in other places, it's not connected to the talent pools whose tides are rising. If not addressed, the very sustainability of our organizations could be at stake.

- It's well known there will be 10 to 20 million jobs that will go unfilled in the coming decade due in large part to the Baby Boomer retirement bubble, yet two-thirds of CEOs haven't taken any steps to address the aging workforce.[1]

- Minorities comprise more than 30 percent of the United States workforce, according to the Bureau of Labor Statistics. That number is expected to hit nearly 40 percent by 2020. Yet 95 percent of all executive-level positions in the United States are still held by White males, according to authors David A. Thomas and John J. Gabarro in *Breaking Through: The Making of Minority Executives in Corporate America*.[2]

- Among Fortune 500 companies, 50 percent expect to lose half of their senior management team over the next five to six years, according to RHR International. These corporations also anticipate a shortfall in the number of middle management candidates prepared to take on greater responsibilities.

When the spotlight is directed at the advancement of multicultural leadership talent, the outlook gets even worse. In the 2008 Chicago United Corporate Diversity Profile, which assessed leadership representation among people of color in the Windy City, the organization found that the number of minority directors hadn't increased since the 2006 report, but the number of director seats had increased by ten. The report observed that if organizations maintained that current pace, it would take nearly 90 years for boards of directors to be representationally diverse.

It was then anticipated that the 2012 study would give some reason for hope by showing progress. But when the results came in, it was clear that little had changed since 2008. The 2012 Profile found that minorities accounted for only 12 percent of the boards of directors at Chicago's 50 largest firms, compared to 15 percent at the 200 largest S&P 500 firms. Nine of those 50 firms have no diversity in their boardrooms, and only three companies have boards with 25 percent people of color. Across the top levels of leadership, there is a dearth of representation by people of color, particularly among CEOs, chief financial officers, those in other C-level positions, and other top executives.[3]

Making matters worse, while 96 percent of executives in a 2013 Korn Ferry study on diversity believe that having a diverse and inclusive workforce can improve employee engagement and business performance, only 23 percent of them said their firms gave senior executives financial incentives to promote inclusion.[4] A follow up Korn Ferry study in 2015 indicated that despite 70 percent of executives saying their organizations had a high programmatic commitment to diversity and inclusion, only 56 percent of them felt these programs enhanced retention of traditionally underrepresented groups.[5]

Not only does this give little hope for progress, but it also shows a disconnect between the expectations for corporate diversity initiatives and their impact on the workplace.

This is bad news in terms of our ability to address the broader talent shortage. If our companies are going to continue to be viable, we're going to have to nurture and find talent in *all* labor pools.

As has often been said, what gets measured gets done. Well, here's one case where we are measuring and we are still not getting it done! Many companies deliberately don't track certain demographics because once they identify a gap in their corporate culture, they are forced to deal with it. The perception is that this could lead to added expense, which would detract from the bottom line. What's missing here is accountability—which is really no different than the challenge businesses face when they try to drive any kind of improvement.

Seriously compounding the problem is the fact that too few people of color are finishing high school and going on to college. According to the National Center for Education Statistics, high school graduation rates for Latinos and African Americans hover around 60 percent.[6] Of these, only *half* go to college.

Of those that do go to college, only 40 percent actually graduate. That gets us to a 10 percent college graduation rate.[7]

This is no longer merely a social service issue. This is a bottom-line business issue. Our collective talent lifeblood is retiring at one end of the pipeline and getting siphoned off at the other. Nothing less than our economic sustainability is at stake.

A 2009 study by management consulting firm McKinsey & Company illustrates just how devastating this broken, leaking, clogged-up pipeline has become. According to the report, "The Economic Impact of the Achievement Gap in America's Schools," if the United States had closed the educational achievement gap between the United States and better-educated countries (such as Finland and Korea), the 2008 Gross Domestic Product (GDP) could have been $1.3 trillion to $2.3 trillion higher—that's 9 to 16 percent of GDP. Noteworthy gains also could have been achieved by closing the gap between Whites on the one hand and Blacks and Latinos on the other or by closing the gap between low-income students and the rest. As the report dramatically asserts, these ongoing achievement gaps result in an economic equivalent of a permanent national recession for the United States.[8]

And the situation does not appear to be improving. McKinsey followed that 2009 report with a 2012 blueprint, "Education to Employment: Designing a System that Works," that analyzed the gap between employers, youth, and educational institutions. The study found:

- Globally, 75 million young people are unemployed and three times less likely than their parents to have a job.
- Roughly half of young people don't see the connection between jobs and education, even those with some college experience.
- Only 43 percent of employers can find enough entry-level workers with the necessary job skills.
- By 2020, there will be a shortage of 85 million skilled workers across the globe.

This shortage of skills and jobs is further exacerbated by the different interpretations of the situation by employers, educational institutions, and students—it's as if these three key players exist in parallel universes. Such circumstances distress the global economy and present national security threats to countries around the world.[9]

Insights

After two decades of explicitly addressing issues of diversity, the United States isn't advancing at the required pace. Good intentions are not enough! And we just can't will "talent of color" into positions of leadership. We have to discover new ways of finding and nurturing that talent. And we need to look within the pipeline to identify top-performing multicultural talent that may contribute in ways that aren't yet recognized as valuable *because of the limitations of our own experiences.*

As we've seen, the number of people of color entering the corporate talent pipeline is too low, according to findings from the Chicago United report. At the same time, other studies reveal that the attrition rate of this very same talent is too high. In effect, we compete intensely with each other for this coveted yet limited-in-numbers talent, creating a revolving door of multicultural employees. The reports also point out that top talent of color serves on an average of almost four boards compared to the norm of three. We appear to be overtaxing this talent by asking the same people to meet our board diversity representation goals.

The weaknesses in the multicultural talent pipeline also reflect the weakness of overall leadership development. If we don't have strong leadership development programs, it doesn't matter what kind of focus we have on filling the pipeline with diverse talent. Progress will be hampered. The reverse is also true: by focusing development resources on multicultural leadership, companies will benefit by building bench strength in an increasingly global and competitive marketplace.

The shortage of multicultural talent is a business issue that must be tackled like any other business issue—with a keen focus on specific objectives. As business leaders, we must put a relentless focus on repairing the pipeline. Today's global marketplace is very different from the one many of us grew up in, requiring new approaches and a diverse leadership team in terms of worldviews, experiences, and thought processes.

As we think about solutions to our most pressing challenges, it's important to be clear about the outcomes we're trying to achieve:

- Will we have a competitive workforce in our various geographic global markets?
- Will we have a workforce that mirrors the marketplace to help us produce relevant and profitable products and services?

- Will we have the leadership we need to sustain our growth?

- Do we have leaders who can lead diverse, multicultural, and global teams?

Let's turn our attention to some of the ways we can address these challenges.

The solutions

Cultivating the talent and leadership necessary to fuel our futures cannot be resolved by just one or two interventions. The required solutions are not all that complex—but they require deliberate action and holding ourselves accountable for the results.

Clearly, we must find ways to increase the flow of talent going into the pipeline in the first place, remove clogs that are blocking the advancement of talent of color, and plug leaks where we're losing talent to competitors or to fields outside the corporate world. Here are three suggestions for doing this.

1. We must widen the entrance to the pipeline.

Admittedly, this recommendation is one that will not yield results in the short-term, but if we don't find a way to *begin* widening the entrance to the pipeline, we're going to face a talent shortage in the next decade that we might have difficulty recovering from. IBM's former diversity leader Ron Glover explains, "There are some skills that in any industry or any society are in overabundance. The real question for us is, will we take this downturn as an opportunity as a nation and across the globe to begin to re-skill people for the coming opportunities?" As a society, we must find a way to increase the number of students of all backgrounds graduating from high school and college.

There are several highly successful school programs that, if replicated nationwide, could significantly boost the amount of talent entering the pipeline. In his 2008 book, *Outliers: The Story of Success*, Malcolm Gladwell tells the story of the KIPP Academy, an experimental public middle school in the South Bronx, one of the poorest neighborhoods in New York City. Roughly half of the students are African American, the rest Latino. Ninety percent are below, at, or just hovering above the poverty level. And yet, writes Gladwell, "By the end of eighth grade, 84 percent of the students are performing at or above their grade level in math...as well...as the privileged eighth graders in America's wealthy suburbs."[10]

To find out why, I highly recommend you read the chapter, "Marita's Bargain," in Gladwell's book. It's an uplifting, yet practical read. You'll see why there are now 125 KIPP Academies across the United States and more on the way. The KIPP methodology is well-thought-out and backed by organizational, parental, and student willpower and discipline. The underlying message is: *Despite well-worn arguments about why it can't happen—poverty, single-parent households, crime, and ineffective infrastructure—solutions do exist.*

New York Times columnist David Brooks wrote about another innovative program, the charter schools operated by the Harlem Children's Zone.[11] Like KIPP, these schools have a specific philosophy and methodology for dramatically—not just incrementally—improving the academic scores of low-income minority students. Again, major breakthroughs are possible. A Harvard economist who assessed the program wrote, "[This] study has changed my life as a scientist." Bottom line: Promise Academy eliminated the achievement gap in math between its Black students and the city average for White students.

Closing the math gap is crucial, not only for Promise Academy students, but for our nation as a whole. A report by the Brookings Institution stated, "American companies urgently need professionals trained in science, technology, engineering, and mathematics (STEM) fields, but there are not enough workers with the necessary skills, and too few Americans earn post-secondary STEM credentials."[12] STEM jobs represent the lifeblood of innovation and economic expansion for the United States and the world. Yet only about 16 percent of all US undergraduates major in science or engineering, compared with 25 percent in Europe, 38 percent in South Korea, and 47 percent in China.[13] And according to a Commerce Department report, "Although women fill close to half of all jobs in the US economy, they hold less than 25 percent of STEM jobs. This has been the case throughout the past decade, even as college-educated women have increased their share of the overall workforce."[14]

The situation is just as dire for students of color. For instance, African Americans received just 7 percent of bachelor's degrees in STEM fields, 4 percent of master's degrees, and a paltry 2 percent of PhDs. In 2009, slightly more than 5,000 doctoral degrees were awarded in chemistry, physics, and other physical sciences, but Blacks received 89, or less than 2 percent.[15]

But it's not just rocket scientists or biochemists that populate STEM jobs. The reason STEM is so important is because it represents the next phase of middle-class jobs in this country. A 2012 conference that focused on the "State of STEM" and was hosted by *US News and World Report*, observed, "The sweep of industries affected by the STEM skills shortage was revealing, from healthcare, energy production and distribution, and autos to the whole slowly renewing domestic manufacturing area, transportation, and agriculture. 'There are no more jobs that require a strong back,' said Tom Luce, the force behind the successful National Math and Science Initiative. 'We have to explain to parents and kids that 30 years ago you could have a living wage job and not be STEM capable. Today that is not possible.'"[16]

In the Obama Era, educating youth has been a priority. But implementing successful programs at every school that needs help will require sustained funding. While this is largely the responsibility of school districts, local, and federal government, there is a place for corporations to partner with schools and not-for-profits to help build tomorrow's diverse workforce. This means providing grants through foundations and volunteer hours through employees. While this type of giving has been beneficial, I believe there is opportunity for more coordinated efforts to drive greater returns on our philanthropic investments. Glover suggests making it a question of business sustainability. "It's a simple answer. It says you find a problem, you recognize that no company can fix it on its own, and reach out to others across government, industry, and the public sector to help you to figure out how to manage this challenge."

A growing number of companies have started to recognize the seriousness of the situation and are doing exactly what Glover advises—reaching out to school systems, community groups, and others to address it. IBM, for one, is putting significant resources where its sentiments are. Big Blue is partnering with schools in New York and Chicago to increase student understanding of the STEM field. Selected schools adopt an innovative 9th through 14th grade curriculum that graduates students with an associate's degree, and the skills (and option) to get an information technology job or to continue toward a bachelor's degree. Students are paired with mentors and other industry professionals who provide a real-world view of the field.[17]

Here's another example. Microsoft targets girls for STEM careers across the globe and sponsors DigiGirlz High Tech Camp and DigiGirlz Day. The camp, for girls 13 years and up, is a three-day hands-on experience with technology, meeting tech rock stars, and networking with industry leaders. The DigiGirlz Day is a one-day event held at Microsoft offices around the world and uses fun-filled technology exercises to entice middle school and high school girls to think about career paths in the field.[18]

Another example of corporate involvement is an initiative sponsored by the Mexican American Legal Defense and Educational Fund (MALDEF) and Sodexo that seeks to educate Chicago Public School students and parents about healthy eating and wellness. According to Sodexo's CDO Rohini Anand, "We have a chef and a dietician working with us on four sessions a year. In the process, we are exposing the kids and parents to who Sodexo is and careers at Sodexo." While not a direct recruitment initiative, this program certainly raises awareness of Sodexo among kids and parents, and may indirectly influence these students to apply at Sodexo when they enter the workforce.

Twenty-first century core skills

What kind of employees, with which competencies, do our companies need? And how can we influence the educational institutions so they are adequately preparing today's youth for the types of jobs and work environments that will be awaiting them?

We need a generation of employees who possess the technical skills required in our respective industries. They must also have developed **crosscultural agility,** along with **adaptability, learning agility,** and **creative problem solving.** The marketplace is changing so rapidly that technical skills become obsolete every five years. Good companies and smart employees find ways to ensure that talent remains current with emerging technical skills.

But what's harder to learn on the job is the mindset, emotional intelligence, and personal mastery skills required to flex, bob, and weave with the constantly evolving marketplace. Our companies will continue to restructure, reengineer, de-layer, and off- and on-shore work. The talent supply chain now extends across the globe, and we're inventing new ways to deploy resources and work around the world.

If the emerging workforce is not equipped with flexibility and adaptation skills, they will not be successful. Technological breakthroughs are creating new products at warp speed, while local politics and economics affect everything from the price of oil, the Dow Jones index, and immunization plans. The competency of problem solving is more critical than ever. We'll continue to face unprecedented challenges for which there are no guidebooks, no benchmarks, and no best practices. The most valuable talent will be those who can develop solutions to never-before-seen problems.

Sure, we need to see a higher percentage of tomorrow's diverse workforce graduate. But we also need them to graduate with the required competencies. Admittedly, this raises the bar for the types of skills we need, which only heightens the urgency for various stakeholders—including government, educational institutions, and business leaders—to address the issue of widening the entrance into the pipeline.

2. We must unclog the pipeline by rethinking how we assess and advance those who are different.

To have the leadership we need to sustain our growth, we must accelerate the advancement of talent of color by unclogging the barriers that slow down their advancement. Already, some new best practices have yielded good results in encouraging the advancement of multicultural talent:

- Many companies make it a requirement that all succession plan boxes include people of color and female talent. While this is a start, we need to go beyond this practice and find new ways to address the unintended barriers.

- Often, we find talent one or two jobs away from a coveted open role, with too little experience to take a risk. By implementing a rotational assignment program, top talent of color can gain exposure and experience under the watchful eye of an experienced leader who can work to accelerate their advancement.

Leadership studies by various HR consultancies have declared that companies who excel at leadership clearly differentiate their high-potential talent. However, we may be overlooking some high-performing talent within the multicultural talent pipeline due to the lack of crosscultural competence in our leadership assessments.[19]

In an increasingly multicultural and global economy, we need diverse styles of leadership. If we continue only to recognize potential new leadership through behaviors that are familiar to us, we'll never accelerate the advancement of people of color. Instead, that talent will remain stuck and frustrated. Thus, we must begin valuing experiences that we traditionally have not valued.

When leadership teams are not diverse, they may not realize that their assessment of what makes a good leader can be culturally biased. Strong leadership can look very different in US subcultures and in national cultures. We're familiar with the European-American leadership model of assertiveness—speaking one's mind and challenging others openly. But there are other strong leadership models (such as in some Asian cultures) that emphasize building consensus while minimizing confrontation.

Development of different types of skills is what's required to answer the question: Do we have leaders who can lead diverse, multicultural, and global teams? Without crosscultural competence, our leaders will not be successful at leading these increasingly diverse teams. "And if they get good at this," adds Aon Hewitt Principal Mollie Kohn, "leaders with this type of competence will also be more effective across the board, because they will be able to manage other types of individual differences—such as in personality, style, and thinking patterns—that may not be attributable to a particular cultural group."

It's also beneficial to require global experience as a prerequisite for senior positions. Doing so requires the investment to create rotational assignments for high-potential talent. The employee excited by these opportunities probably already possesses a natural openness to experiencing and mastering a more diverse work environment.

3. We must seal the leaks by recognizing our high-performing talent of color.

In Chapter 13, "The four pillars of what makes people of color stay and thrive," I made the case about the importance of recognition. Recognition is one of the four pillars for the engagement and retention of people of color, and it is an essential tool for repairing the broken pipeline. I encourage you to revisit that chapter as you develop your own case for strengthening your organization's pipeline.

The key point to internalize is that, for racial and ethnic groups that traditionally have been marginalized, the deep significance of public recognition should not be underestimated. A powerful affirming message can run counter to generations of destructive messages. Given the communal nature of various minority groups, recognizing an individual within that group also speaks to that individual's broader community, which can generate additional goodwill and positive public branding for the organization.

Companies that understand the power of public recognition and that actively advance technically skilled talent of color will be able to prevent their top diverse talent from leaving. These companies will also become more attractive to new talent of color outside the organization and provide a compelling reason for them wanting to join the company...and to stay.

By identifying and recognizing minority talent that exhibit adaptability, agility, and problem-solving competencies, we can get to know those who may often be overlooked in our organizations.

Green shoots of hope

If we don't take steps now to repair the shaky pipeline of multicultural talent, it will mean waiting 40-plus years to see true parity in leadership representation. The three key strategies I've just outlined can help create a pipeline with a stronger influx of qualified talent at the front end, remove hindrances to career progress, and seal the leaks of our most promising talent along the way. Only by taking both immediate and systemic actions will we accelerate the advancement of top talent of color.

So what does this all mean within the context of the Obama Era? Does a president who reflects the diversity of our culture automatically mean that we will see an increase in diversity and inclusion initiatives throughout corporate America? Not necessarily.

According to an article published in the February 2009 issue of *Workforce Management*, within days of his first Inauguration, critics of affirmative action were telling HR managers that the fact the United States has a Black president meant there was no longer a need for diversity practices because the country had fully embraced diversity.[20] According to this same article, however, companies with long-standing affirmative action programs could expect the Equal Employment Opportunity Commission (EEOC) and the Office of Federal Contract Compliance Programs (OFCCP) to be granted more resources under Obama. And this indeed has been the case, as there was an upturn in the enforcement of these types of programs, with greater emphasis placed on how companies compensate minorities as opposed to non-minorities.

Marc Bendick, a partner at Bendick and Egan Economic Consultants, says, "HR staffs within companies that have affirmative action will now have more ammunition with which to go to the CEO and make their case, because enforcement is going to be more stringent."

Another green shoot during the Obama Era has been the expected emphasis on education—in both policy and funding—with particular emphasis on significantly increasing graduation rates and equipping students with the right skills to thrive in a global economy.

Whether the issue is early childhood education or higher education and worker retraining, President Obama has lead one of the most aggressive education reform efforts in our nation's recent history. During his administration, he said, "If we want America to lead in the twenty-first century, nothing is more important than giving everyone the best education possible—from the day they start preschool to the day they start their career."

For the youngest students, the administration targeted $600 million for the Race to the Top – Early Learning Challenge, which incents states to transform their childcare and pre-K school systems (public and private); expand Head Start; and boost the quality of childcare while increasing the number of children served. Once students reach elementary and high school, the groundbreaking Race to the Top (RTT) initiative, with its $4.2 billion federal backing, comes into play. RTT represents a bold initiative to improve standards, teaching, and prepare students for education beyond high school. And to recognize and encourage teachers in STEM subjects, the STEM Master Teacher Corps will recognize 10,000 of the nation's best STEM classroom teachers.[21]

While those and other important pre-K through 12th grade initiatives address the long-term education challenges faced by school-aged students, it's been the administration's efforts on behalf of higher education and worker retraining that has promised more immediate progress. Just a few examples of Obama-Era initiatives:

- Raising the maximum Pell Grant award to $5,500 and helping 9.5 million students in the 2012–13 school year.

- Providing families with up to $10,000 for college tuition assistance through the American Opportunity Tax Credit.

- Fostering partnerships between industry, business, and community colleges through the Skills for America's Future, which plans to provide 500,000 Americans with the skills needed for the new workplace.[22]

Along with his commitment to education, President Obama set the goal for the United States to have the highest proportion of college graduates by 2020, which includes an additional 5 million community college graduates.

It's only fitting that such resources be targeted to higher education and worker retraining. In a speech before the Hispanic Chamber of Commerce, President Obama said, *"We know that economic progress and educational achievement have always gone hand-in-hand in America.... The source of America's prosperity has never been merely how ably we accumulate wealth, but how well we educate our people. This has never been truer than it is today.... Education is no longer just a pathway to opportunity and success, it's a prerequisite for success."*

This focus on education targets all Americans, but as the data shows, some of the greatest dividends from these initiatives will go to women and students of color, who lag far behind on too many national and international academic and economic indicators. And it's those same women and racial/ethnic minorities who are desperately needed in the talent pipeline by today's companies.

There is yet another sign of hope. *New York Times* columnist Thomas Friedman wrote about a call he received in April of 2009 from Wendy Kopp, founder of Teach for America. Kopp "shared the following statistics about college graduates signing up to join her organization to teach in some of our neediest schools in the coming school year: 'Our total applications are up 40 percent. Eleven percent of all Ivy League seniors applied, 16 percent of Yale's senior class, 15 percent of Princeton's, 25 percent of Spelman's, and 35 percent of the African-American seniors at Harvard. In 130 colleges, between 5 and 15 percent of the senior class applied.' In part, said Kopp, this could be attributed to a lack of jobs elsewhere. But part of it is 'students responding to the call that this is a problem our generation can solve.'"[23]

Which begs the question: What would be possible if today's CEOs and their prospective companies also rose to meet this challenge?

President Obama has said the United States needs to look beyond race when evaluating its policies on diversity. Either way, greater diversity in leadership ranks means greater economic strength throughout the pipeline. A strong and healthy multicultural pipeline, armed with education and skills, means prosperity for all. ⌕

SUMMARY POINTS

- The talent pipeline is cracked, leaking, and broken. In some places, it's connected to talent pools that are drying up. In other places, it's not connected to the talent pools whose tides are rising. Compounding the problem, too few people of color are finishing high school and going on to college.

- We just can't will people of color into positions of leadership. We have to discover new ways of finding and nurturing that talent.

- We must identify top-performing, multicultural talent that makes its contributions in ways we don't recognize as valuable because of the limitations of our own experiences.

- We need a generation of employees who have developed the competencies of adaptability, learning agility, and creative problem solving.

- Corporations need to partner with schools and not-for-profits to help build tomorrow's diverse workforce.

- More than ever, companies and the national economy need students skilled in STEM subjects.

- STEM jobs represent the next phase of middle-class jobs.

SHAPING YOUR STRATEGY

- How healthy is your organization's talent pool? How do you recruit new employees? What percentage of those employees are people of color or from minority backgrounds?

- How well does your organization identify top-performing, multicultural talent? Can you identify situations where you may have missed out on recruiting some of these top-performers due to the limitations of preferences within your own worldview?

- How can you influence your company and others within your industry to partner together to contribute to the strengthening of the talent pipeline in primary schools and high schools?

CONCLUSION:
BE THE CHANGE YOU WISH TO SEE IN THE WORLD

Conclusion: Be the change you wish to see in the world

From the top of Inspiration Mountain, vision and purpose seem very clear. But change in *any* era is a pretty tall order. And change across all sectors in the Obama Era and beyond has required no less courage, smarts, perseverance, and passion than have other transformational times. To land right-side-up in an upside-down world demands much more than quoting our favorite orators. The acid test is whether we have the fortitude and skills to change our *own* preconceptions, habits, and preferences so we can, in turn, influence other individuals and entire organizations to make the transformational changes required to survive and thrive in the new world order.

Up to this point, the Inclusion Paradox has focused on the transformative and positive power of constructively calling out our differences to build greater inclusion. But I would be remiss if I didn't acknowledge that which psychologist Carl Jung explored in depth—that every psychological archetype has a potential "shadow side." It is almost like a flip side—or the potential negative element—of an archetype.

Some Jungian psychologists allege that the shadow sides of the competitive male and the collaborative female archetypes are aggression and passivity, respectively. This same potential for a shadow side exists for *any* philosophy, ideology, theology, or business model. One could argue that the shadow side of Christianity's quest for truth was the Inquisition. The shadow side of liberty could be licentiousness. And the shadow side of national security, restricted civil rights.

Being aware of the potential pitfalls of one's own beliefs, or worldview, is essential for creating sustainable change without dampening one's passion. When we encounter people who don't share our worldview, we should remember those people may harbor a fear of the shadow side of our particular worldview deep down inside. Consider, for example, the interpretation of time: Those who are clock oriented may secretly fear that an event-oriented approach would lead to chaos and inefficiency. Similarly, event-oriented people may secretly believe a clock-oriented approach is insensitive and dehumanizing.

We must ask, then: What could be the shadow side of the Inclusion Paradox? It could be that we end up focusing too much on how we differ, in the process forgetting to nurture what we have in common. In other words, greater fragmentation, isolation, and insulation. In effect, *exclusion.*

How can we avoid falling into this shadow side? By keeping our focus on *bridging* the differences between ourselves and others, rather than *defending* them. The first approach leads to connection, the latter to polarization.

As we call out differences constructively, we must embrace the legacy paradigm of tolerance and sensitivity. No, this is not coming "full circle." Rather, it's embracing a paradoxical "both/and" approach. Calling out differences requires seeking out our similarities differently. Rather than merely "understanding" each other, we must discover and embrace our similarities so that we can find a common ground on which to constructively call out our differences. Thus, the melting pot becomes a *paella* instead—where the wild variety of ingredients both retain their unique character in terms of flavor, texture, and shape, and yet at the same time, the *combination* of flavors yields something superlatively tasty, attractive, differentiated, and memorable.

What I've sought to offer in *The Inclusion Paradox* is a way to evolve beyond merely focusing on our similarities at the expense of getting to know each other more truthfully. It involves our ability to interact with each other and with groups and organizations in ways that take into account the fact that our differences help us better achieve our goals, wants, and desires. As we've seen, constructively calling out differences affects everything—from interpersonal relationships to healthcare policy to retirement benefits to talent assessment to product design to operational strategies to marketing and much more.

True, the shadow side of the Inclusion Paradox, if not accounted for, could result in greater division and, therefore, destruction. But the promise of the Inclusion Paradox is one of creation—of innovating new responses to address brand-new challenges by making our differences work together. The seeds of creation lie in finding our commonality in the midst of difference.

The central premise for the Inclusion Paradox is not simply, "I do my thing and you do yours." This leads to fragmentation and isolation. Rather, it's about, "I'm different, you're different—how can we connect?"

Coming back to the eight cultural implications of the Obama Era

We started this conversation looking at the cultural implications of the Obama Era. I intended these to be headlights for the rest of the book, illuminating how to apply the Inclusion Paradox to a variety of different dimensions. As we bring this book to a close, let's now see these implications through the rearview mirror.

Inclusion is a transformative force. Inclusion represents a positive value and goal—one everyone must continually work toward. Instead of a perfect storm that threatens to derail us, the Obama Era and the convergence of global trends have offered a chance to create new opportunities for inclusion—for making the mix work—in individual and corporate environments. Plenty of bytes have been expended highlighting the negatives of corporate influence on issues such as work environments, habits, and labor practices.

But here I want to focus on the positive impact corporations are having at a more profound level in helping address one of the most destructive and intractable human issues: the polarizing effect of differences. Despite having a long way to go in achieving true diversity and inclusion, many large corporations have confronted the challenge of inclusion head-on and invested heavily in financial, leadership, and personnel resources to bridge the gap. Those who have made the investments have not only improved the lives of their talent, but improved their own bottom line. Compare the scene at the National Black MBA Association's national conference—with its 10,000 black MBAs courted by the largest multinationals in the world—with what labor conditions were for blacks just a generation ago, and you'll know we are not in Kansas anymore.

Our actions have global impact. While corporations still have a long way to go in fully advancing those different from the mainstream, ironically, multinationals have managed to be an accelerating force for their advancement. Corporations, particularly those rooted in American and European contexts, come from a worldview of meritocracy, where the best performers reap the greatest rewards. Granted, the dearth of minorities and women in top leadership positions proves the meritocracy value has not been lived out fully. Yet, around the world, multinationals have played a significant role in economically lifting diverse groups. Consider women, for example. Fully aware of the dominant corporate male paradigm of both recent and ongoing history, multinationals have been a change agent for advancing women globally, first in the economic powers that arose out of World War II, and now in the emerging markets of Brazil, India, and China.

Diversity and inclusion require intentionality. Workplace power struggles will not be resolved solely by White males or even by the organizational power structure. As I said at the beginning of this book, we must address both power and crosscultural issues. Granted, my focus has mostly been on crosscultural issues. But as we wrap up our journey together, let us reconsider the issue of power and how it is inherent in the various ceilings hindering advancement. Women and minorities need to face their own power issues. Rather than waiting for the dominant group to change, this requires looking within ourselves for how we can act and behave more powerfully *right now*. The decisive role that traditionally marginalized groups have had in the presidential elections of the twenty-first century is evidence of this starting to happen in the public square. Women are starting to really break through in the corporate realm (though people of color are still treading water way too far downstream).

As these traditionally marginalized groups press forward to their rightful place to the fullness of their abilities, these emerging workplace groups must also be ready to acknowledge and address the difference between selling out versus supporting authentic adaptation for their members. Constructively facing these issues helps build the necessary environment for the work of crosscultural competence, which aims at not just cracking, but shattering, the ceiling.

We'll experience a renaissance of values-driven decision making. Organizations need to help workers take care of themselves in ways that benefit both employee and employer. At Korn Ferry, for example, there is a quest to live out one of the four principles of great leadership—service.

The Leveraging Military Leadership Program (LMLP), initiated in 2013, uses executive coaches and talent management experts from Korn Ferry and defense and aerospace company Exelis who volunteer their time to help transitioning Veterans translate their leadership skills to the civilian sector. Veterans of any rank from all branches of the military who have left service within the last two years, or who will be transitioning in the next six months, are eligible to participate in the free, four-month program.

"This program is all about helping Veterans apply their leadership in new environments," says Exelis Chief Inclusion and Diversity Officer Erica Jeffries. "We have had the privilege of coaching some amazingly talented people who have already made considerable sacrifices for their country." A Marine who recently retired called the program "the most effective transition/professional development seminar I have ever attended."

"We owe our Veterans a debt of gratitude for their service," says former Korn Ferry Leadership Development Practice Leader, Noah Rabinowitz. "This program was designed to help Veterans strengthen their personal, interpersonal, and executive communication skills and develop a focused career strategy for the private sector. The outcomes are not only positive for the participants but also for their employers and the economy as a whole."

We must have a heightened focus on results. Well-developed diversity and inclusion efforts can lead to profitability. Accommodating differences and honoring archetypal preferences is not only good diversity practice, it's also in a company's best interests. For example, inclusive healthcare that accommodates individual differences is good for the community and is good cost management. Seeking out diverse talent expands the talent pool and makes an organization stronger. Knowing how to manage differences leads to less workplace friction, which leads to greater efficiency. Knowing how to help members of all groups to save more for retirement is good for individuals, and financially prepared retirees are good for society. Looking forward, we have to find more ways like this to address the many challenges that confront us while still ensuring economic viability.

The bottom-up is as important as the top-down. Barack Obama rose to the presidency in part because he surrounded himself with a highly efficient, top-down team that was motivated and well organized. This team was critical to his success, but it represents only half of the story. Equally critical was a powerful grassroots set of individuals who were hungry for change and just waiting to be tapped. It was a process that gave voice to the voiceless. It was true in 2008 and even more so in 2012 where these grassroots had available to them the most effective and efficient, as well as easy-to-plug-into-and-contribute, electoral ground game ever.

Corporations need to use the same combination of top-down/bottom-up to be effective, particularly in sustaining inclusion efforts. So many answers to the dilemmas organizations face today are buried in the wisdom of the crowds at the grassroots level. Conversely, as grassroots entities themselves, affinity groups need to connect with each other as well as with the larger organization. By connecting with each other, they increase the size and scope of their grassroots activities. The survival and thriving of affinity groups depends on each group finding common ground with other affinity groups, no matter how different they are from one another.

"Both/and" trumps "either/or." The Inclusion Paradox leads to our human need for community and connection. It resembles the paradox of marriage or community. We need to be individuals, yet we need to be connected. We form groups for a variety of reasons. Our groups need to be unified and connected to other groups. If we do not form these vital connections, we can end up with Balkanization—where two or more communities or societies fail to recognize their common concern and subsequently try to destroy each other. The Inclusion Paradox invites us to honor our differences while rediscovering our commonality. It calls us to refute "either/or," "win/lose" solutions, and instead uncover "and/and," "win/win" ones—to find a third, new way for relationships, groups, organizations, and perhaps even nations. Take multinational corporate culture, for example. It tends to reflect the culture of the country of origin. Yet today, corporate cultures forged from inclusion will not be American or Indian or German or Brazilian, but something richer, deeper, and more inclusive than the current model. May our politicians take heed as well!

True diversity and inclusion require calling out our differences, not minimizing them. 'Nuff said!

We've been to the mountaintop

The complexity, high stakes, and myriad possibilities of diversity and inclusion remind me of a passage in one of the Judeo-Christian scriptures that says, "We are perplexed, but not in despair."[1] The work of diversity and inclusion is about finding profitable answers to today's difficult issues. *"Se hace el camino al andar,"* goes the Spanish saying. "We make our path as we walk it."

A reporter once asked me, "If diversity were a climb of a mountain, how close to the top would you say you are?" The images of the Inca trail on the majestic Andes mountain range in Peru immediately came to mind. I could look back and see several passes in the distance, including a 10,000-foot-high one we had climbed after many days of hiking. Our progress through the sleet, scorching sun, and thin air was exhilarating. But then I looked ahead and saw several more passes shimmering in the distance, including one at 15,000 feet. We celebrated our progress so far with trail mix and coca tea. Then we slipped our backpacks on and continued the journey forward. Step by step.

That's where we are on Diversity Mountain. After many years working to diversify and engage a wide variety of people in the workplace, we can indeed enjoy new views from higher up. While we've advanced in the journey, there is so much more to be done to ensure we have a true representative mix, and that the mix is working.

It won't be without struggle. It never has been. But strategy by strategy, leader by leader, conversation by conversation, succession plan by succession plan, hire by hire, we're eroding and dismantling exclusionary processes, structures, and systems. As the Japanese saying goes, "Fall down seven times. Get up eight." The challenges are formidable, our quest audacious, the problems complex. We need to look at each other and say, "I need your differences... and you need mine." It's the only way we can achieve our unity of purpose to make the world a better place to work—for *everyone.*

People often ask me, "So when is this Diversity thing over? When do we 'get there?'" Interculturalist Dianne Hofner Saphiere offers this answer: "Intercultural effectiveness is an ongoing process. It's not like you ever get there and you're done. It's always going to be something else. You never stop discovering, like in any partnership or marriage, that you never totally get the other person or for that matter, yourself." In other words, by touching the core issues of who we are—gender, race, ethnicity, sexual orientation, nationality, physical ability, thinking styles, you name it—the answer of when we get there, of course, is "never." Given that this is a lifelong journey, we must note that the Inclusion Paradox applies to many other topics and issues that we haven't covered in this book such as faith, aging, size/weight, personality, thinking styles, and on.

We can take this further by applying this discussion to product and home design, school curriculum, and classroom management, among other things. "We have to be able to argue about workplace and marketplace and the plethora of other issues," says diversity pioneer Ted Childs. "We can't be one-subject leaders in the diversity movement. We've got to be able to package and debate multiple issues." The purpose of this book has indeed been to contribute to the conversation about creating the next generation of diversity work.

"The greatest danger of all is to allow new walls to divide us from one another," then candidate Obama told more than 200,000 at the Victory Column in Berlin on July 24, 2008. *"The walls between old allies on either side of the Atlantic cannot stand. The walls between the countries with the most and those with the least cannot stand. The walls between races and tribes, natives and immigrants, Christian and Muslim and Jew cannot stand. These now are the walls we must tear down."*

Let's tear down the walls that separate us—not only in the workplace, but in our homes, families, and communities—wherever we have the power to influence change in other people, as well as in ourselves. This has been the message of the Obama Era. It's the message of the Inclusion Paradox.

Share this message, implement what you can, and most importantly, as Mahatma Gandhi said, "You must be the change you wish to see in the world." ᕿ

An invitation

This is an ongoing conversation. As you read this book, you probably found yourself thinking, "Well, what about this?" or "No way!" or "I've got a story, too." No book on this topic could ever be complete in terms of answers and issues. This is why we've created a blog, www.inclusionparadox.com. I update it continuously with links, observations, and other discussions based on the topics covered here, and more. I invite you to check it out and post your own questions, comments, stories, and challenges. Add your two cents, two pesos, two yuan, two rupees, two euros. We'll take any idea currency!

And there's always:

 Twitter: @AndresTTapia

 LinkedIn: LinkedIn.com/in/andrestapia1

 Web: kornferry.com/diversity

 Blog: inclusionparadox.com

Appendix A

Assessing and developing The Inclusive Leader

Can a leader's inclusive abilities be assessed and developed within each of the four quadrants of Korn Ferry's Four Dimensions of Leadership and Talent (KF4D)? We believe so.

In the same way that we can approach assessment and development through a scientifically validated set of competencies for overall leadership, we can use the Korn Ferry Inclusive Leader performance model to anchor a set of assessments and development experiences to help leaders become more inclusive across all dimensions of the KF4D.

In order to assess and develop, it helps to structure The Inclusive Leader competencies in a staged way, following a "progressive" and developmental logic through the various competencies. Our developmental view of inclusiveness is detailed here:

The Inclusive Leader Competencies (developmental view)

Open and aware
- Self-aware
- Develops self
- Nimble learner
- Global mindset
- Resilient

Actively promotes difference
- Values differences
- Attracts diverse top talent
- Develops all talent
- Communicates the value of D&I effectively
- Drives engagement

Optimizes organizational performance
- Drives vision and purpose
- Builds effective diverse teams
- Builds trusting networks
- Cultivates innovation
- Drives results

Builds a trusting and open culture
- Manages ambiguity
- Manages conflict
- Interpersonally savvy
- Courageous
- Instills trust

Influences effectively
- Organizationally savvy
- Situationally adaptable
- Persuasive
- Collaborates
- Balances stakeholders

Measuring and developing inclusive competencies

Here we use an approach closely modeled on our KF4D approach, relying on the Korn Ferry Leadership Architect™ at its foundation. The Inclusive Leader competency set is an extraction from the full assessment that we administer to leaders as part of our larger leader assessment approach.

By applying our Inclusive Leader competency frameworks, we can help leaders understand where their specific development needs may reside. Developmentally, any one of the competencies within The Inclusive Leader subset can be developed through a variety of learning experiences that include coaching, training, self-paced development through the use of the *FYI® for your improvement: Competencies development guide*, case studies, action learning, simulations, and immersions.

One of the specific skill groupings within The Inclusive Leader competencies is crosscultural agility, which involves being self-aware, having a global mindset, having the ability to develop self, being able to manage ambiguity and conflict, being interpersonally savvy and courageous, and instilling trust.

Some of the most effective inclusive leadership development can also take place in real team settings. We believe in creating the conditions for leaders to develop inclusion competencies through "diverse by design teams"—deliberately bringing people of diverse backgrounds, experiences, and identities together to work on solving business problems of strategic importance. By setting the table with diverse stakeholders, leaders must learn quickly and in a real environment how to leverage diversity with inclusive skills.

Measuring and developing inclusive experiences

From an assessment perspective, a well-structured interview is key to extracting the kinds of *experiences* a leader has had that have helped them develop an inclusive mindset and inclusive skill, or whether they have actually been lacking in these experiences.

From a developmental point of view, action learning and immersive experiences are among the best ways to provide leaders with actual new experiences that move them out of what is so well known and into the unknown. We believe that the most powerful learning takes place when leaders' highly successful (and often exceptionally strong) paradigms are challenged and even obliterated. This is the intent behind our highly immersive "in-market" experiences for leaders that help develop specific skills and behaviors identified by competency assessment, while also providing opportunities to practice a new, broader, and more flexible range of leadership behaviors with a larger scope and reach.

For example, an executive leadership team from a major global pharmaceutical headquartered in a developed market had identified growth in the emerging markets as one of their top priorities. As they examined their strategy for Africa, they realized their dominant mental models and vast years of experience trapped them from being able to think differently about how growth in these markets would take place. The immersion experience took them to Namibia where they saw, felt, and touched firsthand the realities of public and private healthcare in an African nation. The program guided them through interactions and collaboration with healthcare providers, patients, customers, and partners. For those who were physicians, they even provided free healthcare in the rural areas, as well as in the shantytowns circling Namibia's major cities.

The one-week immersion was punctuated with moments of reflection as well as decision making on the ground away from all that was familiar to them. Every leader testified to how the immersion was not only expectation and paradigm altering, but that it also led to them making decisions different from what they otherwise would have made.

Implicit in this highly experiential approach to development is the concept that Inclusive Leaders will thrive in this environment. By putting them into the crucible of real strategic issues, in real and ambiguous high-pressure environments, the competencies referred to in the previous section become critical differentiators of success. Self-awareness, adaptable communication, the ability to motivate diverse teams, to name a few—all of these competencies can be developed through highly experiential approaches to leadership learning.

Measuring and developing inclusive traits

As described in Chapter 12, "Must have: The Inclusive Leader," inclusive traits have to do with leaders' stance toward difference. Currently, we use the Intercultural Development Inventory (IDI) created by Dr. Milton Bennett and Dr. Mitch Hammer. Through self-provided answers to a 20-minute online questionnaire, the instrument will place those assessed along a continuum of sensitivity toward difference. This model is explained in detail in Appendix B.

The key to applying this assessment is to understand how it captures in Denial, Polarization, Minimization, and Acceptance the person's predisposition to be unaware, indifferent, resistant, open to others without curiosity, or curious about how the differences can make a difference. It is only really when in Adaptation that the actual competence to navigate the differences can start to get identified.

Knowing where a leader falls along this continuum is key to understanding how open he or she is to the learning experiences that await him or her to fully develop into an Inclusive Leader.

Measuring and developing inclusive drivers

Approaches also exist to identify a leader's cultural drivers. While upbringing and life experiences—and the choices we make along the way on how to respond to them—are not determinant of our preferences for how we interact with others, get things done, or make choices, they are hugely influential. At the end of the day, regardless of the culture (or cultures) in which we were raised, and the significant choices we may already be making to adapt to the new and different other cultures, we all still have a set of core cultural preferences.

To be an Inclusive Leader, it is vital for each of us to be aware of our preferences. Without this awareness, it is difficult to realize how our behaviors may be inadvertently including some and excluding others. An Inclusive Leader not only has this level of self-awareness, but also is aware of how his or her behavior interacts with people around him or her. An aware and grounded Inclusive Leader can use the new and strengthened muscles of crosscultural agility and other competencies to—in a mutually reciprocal way—adapt to others and help them adapt to him or her.

Various tools offer this view. One of our preferred tools is GlobeSmart®. Based on a short self-assessment, the GlobeSmart® profile provides an easy-to-understand mapping of cultural preferences along five scales that represent a selected subset of the eight cultural driver scales identified in Chapter 12.

Once we have the leader's profile, we can compare their scores to the normative behaviors of national cultures that they may be interacting with as well as the profiles of other team members.

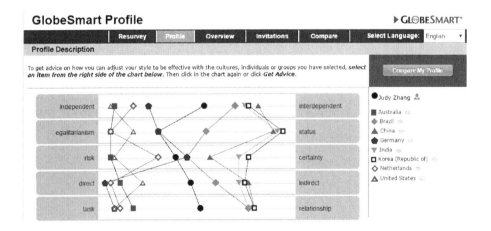

Pulling it all together

As is evident, being an Inclusive Leader is not about an attitude of openness, but rather about a full array of skills, experiences, traits, and drivers that when put together provide a holistic view of a leader's true ability to lead inclusively. All of these elements can be assessed and, in that, a personalized developmental plan can be created for each leader. In addition, the results can be rolled up to obtain collective profiles of a leadership team and, from that, develop a developmental pathway for the entire group.

Appendix B

Figuring out how crossculturally competent you are

Answering the question "Am I crossculturally competent?" requires more than a yes/no answer. Dr. Milton Bennett lays out a more complete answer in his Developmental Model of Intercultural Sensitivity (DMIS), a framework to explain the way in which people commonly develop crosscultural competence (which Dr. Bennett prefers to call "intercultural" competence).

Because I have found it simple to grasp, relevant around the world, and practical in its application, the DMIS is one of the underlying frameworks on which I have constructed the concept of the Inclusion Paradox.

As Dr. Bennett explains it, the DMIS can be used to explain the reactions of people to cultural differences.[1] The underlying assumption of the model is that as one's experience of cultural differences becomes more complex, one's potential competence in intercultural interactions increases. Dr. Bennett has identified a set of fundamental cognitive structures he refers to as "worldviews" that act as orientations to cultural difference. The worldviews vary from more ethnocentric to more ethnorelative. In the DMIS model, there are three stages of development within each worldview.

Ethnocentrism means that we tend to view others from our own perspective, through our own lens. Our own experiences shape what we see and how we feel about and understand how others and we behave. It is our conditioned response to our upbringing by parents or others, the society we grew up in, the messages we hear in the media, the things we learn in school. Given how formative this perspective is, ethnocentrism is a natural human response to the world around us.

The three stages within ethnocentrism are Denial, Polarization, and Minimization. Those in *Denial* ignore cultural differences and focus instead on the familiar. Those in *Polarization* see differences in stereotyped ways and find them threatening and believe theirs is the "true" culture. And those in *Minimization* reduce the importance of differences by emphasizing common humanity and values.

The Developmental Model of Intercultural Sensitivity (DMIS)

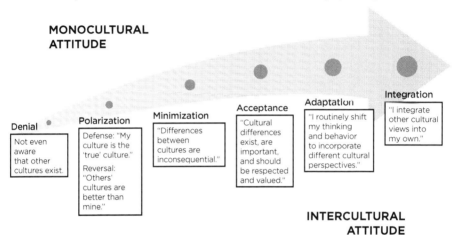

MONOCULTURAL ATTITUDE

Denial

Not even aware that other cultures exist.

Polarization

Defense: "My culture is the 'true' culture."

Reversal: "Others' cultures are better than mine."

Minimization

"Differences between cultures are inconsequential."

Acceptance

"Cultural differences exist, are important, and should be respected and valued."

Adaptation

"I routinely shift my thinking and behavior to incorporate different cultural perspectives."

Integration

"I integrate other cultural views into my own."

INTERCULTURAL ATTITUDE

Ethnorelativism means that a person has developed the ability to imagine events or empathize with experiences from another perspective. As children, we saw the world as revolving around us. As we mature into adulthood, we develop the ability to step back and put ourselves into others' shoes. This ability is reflective of an ethnorelative worldview. There are three stages within ethnorelativism: Acceptance, Adaptation, and Integration. Those in *Acceptance* acknowledge and believe that cultural differences exist in addition to similarities and they are significant. Those in *Adaptation* are able to navigate effectively between the differences, and those in *Integration* have in effect internalized the worldviews of others into their own.

According to the DMIS theory, more ethnorelative worldviews have more potential to generate the attitudes, knowledge, and behavior that constitute intercultural competence. In this DMIS model, ethnorelative competencies can take a lifetime of experience and purposeful reflection to fully develop.

Intercultural Development Inventory (IDI)

The Intercultural Development Inventory (IDI) is a way of measuring where individuals and groups are in their cultural competence as conceptualized by the DMIS. The IDI, developed by Dr. Milton Bennett and Dr. Mitch Hammer, measures an individual's or group's fundamental worldview orientation to cultural difference, and thus, the individual's or group's capacity for intercultural competence.

The IDI is a 50-item, theory-based instrument that can be taken either in paper-and-pencil form or online. The instrument is easy to complete and generates an in-depth graphic profile of an individual's worldview orientation. The IDI is currently in 17 languages (Arabic, Bahasa Indonesian, Chinese, Czech, English, Finnish, French, German, Italian, Japanese, Korean, Norwegian, Portuguese, Russian, Serbian, Spanish, and Turkish). Each language version of the IDI has been rigorously "back translated," ensuring both linguistic and conceptual equivalence in the meaning of each of the items.[2]

Administering and debriefing the instrument and coaching individuals on the best way to develop require people certified in the IDI. At Korn Ferry, we have many IDI certified consultants around the world who conduct coaching debriefs with leaders. Certification is available from IDI, LLC, led by Dr. Hammer (www.idiinventory.com).

The DMIS and the next generation of diversity learning

In Chapter 5, "I need your differences … and you need mine," I made the case for moving from the paradigm of tolerance and sensitivity to one of crosscultural competence. Using DMIS language, tolerance and sensitivity helped individuals, organizations, and societies move from the intercultural competency stage of Polarization (quite prevalent during the time of Civil Rights and early Affirmative Action) and into Minimization. It was a successful strategy in that it helped create more tolerant environments. However, by reinforcing Minimization, diversity work has been struggling to break out of a legacy approach of addressing differences and shaping a new way that effectively addresses the explosion in diversity among workers.

Moving to the paradigm of crosscultural competence, using DMIS language, is to move from Minimization to Acceptance and Adaptation. I have made the claim throughout *The Inclusion Paradox* that this worldview can be more conducive toward achieving true inclusion. I don't make the case, however, that it is necessary to develop into the Integration phase. Whether one internalizes others' worldviews into one's own is not necessary to create inclusion, but being able to accept and adapt to those differences behaviorally and in action and mindset is.

Appendix C

A groundbreaking study that shows race trumps income when it comes to who saves more

An excerpt from "401(k) Plans in Living Color: The Ariel/Hewitt Study" published in June 2009.[1] The study also had input from the Chicago Urban League, the Joint Center for Political and Economic Studies, the National Council of La Raza, the National Urban League, and The Raben Group.

In describing the savings gaps between African Americans and Hispanics on the one hand and Asians and Whites on the other, the report summarized its findings this way:

[The gaps] are alarming and require swift and corrective action. Employers, government, and individuals all have a role to play if there is to be real change.

- **Savings and participation rates:** While age and salary play a clear role in driving retirement savings, the meaningful role race and ethnicity also play has been obscured until now. Regardless of age and income, African-American and Hispanic workers are less likely to participate in their company 401(k) plans, and when they do contribute, they save at much lower rates than Whites do. Asian employees have the highest participation and savings rates of all ethnic groups studied.

- **Stock exposure:** African-American workers are less likely than other workers to invest in equities, a behavior that may limit the long-term growth potential of their accounts, since historically, equities have been the highest yielding investment over the long-term.

- **Loans and hardship withdrawals:** African Americans are more likely to take a loan and more than twice as likely to take a hardship withdrawal as the study population overall. Hispanics also borrow from their retirement accounts at a higher rate than Whites do, but not to the same degree as African Americans. By contrast, Asian employees are the least likely to take early distributions from their 401(k) plan accounts.

- **Account balances:** Lower participation, contribution rates, and equity exposure, coupled with higher withdrawal rates, lead to smaller average account balances. Consider, for instance, individuals who earn between $30,000 and $59,999. Employees with a similar range of income show a significant difference in account balances: African Americans ($21,224), Hispanics ($22,017), Asians ($32,590), and Whites ($35,551). Naturally, these results are influenced by other factors, such as age, job tenure, and pay within the range, but variations exist, even after adjusting for these factors.

Later in the study, the following scenario is painted:

When the data are controlled for factors such as salary, job tenure, and age, they show that African Americans contribute 11 percent less and Hispanics 6 percent less as a portion of pay than do Whites. Imagine four employees working side by side, doing the same job, making the same amount of money, contributing to their 401(k) plans, and expecting to retire at the same time. Chances are that the African-American and Hispanic employees are saving somewhat less per month than the White employee is, and the Asian employee is saving somewhat more. Now, let that difference in today's dollars grow through compounding, and the difference at retirement is significant. These four employees will find themselves experiencing considerably different comfort levels in their retirements.

The report then goes on to make the following recommendations:

Recognizing the problem and finding solutions

When 401(k) account balances are so quantifiably different by race and ethnicity, it is highly likely that financial comfort levels during retirement will be decidedly unequal for different groups. This phenomenon prompts a call to action to ensure that all employees have both the knowledge and opportunity to secure a financially sound retirement for themselves. This phenomenon prompts a call to action to ensure that all employees have both the knowledge and opportunity to secure a financially sound retirement for themselves.

The answer is not a simple, singular action. We need to balance the remedies with reality. Some easier solutions may be costly to implement or could put an undue burden on employers—an unrealistic outcome, especially in the current economic climate. However, failure to act could create a future in which whole categories of workers will be financially insecure, which ultimately affects society as a whole. We encourage policymakers and employers to act on the following recommendations.

Recommendation #1: Design 401(k) plans in a way that benefits a broad, diverse employee base. Employers should consider making the following changes to plan design:

- Implement automatic 401(k) plan enrollment for new employees. Additionally, do a one-time sweep to add non-participants into the 401(k) plan, unless they have previously opted out.

- Set a default contribution rate for employees automatically enrolled in a 401(k) plan so that employees get the full company match, and contribution rates are automatically increased over time to exceed the match threshold.

- Offer investment advice and various tools for investing to meet the needs of all participants. Investment advice can be effective at providing guidance for people with different needs, and possible tools for investing can range from simple suggestions to detailed recommendations to turning over a portfolio to an investment professional.

Recommendation #2: Provide necessary communication, education, and resources to help individuals make wise choices. For example, employers can:

- Promote greater awareness of the costs and consequences of taking loans from 401(k) plans, including strong and compelling education at the point of loan initiation.

- Provide retirement planning resources such as workshops (and company time to attend these), call centers, and online tools and education to enable individuals to make more effective use of their 401(k) plans.

- Create user-friendly and easily understood communication, enabling workers to learn more about how to effectively manage and grow their savings. Information should be made available in multiple forms, recognizing differences in the population. Effective communication that targets specific behaviors (loan usage, the need to save, and so on) should be used when gaps between categories of employees are identified in the data analysis.

- Incorporate different cultural perspectives in broad-based employer communications about 401(k) plans that resonate with diverse groups of employees. The information could be promoted via employer affinity groups.

Recommendation #3: Encourage employers to voluntarily collect and report their 401(k) plan data by race and ethnicity of participants. The federal government could:

- Encourage voluntary collecting and reporting of data about 401(k) plan participants that would enable employers to know where gaps exist among their employees. The types of data to be collected could include account balance, contribution rate, equity exposure, percentage with loans, and percentage taking hardship withdrawals.

- Provide guidelines for the data collection process, such as what measures to use, how to collect data, and the frequency for collecting data. Additionally, if these data were compiled across participating companies, they could be used for benchmarking purposes, and employers could compare their own results with others in their industry and beyond. The resulting information would enable employers to take steps to improve overall outcomes and close any gaps that may exist.

Recommendation #4: Modify loan requirements in 401(k) plans to decrease the likelihood of default when an employee terminates employment.

Though the availability of loans from 401(k) account balances makes investing in these plans attractive, taking loans is likely to reduce account balances. In challenging economic times such as these, employee terminations and loans against 401(k) accounts that are not repaid are both likely to increase.

Most 401(k) plans currently require that employees who terminate with an outstanding loan must repay the loan (often within 60 days[2]) or default. For a person who has just been laid off during a time when unemployment is high and new jobs are scarce, and who is worried about paying the mortgage and other day-to-day bills, it is virtually impossible to pay off a 401(k) loan on time. When a default occurs, the loan is considered a distribution from the plan and is thus taxable. If the employee is not yet retirement age, an additional penalty may apply. In this way, a distribution permanently reduces an employee's retirement savings.

Extending the amount of time a terminating employee has to pay off a loan may improve overall retirement savings. Modifying the current loan rules could help African-American and Hispanic employees in particular retain assets in their 401(k) accounts.

Rules could be changed (which may require legislation) to the following:

- Provide a longer period for repayments. Instead of requiring departing employees to pay off a loan within 60 days of termination, they could be given a longer period of time, perhaps up to six months. At the end of this period, if the loan has not been repaid, it would become a distribution. Or, more narrowly, consider suspending the loan repayment requirement for a given period of time for employees who involuntarily lose their job.

- Allow loan repayments after termination. A second way to decrease defaults on loans is to allow periodic loan repayments that follow the initial timetable even after termination. Currently, most employers do not accept loan repayments after employee termination, largely because payments can no longer be made via payroll deduction. Instead, employees could be allowed to repay a loan by regular payments from their personal accounts at financial institutions.

- Make loans portable. If a 401(k) account balance, plus the outstanding loan against it, could be easily rolled over from one corporate employer to another, employees could be encouraged to roll over their 401(k) and continue loan repayments. This option would be much better than cashing out the account altogether.

Recommendation #5: Provide financial education as a mandated component of both public and private school curricula at all levels, from kindergarten through secondary school.

- Improve financial literacy by providing financial education at younger ages. While this recommendation takes a longer-term perspective, it may ultimately be more successful than other approaches, especially when it comes to closing the sizable racial and ethnic gaps in 401(k) account balances. This is a key component for long-term success.

- Implement financial literacy curriculum in schools to provide future generations with a comprehensive understanding of both the mechanics and importance of sound money management, saving, and investment. Although some schools include financial and investment education throughout their K–12 curricula, most do not. Furthermore, state school systems that offer financial and investment curricula do not uniformly mandate that students enroll in or complete these courses.

Appendix D

Driving up minority 401(k) participation at a medical institution

To increase the 401(k) retirement savings plan participation rate on the part of African-American employees at a large medical center, Hewitt, in collaboration with Ariel Investments President Mellody Hobson, designed and implemented the following five-pronged approach:

1. Selected Black History Month as the timing for the education and enrollment campaign so it could be coupled with other messages appealing to African-American employees.

2. Emphasized face-to-face workshops that would appeal to the more oral (versus written) preference of African-American culture. This also leaned on a communal approach to a call to action. A parallel can be drawn to the communal power of the African-American church experience in influencing behavior. Call it *communal peer pressure.*

3. Set up financial education workshops co-led by African-American leaders. In this case, it was the diversity leader at the medical center and one of Hewitt's consultants with deep expertise in financial education. The idea was to help overcome Black skepticism about the value of long-term investing, which has been documented in more than 10 years of research in the Ariel/Schwab Black Investor study. The premise was that the trust gap could be narrowed by having members of their own community serve as the advocates as well as the subject-matter experts.

4. Tailored the messages in the workshop to address both the opportunities and reticence the African-American worldview may pose toward greater 401(k) participation. For example, when the audience was presented with the data that Blacks tend to put saving for college education over retirement, the question posed was, "Who are you looking to take care of you when you retire?" The answer often came back: "My children." This then led to an eye-opening conversation about how putting that burden on their children may be undermining the very economic advancement they were banking on by sending them to college. Further, it was pointed out that while there are multiple sources to pay for college (many types of scholarships, low-interest loans, etc.), there are very few additional sources for retirement other than one's ability to have saved for it over a period of time.

5. Applied techniques that have worked in general, regardless of multicultural demographics. These have to do with making it logistically easy for employees to enroll right at the workshop itself. So, participants were allowed to fill out enrollment cards at the end of the workshop.

Results

In this project, 42 percent of attendees who had been non-participants before the workshop enrolled during the workshop.

Bibliography

Ariel Investments and Charles Schwab Corporation. *The Ariel/Schwab Black Investor Survey: Saving and Investing Among Higher Income African-Americans and White Americans.* Black Investor Survey, 2008.

Benitez, Cristina. *Latinization: How Latino Culture Is Transforming the US.* Ithaca, NY: Paramount Market Publishing, 2007.

Bennett, Milton J., editor. *Basic Concepts of Intercultural Communication.* Yarmouth, ME: Intercultural Press, 1998.

Broom, Michael F., and Donald C. Klein. *Power: The Infinite Game.* Ellicott City, MD: Sea Otter Press, 1999.

Catalyst. *The Bottom Line: Connecting Corporate Performance and Gender Diversity.* Research study. January, 2004.

Cohen, Adam, and Elizabeth Taylor. *American Pharaoh: Mayor Richard J. Daley – His Battle for Chicago and the Nation.* London: Little, Brown, May, 2000.

de Tocqueville, Alexis. *Democracy in America.* [Originally published 1835.]

Forman, Seth. "Obama's America in Black & White." *National Review Online,* June 23, 2011. <http://www.nationalreview.com/article/270291/obamas-america-black-white-seth-forman>

Gladwell, Malcolm. *Blink: The Power of Thinking without Thinking.* New York, NY: Little, Brown and Company, 2005.

Gladwell, Malcolm. *Outliers: The Story of Success.* New York, NY: Little, Brown and Company, 2008.

Hewlett, Sylvia Ann. *Off-ramps and On-Ramps: Keeping Talented Women on the Road to Success.* Boston, MA: Harvard Business School Publishing, 2007.

Hewlett, Sylvia, Carolyn Buck Luce, Peggy Shiller, and Sandra Southwell. "The Hidden Brain Drain: Off-Ramps and On-Ramps in Women's Careers." *Harvard Business Review.* February 24, 2005.

The Huffington Post. "Obama: I Never Thought My Election Meant America Was Post-Racial." April 26, 2012. <http://www.huffingtonpost.com/2012/04/26/obama-on-race-in-america_n_1455275.html>

Johansson, Frans. *The Medici Effect.* Boston, MA: Harvard Business School Publishing, 2006.

Kochman, Thomas. *Black and White Styles in Conflict.* Chicago, IL: University of Chicago Press, 1981.

Korn Ferry. *FYI® for Your Improvement: Competencies Development Guide.* Minneapolis, MN: Korn Ferry, 2014.

Korn Ferry. *Leadership Architect™ Research Guide and Technical Manual.* Minneapolis, MN: Korn Ferry, 2015.

Korn Ferry Institute. "Diversity and Inclusion Program Doubles Representation of Women of Color Executives in 4 Years." October 22, 2014. <http://www.kornferry.com/institute/diversity-and-inclusion-program-doubles-representation-women-color-executives-4>

Korn Ferry Institute. "Futurestep Survey Finds Compensation One of the Least Important Factors for Recruiting Millennial Talent." March 5, 2015. <http://www.kornferry.com/press/futurestep-survey-finds-compensation-one-of-the-least-important-factors-for-recruiting-millennial-talent/>

Korn Ferry Institute. "The Power of Culture Transformation," March 5, 2015. <http://www.kornferry.com/institute/power-culture-transformation>

Korn Ferry Institute. "Precision Talent Intelligence." June 23, 2014. <http://www.kornferry.com/institute/precision-talent-intelligence-definitive-four-dimensions-leadership-and-talent>

Korn Ferry Institute. Real World Leadership Report Series. 2015. <http://www.kornferry.com/real-world-leadership>

Lee, Malcolm D., director. *Undercover Brother.* DVD. Universal City, CA: Universal Pictures, 2002.

Libert, Barry, Jon Spector, Don Tapscott [foreword], and thousands of contributors. *We Are Smarter Than Me: How to Unleash the Power of Crowds in Your Business.* Upper Saddle River, NJ: Wharton School Publishing, 2007.

Macintosh, Peggy. "White Privilege: Unpacking the Invisible Knapsack." Excerpted from Working Paper 189. "White Privilege and Male Privilege: A Personal Account of Coming to See Correspondences through Work in Women's Studies." Wellesley, MA: Wellesley College Center for Research on Women, 1988.

McKinsey & Company. *The Economic Impact of the Achievement Gap in America's Schools.* Social Sector Office Report. April 2009.

Obama, Barack. *The Audacity of Hope: Thoughts on Reclaiming the American Dream.* New York, NY: Crown Publishers, 2006.

Obama, Barack. *Dreams from My Father: A Story of Race and Inheritance.* New York, NY: Three Rivers Press, 2004.

Obama, Barack. "The Impact of the Obama Economic Plan for America's Working Women." Report. Obama for America. 2009. <www.barackobama.com>

Obama, Barack. "A More Perfect Union" speech. Constitution Center, Philadelphia, PA, March 18, 2008.

Obama, Barack. "Second Inaugural Address," White House, Washington: DC, January 21, 2013.

Obama, Barack. "Second Term Acceptance," speech. McCormick Place, Chicago: IL, November 7, 2013.

Porter, Kira. "Women Leaders: Strategic Yet Invisible Assets." *Link & Learn.* May, 2003.

Rubin, Henry Alex, and Dana Adam Shapiro, directors. *Murderball.* DVD. Hollywood, CA: Paramount Pictures, 2005.

Sevy, Bruce, Vicki Swisher, and Evelyn Orr. "Seven Signposts: The Unmistakable Markers That Identify High Potential Leaders." Korn Ferry Institute. 2013. <http://www.kornferry.com/institute/694-seven-signposts-the-unmistakable-markers-that-identify-high-potential-leaders>

Shelton, Chuck. *Leadership 101 for White Men: How to Work Successfully with Black Colleagues and Customers.* Garden City, NJ: Morgan James Publishing, 2008.

Tammet, Daniel. *Born on a Blue Day: Inside the Extraordinary Mind of an Autistic Savant.* New York, NY: Free Press, 2006.

Tapscott, Don, and Anthony Williams. *Wikinomics: How Mass Collaboration Changes Everything. Expanded ed.* New York, NY: Portfolio, 2010.

Thaler, Richard H., and Cass R. Sunstein. *Nudge: Improving Decisions about Health, Wealth, and Happiness.* Revised and expanded ed. New York, NY: Penguin Books, 2009.

Thomas, David A., and John J. Gabarro. *Breaking Through: The Making of Minority Executives in Corporate America.* Boston, MA: Harvard Business School Publishing, 1999.

Thomas, Roosevelt. *Beyond Race and Gender: Unleashing the Power of Your Total Work Force by Managing Diversity.* N.p.: AMACOM, 1992.

Trompenaars, Fons, and Charles Hampden-Turner. *Riding the Waves of Culture: Understanding Diversity in Global Business.* 2nd ed. New York, NY: McGraw Hill, 1998.

Winters, Mary-Frances, and Andrés Tapia. "Crosscultural Learning Partners Program." Proprietary program of Winters Consulting Group and Hewitt Associates. Lincolnshire, IL: N.d.

Endnotes

Author's note

1 Greenstone, Michael, and Adam Looney, "Unemployment and Earnings Losses: The Long-Term Impacts of the Great Recession on American Workers," November 4, 2011, http://www.hamiltonproject.org/papers/unemployment_and_earnings_losses_a_look_at_long-term_impacts_of_the_gr

Introduction

1 Baxter 2007 Sustainability Report, http://www.baxter.com.cn/downloads/sustainability/report/sustainability_report_2007.pdf

PART 1: THE URGENCY OF INCLUSION

No notes.

Chapter 1: An upside-down world

1 "The World in 2050: Will the Shift in Global Economic Power Continue?" February 2015, http://www.pwc.com/gx/en/issues/the-economy/assets/world-in-2050-february-2015.pdf

2 Patrick Gillespie, "How Columbia Went from Murder Capital to Tech Powerhouse," CNN.com, http://money.cnn.com/2015/03/13/investing/colombia-tech-silicon-valley

3 Sophia Yan, "China Retakes Spot as Biggest Holder of US Debt," May 18, 2015, http://money.cnn.com/2015/05/18/news/economy/china-us-debt/

4 Javiera Quiroga, "Chile Immigration Up on Influx from Andean Neighbors," *BloombergBusiness,* July 3, 2014, http://www.bloomberg.com/news/articles/2014-07-02/chilean-immigration-jumps-24-as-foreigners-boost-labor-market

5 Tom Whitehead, "Migrants to Send Britain's Population Soaring to Largest in EU," *The Telegraph,* October 26, 2011, http://www.telegraph.co.uk/news/uknews/immigration/8851902/Migrants-to-send-Britains-population-soaring-to-largest-in-EU.html

6   Giampaolo Lanzieri, "Population and Social Conditions, Statistics in Focus," Eurostat, August 2008; and Nadja Milewski, (INED), "Immigrant Fertility in West Germany: Socialization Effects in Transition to 2nd and 3rd Births," [PowerPoint Presentation], Conference on Effects of Migration on Population Structures in Europe, Vienna Institute of Demography, December 2008; and Luke Harding, "German Birth Rate Falls to Lowest in Europe," *The Guardian* on the web, March 15, 2006.

7   "The Future of World Religions: Population Growth Projections, 2010-2050," Pew Research Center, April 2, 2015, http://www.pewforum.org/2015/04/02/religious-projections-2010-2050/

8   "Hispanic Americans by the Numbers," US Census Bureau, http://www.infoplease.com/spot/hhmcensus1.html

9   DW Staff, "Top Diversity Leaders," *Diversity Woman,* http://diversitywoman.com/top-diversity-leaders/

10 Eurostat, 2012.

11 Steven Erlanger, "After US Breakthrough, Europe Looks in Mirror," *New York Times*, November 11, 2008.

12 Abul Taher, "UK's First Official Sharia Courts," *The Sunday Times*, September 14, 2008.

13 United Nations Committee on the Elimination of Discrimination Against Women; and www.WomenCount.com

14 New Mexico last voted Democratic in 2004, but has voted Republican 4 out of 5 times since 1992; and Nevada last voted Democratic in 1996; and Colorado last voted Democratic in 1992, "New York Times 2008 Election Results," January 6, 2009, www.nytimes.com

15 Mark Hugo Lopez and Paul Taylor, "Latino Voters in the 2012 Election," Pew Research Hispanic Center, November 7, 2012, http://www.pewhispanic.org/2012/11/07/latino-voters-in-the-2012-election/

16 Ryan Lizza, "The Party Next Time," *The New Yorker*, November 19, 2012, http://www.newyorker.com/reporting/2012/11/19/121119fa_fact_lizza? currentPage=all

17 Geoffrey Colvin, "The End of a Dream," *Fortune*, June 20, 2006.

18 Tammy Flanagan, "Can You Count on Social Security?" Government Executive, July 31, 2014, http://www.govexec.com/pay-benefits/retirement-planning/2014/07/can-you-count-social-security/90260/

19 Shawn Pogatchnik, "Airline Pay Toilets? Ignore That Beverage Cart," *The Associated Press*, February 27, 2009.

20 "Total Retirement Income at Large Companies: The Real Deal," Study by Hewitt Associates, 2008.

21 Jeanne Meister, "Job Hopping Is the 'New Normal' for Millennials: Three Ways to Prevent a Human Resource Nightmare," August 14, 2012, http://www.forbes.com/sites/jeannemeister/2012/08/14/job-hopping-is-the-new-normal-for-millennials-three-ways-to-prevent-a-human-resource-nightmare/

22 Nancy Scola, "White House Launches 'US Digital Service,' with Healthcare.Gov Fixer at the Helm," *The Washington Post*, August 11, 2014, https://www.washingtonpost.com/blogs/the-switch/wp/2014/08/11/white-house-launches-u-s-digital-service-with-healthcare-gov-fixer-at-the-helm/

23 Adam Vaughan, "Obama's Clean Power Plan Hailed As US's Strongest Ever Climate Action," *The Guardian,* August 3, 2015, http://www.theguardian.com/environment/2015/aug/03/obamas-clean-power-plan-hailed-as-strongest-ever-climate-action-by-a-us-president

24 Michael Grunwald, *The New New Deal: The Hidden Story of Change in the Obama Era*, New York, NY: Simon & Schuster, 2012.

25 Clifford Krauss, "Energy Independence in the United States? Don't Pop the Cork Yet," *The New York Times,* November 13, 2012, http://www.nytimes.com/2012/11/14/business/energy-environment/energy-independence-in-america-would-not-be-fully-independent.html

26 Alan S. Blinder, "How Many US Jobs Might Be Offshorable?" *World Economics: The Journal of Current Economic Analysis and Policy*, November 2, 2009.

27 "World Employment Report 2001: Life at Work in the Information Economy," International Labour Organization, 2001.

28 Andria Cheng, "Record Number of Manufacturing Jobs Returning to America," Market Watch, May 1, 2015, http://www.marketwatch.com/story/us-flips-the-script-on-jobs-reshoring-finally-outpaced-offshoring-in-2014-2015-05-01

29 "Future of Work Overview," New Zealand Department of Labour, 2002.

30 "Do 10,000 Baby Boomers Retire Every Day?" http://www.washingtonpost.com/blogs/fact-checker/wp/2014/07/24/do-10000-baby-boomers-retire-every-day/

31 A. P. Carnevale, N. Smith, and J. Strohl, "Help Wanted: Projections of Jobs and Education Requirements through 2018," Washington, DC: Georgetown University, 2010, https://cew.georgetown.edu/wp-content/uploads/2014/12/fullreport.pdf

32 Business Roundtable, "Getting Ahead – Staying Ahead: Helping America's Workforce Succeed in the 21st Century," Business Roundtable: The Springboard Project, 2009.

33 National Science Board, Science and Engineering Indicators 2014, http://www.nsf.gov/statistics/seind14/index.cfm/chapter-3/c3s.htm

34 "No Llegarán a Ejecutarse Millones en Inversión," El Comercio, December 25, 2012.

35 Susan F. Martin, "Heavy Traffic," *The Brookings Review*, Fall 2001.

36 Justin A. Heet, "Beyond Workforce 2020: The Coming (and Present) International Market for Labor," Hudson Institute, 2004.

37 "Employer Perspectives on Global Sourcing," Hewitt Associates, 2004; and Robert Gandossy and Tina Kao, "Overseas Connections," *Across the Board*, Hewitt Associates, November/December 2004.

38 Korn Ferry, Next Africa, https://nextafrica.kornferry.com

39 "Employer Perspectives on Global Sourcing," Hewitt Associates, 2004; and Robert Gandossy and Tina Kao, "Overseas Connections," *Across the Board*, Hewitt Associates, November/December 2004.

40 Linda Levine, "Offshoring (or Offshore Outsourcing) and Job Loss Among US Workers," Congressional Research Service, January 21, 2011, https://www.fas.org/sgp/crs/misc/RL32292.pdf

41 Patrick Thibodeau, "Workers Losing Jobs at IBM Get Overseas Option," *Computerworld*, February 16, 2009.

42 www.ibm.com

43 Robert Gandossy and Tina Kao, "Channels to Anywhere," Hewitt Associates, 2004.

44 Dan Bilefsky, "In Romania, Children Left Behind Suffer the Strains of Migration," *New York Times*, February 15, 2009; and John Tagliabue, "Eastern Europe Becomes a Center for Outsourcing," *New York Times*, April 17, 2007.

45 Louise Story, "Leaving Wall Street for a Job Overseas," *New York Times*, August 11, 2008.

46 Joerg Dietz, "Firms Doomed if They Fail to Tap Diverse Talent Pool," *Toronto Star*, July 27, 2007.

47 Alina Tugend, "It's Unclearly Defined, but Telecommuting Is Fast on the Rise," *The New York Times,* March 7, 2014, http://www.nytimes.com/2014/03/08/your-money/when-working-in-your-pajamas-is-more-productive.html?_r=0%20%20; and http://globalworkplaceanalytics.com/telecommuting-statistics

48 Rachel Emma Silverman, "Your Next Office: At Home?" *Wall Street Journal Online,* June 20, 2012, http://blogs.wsj.com/atwork/2012/06/20/working-from-home-numbers-jump/

49 Center for Creative Leadership, "Always On, Never Done?" August 2013, https://s3.amazonaws.com/s3.documentcloud.org/documents/1148838/always-on-never-done.pdf

50 Clive Thompson, "Are You Checking Work Email in Bed? At the Dinner Table? On Vacation?" Mother Jones, June 2014, http://www.motherjones.com/environment/2014/04/smartphone-addiction-research-work-email

51 Keith H. Hammonds, "You Can Do Anything, But Not Everything," *Fast Company*, May 2000.

52 Chuck Salter, "Solving the Real Productivity Crisis," *Fast Company*, January 2004.

53 Paula Rayman, "Life's Work: Generational Attitudes Toward Work and Life Integration," Radcliffe Public Policy Center; and Lynn Miller, "Upper-Level Workers Say Time Is Better Than Money," Radcliffe Public Policy Center; and Gary Challenger and Cornell Christmas; and "University surveys," *HR Magazine*, 2000.

54 Barry Libert, Jon Spector, Don Tapscott, and thousands of contributors, *We Are Smarter Than Me: How to Unleash the Power of Crowds in Your Business*, Upper Saddle River, NJ: Wharton School Publishing, 2007.

55 "Employment and Unemployment Among Youth Summary," Bureau of Labor Statistics, August 2014, http://www.bls.gov/news.release/youth.nr0.htm

56 Catherine Loughlin and Julian Barling, "Young Workers' Work Values, Attitudes, and Behaviours," *Journal of Occupational and Organizational Psychology*, November 2001.

57 The World Bank, "Population Ages 65 and Above," http://data.worldbank.org/indicator/SP.POP.65UP.TO.ZS

58 David McNeil, "Japan: The Grey Planet's Ticking Time Bomb," *The Independent*, October 1, 2012, http://www.independent.co.uk/news/world/asia/japan-the-grey-planets-ticking-timebomb-8191524.html

59 The World Factbook, China, https://www.cia.gov/library/publications/the-world-factbook/geos/ch.html

60 Peter Schwartz, *Inevitable Surprises*, New York, NY: Gotham Books, 2003.

61 Karen Schwartz, "Some Finding Retirement Is Only a Temporary State," *Chicago Tribune*, March 17, 2004.

62 Prepared for AARP by RoperASW, "Baby Boomers Envision Retirement II – Key Findings," May 2004.

63 US Equal Employment Opportunity Commission, Charge Statistics FY 1997 through FY 2014, http://eeoc.gov/eeoc/statistics/enforcement/charges.cfm

64 "Facts on Women at Work," International Labour Organization, 2003.

65 Chad Steinberg, "Can Women Save Japan (and Asia Too)?" International Monetary Fund, October 2012, http://www.imf.org/external/pubs/ft/fandd/2012/09/steinberg.htm

66 Kathleen Davis, "Has Gender Equality Progress Stagnated in the Last 20 Years?" *Fast Company,* March 10, 2015, http://www.fastcompany.com/3043438/strong-female-lead/has-gender-equality-progress-stagnated-in-the-last-20-years

67 Stephanie Armour, "More Men Train to Be Nurses, Midwives, Secretaries," *USA Today*, July 10, 2003.

68 Mark Dolliver, "Just Think How Cheery They'd Be if They Weren't Discriminated Against," *Adweek*, December 1, 2003.

69 Lynn A. Karoly and Constantijn W. A. Panis, *The 21st Century at Work*, Santa Monica, CA: Rand Corporation, 2004.

70   "Census Releases Immigrant Numbers for Year 2000," Center for Immigration Studies, June 4, 2002.

71   United Nations Population Fund, "Migration: Overview," http://www.unfpa.org/migration

72   Maddy Dychtwald, *Cycles,* New York, NY: The Free Press, 2003.

73   Glassdoor, "Employee Confidence Survey 2015," http://www.glassdoor.com/blog/1-3-employees-job-2015-receive-pay-raise-glassdoor-employment-confidence-survey-q4-2014/

Chapter 2: Sustainable diversity: Relevant, profitable, and game-changing

1   "The View from the Front Lines," 2008 CEO Diversity Leadership, Diversity Best Practices.

2   The Safe Space program started at AT&T more than a decade ago and has been adopted by other companies and universities. It promotes a way for organizations to indicate areas where it's 'safe' to be out as LGBT. The Safe Space logo is a registered trademark of EQUAL! www.equal.org

3   Boris Groysberg and Katherine Connolly, "Great Leaders Who Make the Mix Work," *Harvard Business Review*, September 2013, https://hbr.org/2013/09/great-leaders-who-make-the-mix-work

4   "Multicultural Insights and Opportunities," Bank of America, https://agentresources.bankofamerica.com/neighborhoodlending/multicultural_market#topic

5   Silvina Salazar, "Bank of America: Investing in the Hispanic Community," *Diversity Journal,* January 13, 2015, http://www.diversityjournal.com/14517-bank-america-investing-hispanic-community/

6   "LGBT Marketing and Advertising," Human Rights Campaign, http://www.hrc.org/resources/entry/lgbt-marketing-and-advertising; and Nick Horton, "Chinese Businesses Eye Purchasing Power of LGBT Community," Market Watch, March 19, 2015, http://www.marketwatch.com/story/chinese-businesses-eye-purchasing-power-of-lgbt-community-2015-03-19

7   Darren Bates, "10 Ways to Target the Disability Market & Keep a Competitive Edge," LinkedIn, July 3, 2014, https://www.linkedin.com/pulse/20140703000007-11466134-top-10-ways-to-market-to-people-with-disabilities-and-boost-your-roi

8   Phred Dvorak, "A Firm's Culture Can Get Lost in Translation," *Wall Street Journal*, April 5, 2006.

9   "The Power of Culture Transformation," Korn Ferry Institute, March 5, 2015, http://www.kornferry.com/institute/power-culture-transformation

10   "Korn Ferry Executive Survey: Companies Struggle to Align Culture with Business Strategy," Korn Ferry Institute, September 8, 2014, http://www.kornferry.com/press/15195

11   1997 Diversity Conference, Conference Board, March 1997.

12   "Real World Leadership," Korn Ferry Institute, 2015, http://www.kornferry.com/real-world-leadership

Chapter 3: Deeply embed D&I into your talent management systems

1   *Seven signposts: The unmistakable markers that identify high potential leaders,* by Bruce Sevy, Vicki Swisher, and Evelyn Orr (Korn Ferry Institute) available at kornferryinstitute.com. Study of over 50,000 high potentials. As a result, you can guess they know an awful lot about the characteristics of a high potential. The seven signposts are:

  - A track record of formative experiences
  - Ability to learn from experience
  - Self-awareness
  - A disposition for leadership
  - Motivation to be a leader
  - An aptitude for logic and reasoning
  - Managed derailment risk

2   Data from various Aon Hewitt studies.

3   www.Xerox.com

4   www.ml.com

5   Society for Human Resource Management, "Human Resource Standards: Active Standards Projects," (last accessed December 22, 2012) http://www.shrm.org/HRStandards/ActiveStandardsProjects/Pages/default.aspx

Chapter 4: This thing is global!

1   Tanya Kateri Hernandez, *Racial Subordination in Latin America: The Role of the State, Customary Law, and the New Civil Rights Response*, 2013, https://books.google.com/books?isbn=1107024862

2   Corporate Women Directors International, "2015 CWDI Report: Women Board Directors of 100 Largest Latin American Companies," Washington, D.C., 2015, https://globewomen.org/globalsummit/wp-content/uploads/2015/05/2015-CWDI-Latin-America-Key-Findings.pdf

3   "Women in Senior Management: Still Not Enough," Grant Thornton International Business Report, 2012, http://www.grantthornton.co.nz/Assets/documents/pubSeminars/IBR-2012-women-in-senior-management.pdf

4   Liz Mulligan-Ferry, Mark J. Bartkiewicz, Rachel Soares, Amrita Singh, and Imogene Winkleman, *The 2013 Catalyst Census: Financial Post 500 Women Board Directors,* New York, 2014, http://catalyst.org/knowledge/2013-catalyst-census-financial-post-500-women-board-directors

5   Rebecca Zamon, "The 15 Female Cabinet Members Appointed by Prime Mister Justin Trudeau," *Huffington Post,* November 4, 2015, http://www.huffingtonpost.ca/2015/11/04/female-cabinet-justin-trudeau_n_8471908.html

6   "Catalyst Quick Take: Visible Minorities," Catalyst, 2012, http://catalyst.org/knowledge/visible-minorities; and "Career Advancement in Corporate Canada: A Focus on Visible Minorities," Catalyst, February 2007, www.catalyst.org

7   Human Resources and Skills Development Canada, last accessed January 2013, http://www.hrsdc.gc.ca/eng/labour/equality/employment_equity/tools/eedr/2006/data_reports/page11.shtml

8   "Report on Equality Rights of People with Disabilities," Canadian Human Rights Commission, 2012, http://www.chrc-ccdp.gc.ca/sites/default/files/rerpd_rdepad-eng.pdf; and "More Disabled People in Canada: Report," *The Canadian Press,* December 28, 2009, http://www.cbc.ca/news/health/story/2009/12/28/disabled-reportcanada.html Canadian, and Human Rights Commission, www.chrc-ccdp.ca

9   Gayle Johnson, "Where Will You Find Your Future Workforce?" The Canadian Institute Conference, Winning HR Practices of the Best Employers in Canada, Toronto, April 22, 2008.

10   Neil Crawford and Andrés Tapia, "Diving Deeper into the Talent Pool," Hewitt Associates, Benefits Canada, January 2008.

11   Tavia Grant, "Diversity: Easier Said Than Done, But, with Tenacity, It Can Be Done," *The Globe and Mail,* April 25, 2008.

12   Chad Steinberg, "Can Women Save Japan (and Asia Too)?" International Monetary Fund, October 2012, http://www.imf.org/external/pubs/ft/fandd/2012/09/steinberg.htm; and Martin Fackler, "Career Women in Japan Find a Blocked Path," *New York Times,* August 6, 2007; and Oscar Johnson, "Job to Increase Women Managers"; and www.focusjapan.com

13   "Japan: Portfolio Strategy Womenomics 3.0: The Time Is Now," Goldman Sachs, October 1, 2010, http://www.goldmansachs.com/our-thinking/investing-in-women/bios-pdfs/womenomics3_the_time_is_now_pdf.pdf

14   Brazilian labor law 8.213/91, *Lex Mundi Labor and Employment Desk Book,* Lex Mundi Ltd, 2008.

15   Paul Taylor and D'Vera Cohn, "A Milestone En Route to a Majority Minority Nation," Pew Research Social & Demographic Trends, November 7, 2012, http://www.pewsocialtrends.org/2012/11/07/a-milestone-en-route-to-a-majority-minority-nation/; and US Census Bureau, "An Older and More Diverse Nation by Midcentury," Press Release, August 14, 2008.

16   Alberto Davila, Marie T. Mora, and Angela Marek Zeitlin, "Better Business: How Hispanic Entrepreneurs are Beating Expectations and Bolstering the US Economy, Partnership for a New American Economy," 2014, http://www.renewoureconomy.org/wp-content/uploads/2014/04/hispanic-entrepreneurs-final.pdf

17   Best Employers Latin America 2006, Hewitt Associates, 2006.

PART 2: CALLING OUT DIFFERENCES IN RELATIONSHIPS

No notes.

Chapter 5: I need your differences ... and you need mine

1   Fay Hansen, "Diversity's Business Case: Doesn't Add Up," *Workforce*, April 23, 2003, www.workforce.com; and Elizabeth Levy Paluck and Donald P. Green, "Prejudice Reduction: What Works? A Review and Assessment of Research and Practice," *Annual Review of Psychology, 60,* (2009), pp. 339-367.

2   Fons Trompenaars and Charles Hampden-Turner, *Riding the Waves of Culture: Understanding Diversity in Global Business* (2nd ed.), New York, NY: McGraw-Hill, 1998.

3   Fons Trompenaars and Charles Hampden-Turner, *Riding the Waves of Culture: Understanding Diversity in Global Business* (2nd ed.), New York, NY: McGraw-Hill, 1998.

4   Michelle Hunt, former Vice President of Herman Miller Inc., interview, March 2006; and "If the Chair Fits: All Shapes and Sizes," *Herman Miller Newsletter*, Herman Miller Inc., 2001.

5   "The Cost of Employee Turnover Due to Failed Diversity Initiatives in the Workplace – The Corporate Leavers Survey 2007," Study by Korn Ferry and Level Playing Field Institute, 2007.

6   Thomas Kochman, *Black and White Styles in Conflict*, Chicago, IL: University of Chicago Press, 1983.

Chapter 6: Are you evil, clueless, or just plain incompetent?

1   The Myers-Briggs Type Indicator® is an assessment tool used to determine 16 different personality types. The MBTI is used in the workplace, schools, and other organizations, www.myersbriggs.org

PART 3: CALLING OUT DIFFERENCES IN GROUPS

1   Mark Landler and David Sanger, "World Leaders Pledge $1.1 Trillion to Tackle Crisis," *New York Times*, April 2, 2009.

Chapter 7: I see White people

1   "US Census Bureau Projections Show a Slower Growing, Older, More Diverse Nation a Half Century from Now," US Census Bureau, December 2012, https://www.census.gov/newsroom/releases/archives/population/cb12-243.html

2   "Millennials Outnumber Baby Boomers and Are Far More Diverse, Census Bureau Reports," US Census Bureau, June 25, 2015, https://www.census.gov/newsroom/press-releases/2015/cb15-113.html

3   Eric Schmitt, "Whites in Minority in Largest Cities, Census Shows," *New York Times*, April 30, 2001.

4   Michael Broom and Donald Klein, *Power: The Infinite Game*, Ellicott City, MD: Sea Otter Press, 1999.

5   Malcolm D. Lee, director, *Undercover Brother*, Universal Pictures, 2002.

6   Adam Cohen and Elizabeth Taylor, *American Pharaoh: Mayor Richard J. Daley – His Battle for Chicago and the Nation*, Boston, MA: Little, Brown, May, May 2000.

7   Walter Rucker and James Nathaniel, *Encyclopedia of American Race Riots*, Westport, CT: Greenwood Press, November 2006.

8   "Infant, Neonatal, and Post Neonatal Mortality Rates, by Detailed Race and Hispanic Origin of Mother: United States Selected Years 1983 2010," US Census Bureau, 2013, http://www.cdc.gov/nchs/data/hus/2013/011.pdf

9   Rakesh Kochhar and Richard Fry, "Wealth Inequality Has Widened Along Racial, Ethnic Lines Since End of Great Recession," Pew Research Center, December 12, 2014, http://www.pewresearch.org/fact-tank/2014/12/12/racial-wealth-gaps-great-recession/

10   Laura Sullivan, Tatjana Meschede, Lars Dietruch, and Thomas Shapiro, et al., *The Racial Wealth Gap: Why Policy Matters*, Demos, 2015, http://www.demos.org/sites/default/files/publications/RacialWealthGap_1.pdf

11   "The Condition of Education 2015 (NCES 2015-144)," US Department of Education, National Center for Education Statistics, https://nces.ed.gov/fastfacts/display.asp?id=27

12   Jennifer Manning, Congressional Research Service, *Membership of the 113th Congress: A Profile,* November 24, 2014, https://www.senate.gov/CRSReports/crs-publish.cfm?pid=%260BL%2BR%5CC%3F%0A

13   "McDonald's CEO to Retire; Black Fortune 500 CEOs Decline by 33% in Past Year," *DiversityInc*, January 29, 2015, http://www.diversityinc.com/leadership/mcdonalds-ceo-retire-black-fortune-500-ceos-decline-33-past-year/

14   There is much support for this view. An examination of Aon Hewitt's focus group studies that cross multiple industries and multiple regions in the United States, and the works of Norma Carr-Ruffino's book, *Diversity Success Strategies*; Dr. Daniel Landis, Dr. Milton Bennett, and Dr. Janet Bennett's book, *Handbook for Intercultural Training*; and the work of the diversity consulting group, "White Men As Full Diversity Partners," reveals an overlapping description of European-American worldviews. Here's how "White Men as Full Diversity Partners" describes on their website the values and their interpretation of this culture:

   • Rugged individualism as compared to collectivism

   • Low tolerance for uncertainty and ambiguity

   • Focus on action over reflection (doing as compared to being)

   • Rationality over emotionality

   • Time is linear and future focused

Norma Carr-Ruffino, *Diversity Success Strategies*, Butterworth-Heinemann, 1999; and Dr. Daniel Landis, Dr. Janet Bennett, and Dr. Milton J. Bennett, *The Handbook for Intercultural Training*, (3rd ed.), Thousand Oaks, CA: Sage Publications, Inc., December 2003; and "White Men As Full Diversity Partners," www.wmfdp.com

15 Winters' research is based on a compilation of focus group research and proprietary studies conducted over several years, with many companies and across multiple industries.

16 Aon Hewitt, "Aon Hewitt Engagement Survey Data." Aon Hewitt regularly conducts engagement studies for its clients.

17 Bill Leonard, "Don't Exclude White Males from Diversity and Inclusion Programs," SHRM, February 12, 2013, http://www.shrm.org/hrdisciplines/diversity/articles/pages/whitemales-diversity-inclusion.aspx

18 Chuck Shelton, *Leadership 101 for White Men: How to Work Successfully with Black Colleagues and Customers,* Garden City, NY: Morgan-James Publishing, 2008.

19 The Chicago Dream Dinner was one of many fundraisers designed to raise funds for the Washington, DC, Martin Luther King Jr. National Memorial, which was completed in 2011 on the National Mall, www.mlkmemorial.org

20 Dr. Peggy McIntosh, "White Privilege: Unpacking the Invisible Knapsack," Wellesley College Center for Research on Women, 1988.

21 Dr. Peggy McIntosh, email exchange with author, May 2009.

22 Dr. Peggy McIntosh, "White Privilege: Unpacking the Invisible Knapsack," Wellesley College Center for Research on Women, 1988. For all 50 statements in Peggy McIntosh's "White Privilege," see http://www.mdcbowen.org/p2/rm/mcintosh.html

23 Yuqing Feng, "Why Black Girls Still Prefer White Dolls," *DiversityInc*, February 9, 2007, www.diversityinc.com

24 "Trayvon Martin Shooting Fast Facts," CNN.com, February 7, 2016, http://www.cnn.com/2013/06/05/us/trayvon-martin-shooting-fast-facts/

25 Nadia Prupis, "Perceptions of Opportunities and Equality Differ Widely Along Racial Lines," Common Dreams, September 21, 2015, http://www.commondreams.org/news/2015/09/21/perceptions-opportunities-and-equality-differ-widely-along-racial-lines

26 Barack Obama, "A More Perfect Union," speech transcript, Philadelphia, Pennsylvania, March 18, 2008, https://my.barackobama.com/page/content/hisownwords/

27 Jann S. Wenner, "Ready for the Fight: Rolling Stone Interview with Barack Obama," *Rolling Stone,* April 25, 2012, http://www.rollingstone.com/politics/news/ready-for-the-fight-rolling-stone-interview-with-barack-obama-20120425#ixzz1t9JAOTHw

28 Stacy Khadaroo, "Obama vs. Romney 101: 5 Differences on Education," *Christian Science Monitor,* August 27, 2012, http://www.csmonitor.com/USA/DC-Decoder/2012/0827/Obama-vs.-Romney-101-5-differences-on-education/K-12-spending

Chapter 8: Women in leadership: Why current best practices will not be enough to shatter the glass ceiling

1 International Labour Organization, *Global Employment Trends 2014: Risk of a jobless recovery?* January 2014, http://www.ilo.org/wcmsp5/groups/public/---dgreports/---dcomm/---publ/documents/publication/wcms_233953.pdf

2 The World Bank, Labor Force Participation Rate, Female, http://data.worldbank.org/indicator/SL.TLF.CACT.FE.ZS

3 "Quick Take: Women in Management, Global Comparison," Catalyst, April 28, 2014, http://www.catalyst.org/knowledge/women-management-global-comparison

4 "The State of Women-Owned Businesses," 2014, http://www.womenable.com/59/the-state-of-women-owned-businesses-in-the-us:-2014. Indeed, the growth in the number (up 68%), employment (up 11%), and revenues (up 72%) of women-owned firms over the past 17 years exceeds the growth rates of all but the largest, publicly-traded firms—topping growth rates among all other privately-held businesses over this period.

5 "Obama Signs Lilly Ledbetter Act," *Washington Post,* January 29, 2009, http://voices.washingtonpost.com/44/2009/01/29/obama_signs_lilly_ledbetter_ac.html

6 "Commission on Status of Women," United Nations, March 11, 2005, www.un.org

7 Comparison of Gross National Product per capita measured by purchasing power (from the Atlas of Global Inequality, 2000); and UN Gender Development Index (from the UN Development Programme 2003). Corroborated by "Engendering Development," a World Bank report documenting that societies that discriminate by gender tend to experience slower economic growth and greater poverty.

8 Grant Thornton, "Corporate Governance: The Tone From the Top," March 2015, http://www.grantthornton.global/globalassets/1.-member-firms/global/insights/article-pdfs/2015/corporate-governance-final-a4-lr.pdf

9 "Gender Equality in Mexico," www.wikigender.org

10 "Women in Management, Global Comparison," Catalyst, April 28, 2014, http://www.catalyst.org/knowledge/women-management-global-comparison

11 "2013 Catalyst Census: Fortune 500 Women Executive Officers and Top Earners," Catalyst, December 10, 2013, http://www.catalyst.org/knowledge/2013-catalyst-census-fortune-500-women-executive-officers-and-top-earners

12 "Pyramid: Women in S&P 500 Companies," Catalyst, April 3, 2015, http://www.catalyst.org/knowledge/women-sp-500-companies

13 "Women Entrepreneurs: Why Companies Lose Female Talent and What They Can Do About It," Catalyst, 1998, www.catalyst.org

14 US Department of Education, National Center for Education Statistics, 2011.

15 "Women Entrepreneurs: Why Companies Lose Female Talent and What They Can Do About It," Catalyst, 1998, www.catalyst.org

16 Hillary Clinton concession speech, June 7, 2008, http://www.theguardian.com/commentisfree/2008/jun/07/hillaryclinton.uselections20081

17 There are many articles on this topic, including: Anna Fels, "Do Women Lack Ambition," *Harvard Business Review*, April 2004; and "Women 'Take Care,' Men 'Take Charge': Stereotyping of US Business Leaders Exposed," Catalyst, October 19, 2005, www.catalyst.org

18 Boris Groysberg, L. Kevin Kelly, and Bryan MacDonald, "The New Path to the C-Suite," *Harvard Business Review*, March 2011.

19 Rochelle Sharpe, "As Leaders, Women Rule," *BusinessWeek*, November 20, 2000, www.businessweek.com

20 Kira Porter, "Women Leaders: Strategic Yet Invisible Assets," *Link & Learn*, May 2003.

21 J. E. Orr (ed.), "Korn/Ferry Institute Talent Management Best Practice Series: Women in Leadership," 2013, Los Angeles, http://www.kornferry.com/institute/best-practice-series-women-leadership

22 Sylvia Ann Hewlett, Carolyn Buck Luce, Peggy Shiller, and Sandra Southwell, "Hidden Brain Drain: Off-Ramps and On-Ramps in Women's Careers," *Harvard Business Review*, February 24, 2005.

23 J. E. Orr (ed.), "Korn/Ferry Institute Talent Management Best Practice Series: Women in Leadership," 2013, Los Angeles, http://www.kornferry.com/institute/best-practice-series-women-leadership

24 Sue Shellenbarger, "Maternity Leave for the CEO: Women Balance Pregnancy and Staying in Charge," *Wall Street Journal*, July 14, 2005, http://online.wsj.com/article/0,,SB112129016232185000,00.html

25 Isobel Coleman, "Why Empowering Women Is Good for Business," *Foreign Affairs,* May/June 2010.

26 "Gender Equality in LAC and the IDB," Inter-American Development Bank, http://www.iadb.org/en/topics/gender-indigenous-peoples-and-african-descendants/gender-equality/gender,1926.html

27 The World's Women 2010, United Nations, 2010, http://unstats.un.org/unsd/demographic/products/Worldswomen/WW2010Report_by%20chapterBW/Work_BW.pdf

28 Ricardo Hausmann, Laura D. Tyson, and Saadia Zahidi, "The Global Gender Gap Report 2010," World Economic Forum, 2010, http://www3.weforum.org/docs/WEF_GenderGap_Report_2010.pdf

29 Latin American statistics gathered by Andrés Tapia from a variety of formal and informal sources including journalists, human resources professionals, and marketers on trip to Peru, Chile, Argentina, and Brazil in February 2007.

30 "Pyramid: Women in S&P 500 Companies," Catalyst, April 3, 2015, http://www.catalyst.org/knowledge/women-sp-500-companies

31 "Women on Boards: Hang Seng Index 2015," Community Business, March 3, 2015, http://www.communitybusiness.org/library/News/2015/20150303_PressRelease-Women_On_Boards_Hong_Hong_2015.pdf

32 Hong Kong Equal Opportunity Commission, (last accessed January 5, 2013), http://www.eoc.org.hk/EOC/GraphicsFolder/InforCenter/Papers/StatisticContent.aspx?ItemID=10943 and http://www.eoc.org.hk/EOC/GraphicsFolder/ShowContent.aspx? ItemID=11042

33 "Japan's Need for Women Workers," *The New York Times,* July 28, 2014, http://www.nytimes.com/2014/07/29/opinion/japans-need-for-women-workers.html? _r=0

34 Niall McCarthy, "These Countries Have the Most Women in Management Positions," *Forbes.com*, January 14, 2015, http://www.forbes.com/sites/niallmccarthy/2015/01/14/these-countries-have-the-most-women-in-management-positions-infographic/

35 "Womenomics Improves Women's Advancement in Japan, but Only Slightly," *Chronicle Online,* October 27, 2015, http://chronicle.northcoastnow.com/2015/10/27/womenomics-improves-womens-advancement-in-japan-but-only-slightly/

36 Faith Karimi, "The Girl the Taliban Wanted Dead," CNN.com, December 24, 2012, http://edition.cnn.com/2012/12/24/us/malala-cnn-most-intriguing-2012/index.html?utm_source=feedburner&utm_medium=feed&utm_campaign=Feed%3A+rss%2Fcnn_world+(RSS%3A+World)

37 UN Development Fund for Women 2008.

38 Lillian Cunningham, "Deloitte Is First of 'Big 4' Firms to Name a Female CEO," February 11, 2015, http://www.washingtonpost.com/news/on-leadership/wp/2015/02/11/deloitte-becomes-first-big-firm-to-name-a-female-ceo/

39 "Diversity and Inclusion Program Doubles Representation of Women of Color Executives in 4 Years," Korn Ferry Institute, October 22, 2014, http://www.kornferry.com/institute/diversity-and-inclusion-program-doubles-representation-women-color-executives-4

40 Many research studies have landed on similar conclusions. But one of the latest contributions to the literature is Hermina Ibarra, Cora Chaired Professor of Leadership and Learning and Professor of Organizational Behavior at INSEAD, *Act Like a Leader, Think Like a Leader*, 2015.

41 Laura Bassett, "Women in Politics Break Records in 2012 Election," http://www.huffingtonpost.com/2012/11/07/women-in-politics-break-records-2012-election_n_2088954.html

42 "Barack Obama's Plan to Support Working Women and Families," April 11, 2015, http://documents.mx/documents/barack-obamas-plan-to-support-working-women-and-families.html

Chapter 9: The Millennials: Why this generation is challenging the workplace like no other

1   Michelle Conlin, "Youthquake," *Businessweek*, January 9, 2008, www.businessweek.com

2   Margaret Hoover, "Opinion: Failure to Attract Millennials Is Sinking GOP," CNN.com, November 14, 2012, http://www.cnn.com/2012/11/14/living/millennials-gop-vote/index.html

3   Ken Walsh, "Obama Turns to Nontraditional Media: President Takes His Message to the People, Bypassing the Mainstream Media, *US News and World Report*, June 24, 2015, http://www.usnews.com/news/blogs/ken-walshs-washington/2015/06/24/obama-turns-to-nontraditional-media

4   Richard Fry, "This Year, Millennials Will Overtake Baby Boomers," Pew Research Center, January 16, 2015, http://www.pewresearch.org/fact-tank/2015/01/16/this-year-millennials-will-overtake-baby-boomers/

5   Ken Dychtwald, Tamara J. Erickson, and Robert Morrison, *Workforce Crisis: How to Beat the Coming Shortage of Skills and Talent,* Boston, MA: Harvard Business School Press, April 2006.

6   Conversation with Carol Evans, Founder and CEO, Working Mother Media, December 2007.

7   "Student Debt and the Class of 2013," The Institute for College Access & Success, November 2014, http://ticas.org/sites/default/files/legacy/fckfiles/pub/classof2013.pdf

8   Decennial Census and American Community Survey, data for Millennials are for those 15 to 34 years old in 2012; Baby Boomers comparisons are for when they were 15 to 34 as surveyed in 1980.

9   "Millennials Are in Search of a Different Kind of Career," *National Journal,* June 12, 2015, http://www.theatlantic.com/business/archive/2015/06/millennials-are-in-search-of-a-different-kind-of-career/426195/

10 "Futurestep Survey Finds Compensation One of the Least Important Factors for Recruiting Millennial Talent," Korn Ferry Institute, March 5, 2015, http://www.kornferry.com/press/futurestep-survey-finds-compensation-one-of-the-least-important-factors-for-recruiting-millennial-talent/

11 Dr. John J. Medina, "Brain Rules: Principles of Thriving at Work," Presentation, Diversity and Inclusion Conference, Society for Human Resource Management, October 23, 2012, http://sessionplanner.shrm.org/conference/shrm-2012-diversity-inclusion-conference-exposition/session/brain-rules-principles

12 Andrés Tapia, "The Multicultural Marketing of Benefits," Hewitt White Paper, 2007.

13 Interview with proud but perplexed father in Norwalk, Connecticut, December 2007; and email exchange with Leah Campbell, February 2008.

14 Don Tapscott and Anthony D. Williams, *Wikinomics: The Expanded Edition*, Portfolio, New York, NY: Penguin Group, April 2008.

15 Sanjay Dholakia, "The Intersection of Web 2.0 and Talent Management," *Talent Management*, January 2008.

16 "Generation in the Workplace in the United States and Canada," Catalyst, May 1, 2012, http://www.catalyst.org/knowledge/generations-workplace-united-states-canada; and "Getting to Know Generation X," *NAS Insights*, NAS Recruitment Communications, 2006, www.nasrecruitment.com

17 RUUP4IT: Are you up for it?

Chapter 10: Disability: The diversity issue we fear the most

1 "20th Anniversary of Americans with Disabilities Act: July 26," Facts for Features, US Census, May 26, 2010, http://www.census.gov/newsroom/releases/archives/facts_for_features_special_editions/cb10-ff13.html

2 Disability and Health Fact Sheet, World Health Organization, December 2014, http://www.who.int/mediacentre/factsheets/fs352/en/

3 Jim Harter and Sangeeta Agrawal, "Many Baby Boomers Reluctant to Retire," Gallup, January 20, 2014, http://www.gallup.com/poll/166952/baby-boomers-reluctant-retire.aspx

4 Matthew W. Brault, "Americans with Disabilities: 2010 – Household Economic Studies," *Current Population Reports*, July 2012, http://www.census.gov/prod/2012pubs/p70-131.pdf

5 Marilynn Marchione, "US Vets' Disability Filings Reach Historic Rate," *USA Today*, May 28, 2012, http://usatoday30.usatoday.com/news/health/story/2012-05-28/veteran-disability/55250092/1

6 "Veterans Day 2012: November 11," Facts for Features, US Census, October 11, 2012, http://www.census.gov/newsroom/releases/pdf/cb12ff-21_veteran.pdf

7 "A Snapshot of Our Nation's Veterans," Census Bureau, 2010, https://www.census.gov/how/pdf/census_veterans.pdf

8 Matthew W. Brault, "Americans with Disabilities: 2010 – Household Economic Studies," *Current Population Reports*, July 2012, http://www.census.gov/prod/2012pubs/p70-131.pdf

9 Matthew W. Brault, "Americans with Disabilities: 2010 – Household Economic Studies," *Current Population Reports*, July 2012, http://www.census.gov/prod/2012pubs/p70-131.pdf

10 Matthew W. Brault, "Americans with Disabilities: 2010 – Household Economic Studies," *Current Population Reports*, July 2012, http://www.census.gov/prod/2012pubs/p70-131.pdf

11 "US Census Bureau, American Community Survey," November 2006 as quoted by Jonathan J. Kaufman; and Jonathan J. Kaufman, "The Search for Talent: Why Hiring and Retaining People with Disabilities Is Good for Business," *CDO Insights*, Diversity Best Practices, December 2007, http://consultspringboard.com/2007/the-search-for-talent-why-hiring-and-retaining-people-with-disabilities-is-good-for-business/

12   Michelle Yin, Dahlia Shaewitz, and Mahlet Megra, "An Uneven Playing Field: The Lack of Equal Pay for People with Disabilities," American Institutes for Research, December 2014, http://www.air.org/sites/default/files/Lack%20of%20Equal%20 Pay%20for%20People%20with%20Disabilities_Dec%2014.pdf

13   Erika Steinmetz, US Census Bureau Current Population Report: Americans with Disabilities: 2002 (p. 70-107).

14   H. G. Gallagher, *FDR's Splendid Deception*, Arlington, VA: Vandamere Press, 1994.

15   "Reauthorization of the Higher Education Act: The Implications for Increasing the Employment of People with Disabilities," National Council on Disability, May 19, 2015, http://www.ncd.gov/publications/2015/05192015/

16   Jonathan J. Kaufman, "The Search for Talent: Why Hiring and Retaining People with Disabilities Is Good for Business," *CDO Insights*, Diversity Best Practices, December 2007, http://consultspringboard.com/2007/the-search-for-talent-why-hiring-and-retaining-people-with-disabilities-is-good-for-business/

17   "Persons with a Disability: Labor Force Characteristics Summary," Bureau of Labor Statistics, June 16, 2015, http://www.bls.gov/news.release/disabl.nr0.htm

18   World Report on Disability 2011, Chapter 8 "Work and Employment," World Health Organization and The World Bank, 2011.

19   Yoji Cole, "Corporate America in a Post-ADA World," *DiversityInc*, November/ December 2007.

20   Yoji Cole, "Corporate America in a Post-ADA World," *DiversityInc*, November/ December 2007.

21   Jeré Longman, "Embracing the Equality of Opportunity," *New York Times*, August 17, 2008.

22   Carol Pogash, "A Personal Call to Invention: Amputee's Prosthetic Design IS Helping Pistorius and Others" *New York Times*, July 2, 2008.

23   Jonathan J. Kaufman, "The Search for Talent: Why Hiring and Retaining People with Disabilities Is Good for Business," *CDO Insights*, Diversity Best Practices, December 2007, http://consultspringboard.com/2007/the-search-for-talent-why-hiring-and-retaining-people-with-disabilities-is-good-for-business/

24   Richard J. McNally and B. Christopher Frueh, "Why Are Iraq and Afghanistan War Veterans Seeking PTSD Disability Compensation at Unprecedented Rates?" *Journal of Anxiety Disorders,* July 2013, http://mcnallylabcom.ipage.com/beta/ wp-content/uploads/mcnally-frueh-2013-jad-disability-rates1.pdf

25   Dan Senor and Saul Singer, *Start-Up Nation: The Story of Israel's Economic Miracle,* New York, NY: Twelve, November 2009.

26   "Fact Sheet: Veteran and Military Spouse Employment Hiring Commitments," April 23, 2015, https://www.whitehouse.gov/sites/default/files/docs/ jf.employmentfactsheet.april23.pdf

27 Bonnie Kavoussi, "Drexel Hamilton, Wall Street Firm, Trains and Hires Disabled Veterans" *The Huffington Post,* June 18, 2012, http://www.huffingtonpost.com/2012/06/18/drexel-hamilton-veterans_n_1605619.html?utm_hp_ref=business

28 Bureau of Workforce Development, "2007 WIA Annual Report Individuals with Disabilities Served," Illinois Department of Commerce and Economic Opportunity, December 26, 2007, http://www.illinois.gov/dceo/AboutDCEO/AboutIllinoisServices/Statutory%20Reports/WIADisabilityReport2007wCoverLtr.pdf

29 "A 25-Year History of the IDEA (archived)," US Department of Education, July 2007, www.ed.gov

30 "Emerging Giant – Big Is Not Enough: The Global Economics of Disability," US Census, US Department of Labor, Statistics Canada, European Central Bank, IPS, IPS Insights, April 2010, www.odenetwork.com/library/global-economics-of-disability-the-april-20-2010

31 "Remarks by the President on Signing of U.N. Convention on the Rights of Persons with Disabilities Proclamation," The White House, July 24, 2009, http://www.whitehouse.gov/the_press_office/Remarks-by-the-President-on-Rights-of-Persons-with-Disabilities-Proclamation-Signing

32 Ramsey Cox and Julian Pecquet, "Senate Rejects United Nations Treaty for Disabled Rights in a 61-38 Vote," The Hill, December 4, 2012, http://thehill.com/policy/international/270831-senate-rejects-un-treaty-for-disabled-rights-in-vote

33 Melanie Trottman, "US Pushes Target for Hiring the Disabled," *Wall Street Journal*, February 29, 2012, http://online.wsj.com/article/SB1000142405297020452020457725130372666294.html

Chapter 11: How my gay friends upended my understanding about most everything

1 Lori Grisham, "What Does the Q in LGBTQ Stand For?" *USA Today,* June 1, 2015, http://www.usatoday.com/story/news/nation-now/2015/06/01/lgbtq-questioning-queer-meaning/26925563/

2 Inaugural invocations by Pastor Rick Warren of Saddleback Church in California (January 20, 2009) and The Right Rev. V. Gene Robinson, Bishop of the US Episcopal Church in the diocese of New Hampshire (January 19, 2009).

3 Hewitt presentation to Talent & Organization Consulting (TOC) North America meeting, May 31, 2007, states: "Hewitt research demonstrates that a 10% increase in attracting and retaining pivotal employees adds approximately $70 million to $160 million to a company's bottom line." This research was conducted by Hewitt's Human Capital Foresight team.

4 Thom Shanker and Patrick Healy, "A New Push to Roll Back 'Don't Ask, Don't Tell,'" *The New York Times*, November 30, 2007, http://www.nytimes.com/2007/11/30/us/30military.html?_r=1

5 "Don't Ask, Don't Tell Repeal Act of 2010," Wikipedia, https://en.wikipedia.org/wiki/Don%27t_Ask,_Don%27t_Tell_Repeal_Act_of_2010

6   Map: Same-Sex Marriage in the United States, CNN.com, June 26, 2015, http://www.cnn.com/interactive/us/map-same-sex-marriage/

7   Karen McVeigh, "Gay Rights Must Be Criterion for US Aid Allocation, Instructs Obama," *The Guardian* online, December 6, 2011, http:// www.guardian.co.uk/ world/2011/dec/07/gayrights- us-aid-criteria

8   Heather Timmons, "India Court Overturns Gay Sex Ban," *The New York Times*, July 2, 2009, http://www.nytimes.com/2009/07/03/world/asia/03india.html?_r=1

9   Susan Donaldson James, "'Gayby Boom' Fueled by Same-Sex Parents," ABCNews.com, August 3, 2009, http://abcnews.go.com/Health/ ReproductiveHealth/story?id=8232392

10 Susan Donaldson James, "'Gayby Boom' Fueled by Same-Sex Parents," ABCNews.com, August 3, 2009, http://abcnews.go.com/Health/ ReproductiveHealth/story?id=8232392

11 David M. Brodzinsky, "Expanding Resources for Children III: Research-Based Best Practices in Adoption by Gays and Lesbians," Evan B. Donaldson Adoption Institute, October 2011, http://adoptioninstitute.org/old/publications/2011_10_ Expanding_Resources_BestPractices.pdf

12 "Corporate Equality Index 2015," Annual Report, Human Rights Campaign, 2015, http://www.hrc.org/campaigns/corporate-equality-index

13 Bill Chappell, "Supreme Court Declares Same-Sex Marriage Legal in All 50 States," NPR News, June 26, 2015, http://www.npr.org/sections/thetwo-way/2015/06/26/417717613/supreme-court-rules-all-states-must-allow-same-sex-marriages

14 "Seven Out of Ten Heterosexuals Today Know Someone Gay," Press Release, Out & Equal, October 10, 2006, www.outandequal.org

15 Katie McDonough, "Remember: It's Still Legal to Fire Someone for Being Gay in the U.S.," Fusion, July 23, 2015, http://fusion.net/story/171850/equality-act/

16 Transgender FAQ, Human Rights Campaign, http://www.hrc.org/resources/entry/ transgender-faq#11

17 "Hate Crime Statistics 2013," Bias Breakdown, Federal Bureau of Investigations, December 8, 2014, https://www.fbi.gov/news/stories/2014/december/latest-hate-crime-statistics-report-released

18 Grace Wong, "One Job, Two Lives: LGBT in the American Workplace," CNN.com, October 30, 2014, http://edition.cnn.com/2014/10/30/us/gays-lgbt-corporate-america/

19 "1,400 LGBT Executives and 118 Sponsors Gathered for the 14th Annual Out & Equal Workplace Summit: Baltimore, October 29-November 1," Press Release, Out & Equal, November 5, 2012, http://outandequal.org/node/514

20 Samir Luther, "Domestic Partner Benefits: Employer Trends and Benefits Equivalency for the GLBT Family," Report by the Human Rights Campaign Foundation, March 2006, www.hrc.org

21   Blake Ellis, "Record Number of US Firms Offering Same-Sex Benefits," CNN.com, December 9, 2013, http://money.cnn.com/2013/12/09/pf/lgbt-corporate-equality/

22   "Corporate Equality Index 2002," Study by the Human Rights Campaign Foundation, August 2002, www.hrc.org

23   "Mobilizing: The Road to Equality," Annual Report, Human Rights Campaign, 2011, http://www.hrc.org/files/assets/resources/AnnualReport_2011.pdf; and 2013 Corporate Equality Index, Human Rights Campaign, 2013, http://www.hrc.org/files/assets/resources/CEI_2013_Final_low.pdf.pdf

24   "Mobilizing: The Road to Equality," Annual Report, Human Rights Campaign, 2011, http://www.hrc.org/files/assets/resources/AnnualReport_2011.pdf; and 2013 Corporate Equality Index, Human Rights Campaign, 2013, http://www.hrc.org/files/assets/resources/CEI_2013_Final_low.pdf.pdf

25   "Corporate Equality Index 2015," Annual Report, Human Rights Campaign, 2015, http://www.hrc.org/campaigns/corporate-equality-index

26   "Buying Power of Gay Men and Lesbians in 2008," Gay Market Report 2009, Witeck-Combs Communications, www.pinkbananamedia.com

27   "America's LGBT 2014 Buying Power Estimated at $884 Billion," Witeck Communications, June 10, 2015, http://www.witeck.com/pressreleases/americas-lgbt-2014-buying-power-estimated-at-884-billion/

28   "Asian American Buying Power Increased by More Than $50 Billion in One-Year-Expected to Hit $1 Trillion by 2018," Nielsen, June 11, 2015, http://www.nielsen.com/us/en/press-room/2015/nielsen-asian-american-buying-power-increased-by-more-than-50B-in-one-year.html

29   "The 2013 LGBT Report: Demographic Spotlight," Experian Market Services, 2013, http://www.experian.com/assets/simmons-research/white-papers/2013-lgbt-demographic-report.pdf

30   "LGBT Adults Strongly Prefer Brands That Support Causes Important to Them and That Also Offer Equal Workplace Benefits," Harris Interactive and Witeck-Combs Communications, July 18, 2011.

31   Michael Wilke, "IBM: Beyond Gay Vague," *The Gully Online Magazine*, January 5, 2004.

32   "Corporate Equality Index 2016," Human Rights Campaign, 2016, http://hrc-assets.s3-website-us-east-1.amazonaws.com//files/assets/resources/CEI-2016-FullReport.pdf

33   Lisa Belkin, "Smoother Transitions," *New York Times*, September 3, 2008.

34   "*Fortune* Magazine Highlights Transgender Inclusion in the Workplace," Human Rights Campaign, July 14, 2015, http://www.hrc.org/blog/entry/fortune-magazine-highlights-transgender-inclusion-in-the-workplace

35   "Corporate Equality Index 2013," Human Rights Campaign, 2013, http://www.hrc.org/files/assets/resources/CEI_2013_Final_low.pdf.pdf

36   Eve Glicksman, "Transgender Today," American Psychological Association, April 2013, http://www.apa.org/monitor/2013/04/transgender.aspx

PART 4: CALLING OUT DIFFERENCES IN ORGANIZATIONS

1   R. Roosevelt Thomas, Jr., "Diversity Management and Affirmative Action: Past, Present and Future," Diversity Symposium, October 7, 2004.

2   Joseph Schumpeter, *Capitalism, Socialism, and Democracy*, New York, NY: Harper & Row, 1942.

Chapter 12: Must have: The Inclusive Leader

1   N. J. Adler, *International Dimensions of Organizational Behavior* (4th ed.), Cincinnati, OH: South-Western College Publishing, 2002, c. Milton J. Bennett, 2008.

2   Shapiro Consulting and Opportunity Now, *Inclusive Leadership: From Pioneer To Mainstream*, 2011, http://gender.bitc.org.uk/system/files/research/inclusive_leadership_-_from_pioneer_to_mainstream.pdf

3   Sylvia Ann Hewlett, Melinda Marshall, and Laura Sherbin, *Innovation, Diversity and Market Growth,* Center for Talent Innovation, 2013, http://www.talentinnovation.org/_private/assets/IDMG-ExecSummFINAL-CTI.pdf

4   Vivian Hunt, Dennis Layton, and Sara Prince, *Why Diversity Matters,* McKinsey & Company, 2014, http://www.mckinsey.com/insights/organization/why_diversity_matters

5   "Precision Talent Intelligence," Korn Ferry Institute, June 23, 2014, http://www.kornferry.com/institute/precision-talent-intelligence-definitive-four-dimensions-leadership-and-talent

6   Korn Ferry, *Leadership Architect™ Research Guide and Technical Manual,* Minneapolis, MN: Korn Ferry, 2015.

7   "Deal–breakers: Retention, Integration and Culture, A Report on the Joint M&A Study from Hewitt," Hewitt and The Deal, Spring 2009.

8   Milton J. Bennett, "Towards a Developmental Model of Intercultural Sensitivity" in R. Michael Paige, (ed.), *Education for the Intercultural Experience*, Yarmouth, ME: Intercultural Press, 1993.

9   "Real World Leadership," Korn Ferry Institute, 2015, http://www.kornferry.com/real-world-leadership

10   Christie Smith and Stephanie Turner, *The Radical Transformation of Diversity and Inclusion: The Millennial Influence*, Deloitte University: The Leadership Center for Inclusion, 2015, pg. 6.

11   Christie Smith and Stephanie Turner, *The Radical Transformation of Diversity and Inclusion: The Millennial Influence*, Deloitte University: The Leadership Center for Inclusion, 2015, pg. 7.

12   Christie Smith and Stephanie Turner, *The Radical Transformation of Diversity and Inclusion: The Millennial Influence*, Deloitte University: The Leadership Center for Inclusion, 2015, pg. 9.

13   Kenji Yoshino and Christie Smith, *Uncovering Talent: A New Model of Inclusion,* Deloitte Development, LLC, 2013, https://www2.deloitte.com/content/dam/Deloitte/us/Documents/about-deloitte/us-inclusion-uncovering-talent-paper.pdf

14   Kenji Yoshino and Christie Smith, *Uncovering Talent: A New Model of Inclusion*, Deloitte Development, LLC, 2013, https://www2.deloitte.com/content/dam/Deloitte/us/Documents/about-deloitte/us-inclusion-uncovering-talent-paper.pdf

15   Kenji Yoshino and Christie Smith, *Uncovering Talent: A New Model of Inclusion,* Deloitte Development, LLC, 2013, https://www2.deloitte.com/content/dam/Deloitte/us/Documents/about-deloitte/us-inclusion-uncovering-talent-paper.pdf

16   Christie Smith and Stephanie Turner, *The Radical Transformation of Diversity and Inclusion: The Millennial Influence*, Deloitte University: The Leadership Center for Inclusion, 2015, pg. 6.

17   Jeanine Prime and Elizabeth R. Salib, *Inclusive Leadership: The View from Six Countries,* Catalyst, 2014, http://www.catalyst.org/system/files/inclusive_leadership_the_view_from_six_countries_0.pdf

18   Jeanine Prime and Elizabeth R. Salib, *Inclusive Leadership: The View from Six Countries,* Catalyst, 2014, http://www.catalyst.org/system/files/inclusive_leadership_the_view_from_six_countries_0.pdf

19   "Executive Survey Finds a Lack of Focus on Diversity and Inclusion Key Factor in Employee Turnover," Korn Ferry Institute, 2015, http://www.kornferry.com/press/executive-survey-finds-a-lack-of-focus-on-diversity-and-inclusion-key-factor-in-employee-turnover/

20   "Executive Survey Finds a Lack of Focus on Diversity and Inclusion Key Factor in Employee Turnover," Korn Ferry Institute, 2015, http://www.kornferry.com/press/executive-survey-finds-a-lack-of-focus-on-diversity-and-inclusion-key-factor-in-employee-turnover/

21   Christie Smith and Stephanie Turner, *The Radical Transformation of Diversity and Inclusion: The Millennial Influence*, Deloitte University: The Leadership Center for Inclusion, 2015, pg. 12.

22   Christie Smith and Stephanie Turner, *The Radical Transformation of Diversity and Inclusion: The Millennial Influence*, Deloitte University: The Leadership Center for Inclusion, 2015, pg. 13.

Chapter 13: The four pillars of what makes people of color stay and thrive

1   "Preparing for the Workforce of Tomorrow," Hewitt Timely Topic Survey, February 2004.

2   Mitra Toossi, "Labor Force Projections to 2012: The Graying of the U.S. Workforce," *Monthly Labor Review*, February 2004, www.bls.gov

3   Conversation with Dr. Jeff Howard, April 2009. Dr. Howard is the founder and CEO of J. Howard & Associates, a diversity consulting firm that became a part of Korn Ferry.

4   2 Corinthians 4:8, *The Holy Bible, New International Version*.

Chapter 14: Why not acknowledging differences can make us sicker and poorer

1   "401(k) Plans in Living Color: A Study of 401(k) Savings Disparities Across Racial and Ethnic Groups," Ariel/Aon Hewitt, 2012, https://www.arielinvestments.com/images/stories/PDF/ariel-aonhewitt-2012.pdf

2   "401(k) Plans in Living Color: A Study of 401(k) Savings Disparities Across Racial and Ethnic Groups," Ariel/Aon Hewitt, 2012, http://www.arielinvestments.com/401k-Study-2012/

3   "401(k) Plans in Living Color: A Study of 401(k) Savings Disparities Across Racial and Ethnic Groups," Ariel/Aon Hewitt, 2012, https://www.arielinvestments.com/images/stories/PDF/ariel-aonhewitt-2012.pdf

4   "2007 Ariel-Schwab Black Investor Survey," Ariel Investments, October 2007, www.arielinvestments.com

5   Ariel Investments, http://www.arielinvestments.com/content/view/1774/1173/

6   "Longer Life Spans, Lower Salaries and Conservative Saving Habits Key Factors in Gap Between How Much Women Need for Retirement and Their Actual Saving Behaviors," Study by Hewitt, July 9, 2008. Study of nearly 2 million employees at 72 large U.S. companies.

7   Excerpts from "401(k) Plans in Living Color: A Study of 401(k) Savings Disparities Across Racial and Ethnic Groups," Ariel/Aon Hewitt, 2012, http://www.arielinvestments.com/401k-Study-2012/

Some reasons for the retirement savings gap between women and men

- Make less and live longer. Despite the fact that women's income has increased 63 percent in the past 30 years, their salaries still trail men's, with the average woman earning just $57,000 a year compared to $84,000 for the average man in Hewitt's study. In addition, women are expected to live almost three years longer than men—an average of 22 years after retirement at age 65 compared to just 19 years post-retirement for men. As a result, most women will need to save more to make their retirement savings last over a longer stretch of time. In addition, because medical costs after retirement are a flat dollar amount for all employees, those costs will consume a higher percentage of women's retirement assets than men's.

- Invest less assertively. 2009 Hewitt research reveals that most women have less money saved in their 401(k) plans than men. The average plan balance for women is $56,320—nearly $47,000 less than men. In addition, women tend to contribute less (7.3 percent of pay versus 8.1 percent for men) to their 401(k) plan, and they are less likely to take advantage of the employer match. Thirty percent of women did not contribute to their 401(k) plans in 2007 and another quarter (24 percent) did not contribute at a level high enough to take advantage of the company match, which, according to Hewitt research, is typically $0.50 for every dollar up to 6 percent of pay per year. Hewitt research also shows that women are less aggressive than men with respect to saving and investing in their 401(k) plans. Women invest less in riskier equity investments (65 percent for women compared to 71 percent for men), and are about half as likely as men to make a trade (13 percent versus 24 percent). Additionally, women tend to choose investments and let them stick more often than men. Just over a quarter (26 percent) make changes to their contribution rate each year compared to 30 percent of men.

- Delay retirement saving and have spotty saving patterns. Not surprisingly, Hewitt's study reveals that the earlier and more consistently employees save for retirement, the greater the impact on increasing overall income replacement rates. Unfortunately, Hewitt's research also shows that women wait two to four years longer than men to start saving for retirement. In addition, they are more likely to be in and out of the workforce for family reasons, which can result in hundreds of thousands of dollars in missed earnings, promotions, raises, and benefits over the course of a career, including larger deficiencies in retirement savings.

How can women close the gap?

Despite the challenges they face, it is possible for women to get to a more comfortable place in retirement. In fact, making a few easy changes to their saving and investing behaviors can have a significant impact in helping women shrink the retirement income gap and get to more appropriate retirement levels.

- Invest earlier and at a more vigorous rate. Hewitt research shows that the age at which employees start saving has a significant impact on their retirement balances. Women could potentially increase their nest egg by 18 percent simply by investing two years earlier than they do now, or 23 percent by investing just four years earlier. In addition, women can increase their projected retirement income rates an average of 7 percent simply by investing just 2 percent of pay more a year in their 401(k)s. A woman who makes an average salary of $57,000 and who increases her annual 401(k) contribution from 2 percent to 4 percent—an increase of just $95 per month—will have accumulated an extra $81,000 by the time she reaches retirement age. What's more, she will tack on an extra $40,500 by having contributed at a rate high enough to take advantage of her employer's company match program.

- Put off retirement for a few years. While most employees, including women, estimate they will retire by age 65, working just 2 years longer to age 67 can increase projected retirement replacement income levels by 13.5 percent for women who contribute to their 401(k) plans. And because women will have more money to live on during their years in retirement, their retiree medical costs—typically a flat dollar amount on an annual basis—won't eat up as large a percentage of their savings had they retired at age 65 or earlier.

For more details go to: http://www.hewittassociates.com/Intl/NA/en-US/AboutHewitt/Newsroom/PressReleaseDetail.aspx?cid=5346

8   Michael Grunwald, "How Obama Is Using the Science of Change," *Time*, April 6, 2009.

9   Michael Grunwald, "How Obama Is Using the Science of Change," *Time*, April 6, 2009.

10   "Redlining," Wikipedia, https://en.wikipedia.org/wiki/Redlining

11   "401(k) Plans in Living Color: A Study of 401(k) Savings Disparities Across Racial and Ethnic Groups," Ariel/Aon Hewitt, 2012, http://www.arielinvestments.com/401k-Study-2012/

12   Amy Gahran, "Why One in Five U.S. Adults Doesn't Use the Internet," CNN.com, April 16, 2012, http://edition.cnn.com/2012/04/13/tech/web/pew-not-using-internet/#

13   Kathryn Zickuhr and Aaron Smith, "Digital Differences," Pew Internet and American Life Project, Pew Research Center, April 13, 2012, http://pewinternet.org/Reports/2012/Digital-differences.aspx

14   "Distribution of the Nonelderly Uninsured by Family Work Status," The Henry J. Kaiser Family Foundation, 2014, http://www.statehealthfacts.org/comparebar.jsp?ind=135&cat=3

15   "About Minority Health," Centers for Disease Control and Prevention, www.cdc.gov

16   Paula Moyer, "AACAP: Ethnicity Linked to Schizophrenia Diagnosis for Black and Latino Teens," Medpage Today, October 25, 2005, http://www.medpagetoday.com/Neurology/Seizures/1994

17   Didier Demesmin, "Recognizing and Addressing Healthcare Disparities in Medication Prescribing Among Racial and Ethnic Minorities with Acute and Chronic Pain," Medscape.org website, December 30, 2009, available at http://www.medscape.org/viewarticle/713641

18   Kristin M. Lefebvre and Stephen Metraux, "Disparities in Level of Amputation Among Minorities: Implications for Improved Preventative Care," University of the Sciences in Philadelphia, 2009, http://works.bepress.com/cgi/viewcontent.cgi?article=1024&context=metraux

19   Mary E. Clark, Stewart Landers, Rhonda Linde, and Jodi Sperber, "The GLBT Health Access Project: A State-Funded Effort to Improve Access to Care," *American Journal of Public Health*, June 2001, http://www.ncbi.nlm.nih.gov/pmc/articles/PMC1446464/pdf/11392930.pdf

20   Robert Bernstein and Tom Edwards, "An Older and More Diverse Nation by Midcentury," Press Release, US Census Bureau, August 14, 2008, www.census.gov

21   "2006 Hewitt Annual Healthcare Survey," Hewitt Associates, 2006, www.hewitt.com

22   "2001 Health Care Quality Survey," The Commonwealth Fund, November 2001, www.commonwealthfund.org

23 "2001 Health Care Quality Survey," The Commonwealth Fund, November 2001, www.commonwealthfund.org

24 Dr. Janet L. Dreachslin and Fred Hobby, "Racial and Ethnic Disparities: Why Diversity Leadership Matters," *Journal of Healthcare Management*, January 2008.

25 Lisa Beyer, "Companies Are Turning to Technology to Help Keep Workers Well," Workforce Management, October 1, 2011.

26 "American Diabetes Association Partners with Numera to Manage Diabetes Using Social Media," Benzina.com, March 2, 2012, http://www.diabetes.org/in-my-community/local-offices/seattle-tacoma-washington/

27 "Barbershops As Hypertension Detection, Referral, and Follow-Up Centers for Black Men," *Hypertension Magazine*, American Heart Association, 2007.

28 Amy Gahran, "Why One in Five US Adults Doesn't Use the Internet," CNN.com, April 16, 2012, http://edition.cnn.com/2012/04/13/tech/web/pew-not-using-internet/#

Chapter 15: Work-life flexibility: The mother of all battles

1   Julia Overturf Johnson and Barbara Downs, "Maternity Leave and Employment Patterns of First-Time Mothers: 1961-2000 – Household Economic Studies," *Current Population Reports*, US Census Bureau, October 2005, www.census.gov

2   Yearly Hewitt benefits surveys.

3   Oriel Sullivan and Scott Coltrane, "Men's Changing Contribution to Housework and Child Care," prepared for the 11th Annual Conference of the Council on Contemporary Families, April 25-26, 2008.

4   Kerstin Aumann, Ellen Galinsky, and Kenneth Matos, "The New Male Mystique," Families and Work Institute, 2011, http://familiesandwork.org/site/research/reports/newmalemystique.pdf

5   Remarks by Michelle Obama, as prepared for delivery, Women's Economic Roundtable, Pontiac, Michigan, July 9, 2008.

6   Sylvia Ann Hewlett, *Off-Ramps and On-Ramps: Keeping Talented Women on the Road to Success*, Boston, MA: Harvard Business School Press, 2007.

7   "About Flexible Work Arrangements," Hewitt Timely Topics Survey, 2008.

8   James W. Loewen, *Lies My Teacher Told Me: Everything Your American History Textbook Got Wrong*, New York, NY: New Press, 2008.

9   Interview with Carol Evans, CEO of Working Mother Media, August 2008.

10 Michael F. Broom and Donald C. Klein, *Power: The Infinite Game*, Ellicott City, MD: Sea Otter Press, October 1999.

11   Tory Johnson, "Flexibility Equals Productivity," ABC News, April 13, 2006, www.abcnews.go.com; and Gregory P. Smith, "Flexible Work Arrangements Promote Productivity," *Business Know-How*, www.businessknowhow.com; and "Survey: Working from Home Boosts Productivity," *Inc.*, February 2007, www.inc.com

12   Jennifer Robison, "Workplace Socializing Is Productive; An MIT Researcher Talks about the Usefulness of Water Cooler Chatter," *Gallup Management Journal*, December 24, 2008.

13   Chris Sullivan, "The Next Workplace Revolution," *Dialogue*, Gensler Publication, 2008.

14   "2008 US Workplace Survey," Report by Gensler Publication, October 2008, www.gensler.com

15   "2008 US Workplace Survey," Report by Gensler Publication, October 2008, www.gensler.com

16   Blair Kamin, "Come See the Silver Sides of the Sears Tower?" *Chicago Tribune*, March 11, 2009.

17   Chris Sullivan, "The Next Workplace Revolution," *Dialogue*, Gensler Publication, 2008; and Helen Kirwan-Taylor, "The Time We Waste," *Management Today*, September 4, 2007, www.managementtoday.co.uk

18   Helen Kirwan-Taylor, "The Time We Waste," *Management Today*, September 4, 2007, www.managementtoday.co.uk

19   "The Most 'Family Friendly' Members of Congress," Carol Evans interview on MSNBC, December 4, 2012, http://video.msnbc.msn.com/the-cycle/50075927#50075927

20   "Forum on Workplace Flexibility: Closing Session," The White House, March 31, 2010, http://www.whitehouse.gov/photos-and-video/video/forum-workplace-flexibility-closing-session#transcript

21   "The Most 'Family Friendly' Members of Congress," Carol Evans interview on MSNBC, December 4, 2012, http://video.msnbc.msn.com/the-cycle/50075927#50075927

Chapter 16: The toughest challenge: The broken, leaking, plugged-up diverse talent pipeline

1   Deb Perelman, "Study: Businesses Unprepared for Aging Workforce," March 16, 2007, *eweek.com*

2   Mitra Toossi, "Labor Force Change, 1950–2050," *Monthly Labor Review*, May 2002, http://www.bls.gov/opub/mlr/2002/05/art2full.pdf

3   Paul Merrion, "Chicago Boardrooms Lag Nation in Diversity," Workforce.com, November 15, 2012, http://www.workforce.com/article/20121115/NEWS01/121119971/chicago-boardrooms-lag-nation-in-diversity#

4   "Executive Attitudes on Diversity Positive, but Actions Lagging, Korn Ferry Institute Survey Finds," Korn Ferry Institute, November 4, 2013, http://www.kornferry.com/press/15143/

5   "Executive Survey Finds a Lack of Focus on Diversity and Inclusion Key Factor in Employee Turnover," Korn Ferry Institute, March 2, 2015, http://www.kornferry.com/press/executive-survey-finds-a-lack-of-focus-on-diversity-and-inclusion-key-factor-in-employee-turnover/

6   "Status and Trends in the Education of Racial and Ethnic Minorities," National Center for Education Statistics, September 2007, www.nces.ed.gov

7   "US College Drop-Out Rate Sparks Concern," MSNBC, November 15, 2005, www.msnbc.msn.com; and Jay P. Greene, Ph.D. and Marcus A. Winters, "Public High School Graduation and College-Readiness Rates: 1991–2002," Education Working Paper, Manhattan Institute for Policy Research, February 2005.

8   "The Economic Impact of the Achievement Gap in America's Schools," Report by McKinsey & Company, April 2009, www.mckinsey.com

9   "Education to Employment: Designing a System that Works," McKinsey & Company, 2012, http://mckinseyonsociety.com/downloads/reports/Education/Education-to-Employment-exec-summary_FINAL.pdf

10   Malcolm Gladwell, *Outliers: The Story of Success*, New York, NY: Little, Brown and Company, 2008.

11   David Brooks, "The Harlem Miracle," *New York Times*, May 7, 2009.

12   Lisa Quast, "Women and STEM Careers: How Microsoft Is Building a Bridge to Future Innovation – One Girl at a Time," *Forbes.com*, October 10, 2012, http://www.forbes.com/sites/lisaquast/2012/10/22/women-and-stem-careers-how-microsoft-is-building-a-bridge-to-future-innovation-one-girl-at-a-time/

13   Jesse Washington, "STEM Education and Jobs: Declining Numbers of Blacks Seen in Math, Science," *Huffington Post,* October 24, 2011, http://www.huffingtonpost.com/2011/10/24/stem-education-and-jobs-d_n_1028998.html

14   Lisa Quast, "Women and STEM Careers: How Microsoft Is Building a Bridge to Future Innovation – One Girl at a Time," *Forbes.com,* October 10, 2012, http://www.forbes.com/sites/lisaquast/2012/10/22/women-and-stem-careers-how-microsoft-is-building-a-bridge-to-future-innovation-one-girl-at-a-time/

15   Jesse Washington, "STEM Education and Jobs: Declining Numbers of Blacks Seen in Math, Science," *Huffington Post,* October 24, 2011, http://www.huffingtonpost.com/2011/10/24/stem-education-and-jobs-d_n_1028998.html

16   Brian Kelly, "The State of STEM and Jobs," *USNews.com*, September 21, 2012, http://www.usnews.com/news/articles/2012/09/21/the-state-of-stem-and-jobs?page=2

17   Rodney C. Adkins, "America Desperately Needs More STEM Students. Here's How to Get Them," *Forbes.com,* July 9, 2012, http://www.forbes.com/sites/forbesleadershipforum/2012/07/09/america-desperately-needs-more-stem-students-heres-how-to-get-them/

18 Lisa Quast, "Women and STEM Careers: How Microsoft Is Building a Bridge to Future Innovation – One Girl at a Time" *Forbes.com*, October 10, 2012, http://www.forbes.com/sites/lisaquast/2012/10/22/women-and-stem-careers-how-microsoft-is-building-a-bridge-to-future-innovation-one-girl-at-a-time/

19 "Top Companies for Leaders 2007," Hewitt Associates, 2007.

20 Jessica Marquez, "Diversity: The Obama Effect," *Workforce Management*, February 5, 2009, www.workforce.com

21 The White House website on Education: http://www.whitehouse.gov/issues/education

22 The White House website on Education: http://www.whitehouse.gov/issues/education

23 Thomas Friedman, "Swimming without a Suit," *New York Times*, April 22, 2009.

CONCLUSION: BE THE CHANGE YOU WISH TO SEE IN THE WORLD

1 2 Corinthians 4:8, *The Holy Bible, New International Version*.

Appendix A: Assessing and developing The Inclusive Leader

No notes.

Appendix B: Figuring out how crossculturally competent you are

1 Dr. Milton Bennett, *Basic Concepts of Intercultural Communication*, Boston, MA: Intercultural Press, 1998.

2 Full details about the design of the IDI are available in *International Journal of Intercultural Relations, Special Issue on Intercultural Development*, *27*(4), July 2003. The entire issue is dedicated to DMIS and IDI.

Appendix C: A groundbreaking study that shows race trumps income when it comes to who saves more

1 "401(k) Plans in Living Color: A Study of 401(k) Savings Disparities Across Racial and Ethnic Groups," Ariel/Aon Hewitt, 2012, https://www.arielinvestments.com/images/stories/PDF/ariel-aonhewitt-2012.pdf

2 The rules regarding loans are complex but do include limits on the time period a person has to repay before default occurs. Many employers simplify the process by establishing a 60-day repayment requirement.

Appendix D: Driving up minority 401(k) participation at a medical institution

No notes.

thank you

הודה

Спасибо

Gracias

谢谢

grazie

Je vous remercie

Danke

ありがとうございました

Acknowledgments

It not only takes a village to raise a child, as the African proverb says, but it also takes one to create a book. Not just for the actual editorial process of researching, interviewing, reviewing, editing, proofreading, designing, marketing, and project managing, but to also actually create something to write about. Here I want to acknowledge those who played a part either in creating the story to tell or in the telling of the story.

Acknowledgments Korn Ferry

The following Korn Ferry colleagues added their contributions either to this third edition of the book itself or to the projects we worked on together.

Gracias to all for the work you do every day, every moment, around the globe, to make the world a better place to work—for everyone.

KORN FERRY LEADERS, CONSULTANTS, ADMINISTRATIVE EXPERTS

For your smartness, support, belief, testing, sharpening, contributions, heavy lifting, encouragement:

Anna Waters | **Audra** Bohannon | **Barbara** Nelson **Barry** Callender | **Bernard** Zen-Ruffinen | **Bill** Westwood **Bryan** Proctor | **Caroline** Crow | **Carolyn** McChesney **Cathi** Rittelmann | **Cecilia** Pinzón | **Darryl** Smith | **Dave** Eaton | **David** Lange | **David** Williams | **Dési** Kimmins **Evelyn** Orr | **Fayruz** Kirtzman | **Fred** Alce | **Gary** Burnison | **Gen** Coleman | **Germayne** Cade | **Gerry** Lupacchino | **Gustavo** Gisbert | **Heather** Krupinski | **Ilene** Gochman | **Jamie** Small | **Jane** Chang | **Jill** Bowman **Jim** Crawford | **Jim** Peters | **John** Mackey | **Jorge** Farías **Julia** Sweeney | **Karen** Opp | **Kat** Zacharia | **Kathleen** Hamblin-Trué | **Kelvin** Falkner | **Kevin** Cashman **Linda** Dziubala | **Ludger** Schwinn | **Luisa** Kurtz | **Maija** Boris | **Mark** Pierce | **Mike** Hyter | **Noah** Rabinowitz

Noni Sutherland | **Oris** Stuart | **Paul** Styrna | **Peggy** Hazard

Pete Ambrozaitis | **Renee** Jackson | **Rodrigo** Araujo

Rolando García | **Rosaleena** Marcellus | **Sara** Larson

Selena Yuan | **Sergio** Averbach | **Stu** Crandell | **Teresa** Shannon | **Tim** Vigue | **Tony** Malinauskas | **Victor** Arias

Wayland Lum | **Wendy** Beecham |

RESEARCH, EDITING, PRODUCTION

For your eagle eyes, relentless pursuit of the elusive stat, perseverance to ensure full accuracy and clarity, managing the process to the finish line:

Amanda Berger | **Bonnie** Parks | **Doug** Lodermeier Sr.

Jeanine Amilowski | **Korn Ferry** India Center of Knowledge | **La Tasha** Reed | **Lesley** Kurke | **Paul** Montei

Shannon Ridgway |

MARKETING

For your elegant, savvy, content rich approach to getting the word out about what we do and why:

Allison Cadogan | **Dan** Gugler | **Marisa** Kacary | **Mike** Distefano | **Renee** Medema | **Sarah** Kesher | **Stacy** Levyn **Tracy** Kurschner |

CLIENTS

To all my dear clients who have opened the doors to partner with them to bring about transformative change. Your dedication! Your persistence! Your trust. Gracias.

To those who contributed to the first and second editions at Hewitt and Diversity Best Practices

Those who partnered in doing the work:

For your commitment, passion, knowledge, and skills:

Tyronne Stoudemire, Elina Rodriguez, Susan McCuistion, Linda DeLavallade, Chuck Adams, Nancy Sedin, Cathy Gallagher-Louisy, Patti Meessmann, Bo Young Lee, Diane Krieman, Carol Sladek, Elaine Masterson, and Kristin Slavish.

Those who believed and were partners in the early pioneering efforts:

For my colleagues, mentors, and leaders where all this got started:

Steve King for the opportunity offered for me to become a CDO. Dale Gifford for the deep and broad sponsorship of the early work. Jack Bruner for the opening into the business. Helen Mills, Brandon Bennett, Gino Pinto, Andy Hiles, John Bomba, Linda Schievelbein, and Sandy Miller for creating marketplace openings. Tracy Keogh and Russ Fradin for sponsoring the first edition of this book. Mary-Frances Winters for that foundation-setting beginning we partnered on.

My editors throughout my career:

David Neff for inculcating the discipline of precision. To Verne Becker for teaching me how to tell a story. To Sandy Close, CEO and executive editor of the New America Media, for providing a platform for finding my author voice.

The ones who kept me together and those around me sane:

My executive assistants, Barbara Grala and Katie Reardon.

The many who agreed to be interviewed for the book and have been quoted throughout.

And finally, there were many who in one way or another moved the work forward internally at Hewitt and with our clients when I served there as CDO, and then when I was president at Diversity Best Practices with our members and clients, or who played a key role in the process of putting this book together in terms of editorial help, graphic design, marketing, and subject-matter expert review. Their names along with those mentioned above show up in the roll call that follows.

Alison Borland, Amanda Wuest, ANDY HILES, Artell Smith, Barbara Grala, Barb Hogg, BECKY KEEN, Bob Campbell, Bo Young Lee, Brandon Bennett, Carol Sladek, Cathy Gallagher-Louisy, Christi Rager-Wise, Chuck Adams, Cindy Dayney, Cosette Yisrael, DALE GIFFORD, Dana Holmes, David Neff, Dawne Simmons, Diane Krieman, ELINA RODRIGUEZ, ERIN PETERSON,

Gino Pinto, Helen Mills, Jack Bruner, **JD Piro,** Jeff Shovlin, *Jill Sherer Murray,* **Jim Konieczny,** JOANNE DAHM, *Jon Leatherbury,* **Jon Malysiak,** *Julie Cook Ramirez,* *JULIE MACDONALD,* Kelley McDonald, *Kelly Salek,* **Kerry LaCoste, KRISTIN SLAVISH,** *Linda Mateja,* **Linda DeLavallade,** Lisa Horuczi Markus, *Lori Miller, MARK BOCIANSKI,* **Mary-Frances Winters,** MARY KELLEY, *Maurissa Kanter,*

Melissa Giovagnoli, MOLLIE KOHN, Monica Francois Marcel, **Nancy Sedin,** Pam Harris, **PAMAY BASSEY,** *PATTI MEESSMANN,* *Ray Baumruk,* Robert Lundin, Ron Dayney, RUSS FRADIN, **SANDY CLOSE,** Sandy Miller, *Steve Bright,* Steve King, **SUSAN MCCUISTION, Susan Welch,** SUZANNE KENNEY, *Tanya McKeel,* Tracy Keogh, **TYRONNE STOUDEMIRE,** *Verne Becker, WENDY RHODES*

About the author

Andrés Tapia is a Senior Client Partner and Global Practice Leader for Korn Ferry's Workforce Performance, Inclusion and Diversity Practice.

Andrés has been one of the leading voices in shaping a contemporary, next-generation approach to diversity and inclusion. The approach is global, deeply integrated into talent systems, and focused on enabling marketplace success. He has over 25 years of experience as a C-suite management consultant, diversity executive, organizational development and training professional, and journalist.

Andrés joined Korn Ferry from Diversity Best Practices, a diversity and inclusion think-tank and consultancy, where he acted as President and was responsible for the organization's overall vision, strategy, and outcomes. Prior to his tenure there, he acted as Chief Diversity Officer and Emerging Workforce Solutions Leader for Hewitt Associates and was responsible for shaping and leading that organization's internal diversity transformation as well as its diversity consultancy.

Throughout Europe, Asia, North America, and his native Latin America, Andrés has served clients in shaping their enterprise-wide diversity and inclusion business cases and strategies across industries—including financial, healthcare, retail, manufacturing, government, not-for-profits, and education—with dozens of Global 500 organizations headquartered in the US, Brazil, South Korea, Switzerland, Italy, and India, such as John Deere, Marriott, United Airlines, Target, Cigna, CJ, Tata, Barilla, and Roche.

Andrés is a globally sought-after speaker on the topic of diversity and inclusion. He has been published in major dailies throughout the US and Latin America primarily through his writing for the New America Media wire service as well as the *Huffington Post.* He is the recipient of numerous leadership and diversity awards and has served on a number of boards, including currently serving on the editorial board of *Diversity Executive* magazine, the corporate advisory board for the Bentley University Center for Women and Business, and the Ravinia Arts Festival.

Andrés received a bachelor's degree in modern history from Northwestern University in the Chicago area with an emphasis in journalism and political science. He grew up in a bilingual/bicultural home in Lima, Perú. He is married to Lori, a musician, and they have an adult daughter, Marisela, who is a professional flamenco dancer.

About Korn Ferry and the Korn Ferry Institute

Korn Ferry is the preeminent global people and organizational advisory firm. We help leaders, organizations and societies succeed by releasing the full power and potential of people. Our nearly 7,000 colleagues deliver services through our Executive Search, Hay Group, and Futurestep divisions. Visit **kornferry.com** for more information.

The **Korn Ferry Institute,** our research and analytics arm, was established to share intelligence and expert points of view on talent and leadership. Through studies, books, and a quarterly magazine, *Briefings*, we aim to increase understanding of how strategic talent decisions contribute to competitive advantage, growth, and success.

Printed in Germany
by Amazon Distribution
GmbH, Leipzig